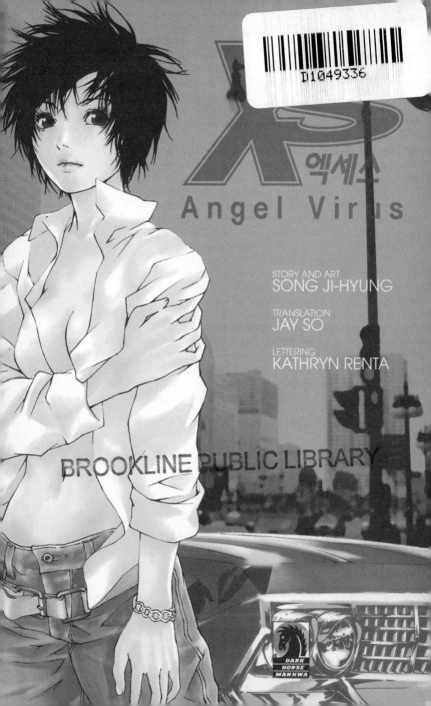

X 엑세스

Angel Virus

STORY AND ART
SONG JI-HYUNG

TRANSLATION
JAY SO

LETTERING
KATHRYN RENTA

GRAPHIC
XS Hybrid
v.2

2nd XS
DENIZENS

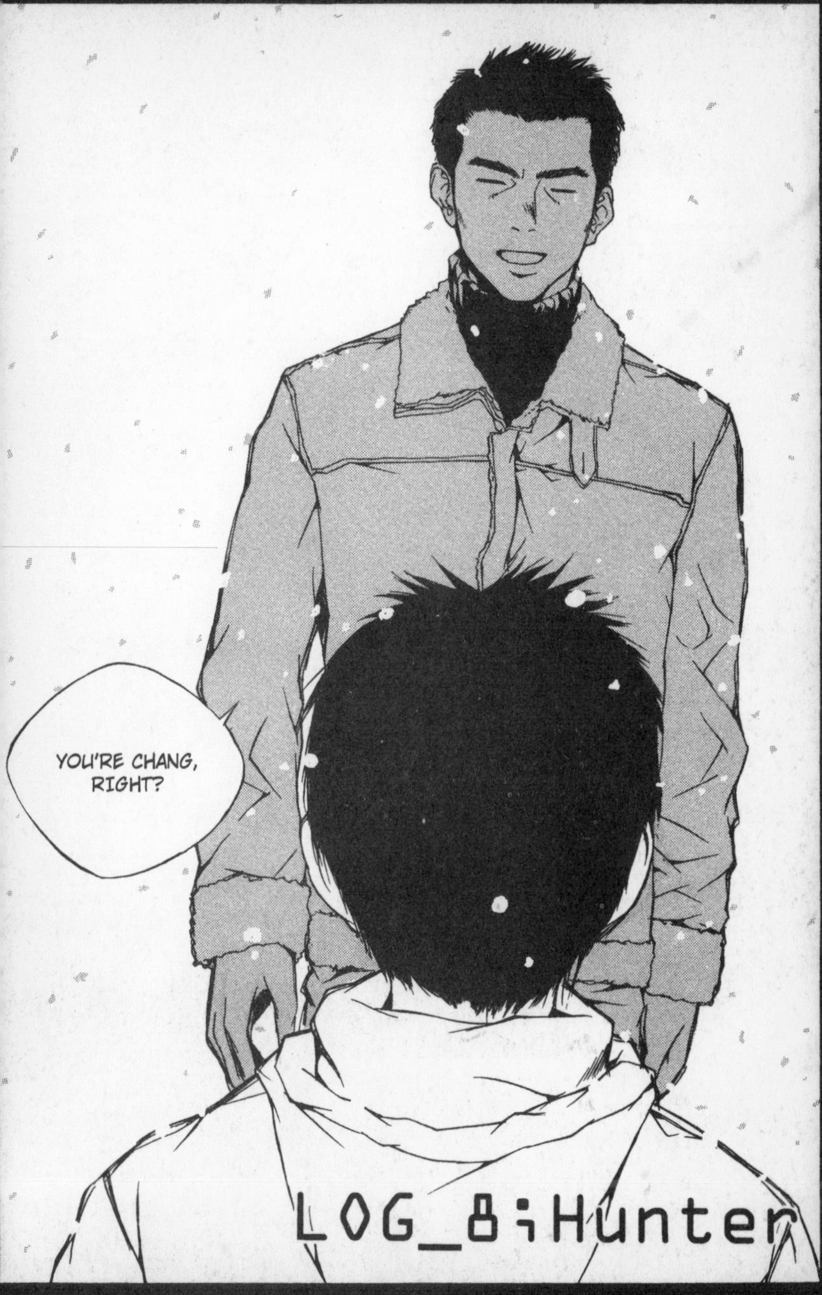
YOU'RE CHANG, RIGHT?
LOG_8:Hunter

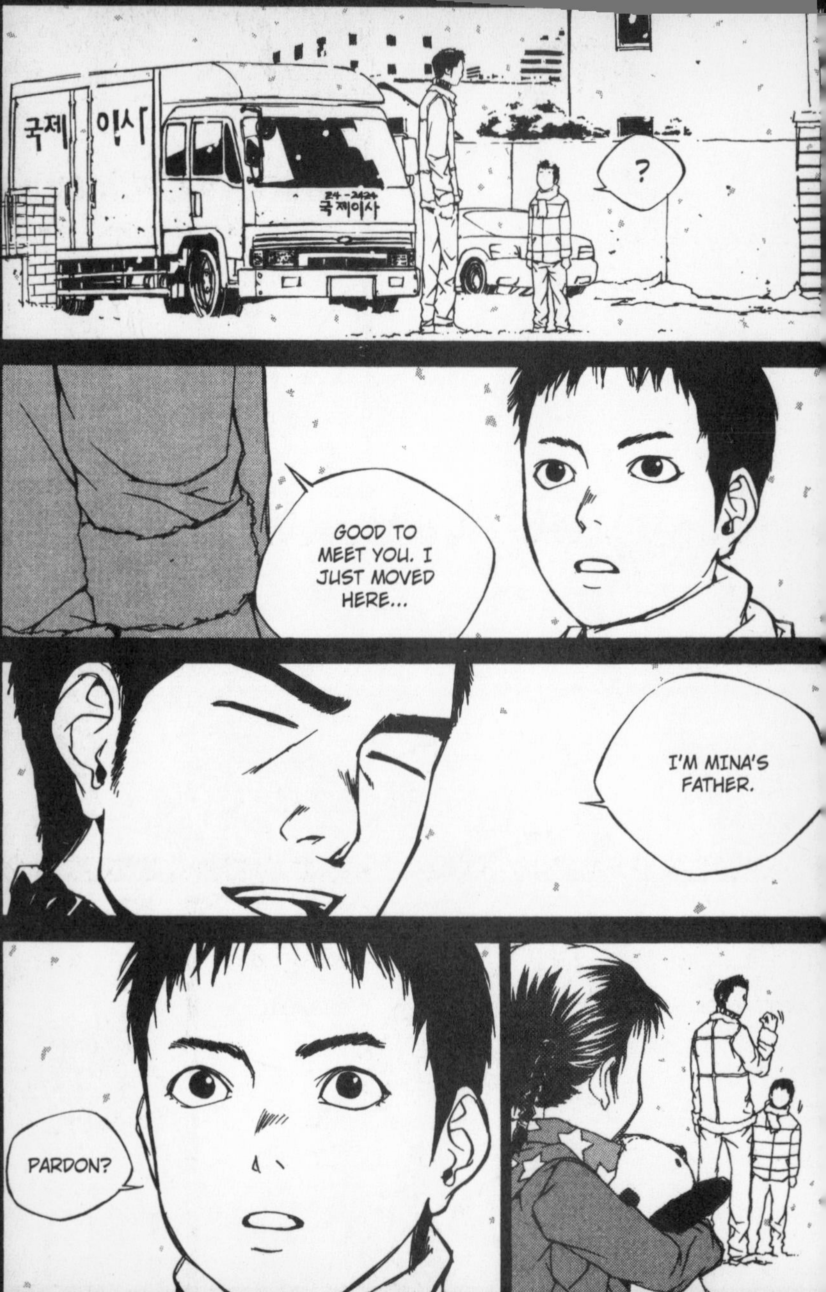
국제 이사
국제이사
?
GOOD TO MEET YOU. I JUST MOVED HERE...
I'M MINA'S FATHER.
PARDON?

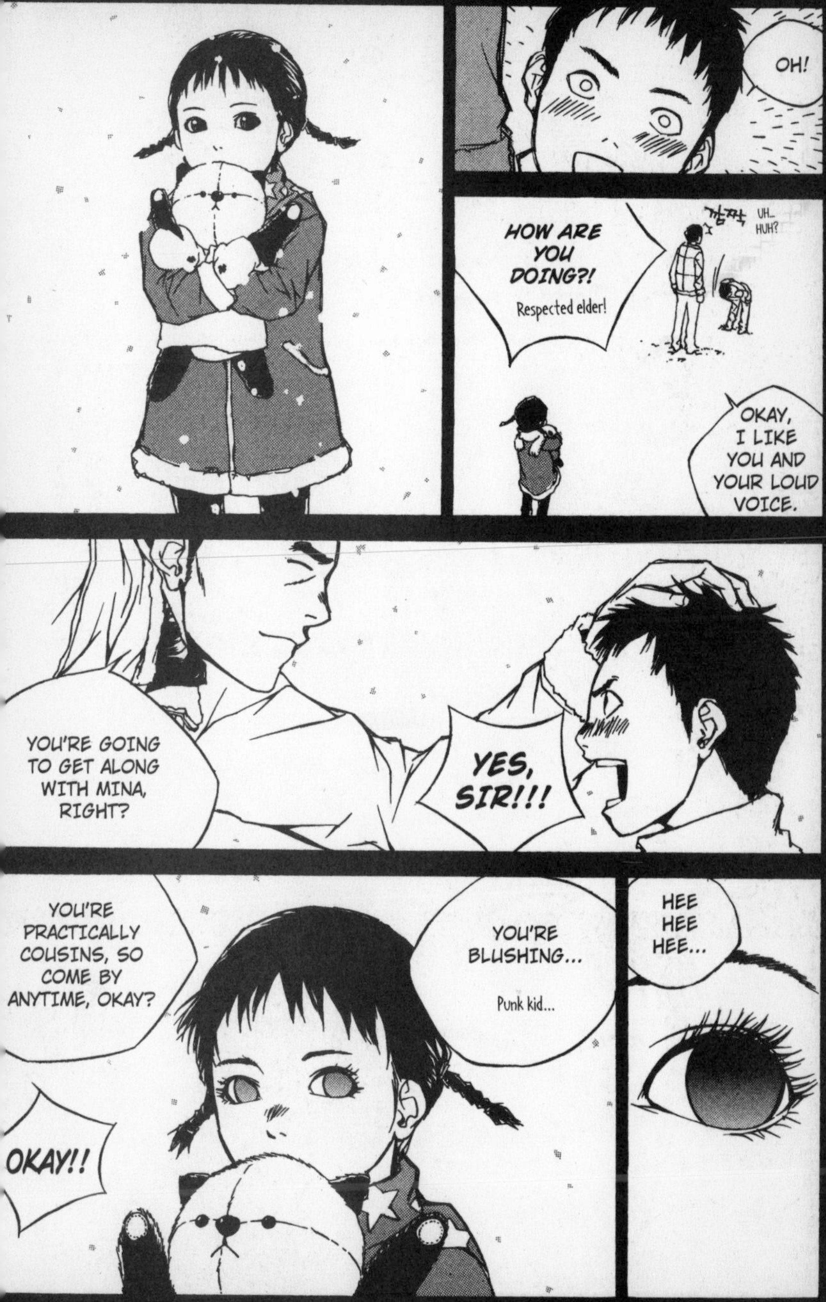
OH!
HOW ARE YOU DOING?!
Respected elder!
깜짝
UH... HUH?
OKAY, I LIKE YOU AND YOUR LOUD VOICE.
YOU'RE GOING TO GET ALONG WITH MINA, RIGHT?
YES, SIR!!!
YOU'RE PRACTICALLY COUSINS, SO COME BY ANYTIME, OKAY?
OKAY!!
YOU'RE BLUSHING...
Punk kid...
HEE HEE HEE...

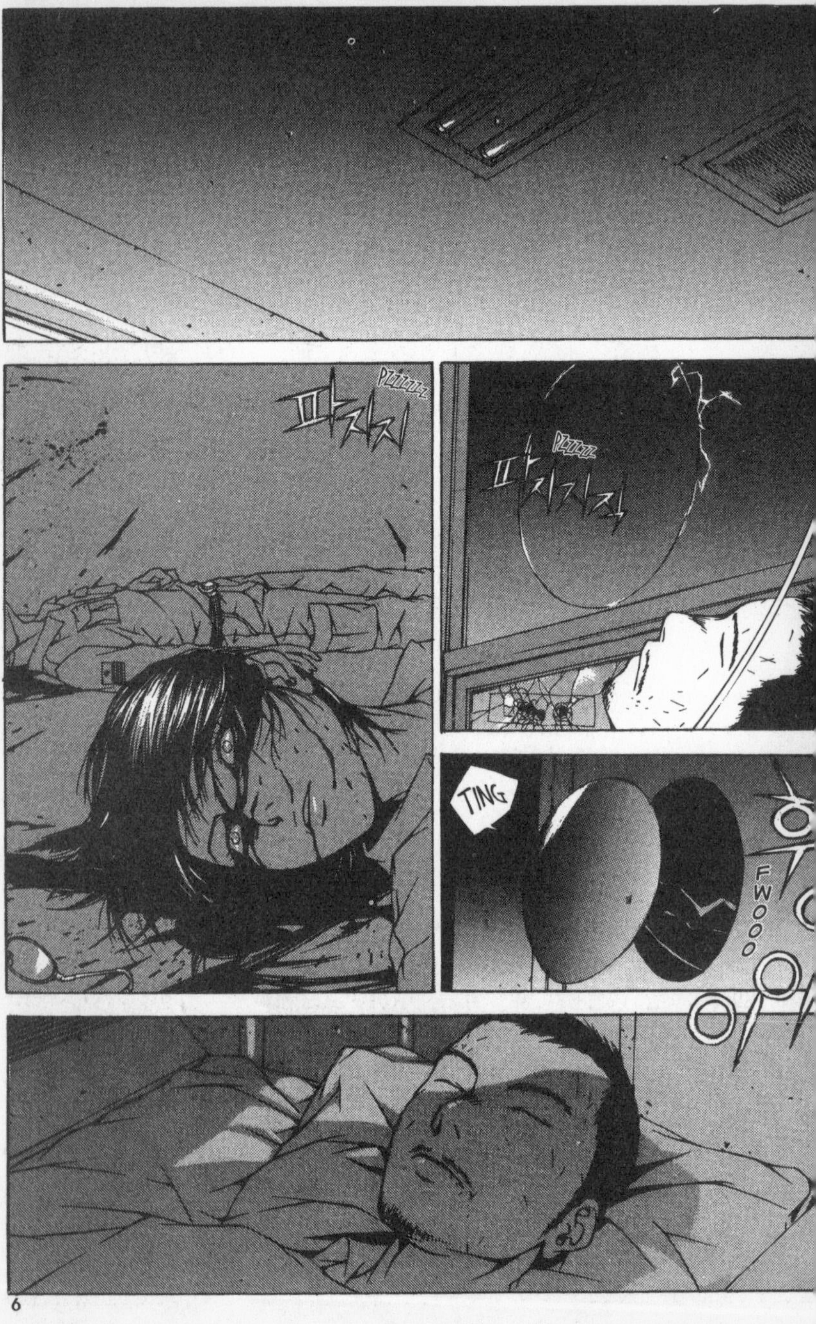

파지지
PZZZZZZ
파지지지직
PZZZZZ
TING
FWOOOO

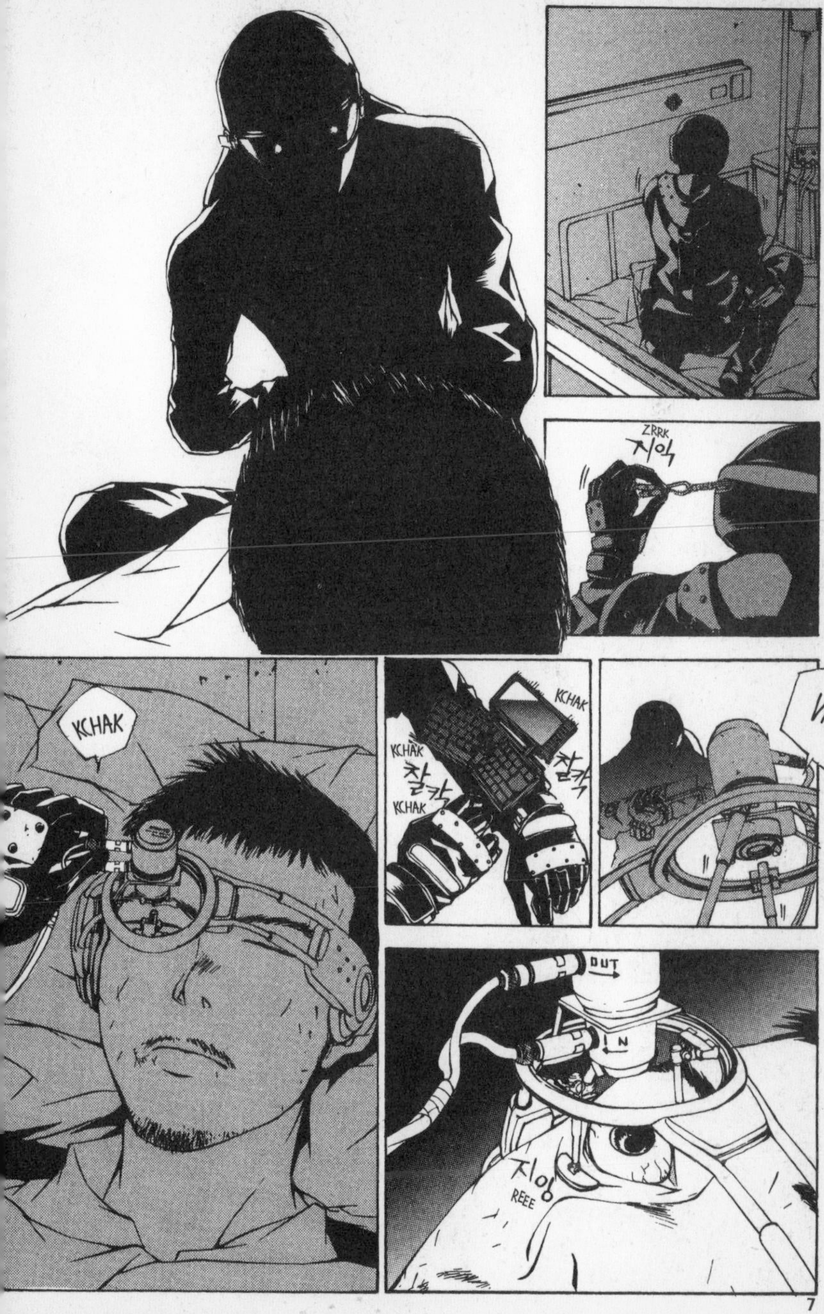
ZRRK
지익
KCHAK
KCHAK
찰칵
KCHAK
KCHAK
찰칵
VREE
OUT
IN
지잉
REEE

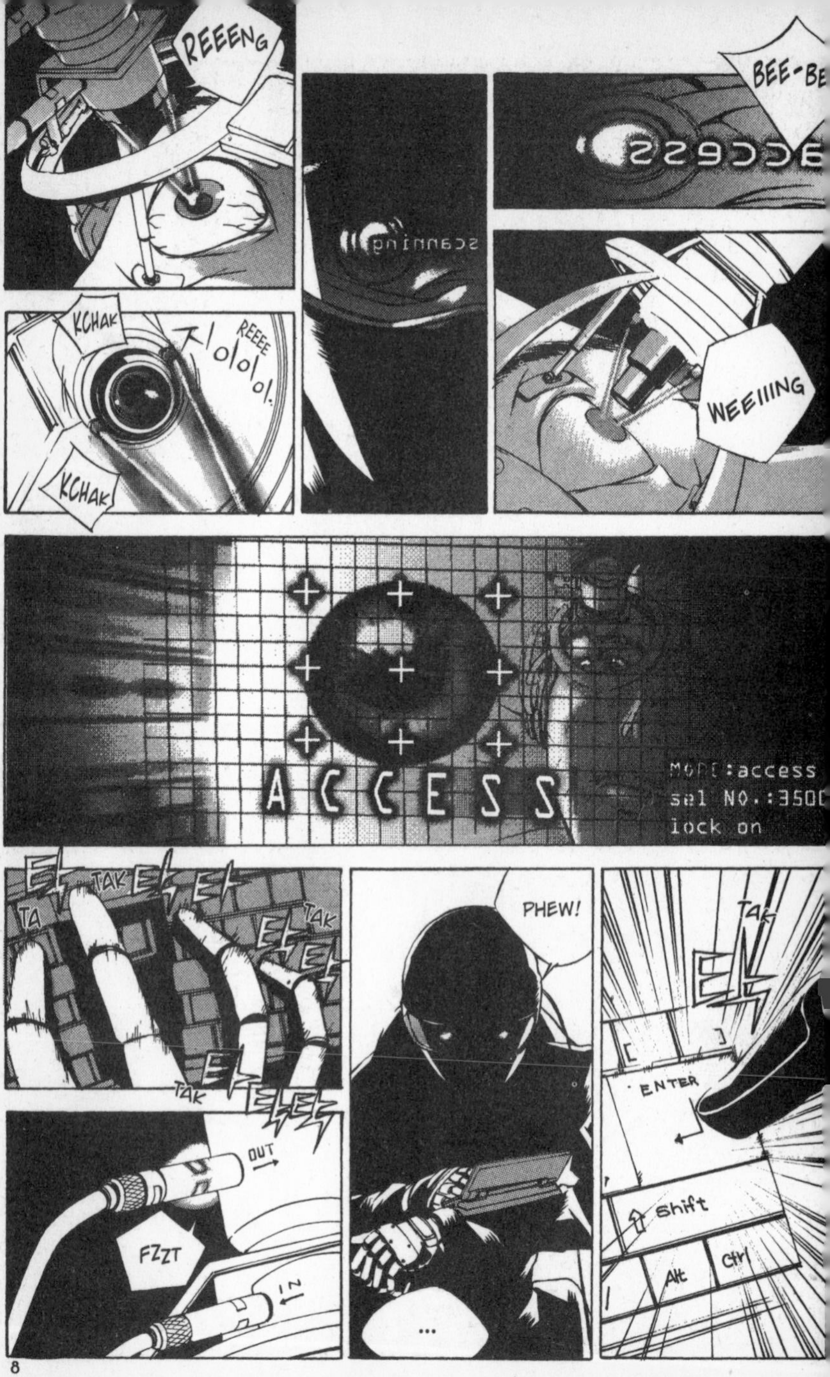

REEENG
KCHAK
REEEE
지이이이이.
KCHAK
scanning
BEE-BE
access
WEEIIING
ACCESS
:access
sal NO.:350
lock on
TA
TAK
TAK
TAK
OUT
FZZT
IN
PHEW!
...
TAK
ENTER
Shift
Alt
Ctrl

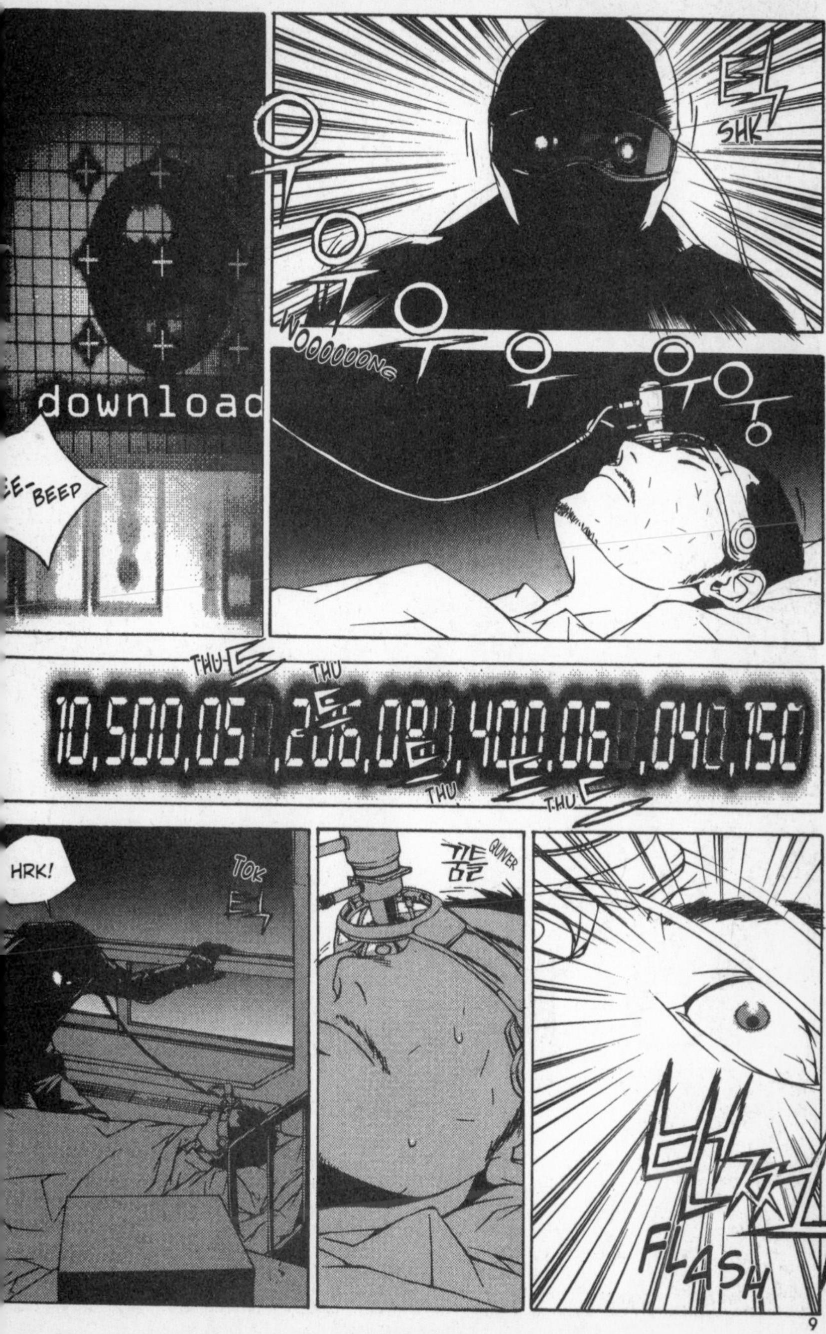
download
EE-BEEP
SHK
WOOOOOONG
THU
THU
10,500,05 ,206,08 ,400,06 ,040,150
THU
THU
HRK!
TOK
QUIVER
FLASH

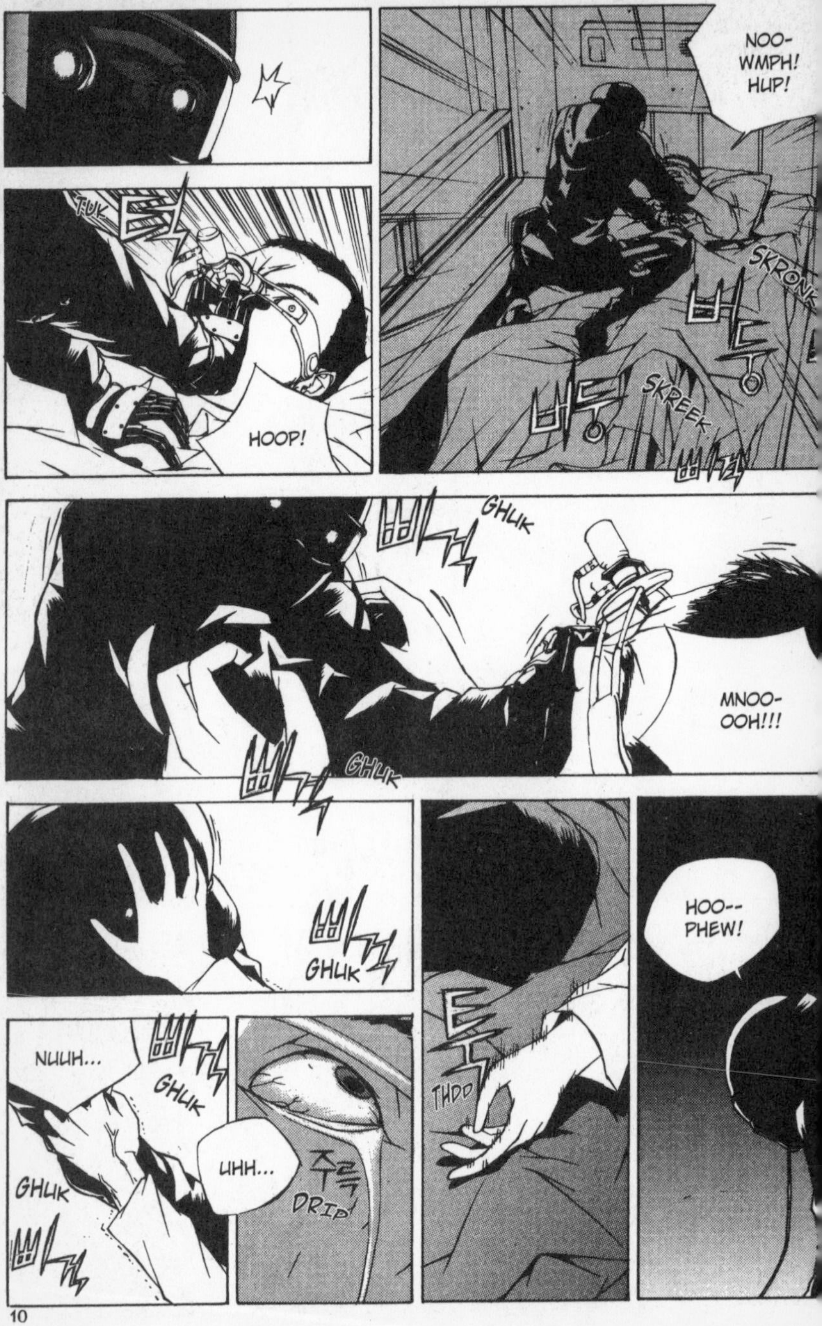

TUK
HOOP!
NOO-
WMPH!
HUP!
SKRONK
SKREEK
GHUK
GHUK
MNOO-
OOH!!!
GHUK
NUUH...
GHUK
GHUK
UHH...
DRIP
THDD
HOO--
PHEW!

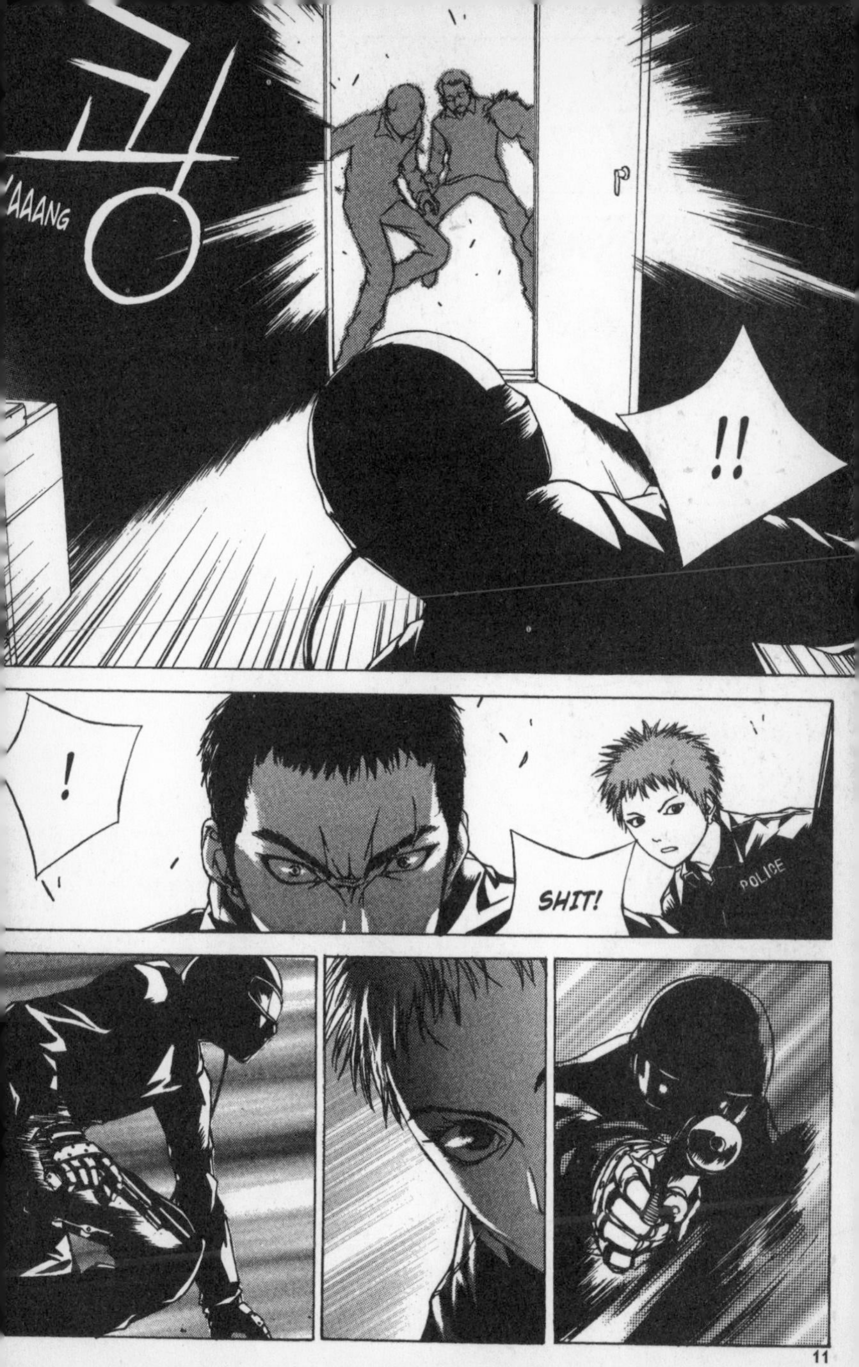
AAANG
!!
!
SHIT!
POLICE

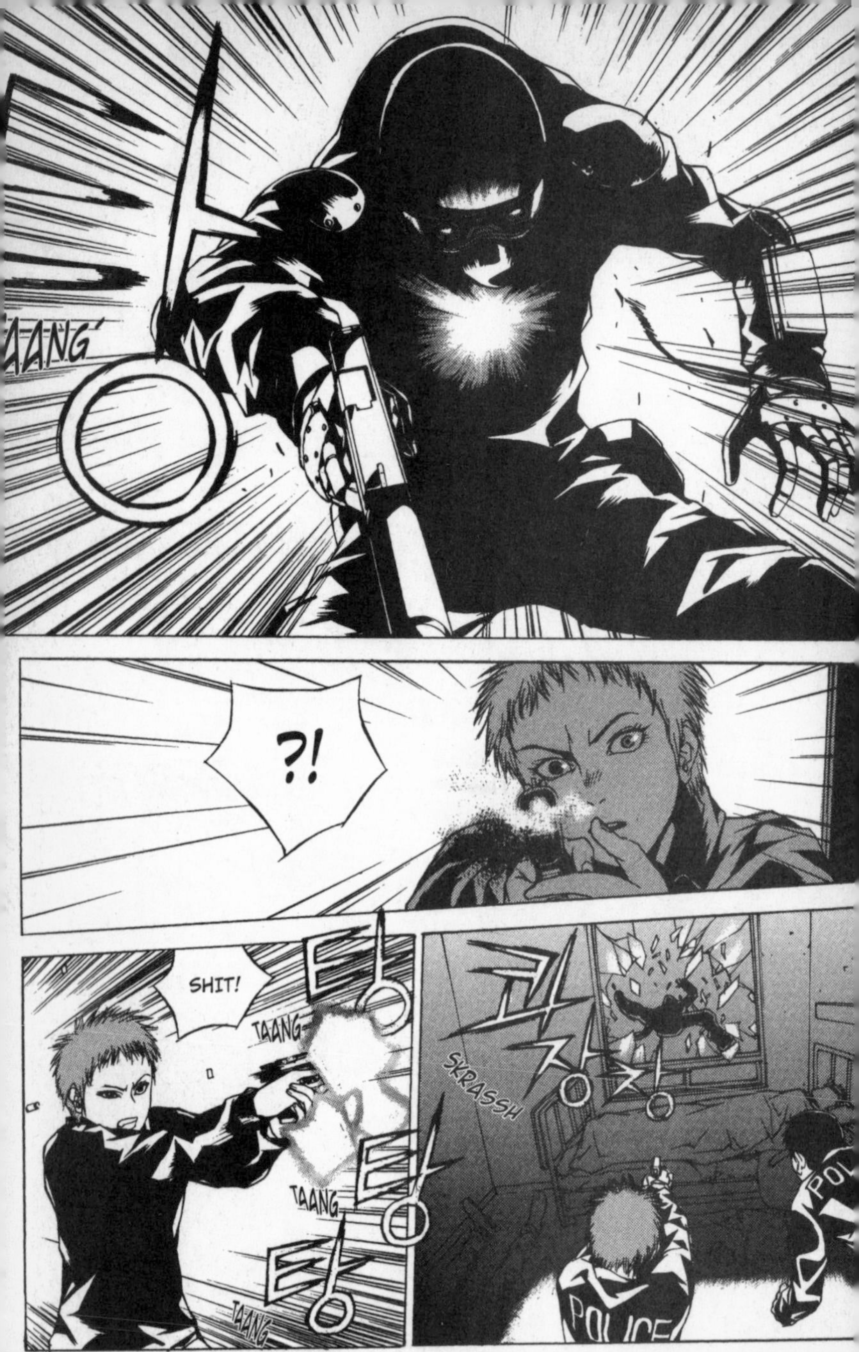
AANG
?!
SHIT!
TAANG
TAANG
TAANG
SKRASSH
POLICE

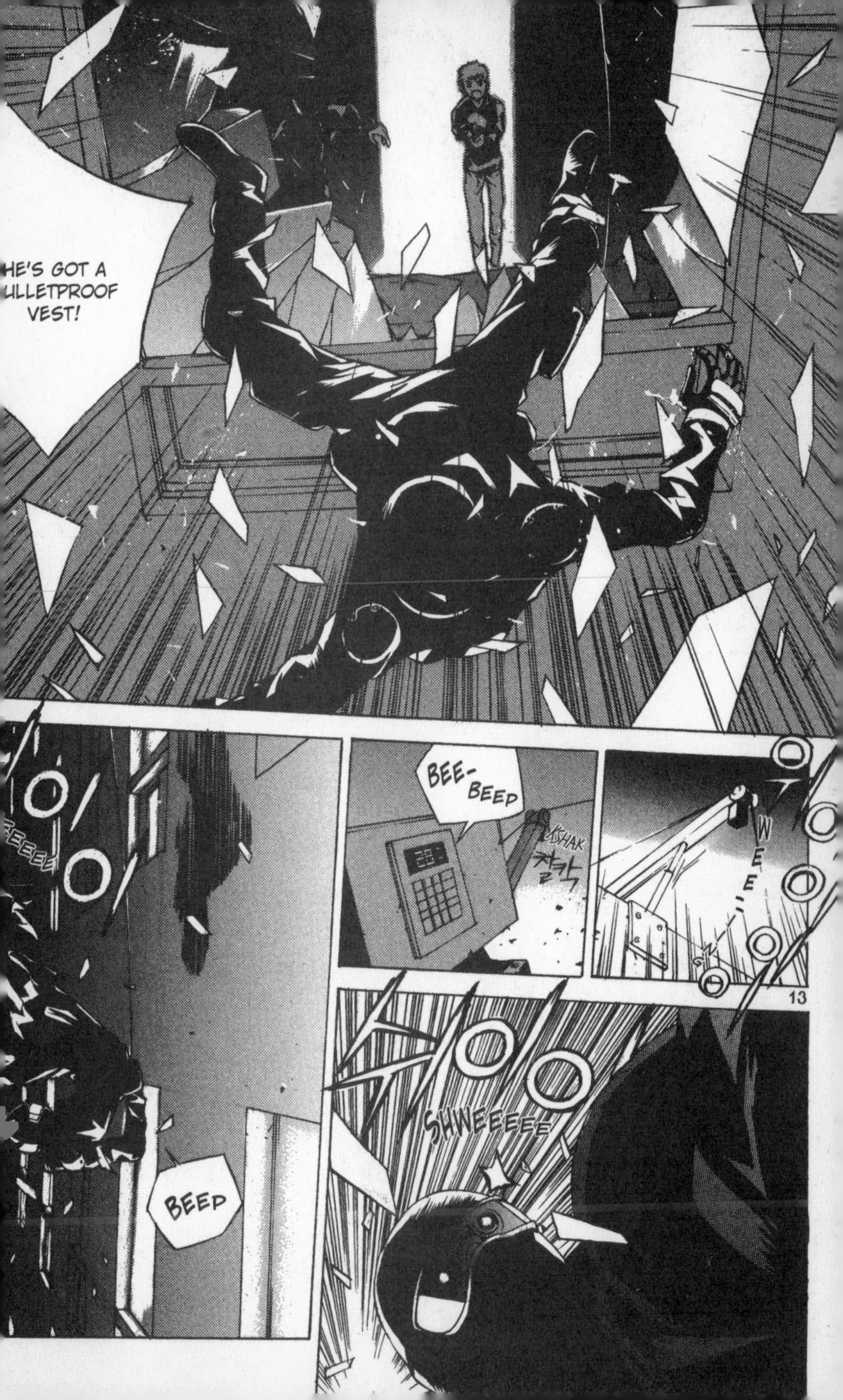
HE'S GOT A
ULLETPROOF
VEST!
EEEEE
BEEP
BEE-BEEP
KSHAK
찰칵
WEE--NG
SHWEEEEEE

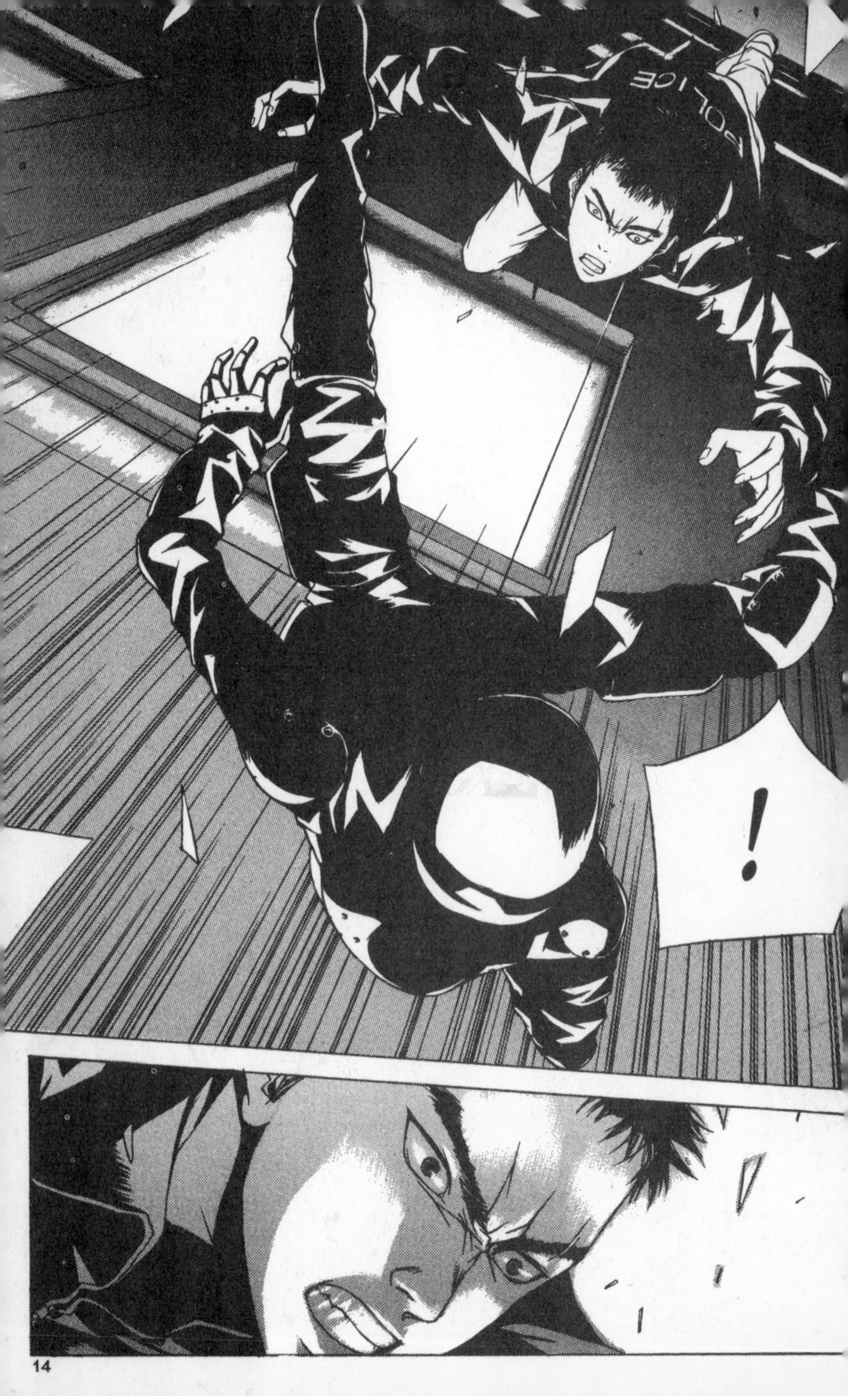
!

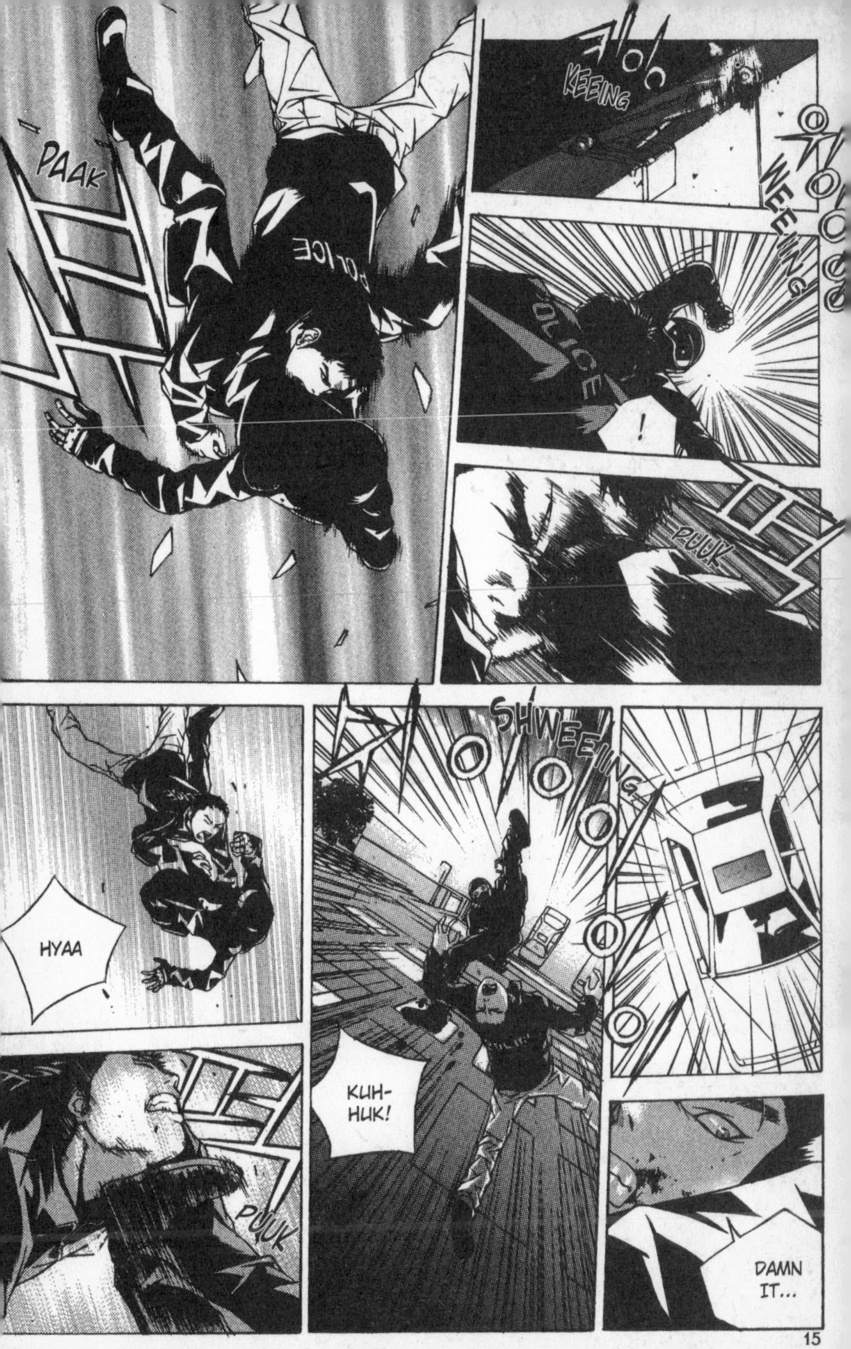
PAAK
KEEING
WEEEING
!
PUUK
HYAA
PUUK
SHWEEEING
KUH-HUK!
DAMN IT...

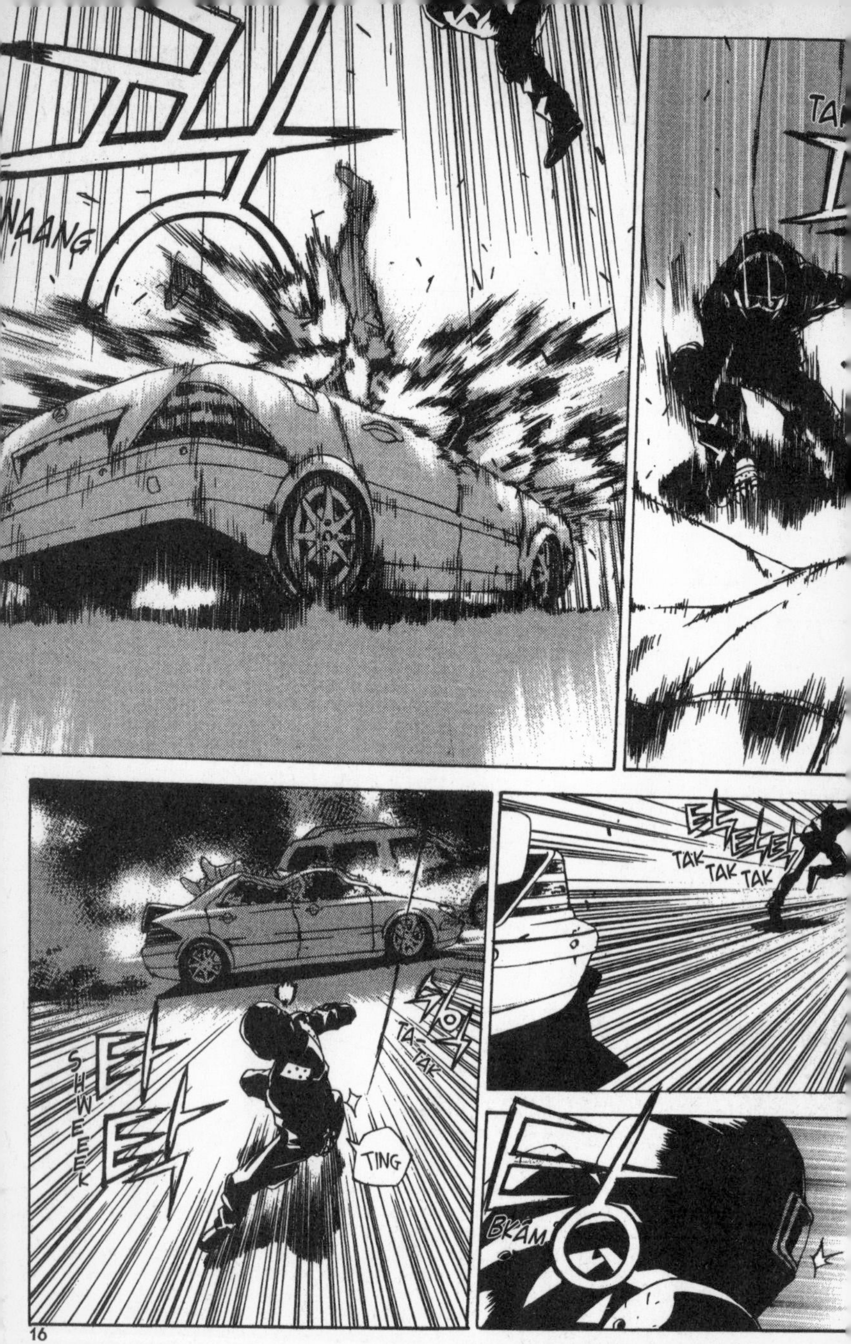
NAANG
TA
SHWEEEK
TA-TAK
TING
TAK TAK TAK
BKAM

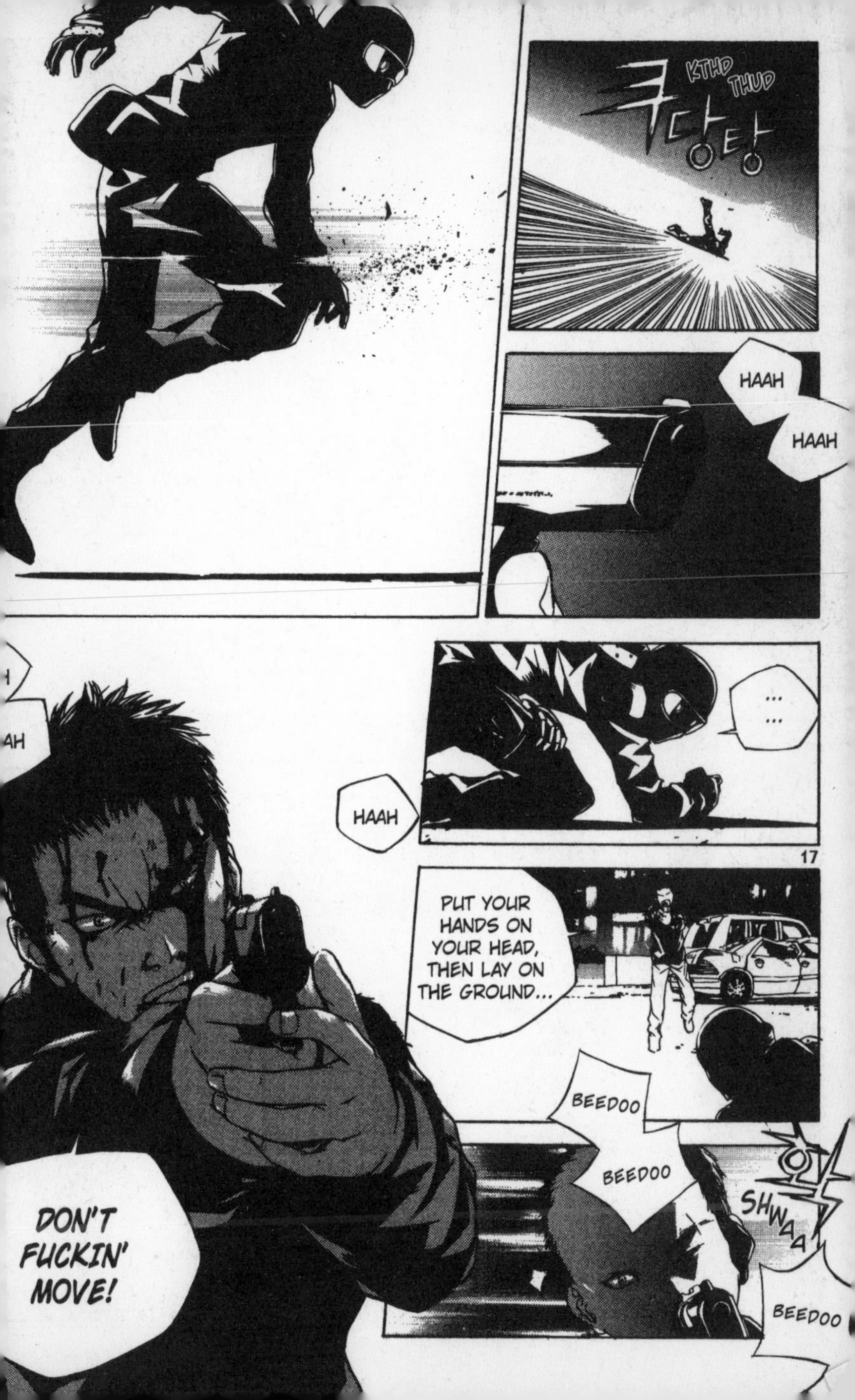
KTHD
THUD
HAAH
HAAH
DON'T FUCKIN' MOVE!
......
HAAH
PUT YOUR HANDS ON YOUR HEAD, THEN LAY ON THE GROUND...
BEEDOO
BEEDOO
SHWAA
BEEDOO

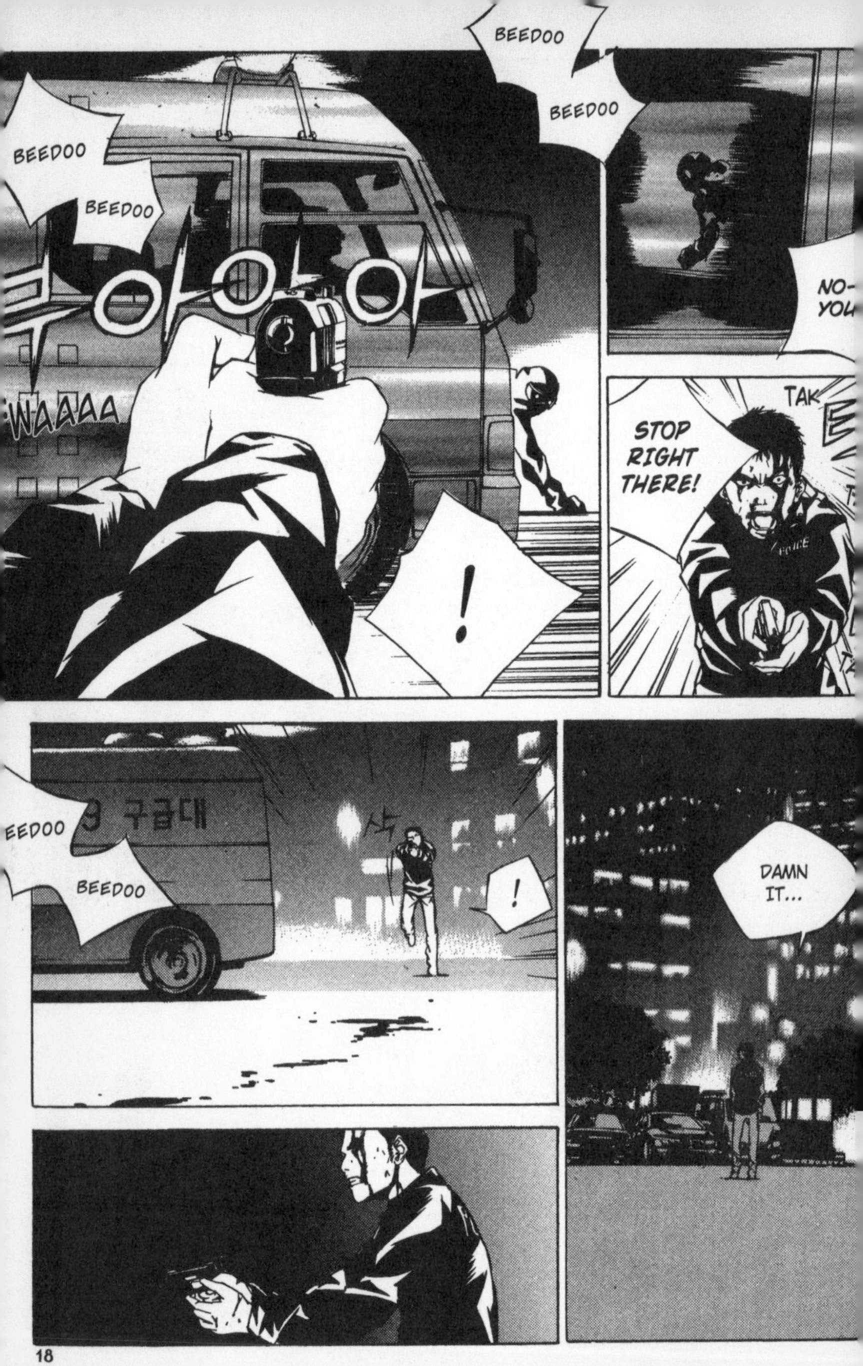
BEEDOO
BEEDOO
BEEDOO
BEEDOO
WAAAA
!
NO-
YOU
TAK
STOP RIGHT THERE!
EEDOO
BEEDOO
구급대
!
DAMN IT...

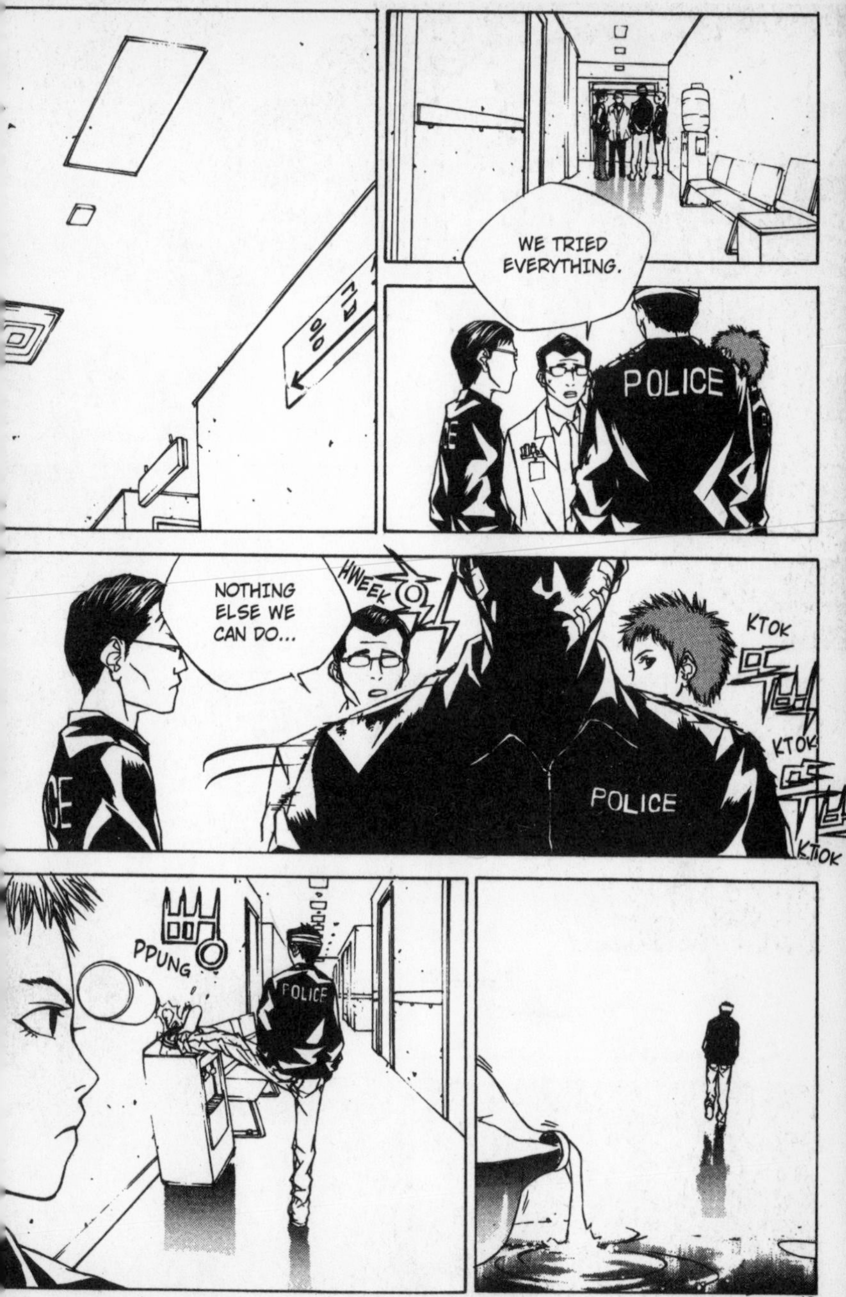
WE TRIED EVERYTHING.
POLICE
NOTHING ELSE WE CAN DO...
HWEEK
KTOK
KTOK
POLICE
KTOK
PPUNG
POLICE

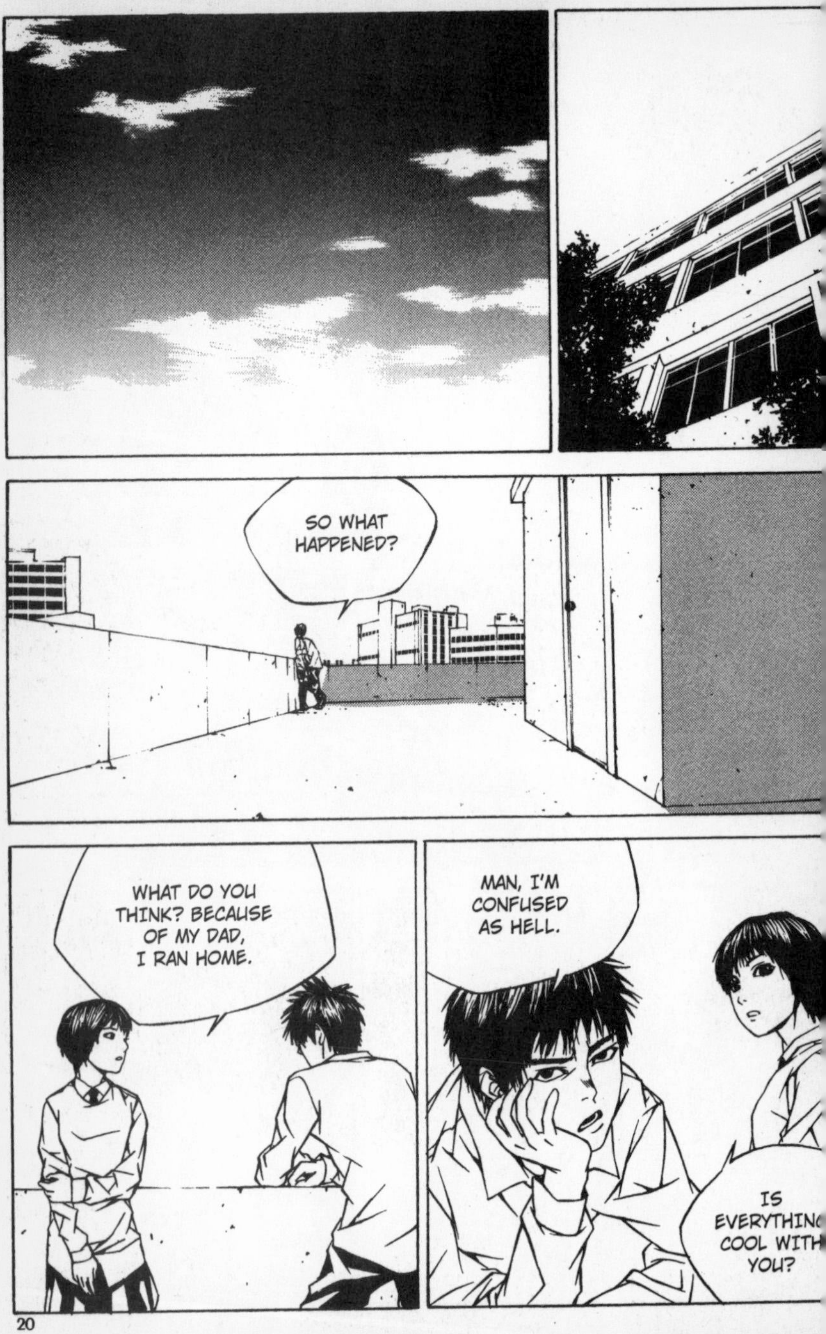
SO WHAT HAPPENED?
WHAT DO YOU THINK? BECAUSE OF MY DAD, I RAN HOME.
MAN, I'M CONFUSED AS HELL.
IS EVERYTHING COOL WITH YOU?

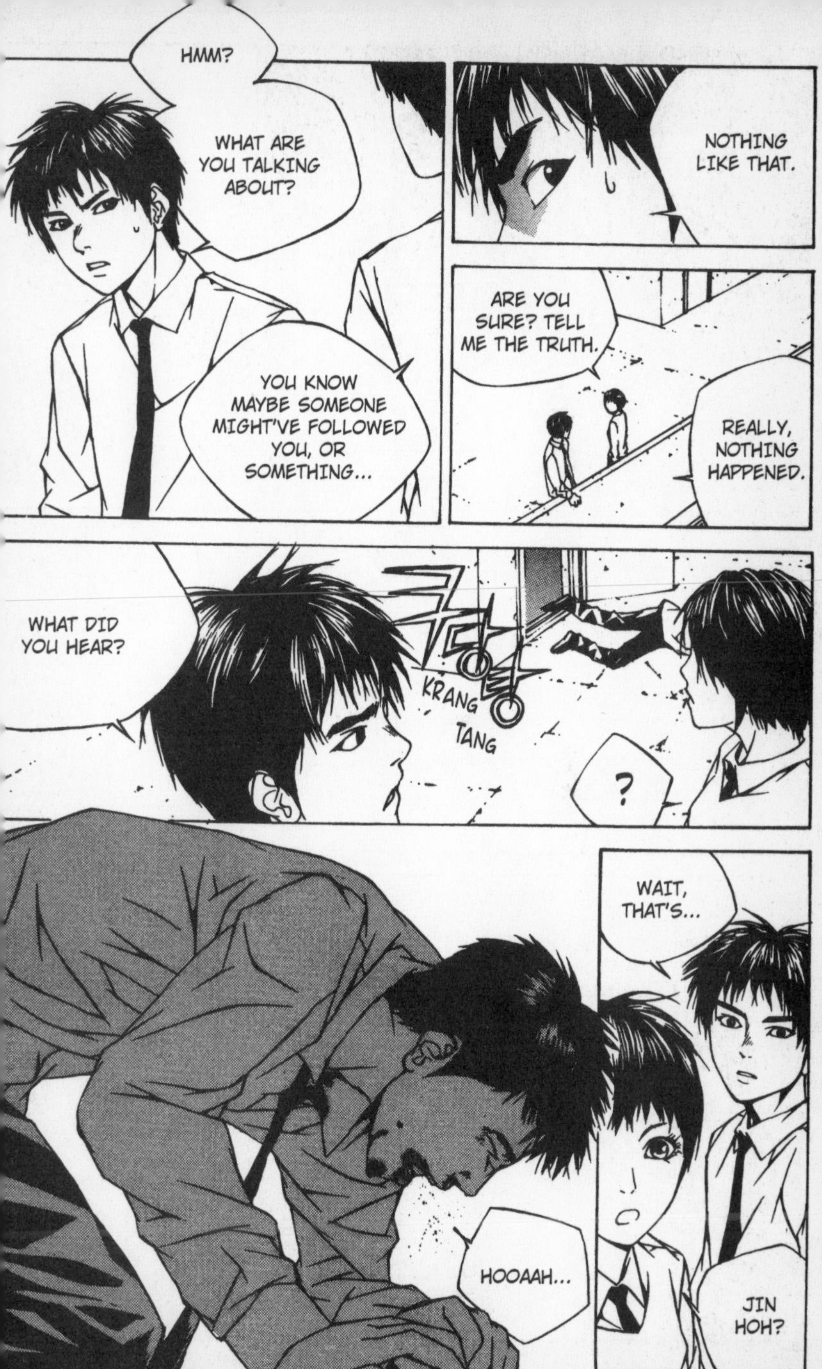
HMM?
WHAT ARE YOU TALKING ABOUT?
YOU KNOW MAYBE SOMEONE MIGHT'VE FOLLOWED YOU, OR SOMETHING...
NOTHING LIKE THAT.
ARE YOU SURE? TELL ME THE TRUTH.
REALLY, NOTHING HAPPENED.
WHAT DID YOU HEAR?
KRANG
TANG
?
WAIT, THAT'S...
HOOAAH...
JIN HOH?

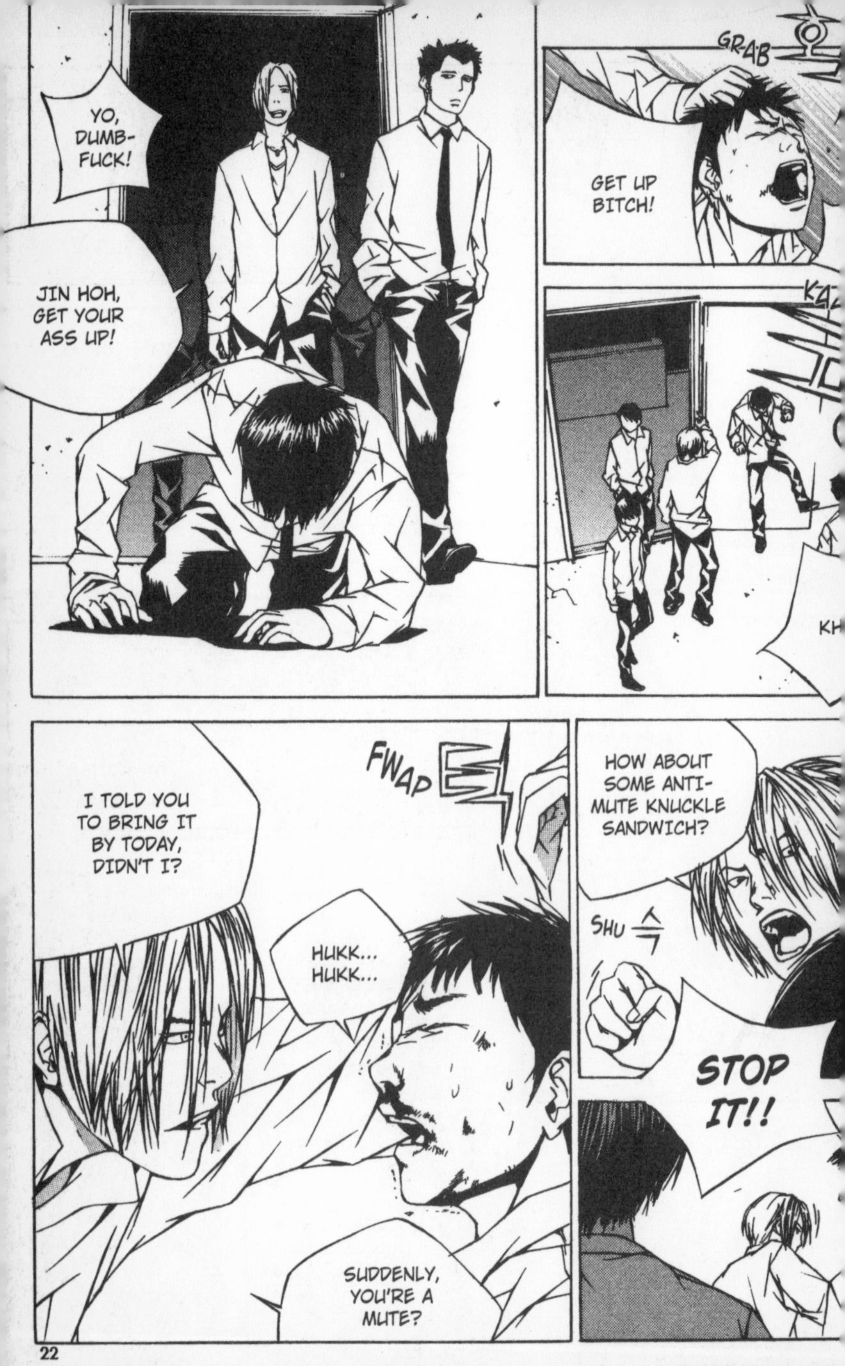

YO, DUMB-FUCK!
JIN HOH, GET YOUR ASS UP!
GRAB
GET UP BITCH!
I TOLD YOU TO BRING IT BY TODAY, DIDN'T I?
FWAP
HUKK... HUKK...
SUDDENLY, YOU'RE A MUTE?
HOW ABOUT SOME ANTI-MUTE KNUCKLE SANDWICH?
SHU 슥
STOP IT!!

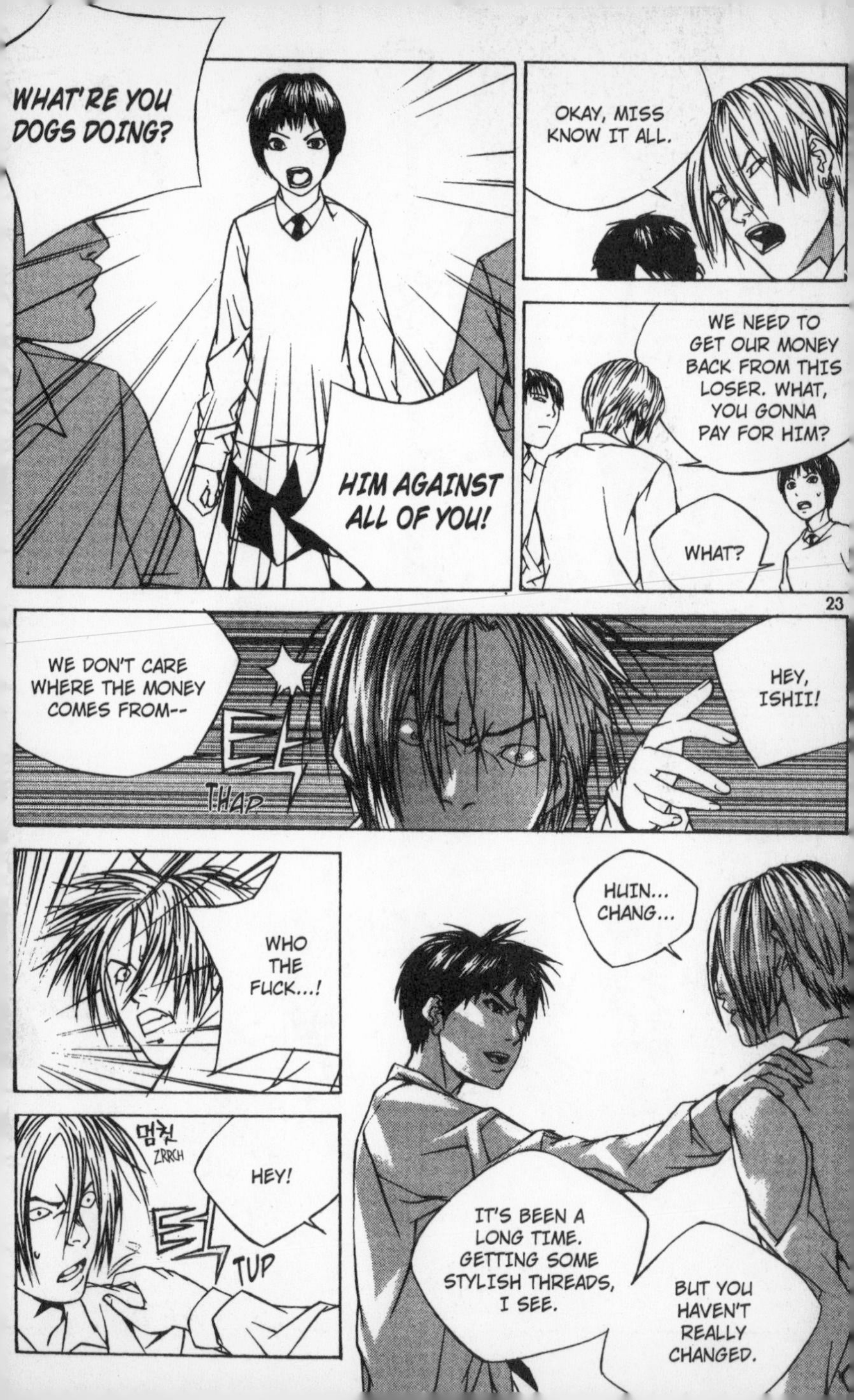
WHAT'RE YOU DOGS DOING?
HIM AGAINST ALL OF YOU!
OKAY, MISS KNOW IT ALL.
WE NEED TO GET OUR MONEY BACK FROM THIS LOSER. WHAT, YOU GONNA PAY FOR HIM?
WHAT?
WE DON'T CARE WHERE THE MONEY COMES FROM--
THAP
HEY, ISHII!
WHO THE FUCK...!
멈칫
ZRRCH
HEY!
TUP
HUIN... CHANG...
IT'S BEEN A LONG TIME. GETTING SOME STYLISH THREADS, I SEE.
BUT YOU HAVEN'T REALLY CHANGED.

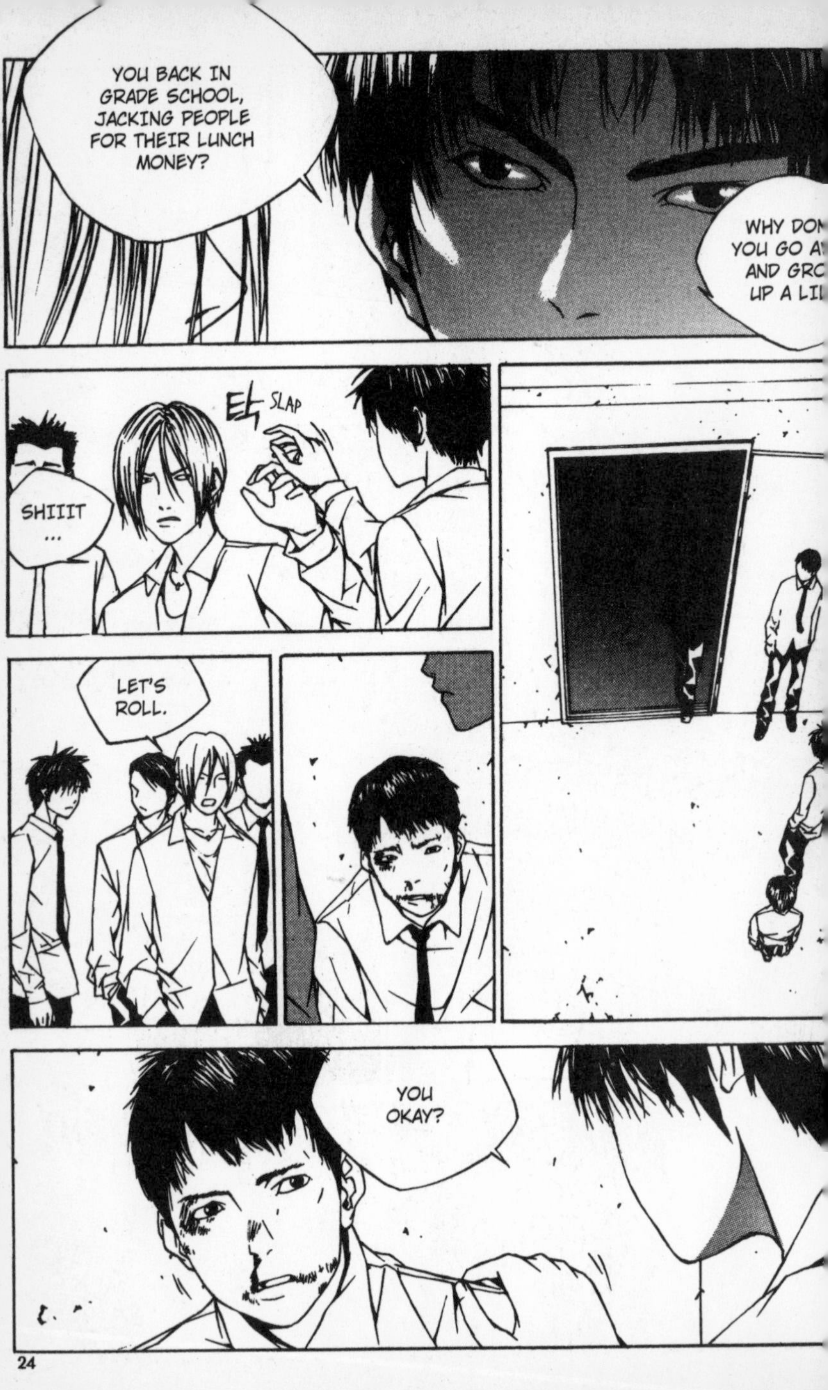

YOU BACK IN GRADE SCHOOL, JACKING PEOPLE FOR THEIR LUNCH MONEY?
WHY DON YOU GO A AND GRO UP A LI
SHIIIT ...
SLAP
LET'S ROLL.
YOU OKAY?

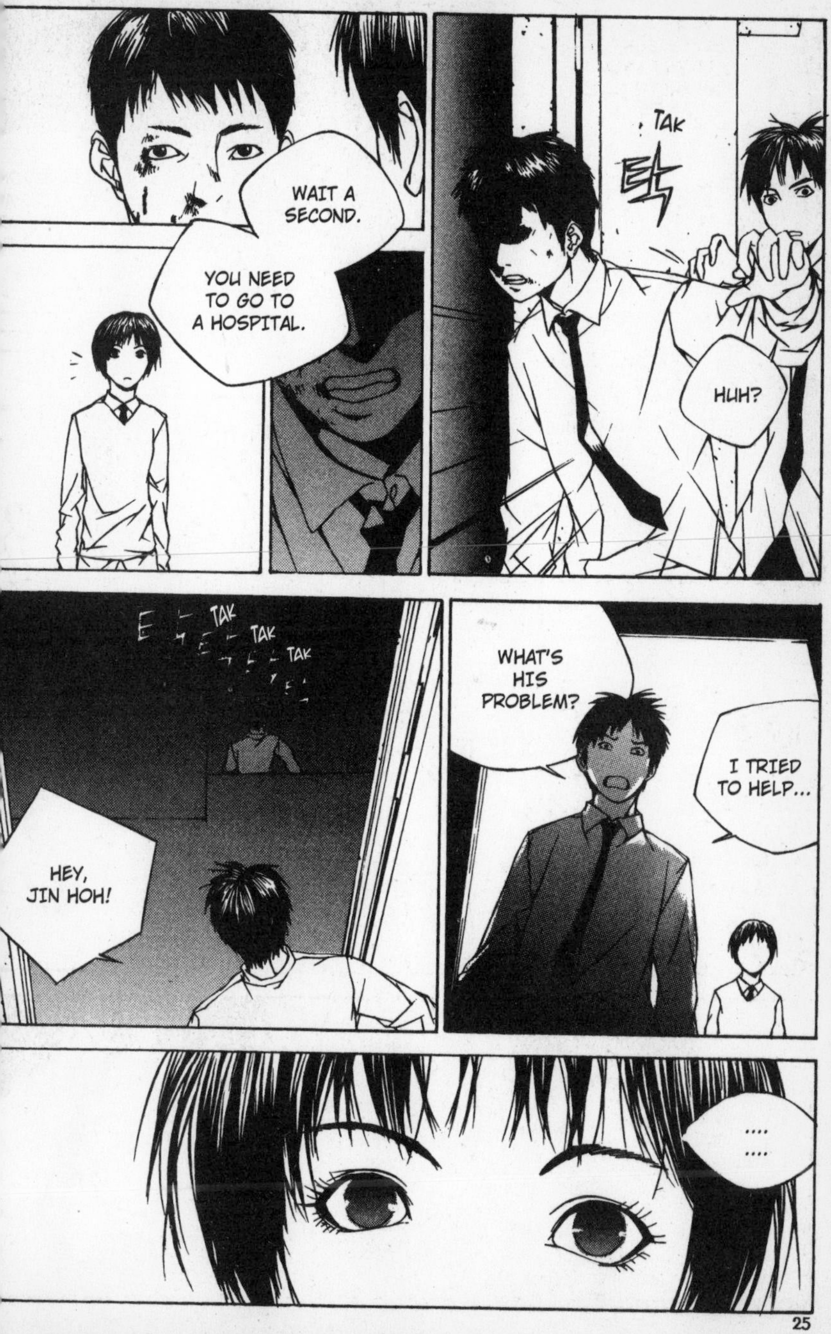
WAIT A SECOND.
YOU NEED TO GO TO A HOSPITAL.
TAK
HUH?
TAK
TAK
TAK
HEY, JIN HOH!
WHAT'S HIS PROBLEM?
I TRIED TO HELP...
....
....

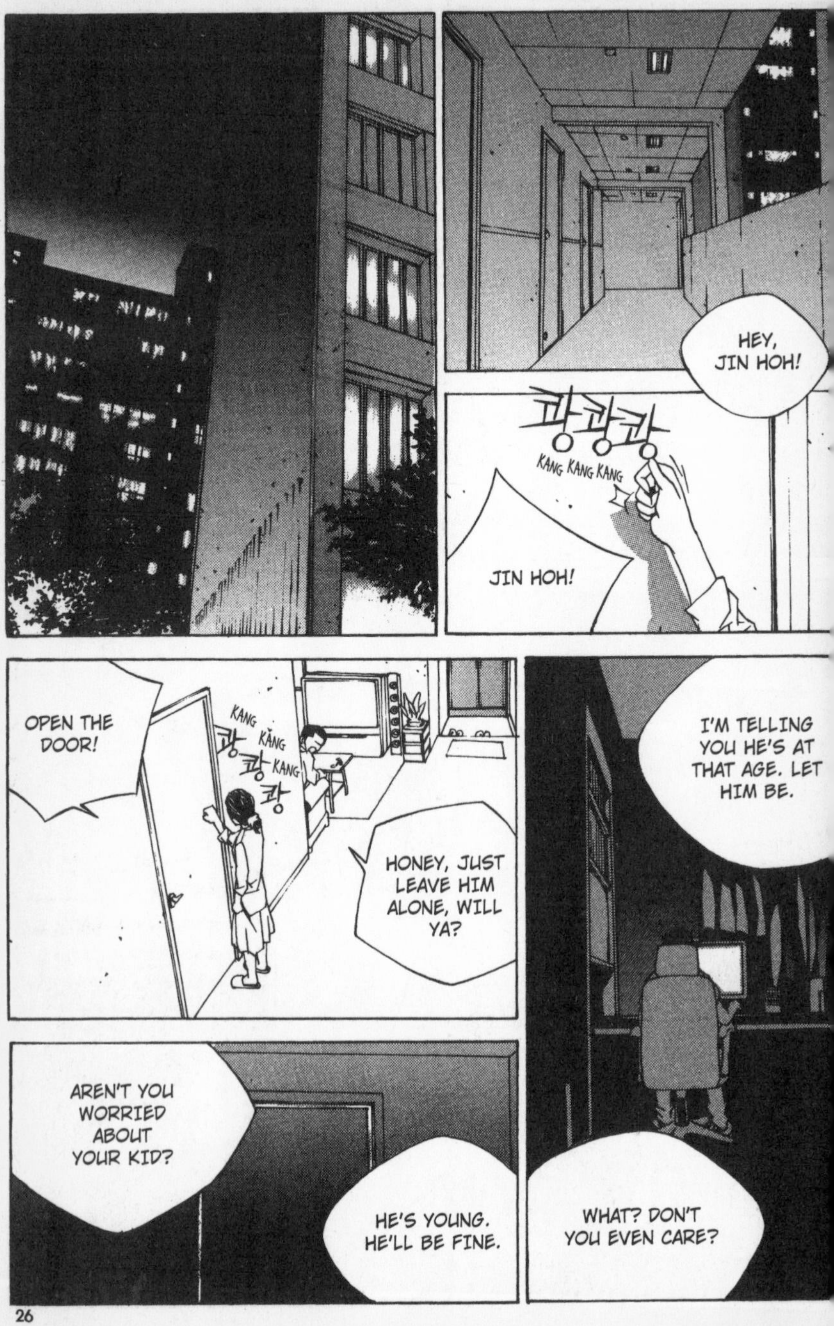
HEY, JIN HOH!
광광광
KANG KANG KANG
JIN HOH!
OPEN THE DOOR!
KANG KANG KANG
광광광
HONEY, JUST LEAVE HIM ALONE, WILL YA?
AREN'T YOU WORRIED ABOUT YOUR KID?
HE'S YOUNG. HE'LL BE FINE.
I'M TELLING YOU HE'S AT THAT AGE. LET HIM BE.
WHAT? DON'T YOU EVEN CARE?

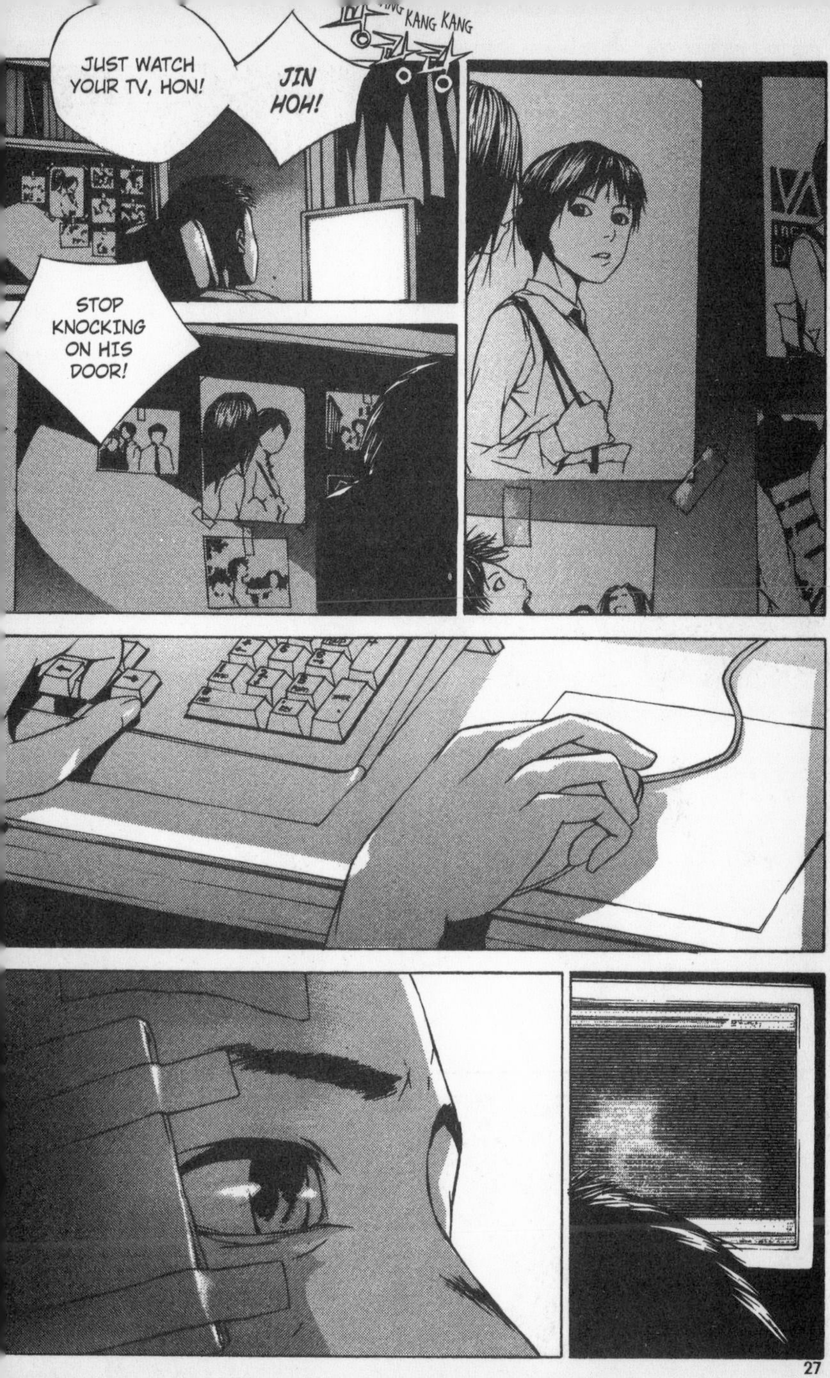
JUST WATCH YOUR TV, HON!
JIN HOH!
KANG KANG
STOP KNOCKING ON HIS DOOR!

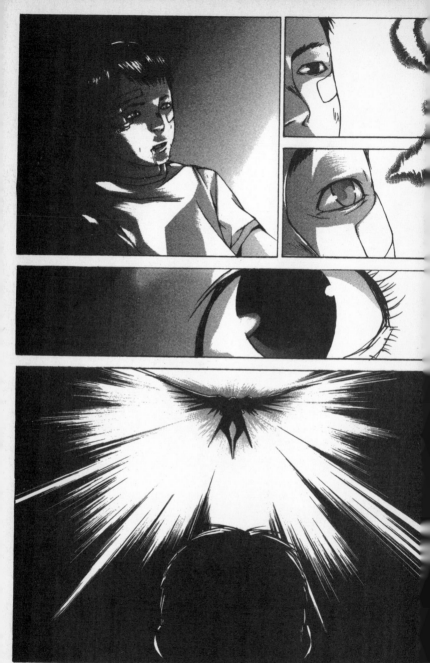

Log-8 END

XS 엑세스

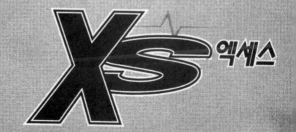

Ducati 996 · EM!

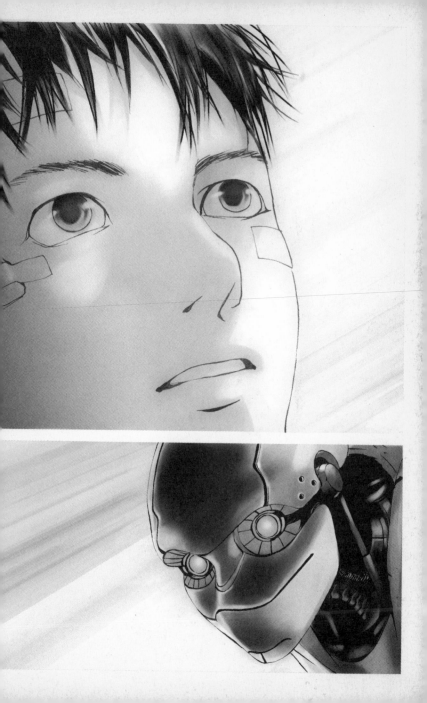

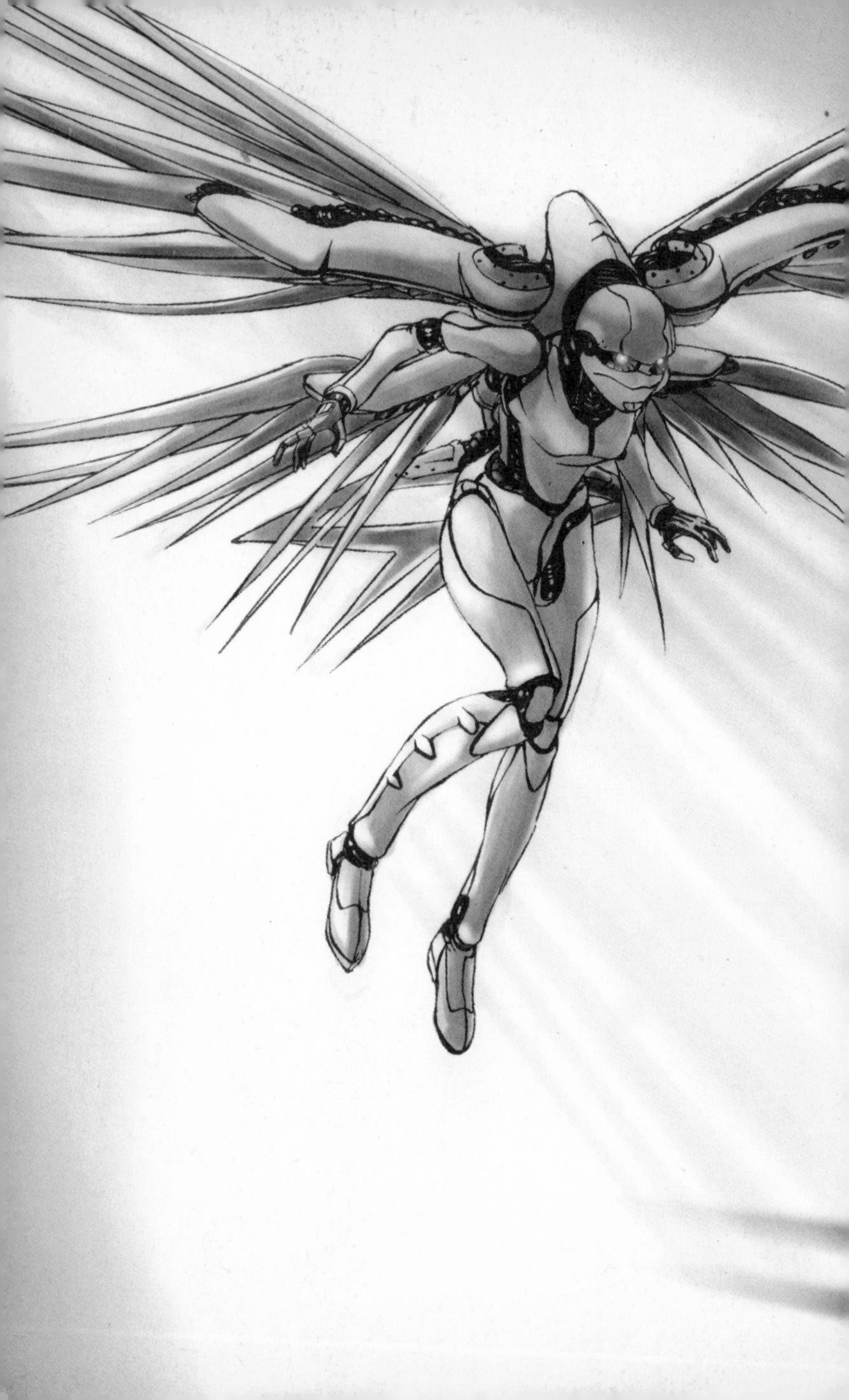

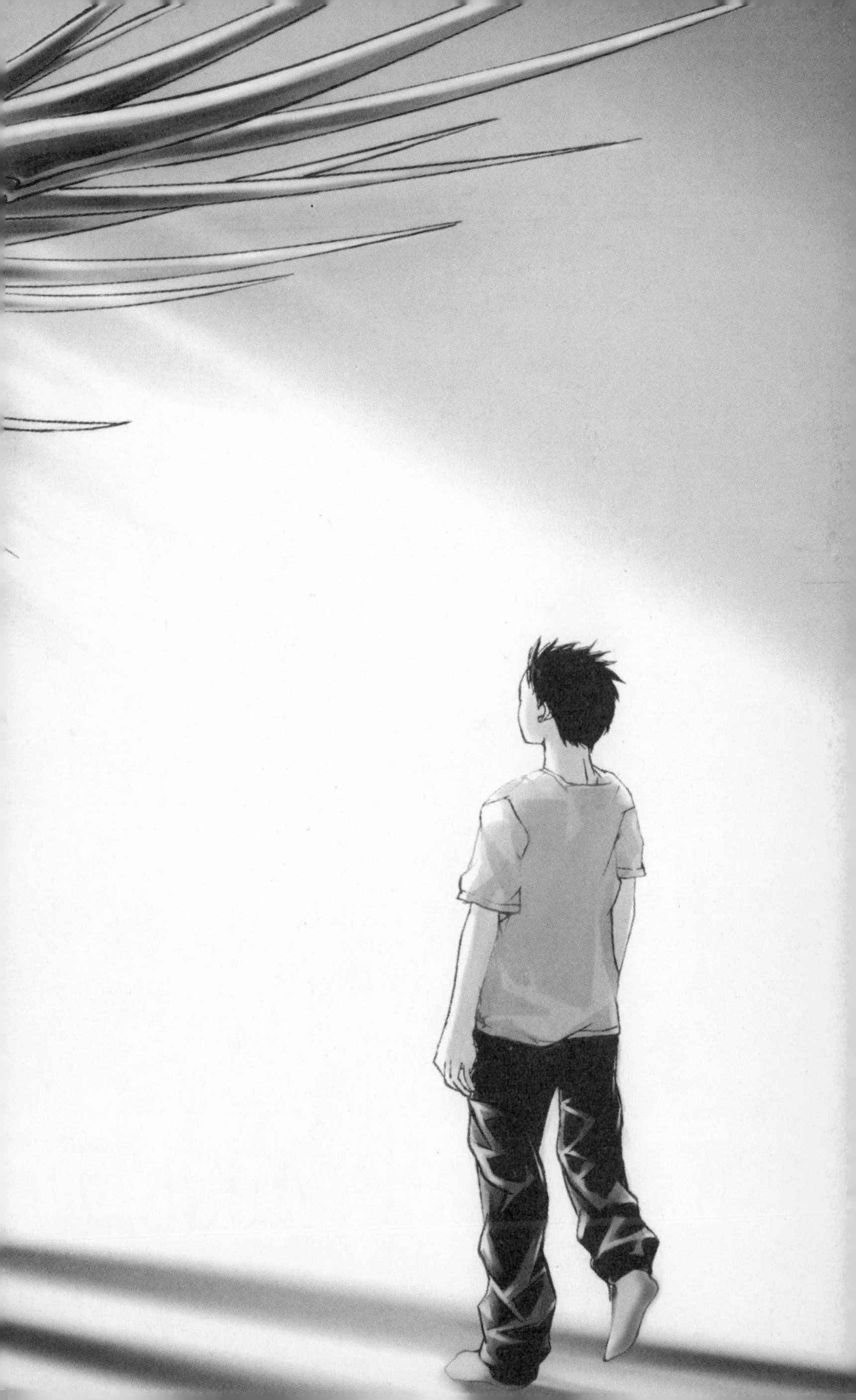

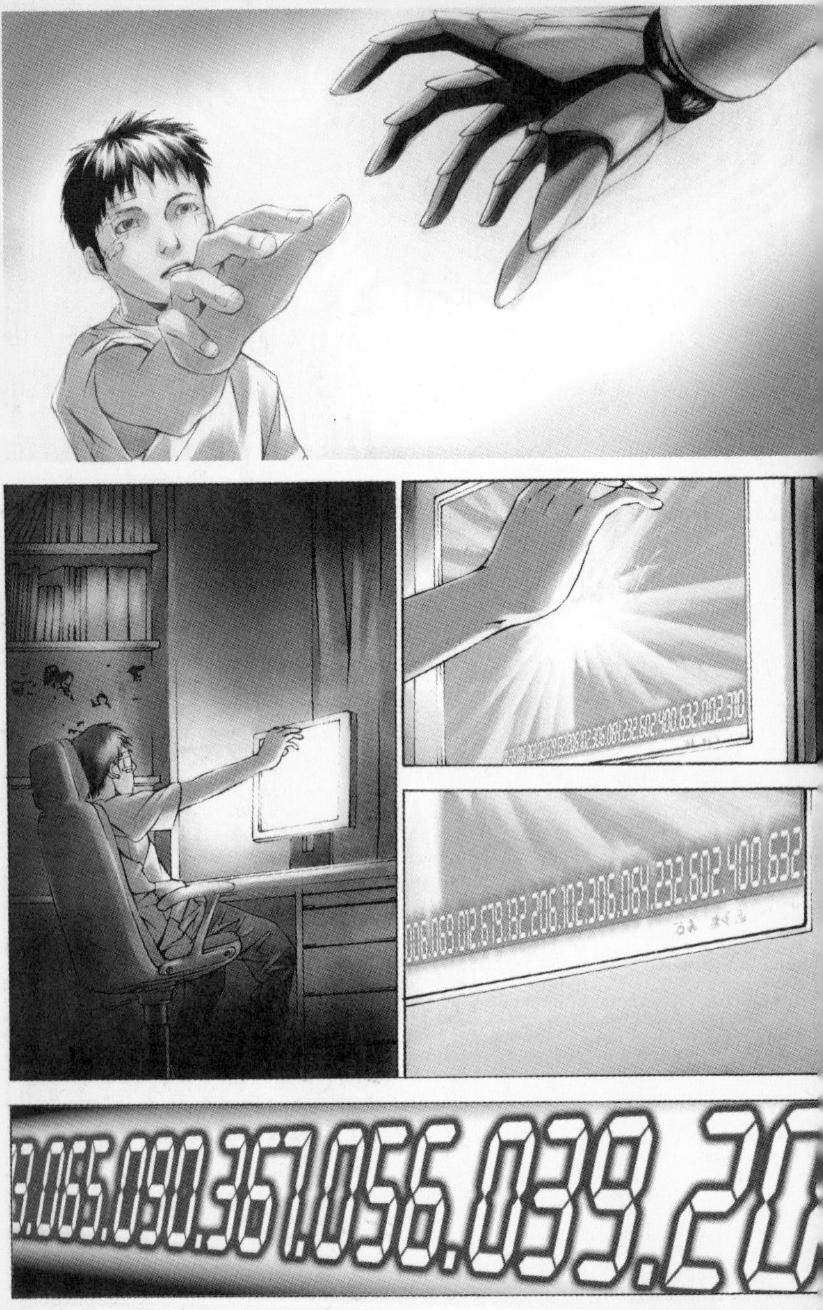
232.602.400.632.002.310
008.069.012.679.132.206.102.306.064.232.602.400.632.
065.080.367.056.039.20

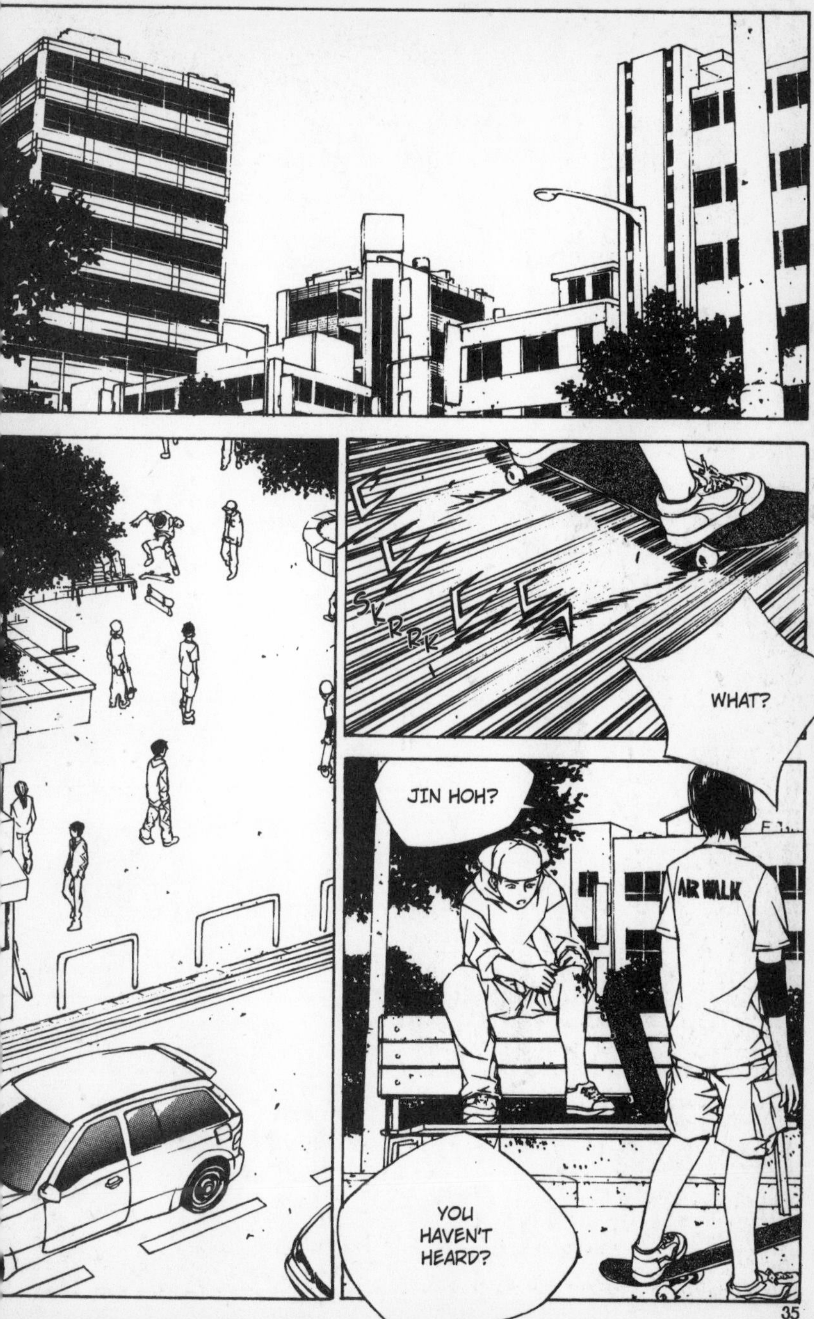
SKRRK
WHAT?
JIN HOH?
AIR WALK
YOU HAVEN'T HEARD?

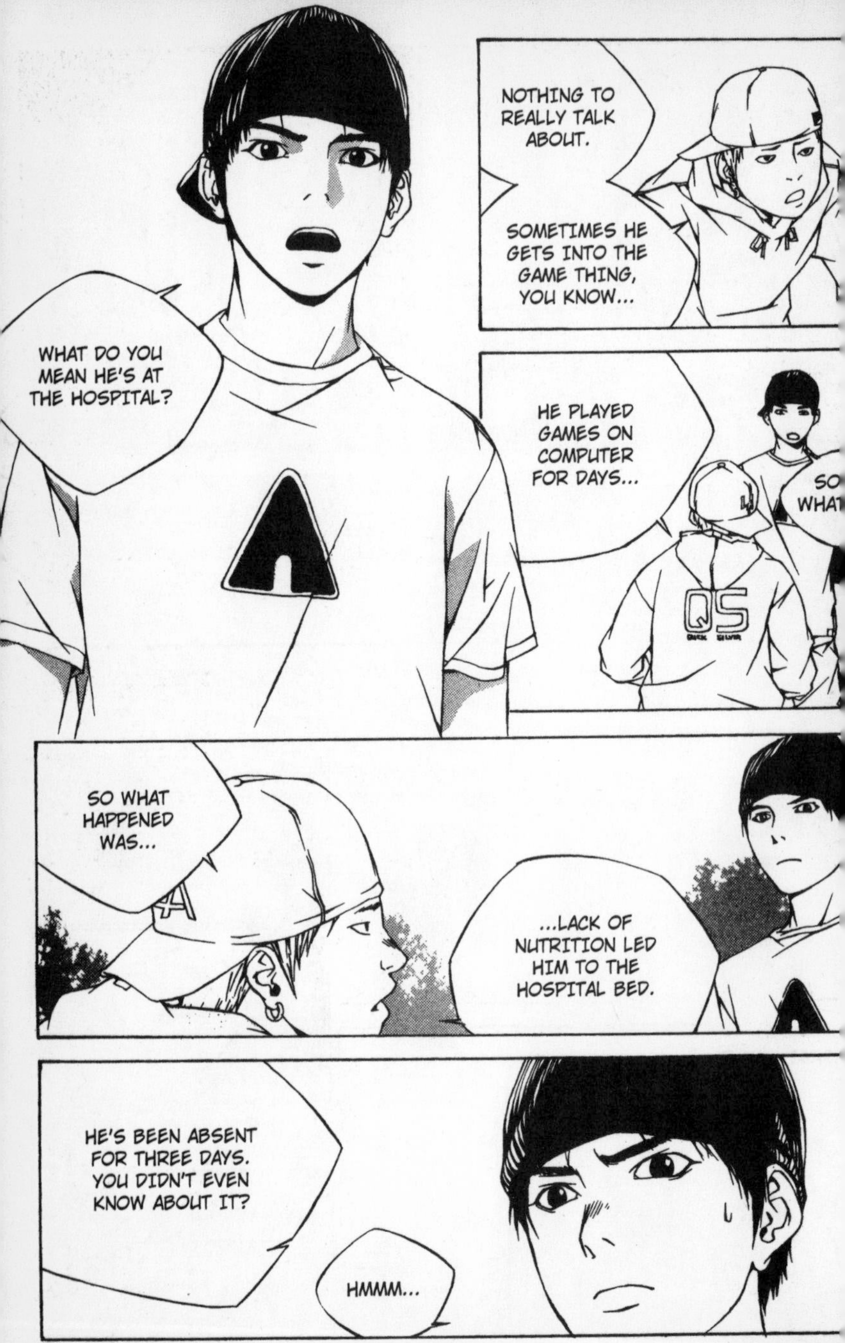
WHAT DO YOU MEAN HE'S AT THE HOSPITAL?
NOTHING TO REALLY TALK ABOUT.
SOMETIMES HE GETS INTO THE GAME THING, YOU KNOW...
HE PLAYED GAMES ON COMPUTER FOR DAYS...
SO WHAT
SO WHAT HAPPENED WAS...
...LACK OF NUTRITION LED HIM TO THE HOSPITAL BED.
HE'S BEEN ABSENT FOR THREE DAYS. YOU DIDN'T EVEN KNOW ABOUT IT?
HMMM...

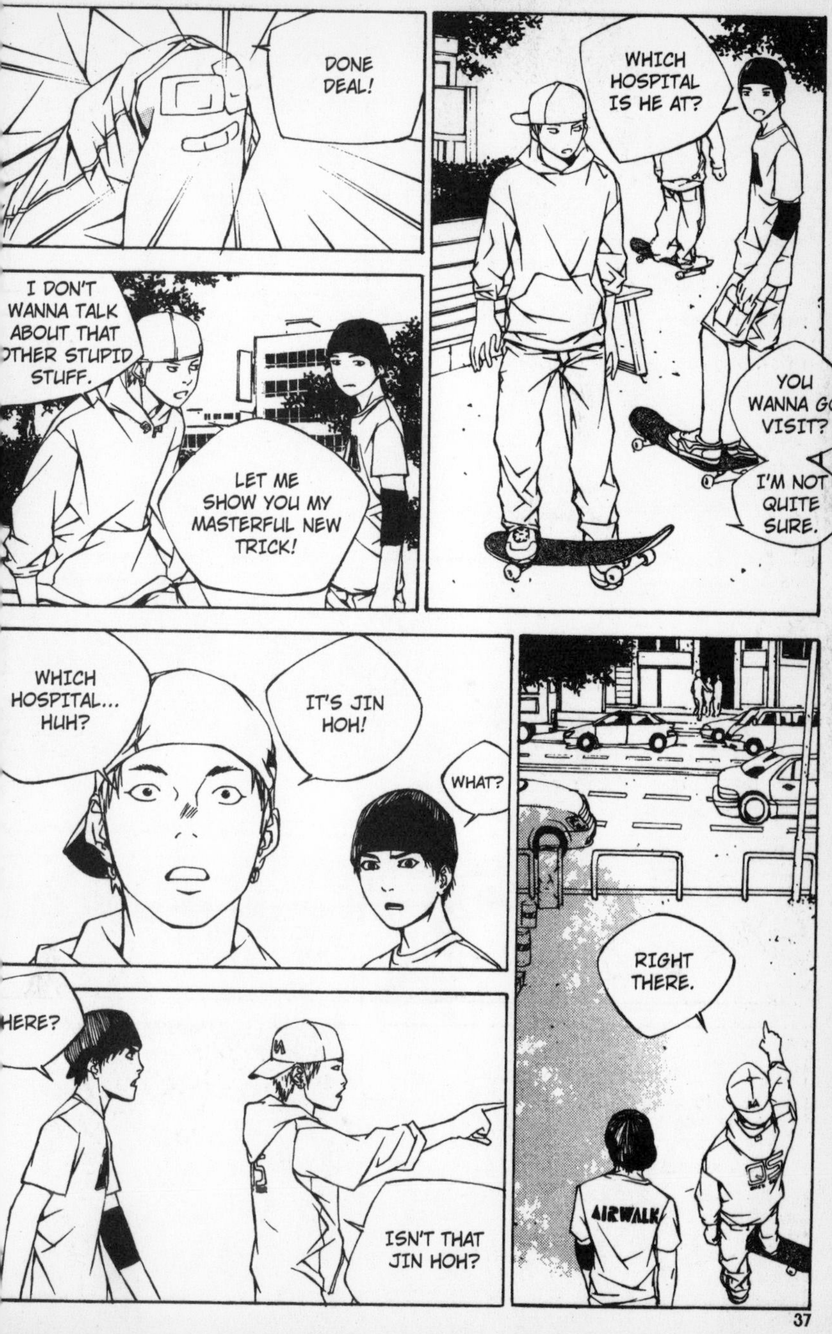
DONE DEAL!
I DON'T WANNA TALK ABOUT THAT OTHER STUPID STUFF.
LET ME SHOW YOU MY MASTERFUL NEW TRICK!
WHICH HOSPITAL IS HE AT?
YOU WANNA GO VISIT?
I'M NOT QUITE SURE.
WHICH HOSPITAL... HUH?
IT'S JIN HOH!
WHAT?
HERE?
ISN'T THAT JIN HOH?
RIGHT THERE.
AIRWALK

I'VE SEEN THOSE GUYS BEFORE.

WHAT'RE THEY DOING WITH JIN HOH?

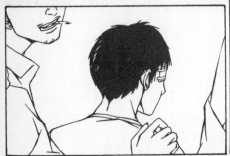

HEY, HEY, I DON'T LIKE THIS SCENE HERE.

THOSE BASTARDS...

TAK TAK TAK TAK

HUH?

HE
CHAN

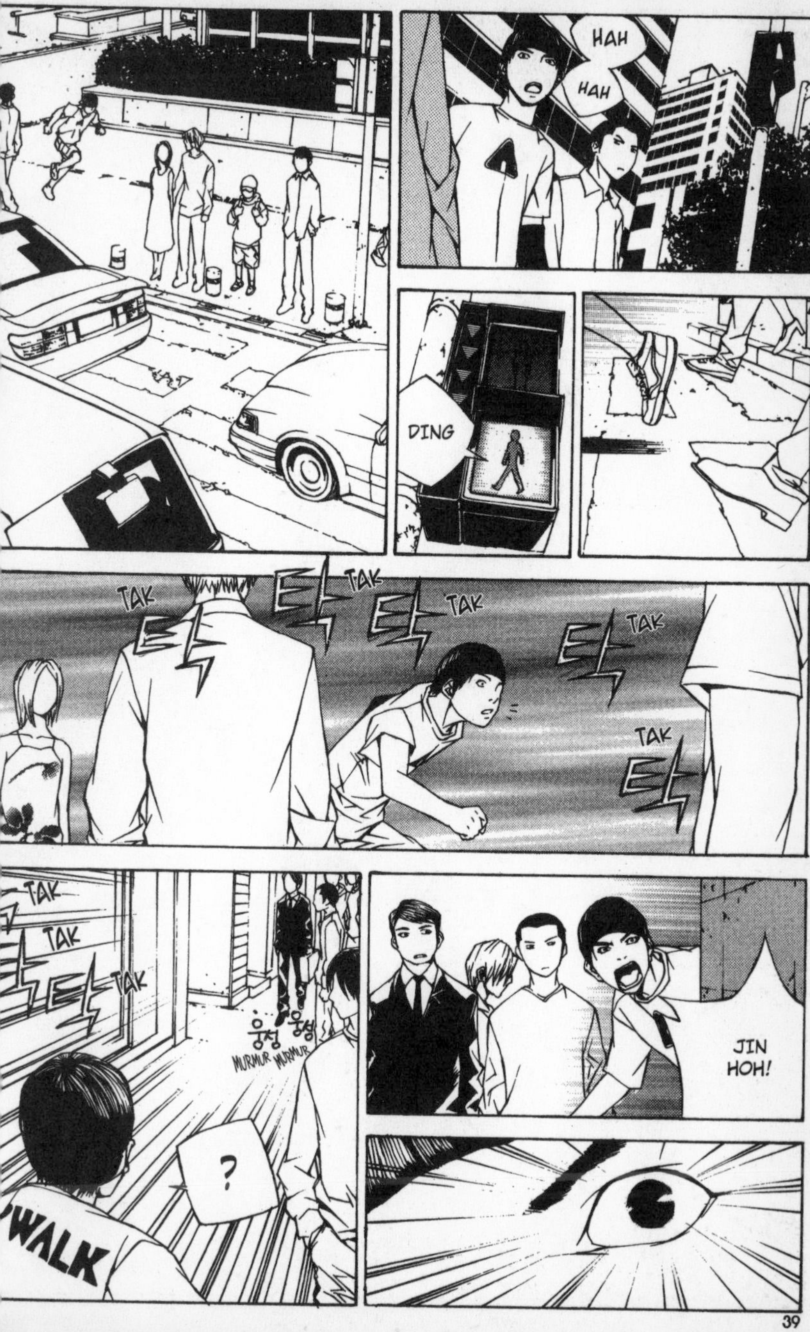

HAH
HAH
DING
TAK
타
타
TAK
타
TAK
타
TAK
TAK
타
TAK
TAK
타
타
TAK
웅성 웅성
MURMUR MURMUR
?
WALK
JIN HOH!

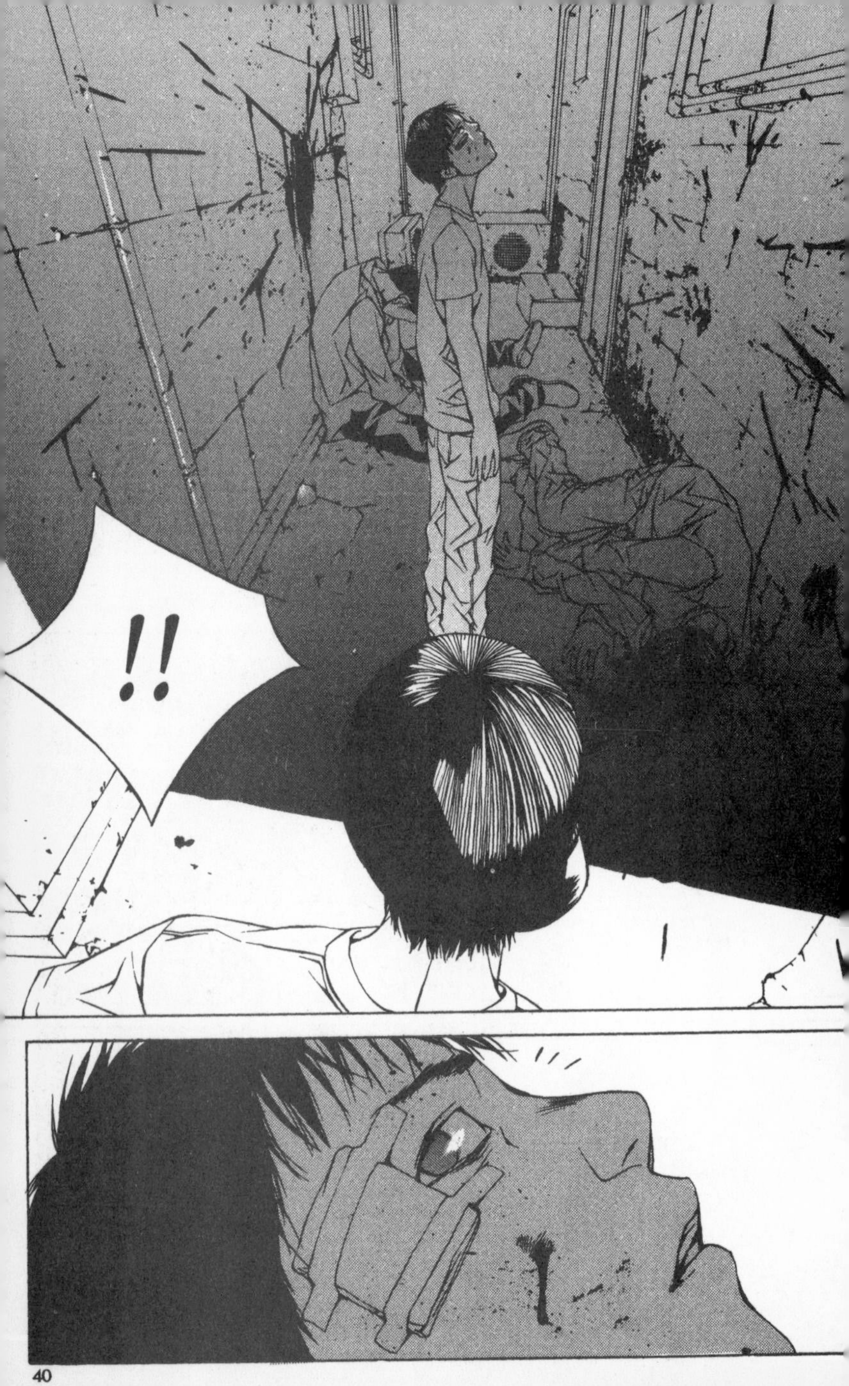
!!

WHA--

WHAT THE--

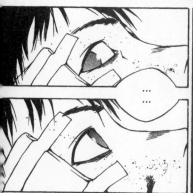

...
...

S...
TEEL...

AN...
GEL...

HUH?

STEEL...
ANGEL?

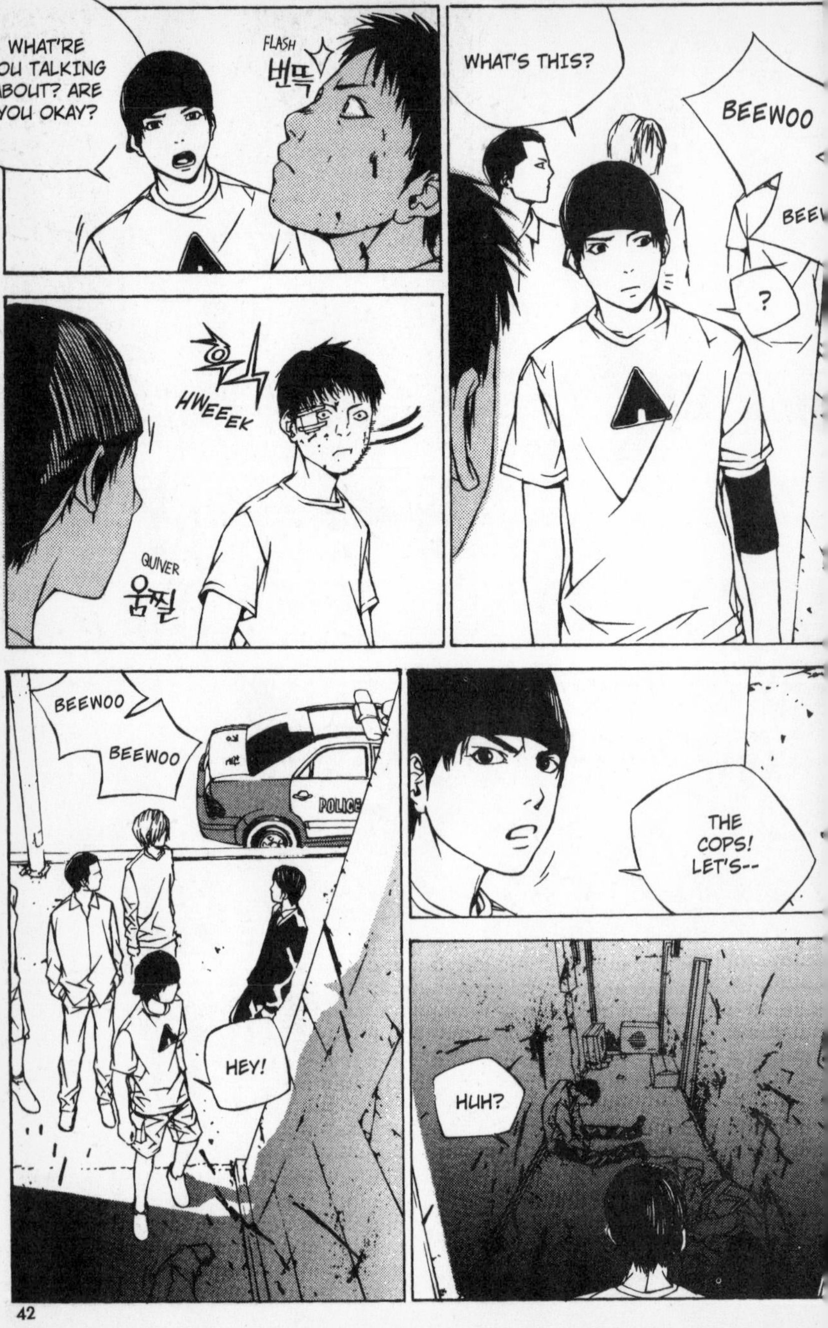
WHAT'RE YOU TALKING ABOUT? ARE YOU OKAY?
FLASH
번뜩
HWEEEK
휙
QUIVER
움찔
WHAT'S THIS?
BEEWOO
BEEW
?
BEEWOO
BEEWOO
POLICE
HEY!
THE COPS! LET'S--
HUH?

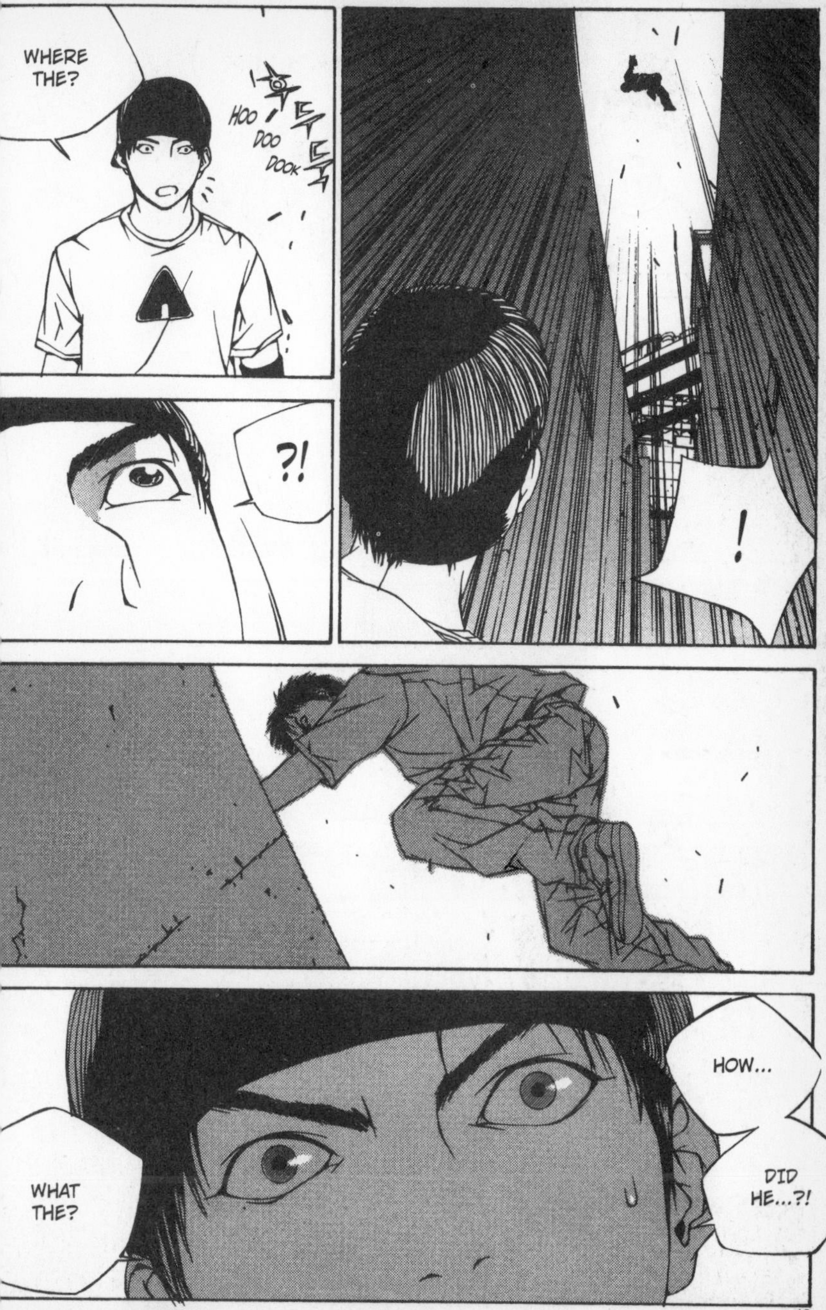
WHERE THE?
HOO DOO DOOK
?!
!
WHAT THE?
HOW...
DID HE...?!

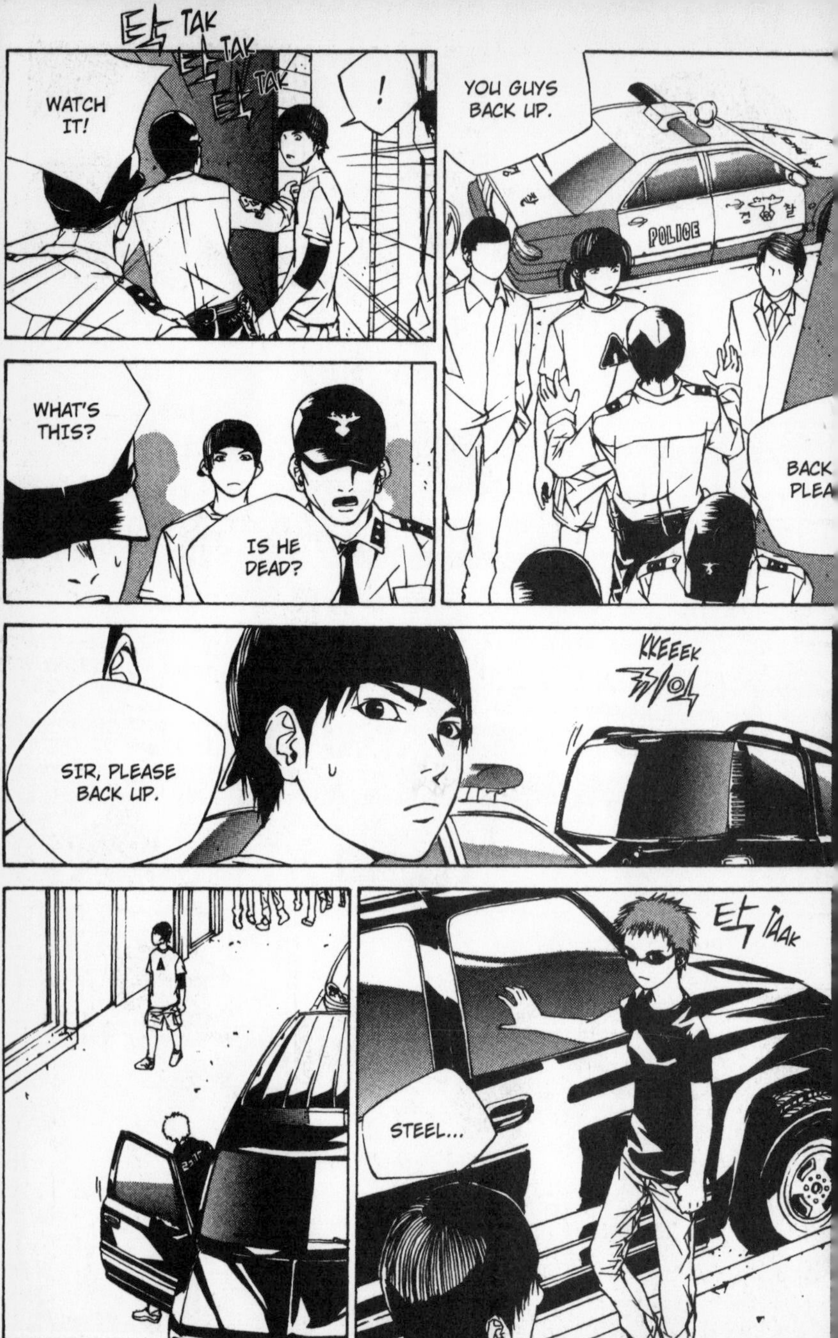
TAK
TAK
TAK
WATCH IT!
!
WHAT'S THIS?
IS HE DEAD?
YOU GUYS BACK UP.
BACK PLEA
SIR, PLEASE BACK UP.
KKEEEK
STEEL...
TAAK

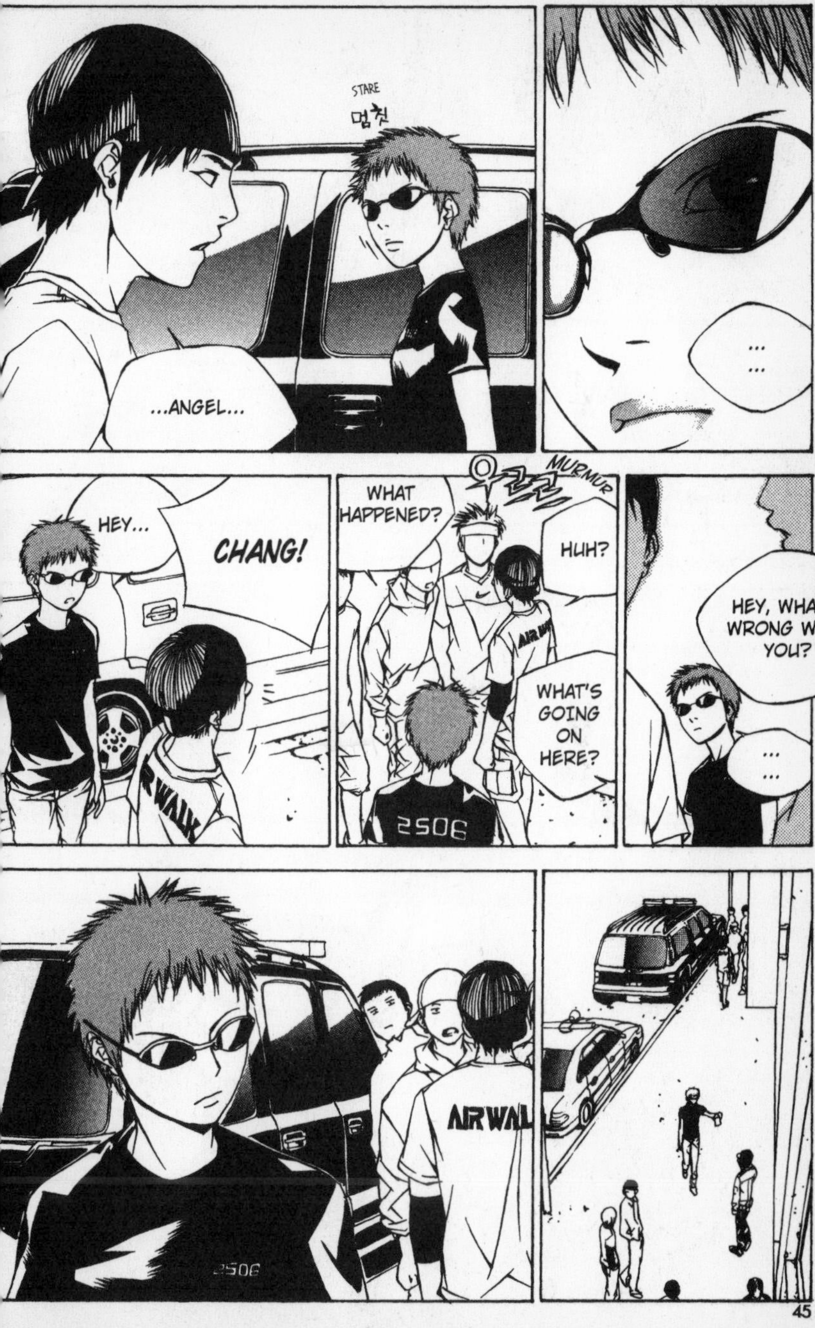
STARE
멈칫
...ANGEL...
...
...
HEY...
CHANG!
WHAT HAPPENED?
우글
MURMUR
HUH?
WHAT'S GOING ON HERE?
HEY, WHAT'S WRONG WITH YOU?
...
...
AIR WALK
2506

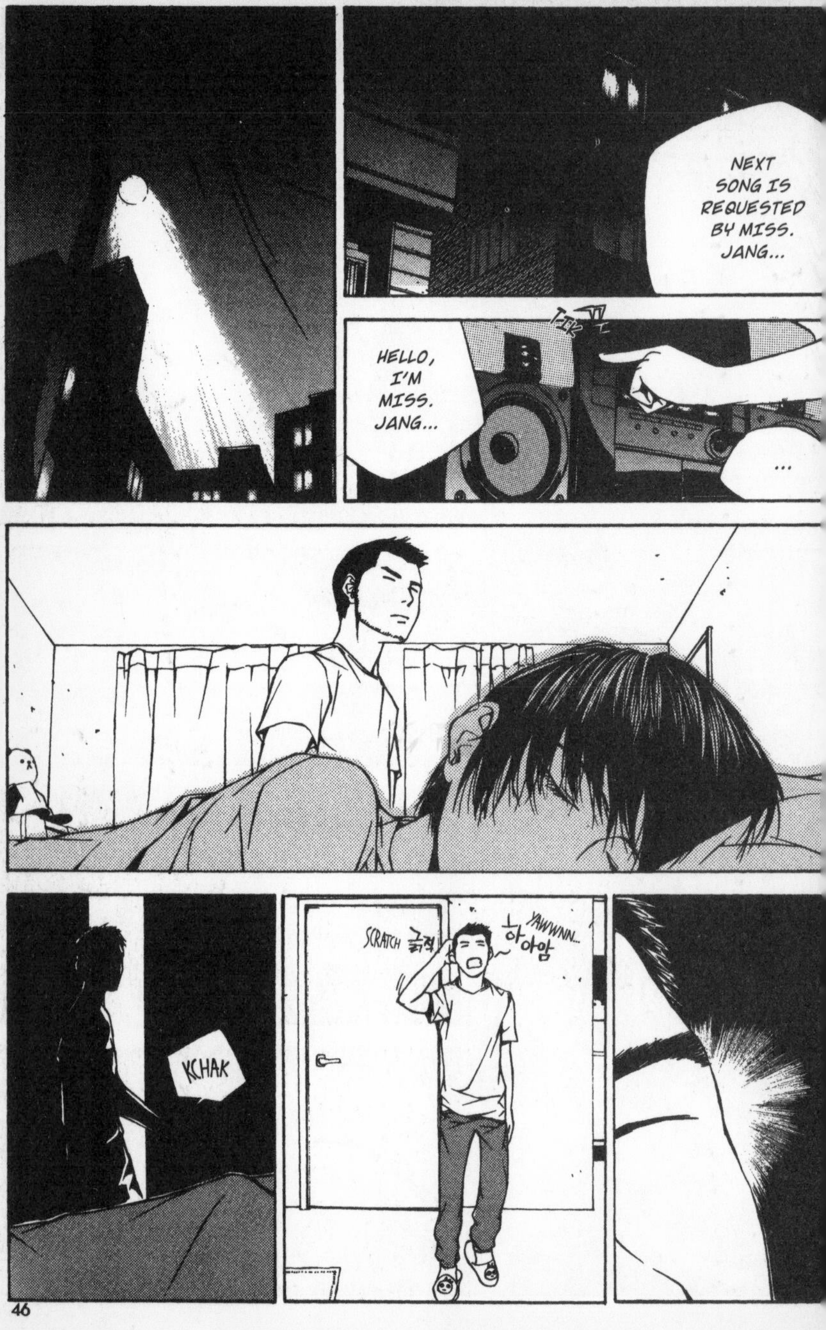
NEXT SONG IS REQUESTED BY MISS. JANG...
TIK
HELLO, I'M MISS. JANG...
...
KCHAK
SCRATCH 긁적
YAWWNN... 하아암

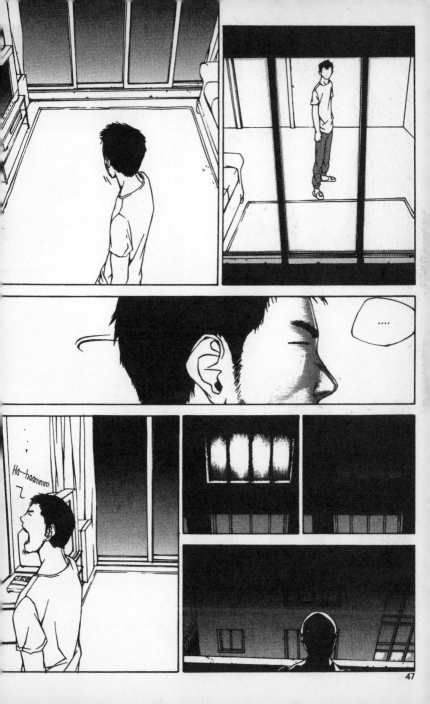

Ha~haammm

47

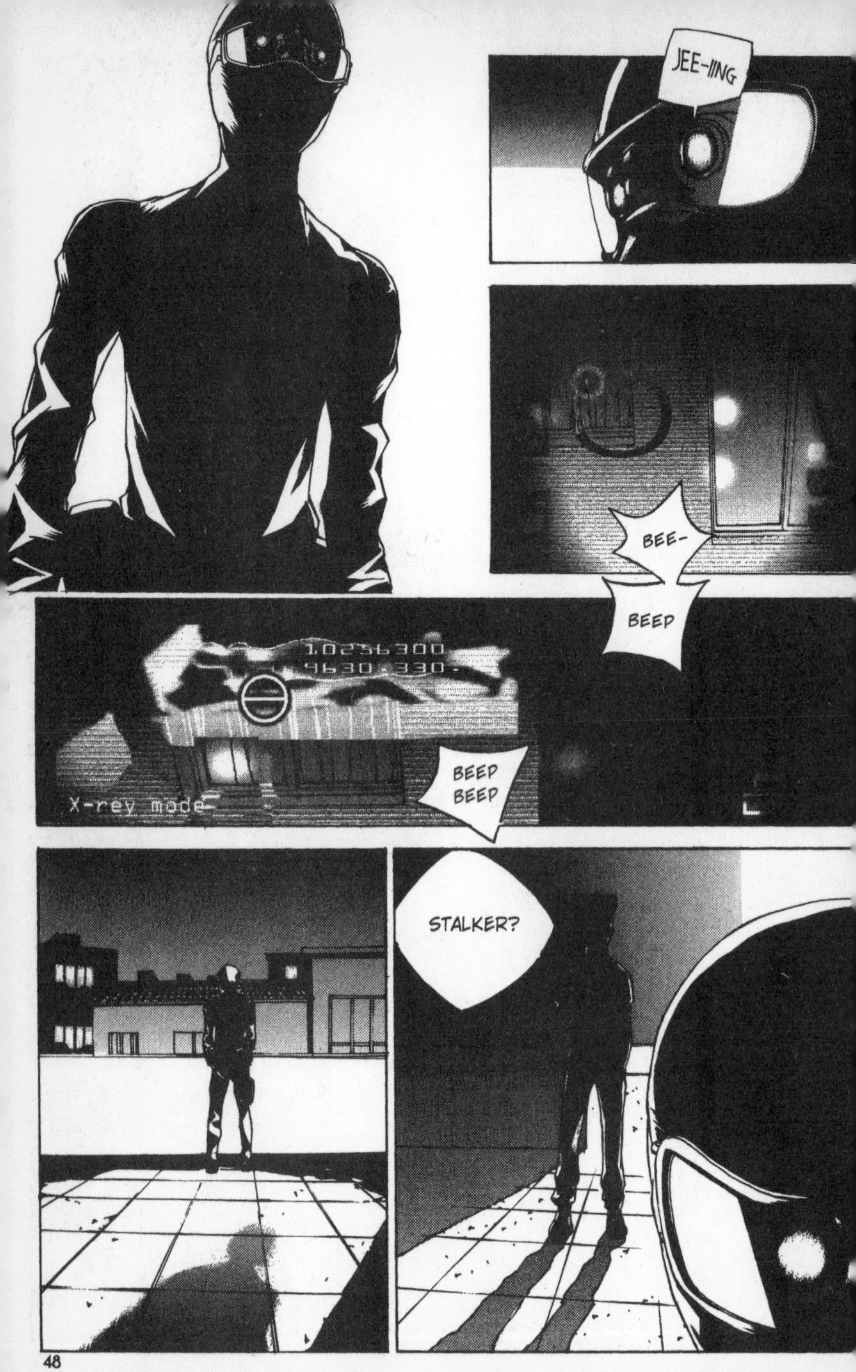
JEE-IING
BEE-
BEEP
1.0256300
9630.330.
X-rey mode
BEEP BEEP
STALKER?

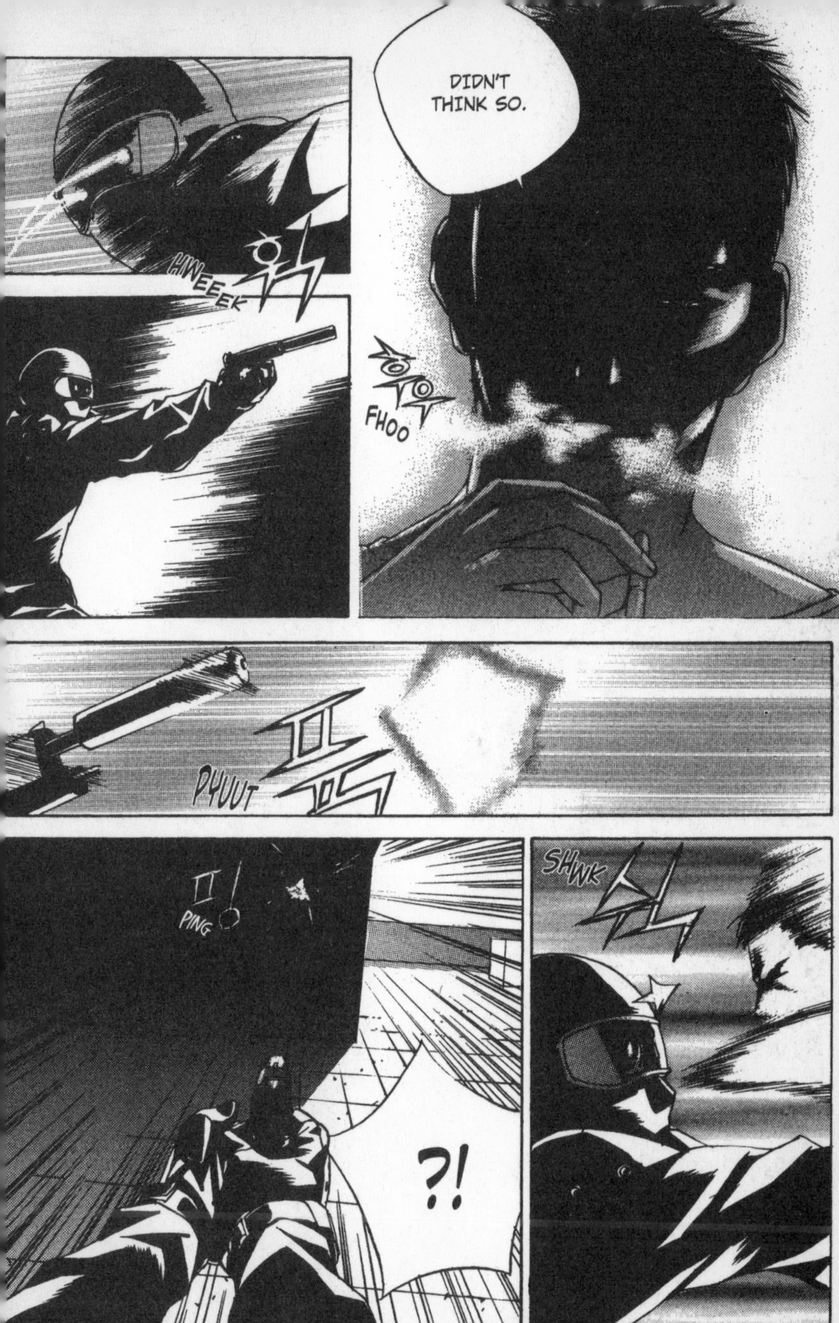
HWEEEK
DIDN'T THINK SO.
FHOO
PYUUT
PING
?!
SHWK

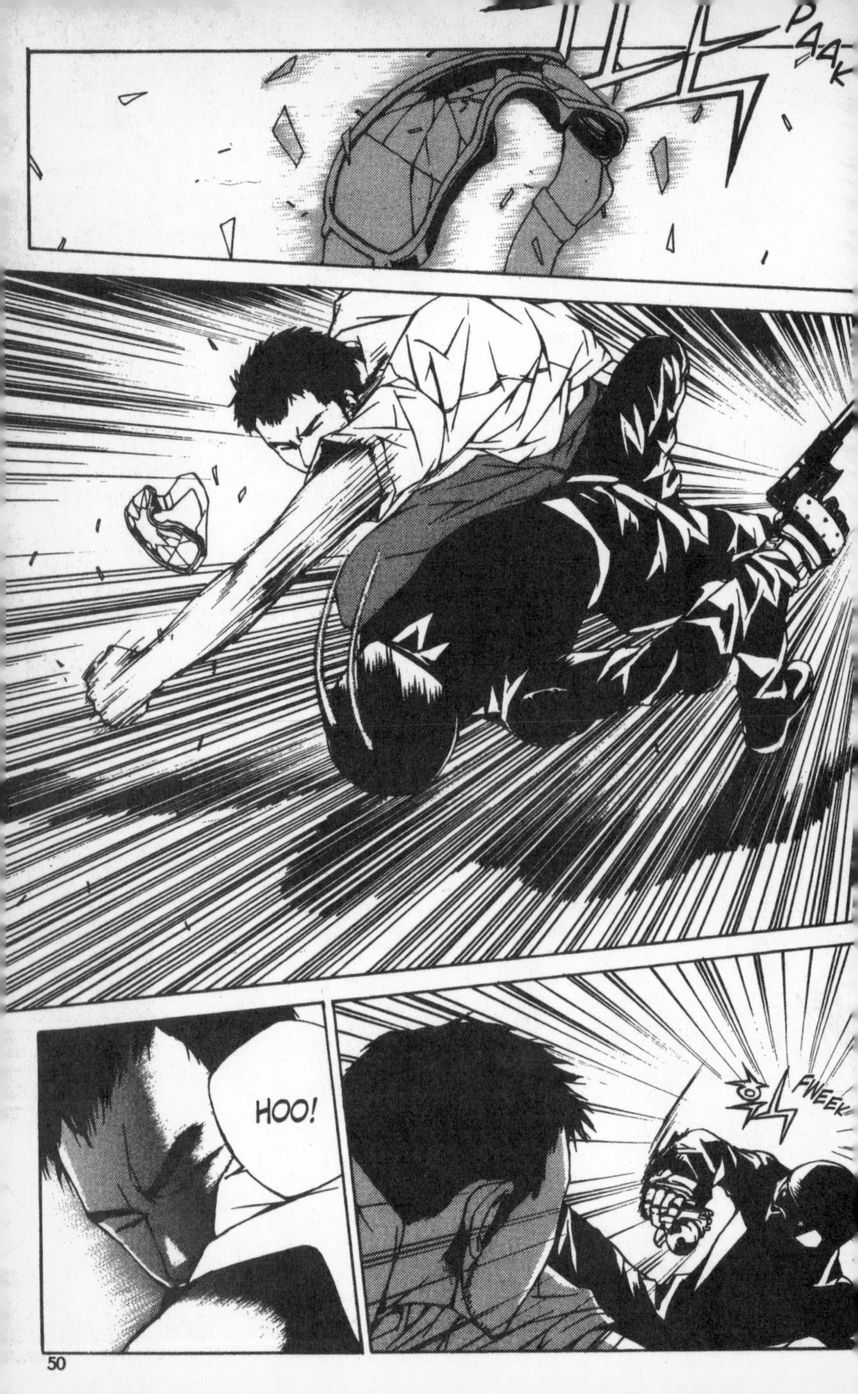
PAAK
HOO!
FWEEK

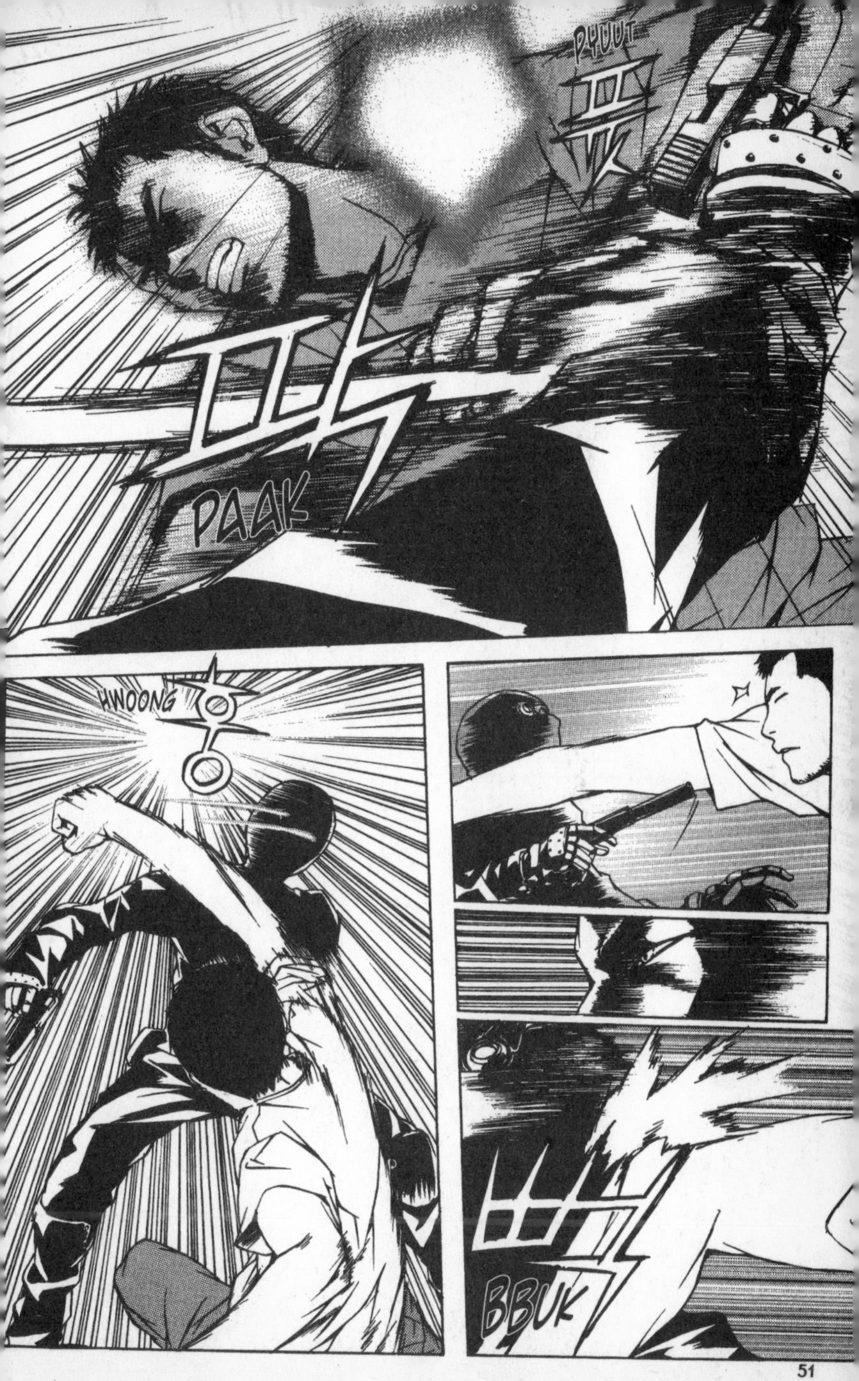
PYUUT
PAAK
HWOONG
BBUK

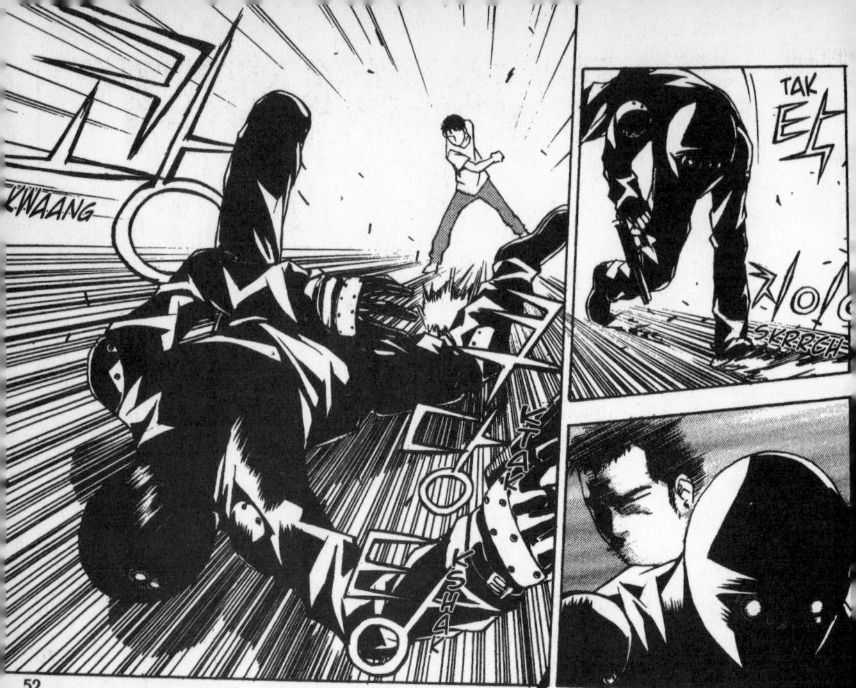
KWAANG
KTAK
KSHAK
TAK
SKRRGH

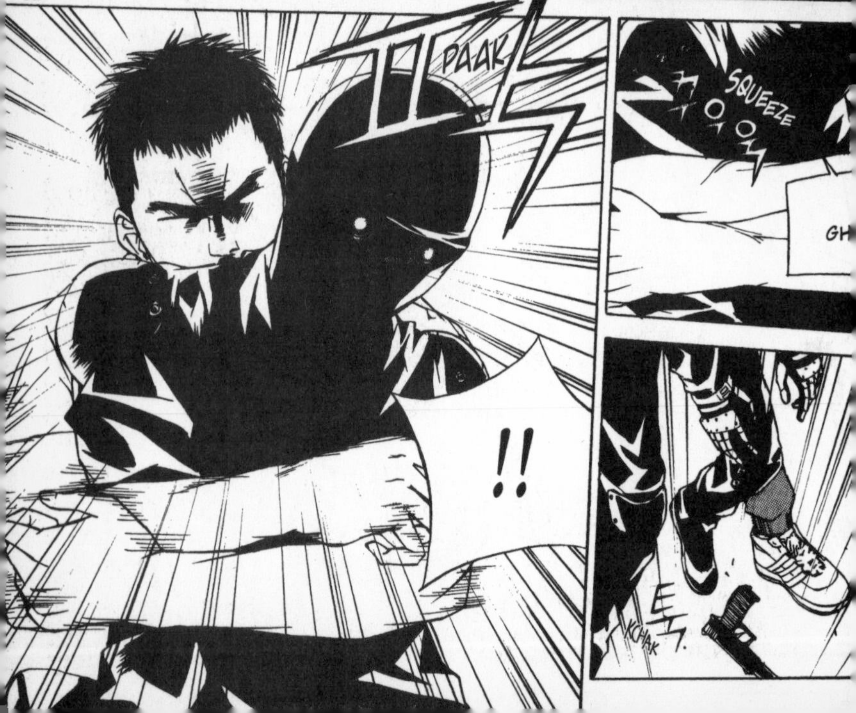
PAAK
!!
SQUEEZE
GH
KCHAK

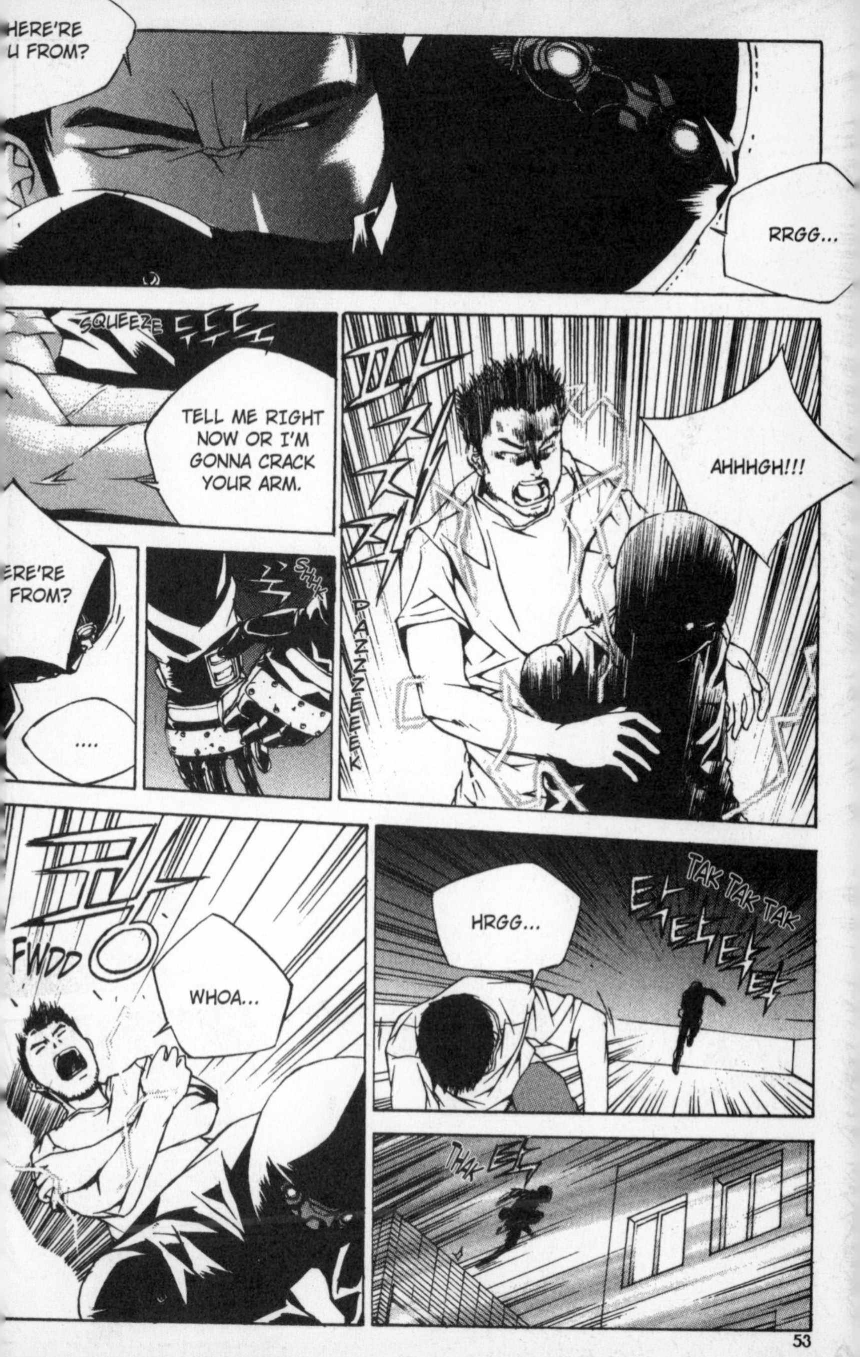
HERE'RE
U FROM?
RRGG...
SQUEEZE
TELL ME RIGHT NOW OR I'M GONNA CRACK YOUR ARM.
ERE'RE
FROM?
....
SHHK
PAZZZEEEK
AHHHGH!!!
FWDD
WHOA...
HRGG...
TAK TAK TAK
THAK

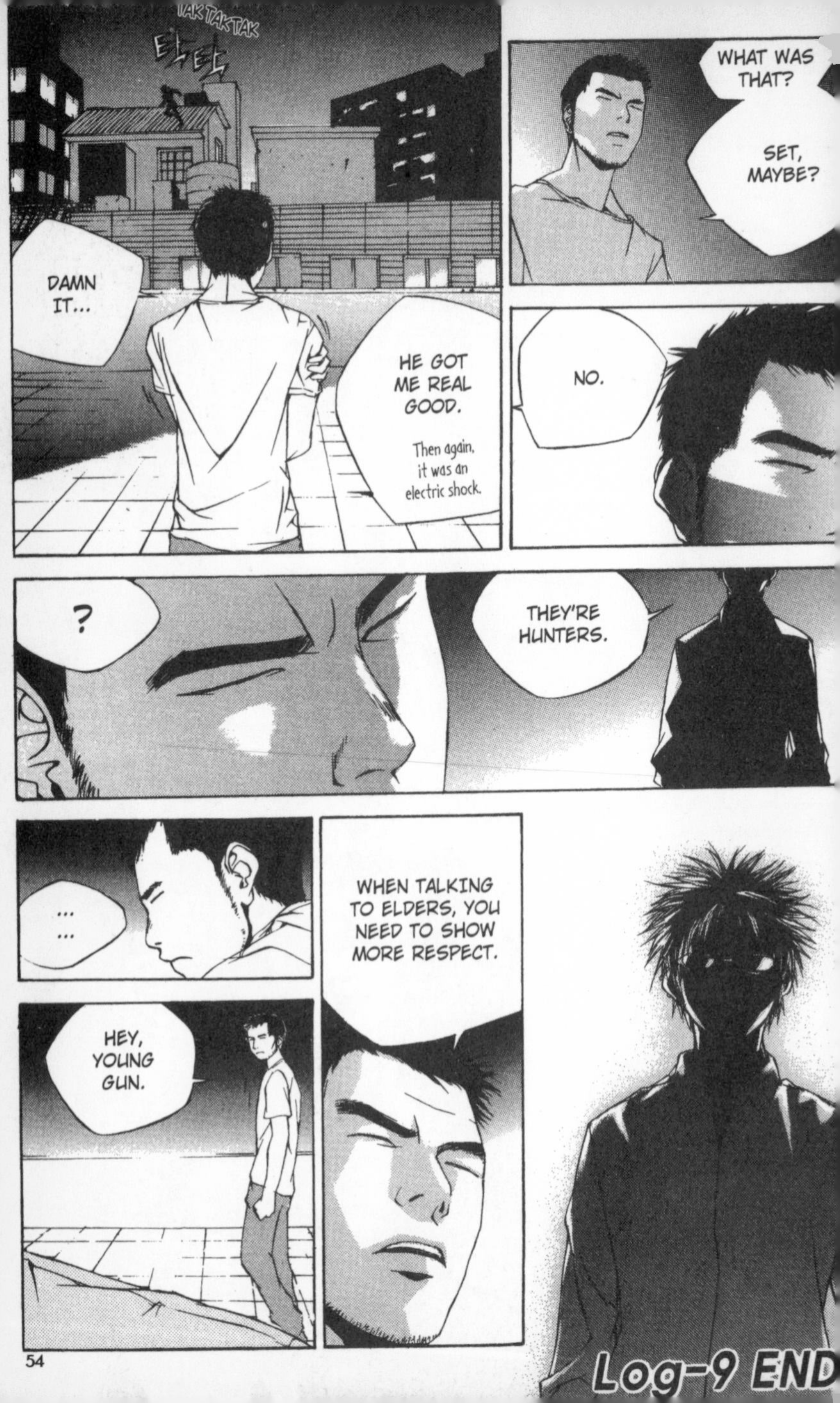
TAK TAKTAK
DAMN IT...
HE GOT ME REAL GOOD.
Then again, it was an electric shock.
WHAT WAS THAT?
SET, MAYBE?
NO.
?
THEY'RE HUNTERS.
...
...
HEY, YOUNG GUN.
WHEN TALKING TO ELDERS, YOU NEED TO SHOW MORE RESPECT.
Log-9 END

OG_10;
teel Angel(2)

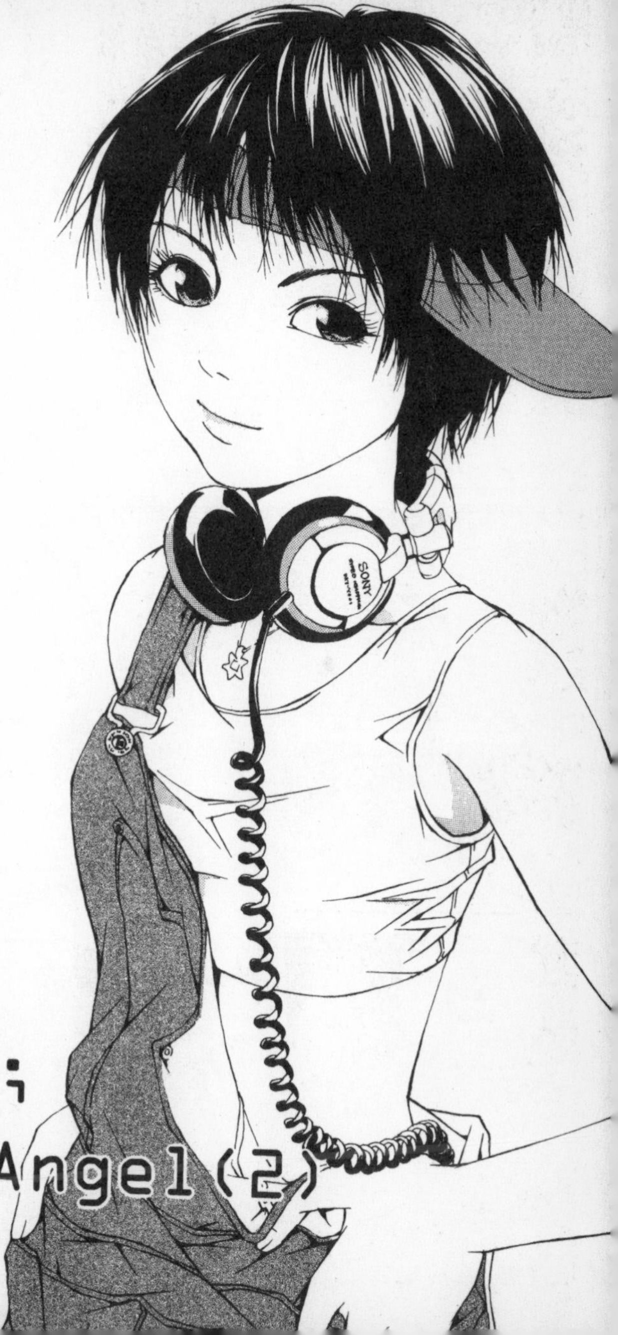
SONY

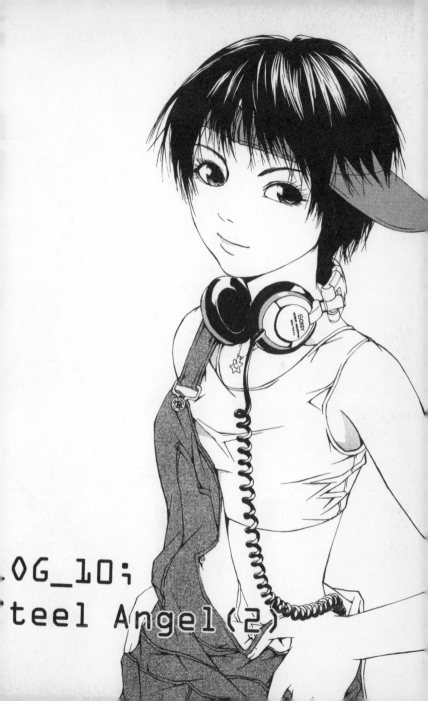

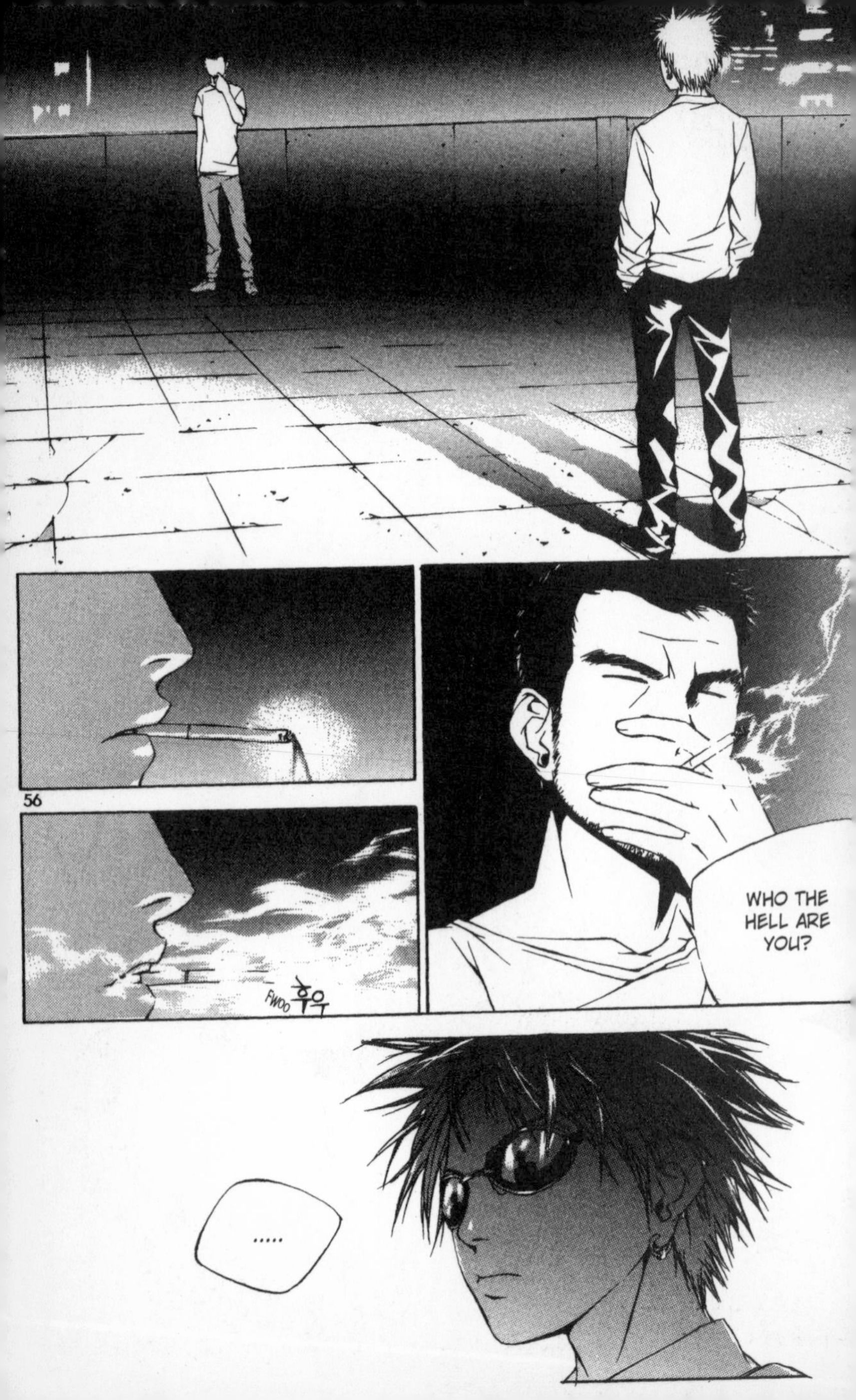
FWOO 후우
WHO THE HELL ARE YOU?
......

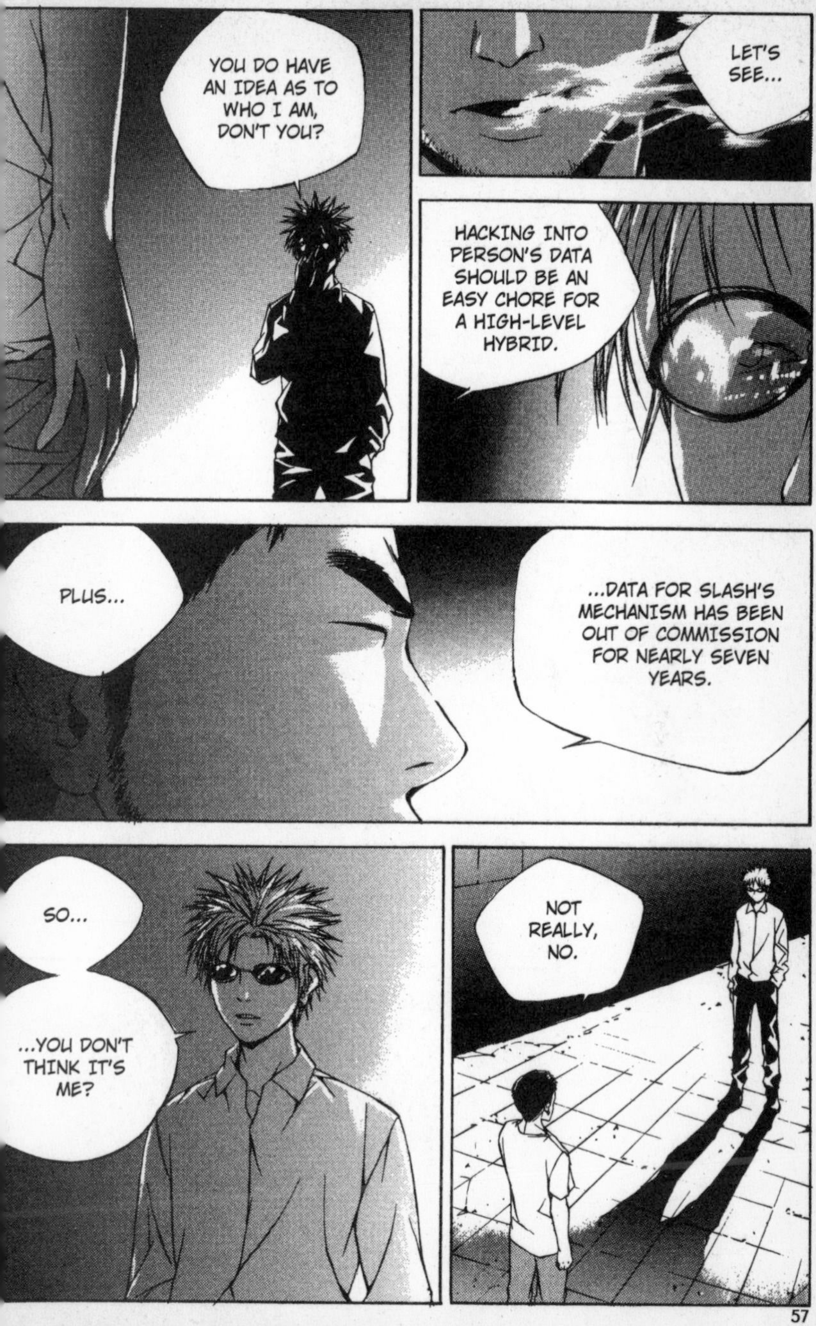
YOU DO HAVE AN IDEA AS TO WHO I AM, DON'T YOU?
LET'S SEE...
HACKING INTO PERSON'S DATA SHOULD BE AN EASY CHORE FOR A HIGH-LEVEL HYBRID.
PLUS...
...DATA FOR SLASH'S MECHANISM HAS BEEN OUT OF COMMISSION FOR NEARLY SEVEN YEARS.
SO...
...YOU DON'T THINK IT'S ME?
NOT REALLY, NO.

THANKS TO YOU, THEY'VE BEEN ABLE TO LOCATE US.

SLASH, SUPPOSEDLY A GUARDIAN, CANNOT MAKE A STUPID MISTAKE LIKE THAT.

WHO ARE YOU, REALLY?

THEN AGAIN, YOU DON'T REALLY HAVE TO EXPLAIN.

......

YOUR ONE-DIMENSIONAL MIND IS STILL THE SAME.

MAYBE I SHOULD...

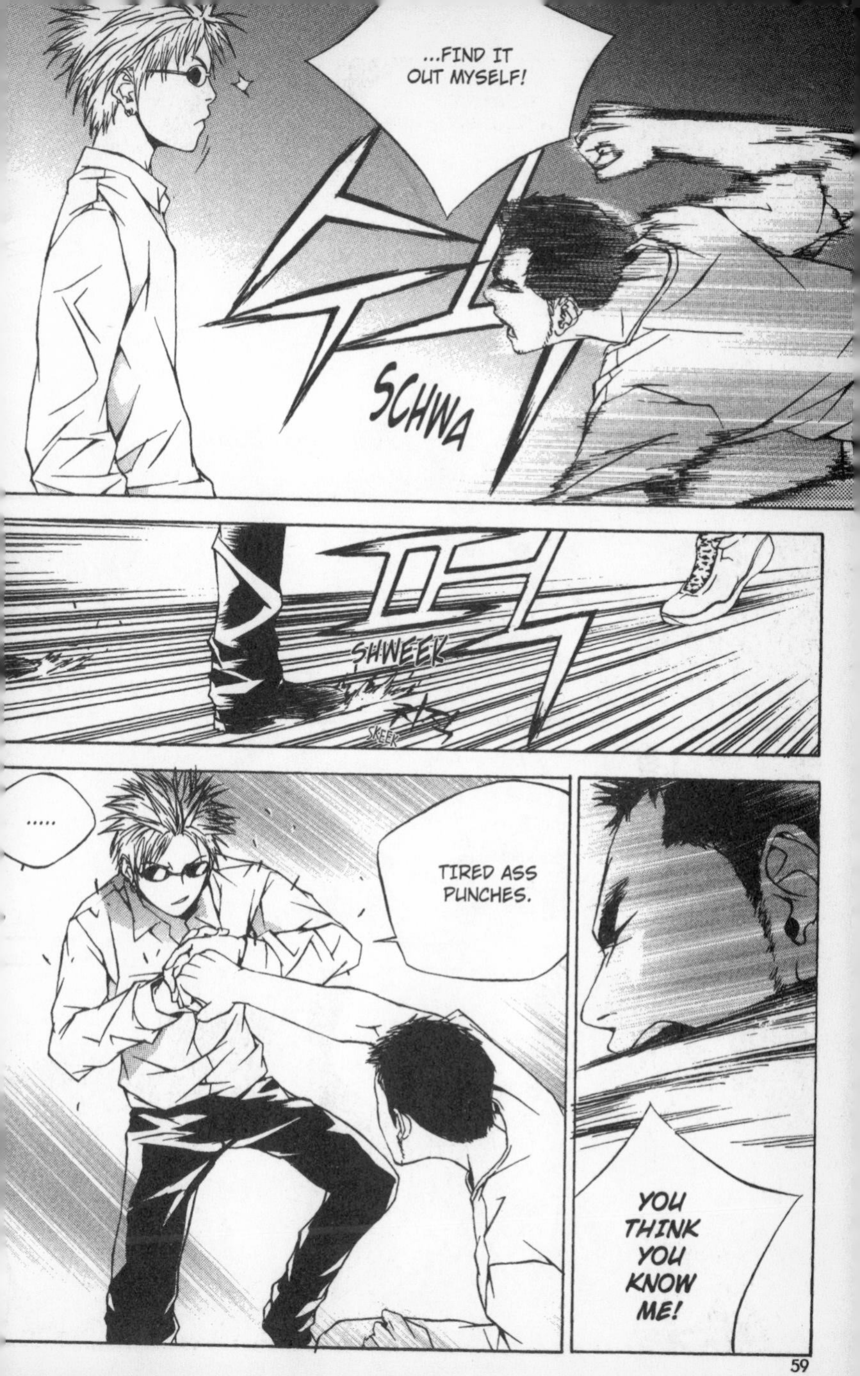
...FIND IT OUT MYSELF!
SCHWA
SHWEEK
SKEEK
......
TIRED ASS PUNCHES.
YOU THINK YOU KNOW ME!

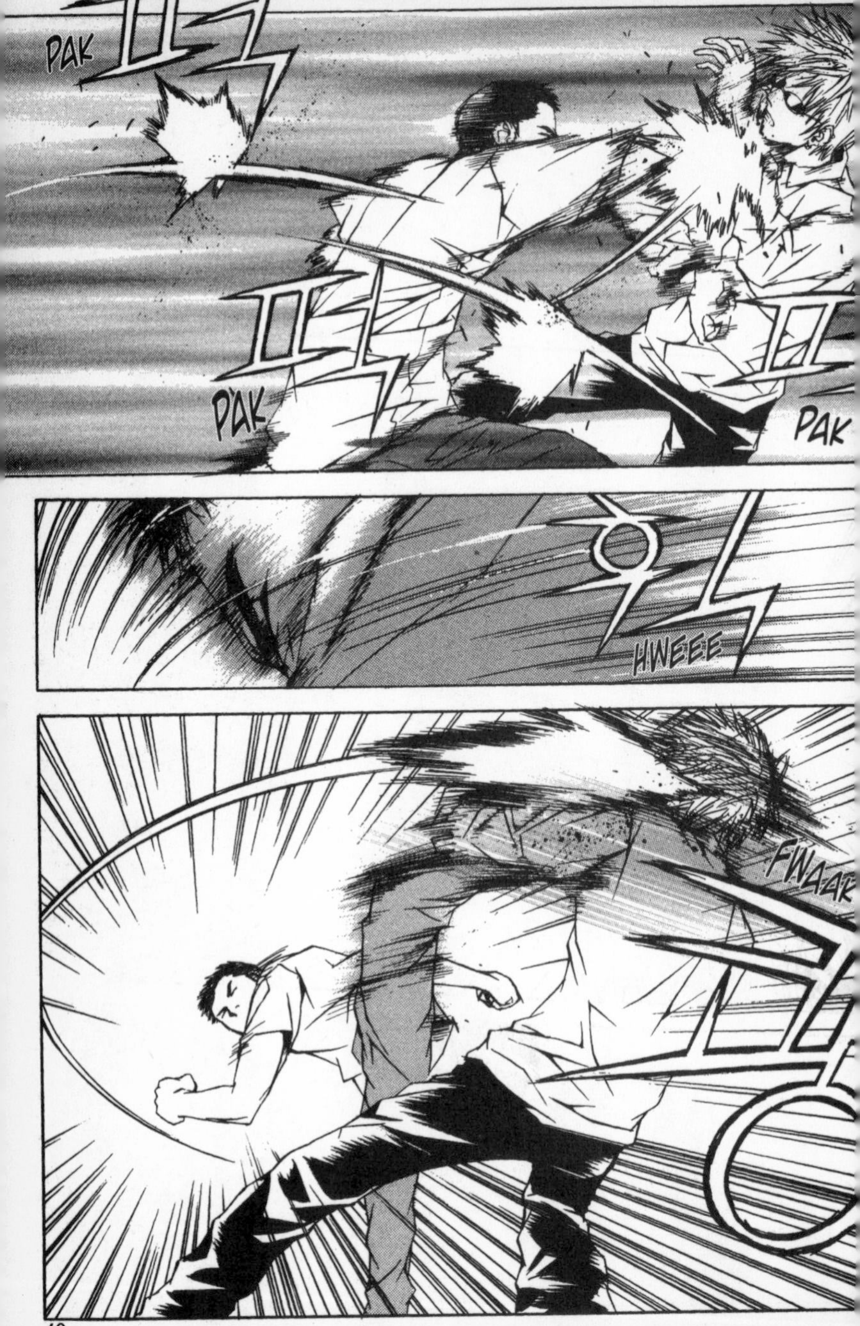
PAK
PAK
PAK
HWEEE
FWAAR

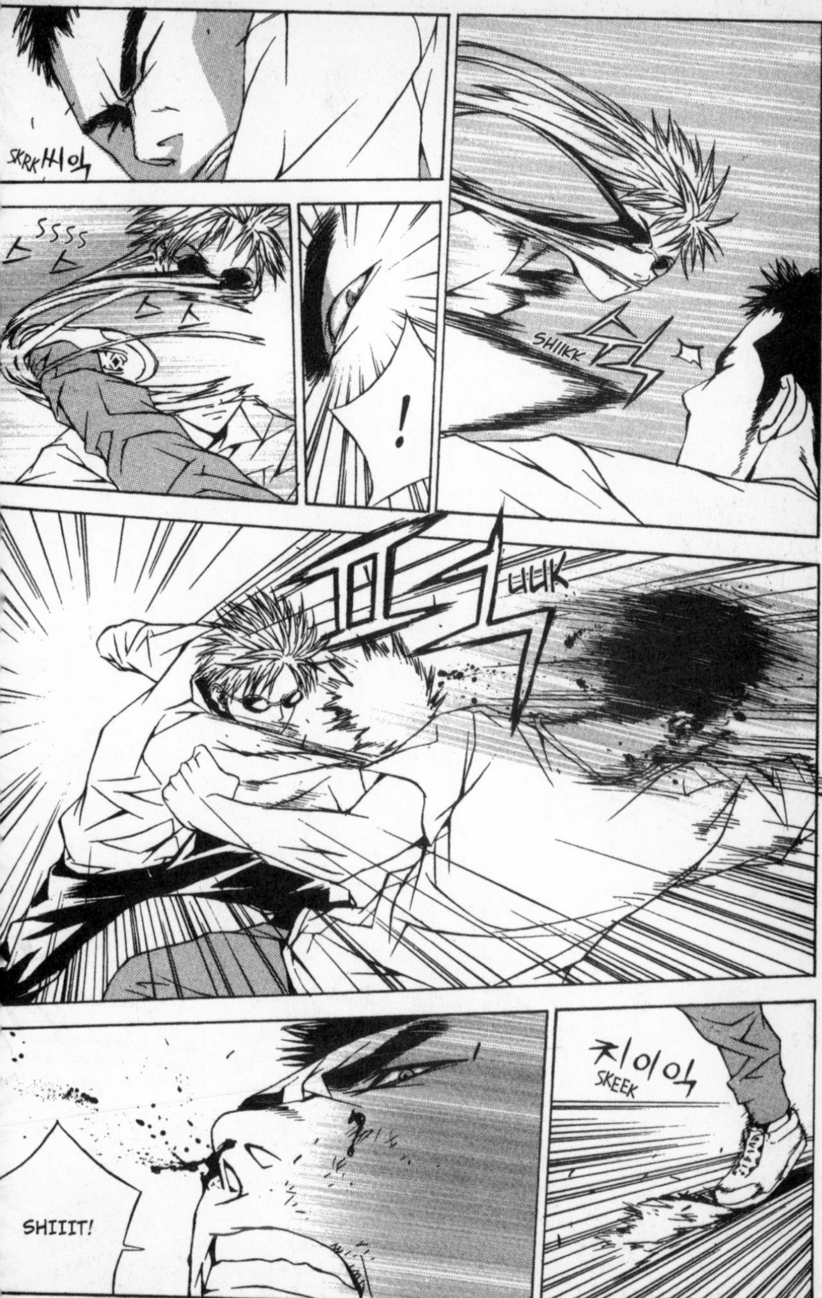
SKRK 쓰아악
SSSS
스스
스스
!
SHIIKK 슥
콰득 UUK
SHIIIT!
치이익
SKEEK

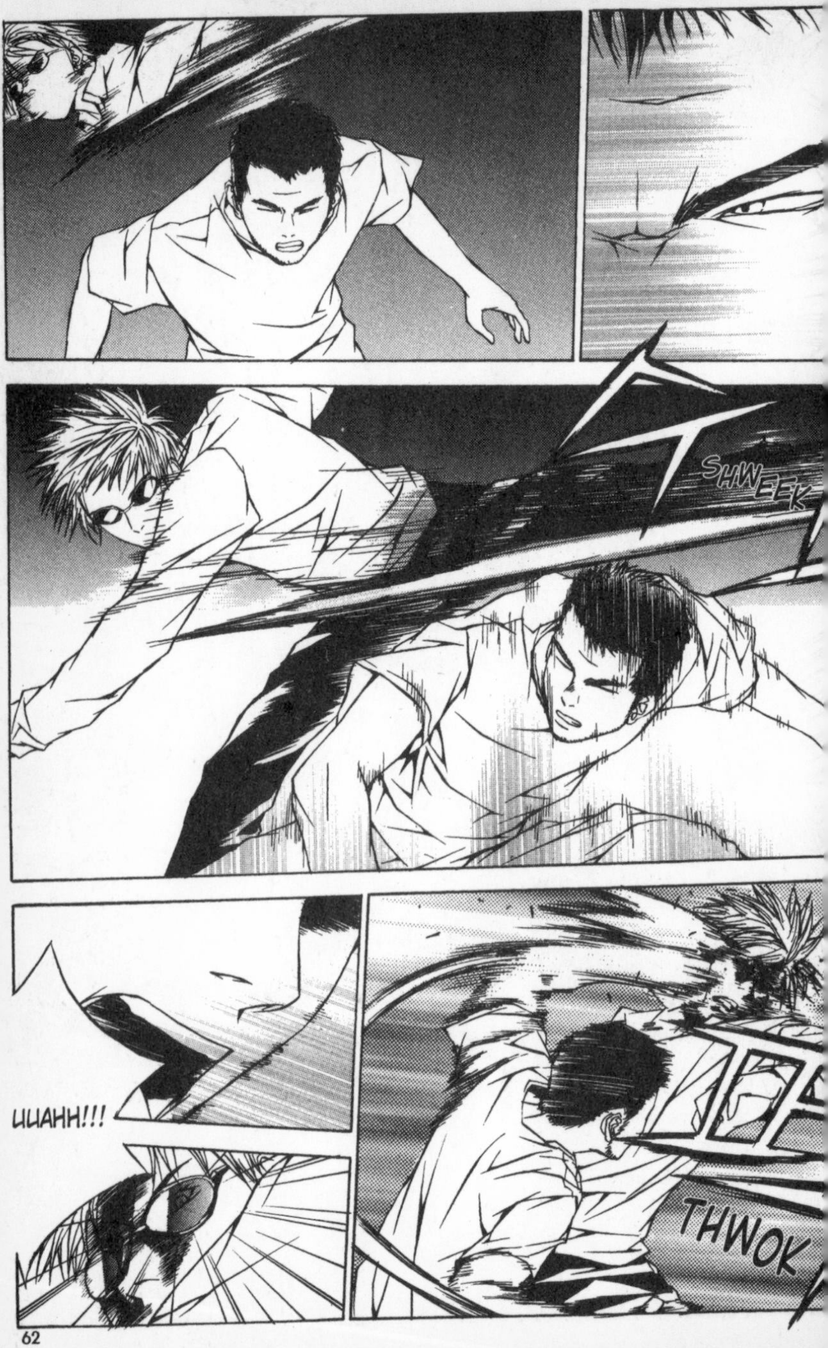
SHWEEK
UUAHH!!!
THWOK

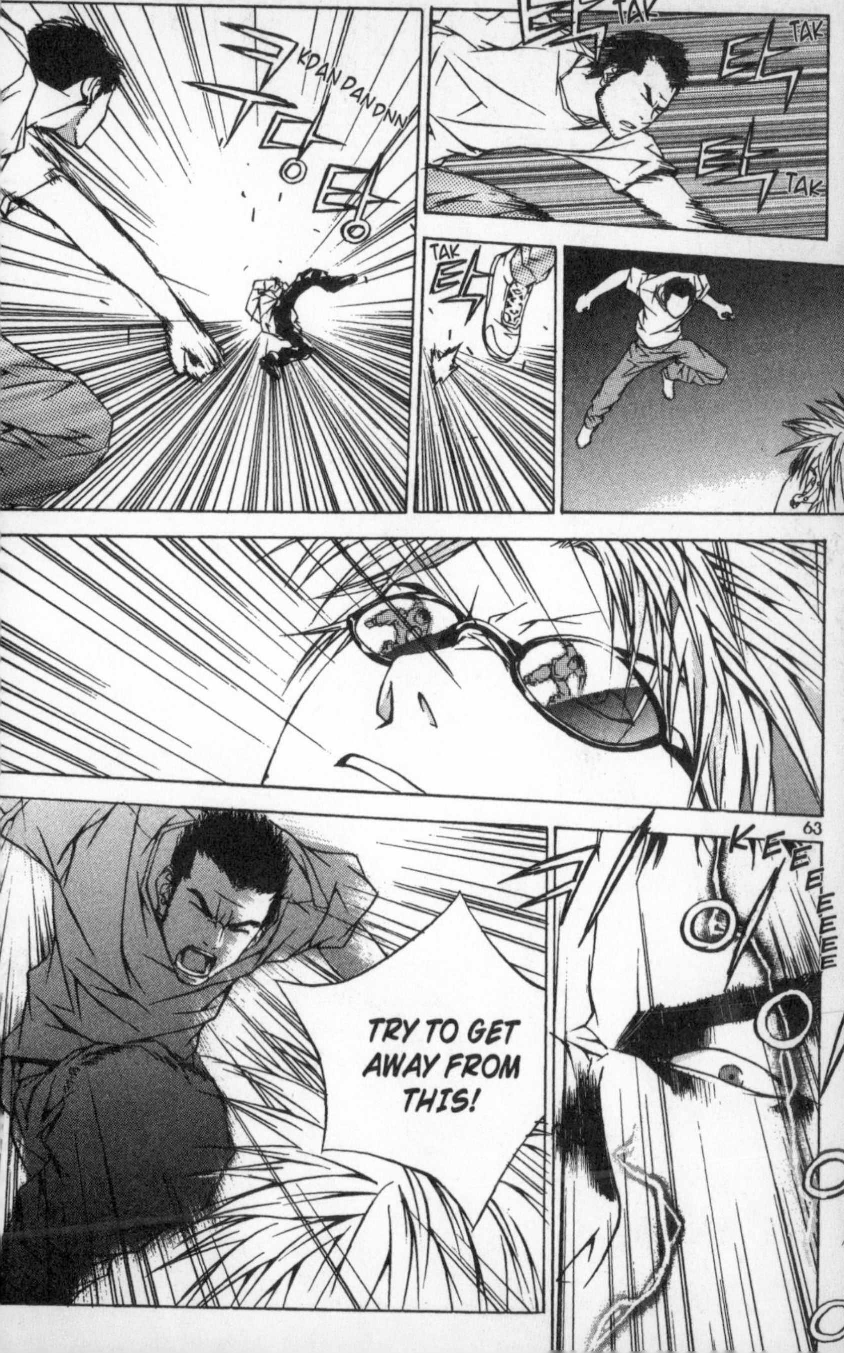
KDANDANDNN
TAK
TAK
TAK
TAK
TRY TO GET AWAY FROM THIS!
KTEEEEEEEE

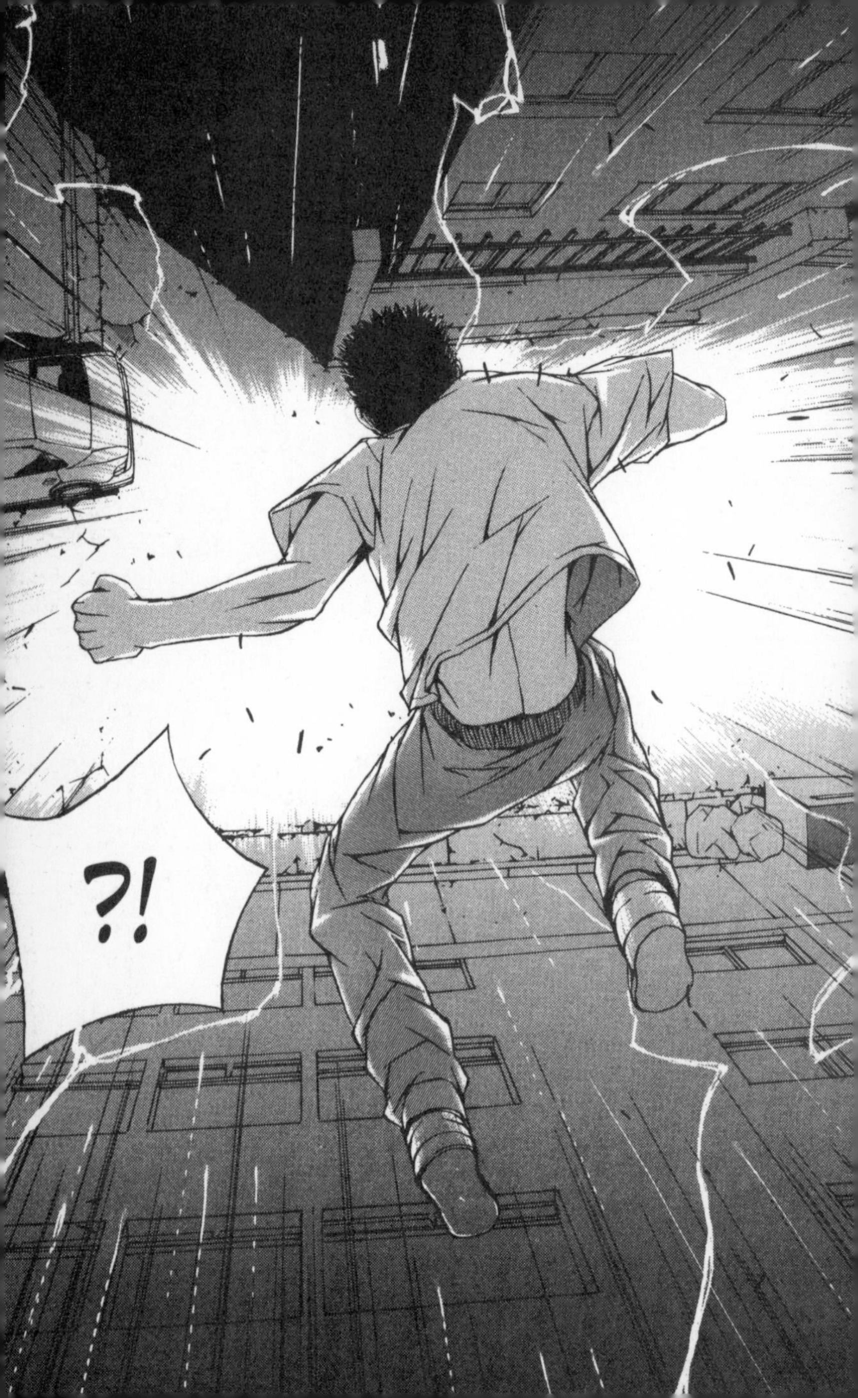
?!

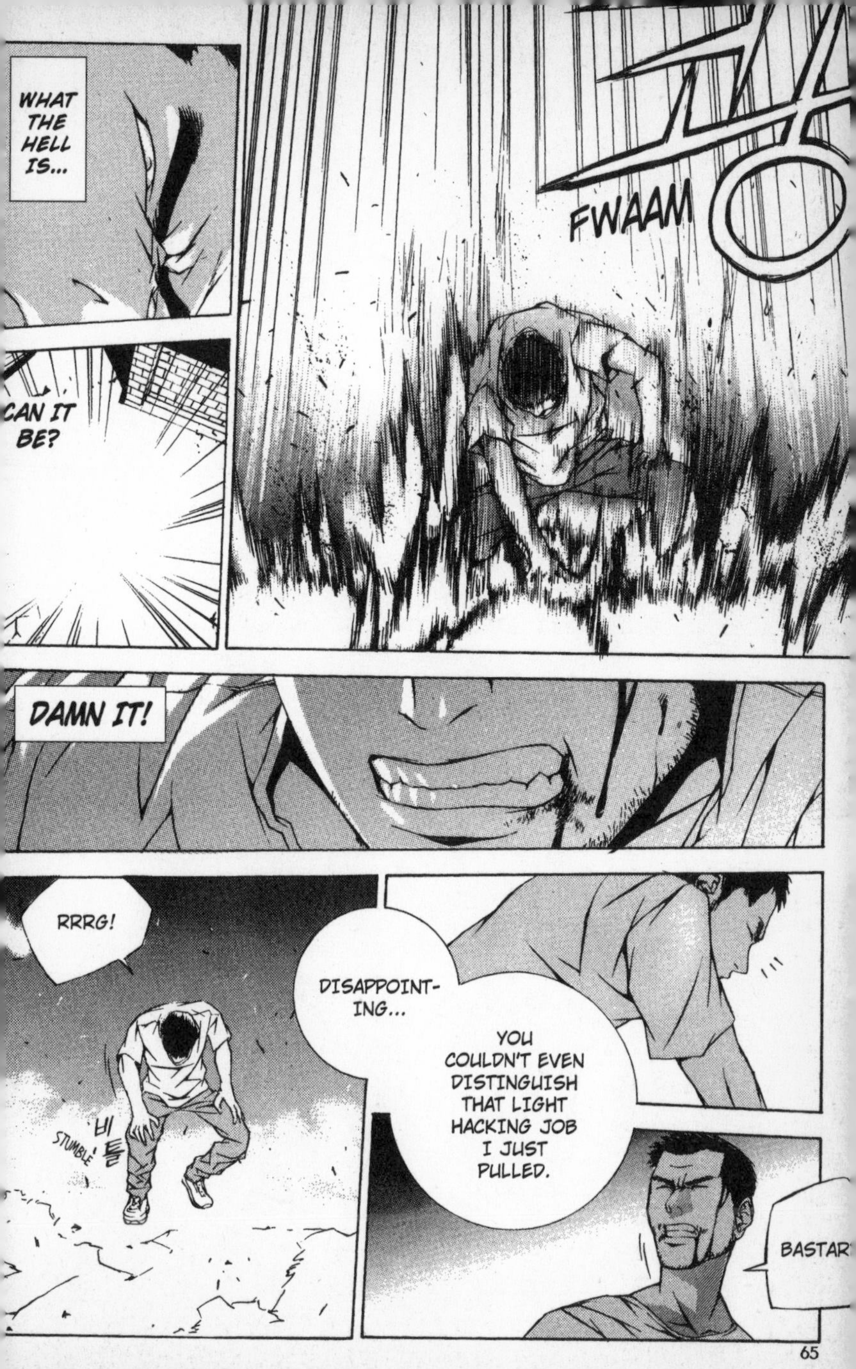
WHAT THE HELL IS...
CAN IT BE?
FWAAM
DAMN IT!
RRRG!
STUMBLE
DISAPPOINT-ING...
YOU COULDN'T EVEN DISTINGUISH THAT LIGHT HACKING JOB I JUST PULLED.
BASTAR

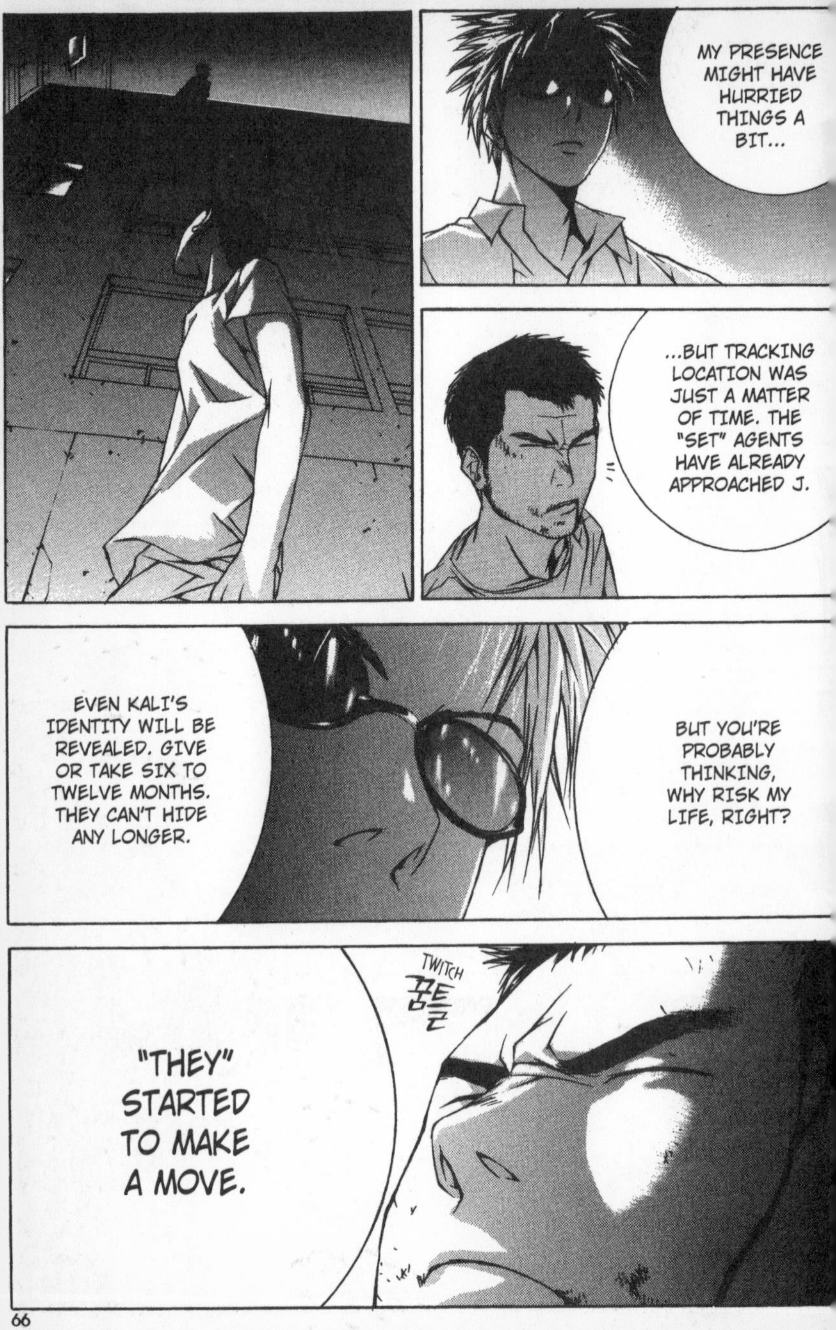
MY PRESENCE MIGHT HAVE HURRIED THINGS A BIT...
...BUT TRACKING LOCATION WAS JUST A MATTER OF TIME. THE "SET" AGENTS HAVE ALREADY APPROACHED J.
EVEN KALI'S IDENTITY WILL BE REVEALED. GIVE OR TAKE SIX TO TWELVE MONTHS. THEY CAN'T HIDE ANY LONGER.
BUT YOU'RE PROBABLY THINKING, WHY RISK MY LIFE, RIGHT?
"THEY" STARTED TO MAKE A MOVE.
TWITCH
꿈틀

WHAT DO YOU MEAN, "THEY"?

WITHOUT KALI?

MMM...

FOR TWENTY PLUS YEARS, THEY PERFECTED THIS SIMULATION PROCESS THAT DOESN'T REQUIRE KALI.

BUT STILL, WE HAVE TO ALERT KALI.

WHAT?

WE'RE RUNNING OUT OF TIME.

KALI?

REVIVE HER?

TURN

PROBABLY THE ONLY WAY TO BLOCK THEM...

.....

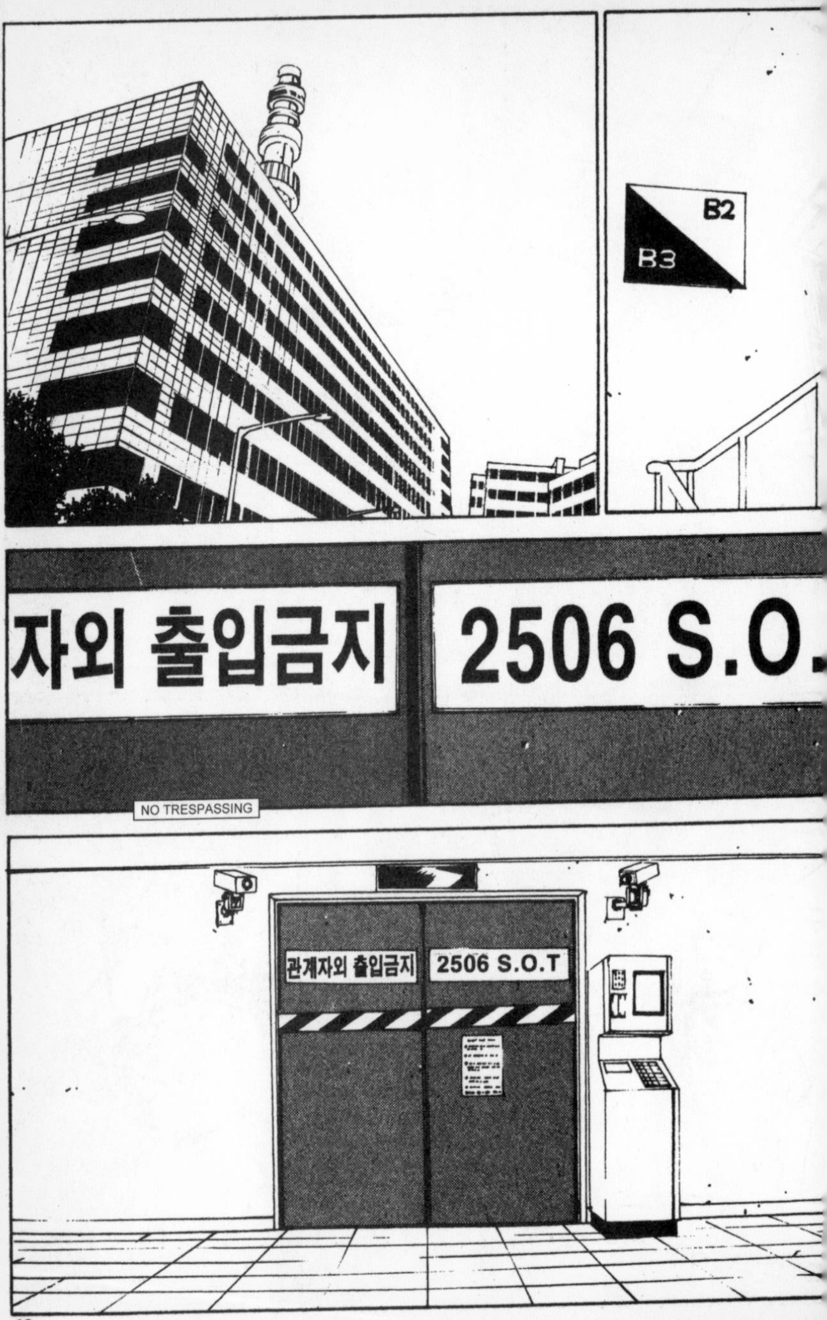
B2
B3
자외 출입금지
2506 S.O.
NO TRESPASSING
관계자외 출입금지
2506 S.O.T

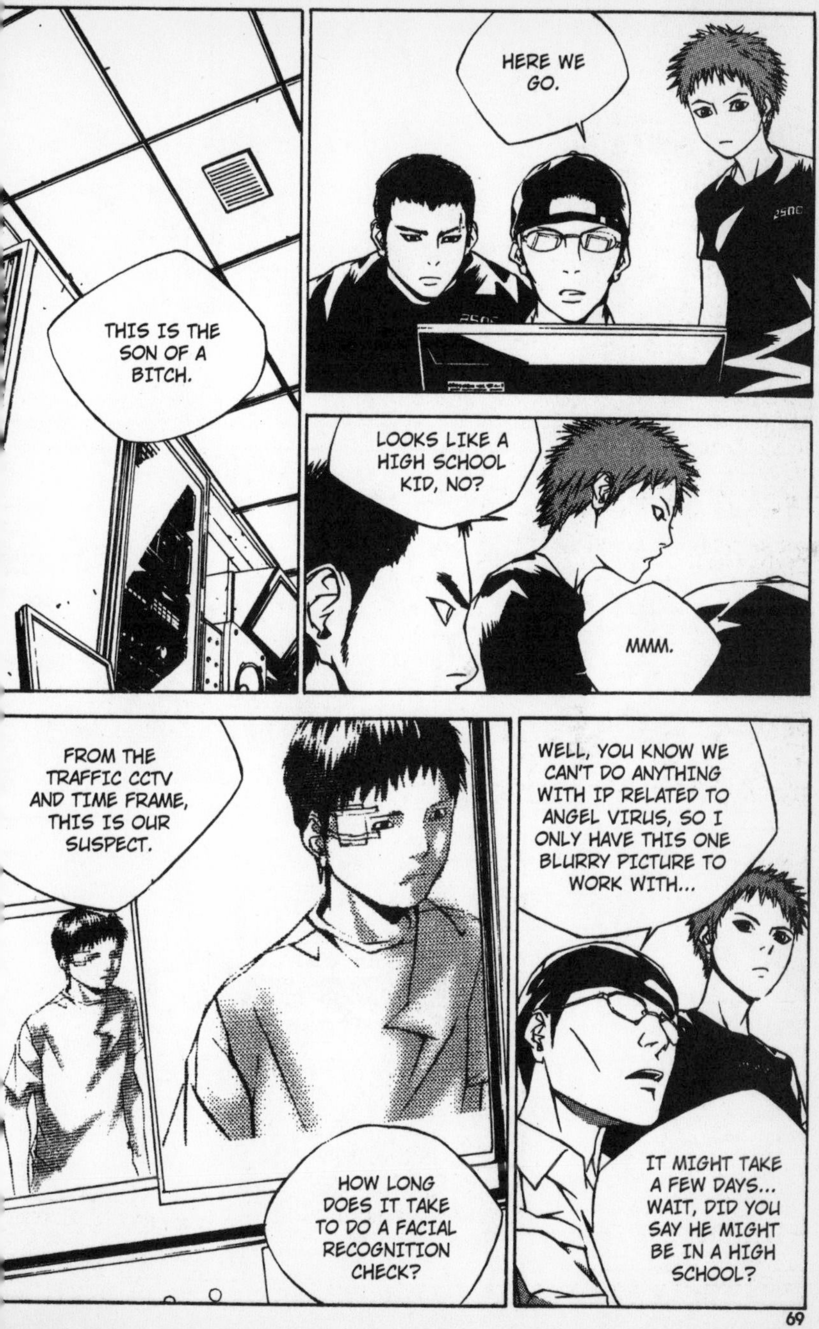
THIS IS THE SON OF A BITCH.
HERE WE GO.
LOOKS LIKE A HIGH SCHOOL KID, NO?
MMM.
FROM THE TRAFFIC CCTV AND TIME FRAME, THIS IS OUR SUSPECT.
HOW LONG DOES IT TAKE TO DO A FACIAL RECOGNITION CHECK?
WELL, YOU KNOW WE CAN'T DO ANYTHING WITH IP RELATED TO ANGEL VIRUS, SO I ONLY HAVE THIS ONE BLURRY PICTURE TO WORK WITH...
IT MIGHT TAKE A FEW DAYS... WAIT, DID YOU SAY HE MIGHT BE IN A HIGH SCHOOL?

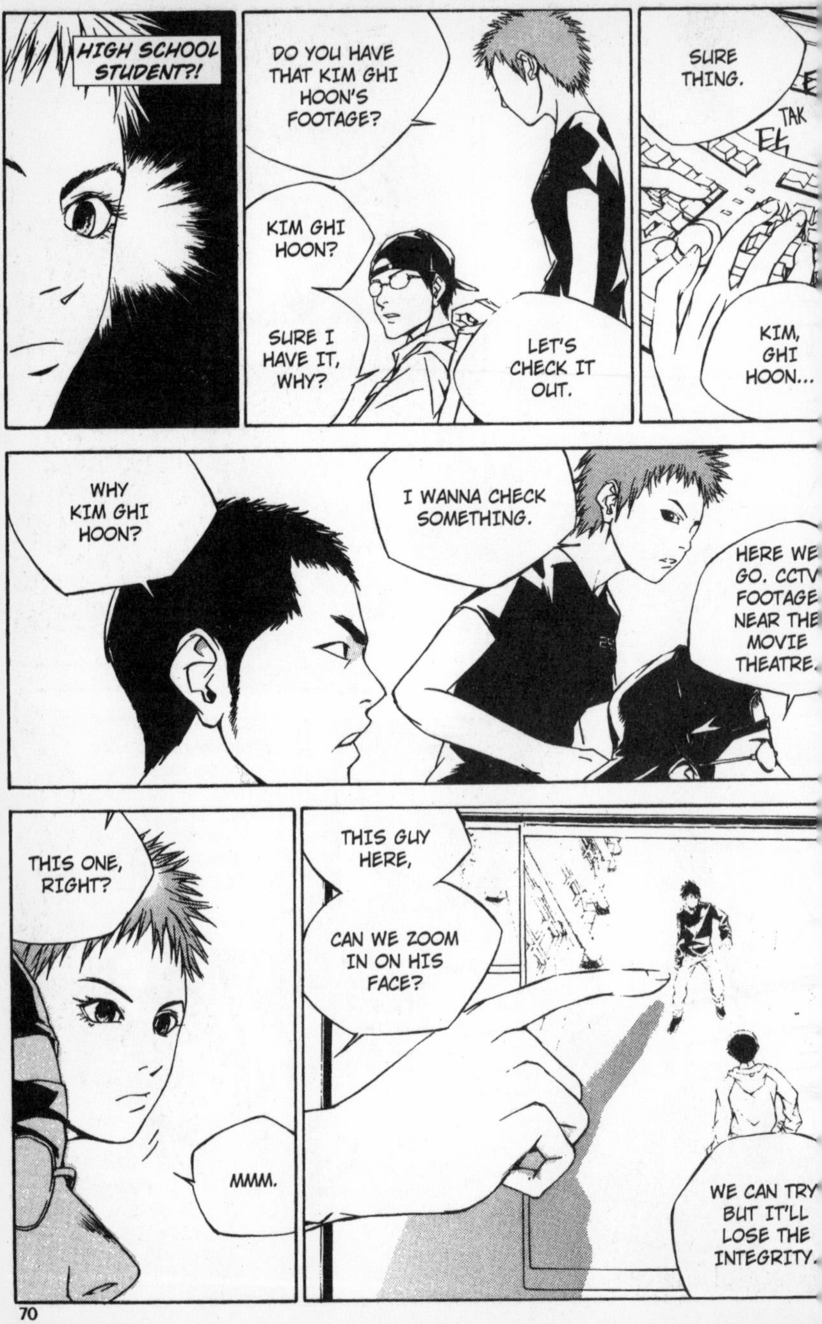
HIGH SCHOOL STUDENT?!
DO YOU HAVE THAT KIM GHI HOON'S FOOTAGE?
KIM GHI HOON?
SURE I HAVE IT, WHY?
LET'S CHECK IT OUT.
SURE THING.
TAK
KIM, GHI HOON...
WHY KIM GHI HOON?
I WANNA CHECK SOMETHING.
HERE WE GO. CCTV FOOTAGE NEAR THE MOVIE THEATRE.
THIS ONE, RIGHT?
MMM.
THIS GUY HERE,
CAN WE ZOOM IN ON HIS FACE?
WE CAN TRY BUT IT'LL LOSE THE INTEGRITY.

LET ME TRY IT THIS WAY,

HERE WE GO.

I SAW THIS GUY A FEW DAYS AGO. I THOUGHT HE LOOKED FAMILIAR.

I KNEW IT.

THIS IS HIM.

?

PARDON?

ARE YOU SURE?

MMM.

SUSPECT'S AGE IS SIMILAR WITH THIS GUY.

HIM JUST SHOWING UP NEAR THE CRIME SCENE, IT DOESN'T FEEL RIGHT.

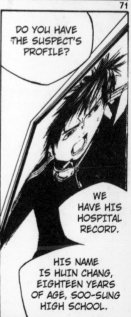

DO YOU HAVE THE SUSPECT'S PROFILE?

WE HAVE HIS HOSPITAL RECORD.

HIS NAME IS HUIN CHANG, EIGHTEEN YEARS OF AGE, SOO-SUNG HIGH SCHOOL.

250

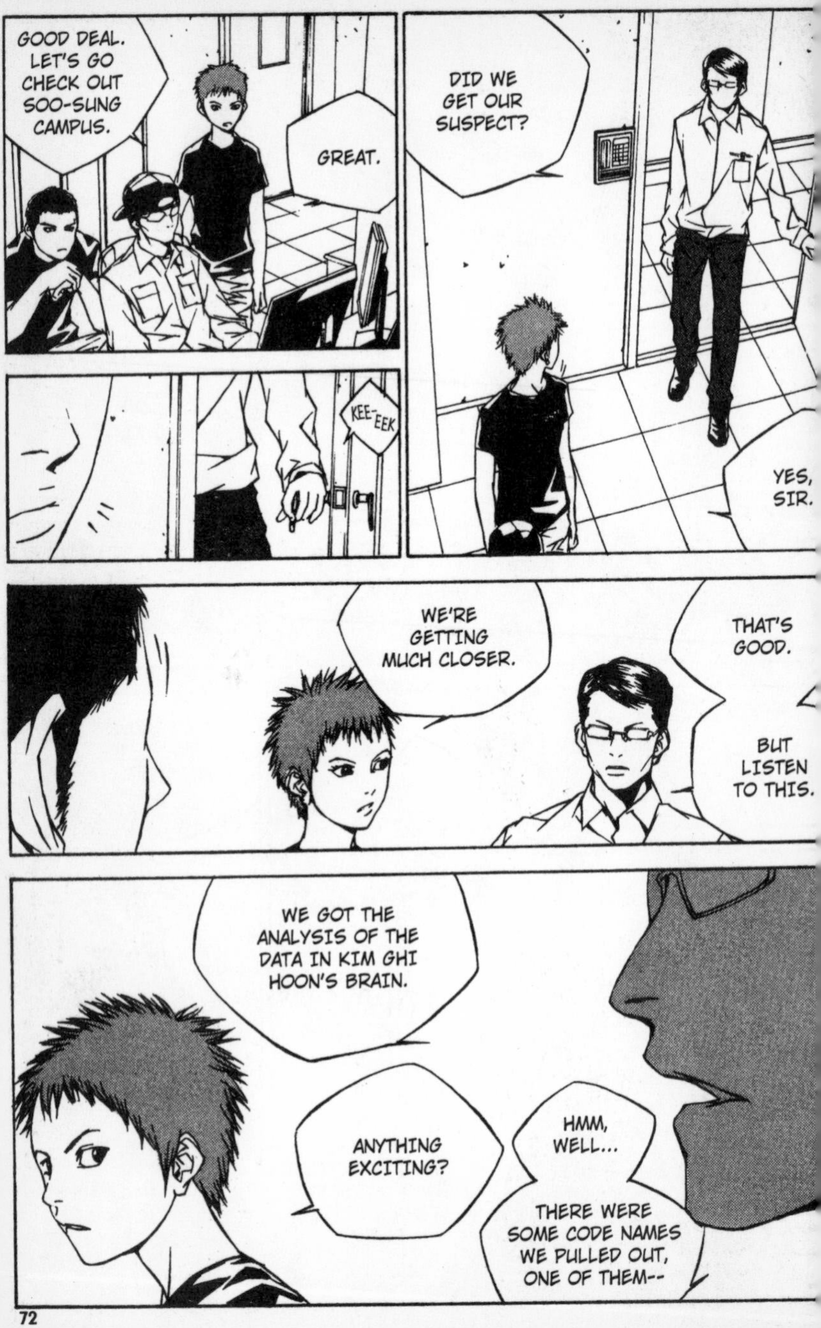
GOOD DEAL. LET'S GO CHECK OUT SOO-SUNG CAMPUS.
GREAT.
KEE-EEK
DID WE GET OUR SUSPECT?
YES, SIR.
WE'RE GETTING MUCH CLOSER.
THAT'S GOOD.
BUT LISTEN TO THIS.
WE GOT THE ANALYSIS OF THE DATA IN KIM GHI HOON'S BRAIN.
ANYTHING EXCITING?
HMM, WELL...
THERE WERE SOME CODE NAMES WE PULLED OUT, ONE OF THEM--

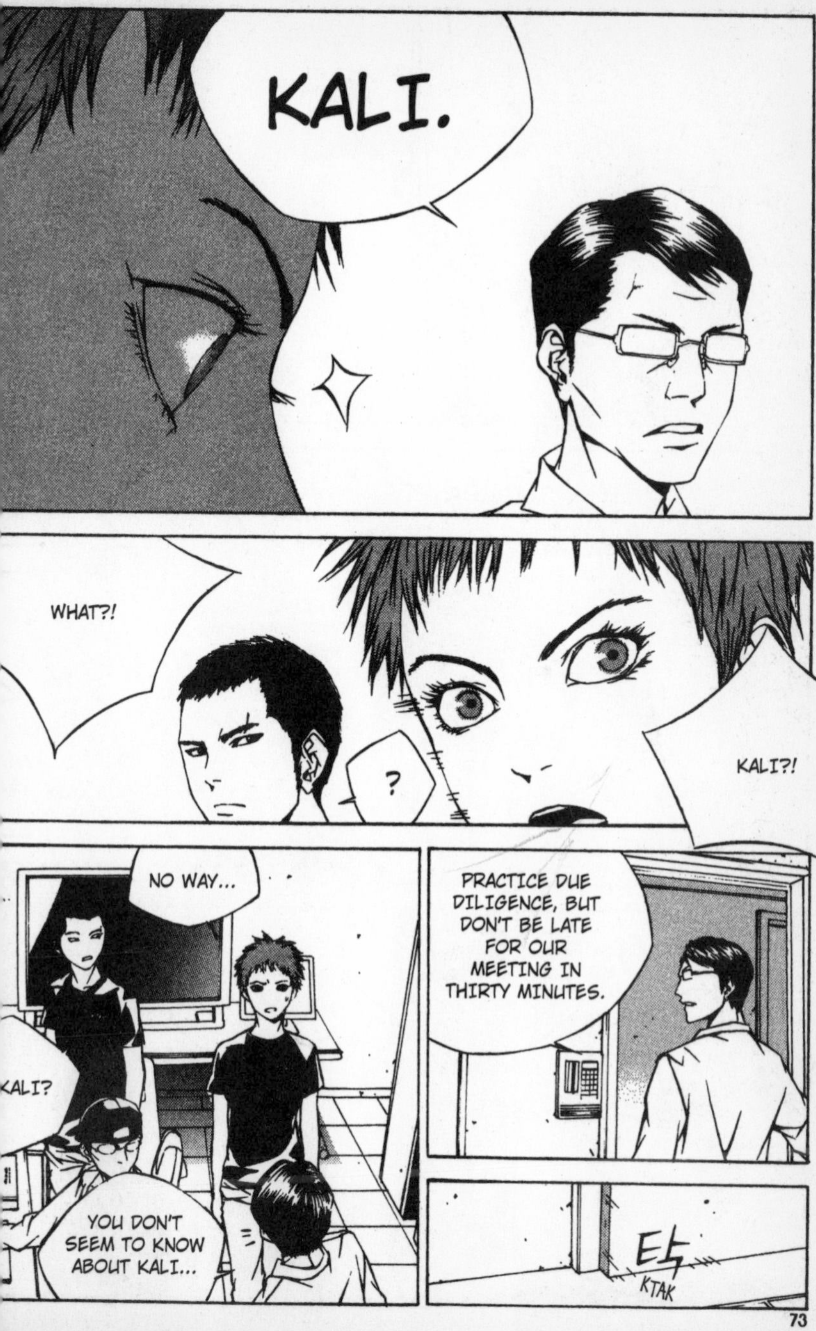
KALI.
WHAT?!
?
KALI?!
NO WAY...
KALI?
YOU DON'T SEEM TO KNOW ABOUT KALI...
PRACTICE DUE DILIGENCE, BUT DON'T BE LATE FOR OUR MEETING IN THIRTY MINUTES.
KTAK

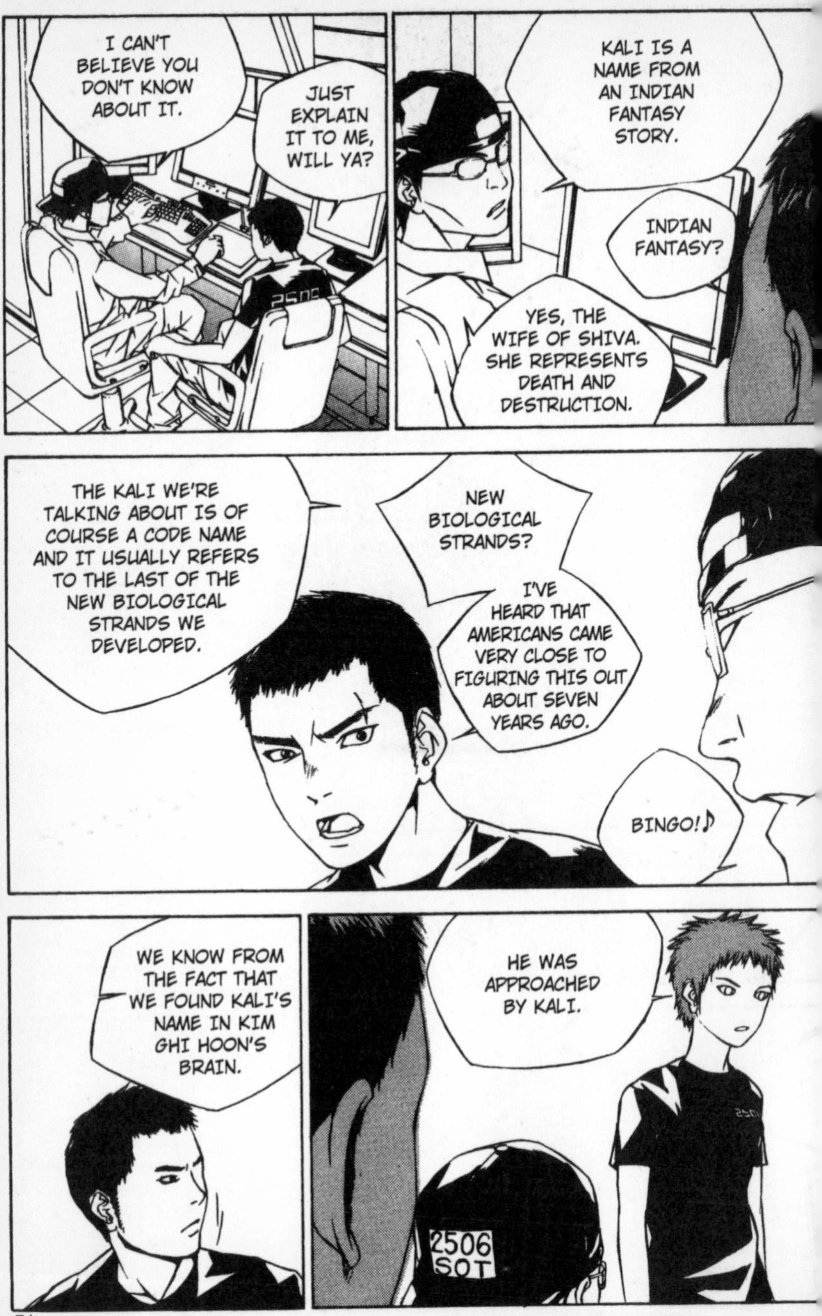
I CAN'T BELIEVE YOU DON'T KNOW ABOUT IT.
JUST EXPLAIN IT TO ME, WILL YA?
KALI IS A NAME FROM AN INDIAN FANTASY STORY.
INDIAN FANTASY?
YES, THE WIFE OF SHIVA. SHE REPRESENTS DEATH AND DESTRUCTION.
THE KALI WE'RE TALKING ABOUT IS OF COURSE A CODE NAME AND IT USUALLY REFERS TO THE LAST OF THE NEW BIOLOGICAL STRANDS WE DEVELOPED.
NEW BIOLOGICAL STRANDS?
I'VE HEARD THAT AMERICANS CAME VERY CLOSE TO FIGURING THIS OUT ABOUT SEVEN YEARS AGO.
BINGO!♪
WE KNOW FROM THE FACT THAT WE FOUND KALI'S NAME IN KIM GHI HOON'S BRAIN.
HE WAS APPROACHED BY KALI.
2506
SOT

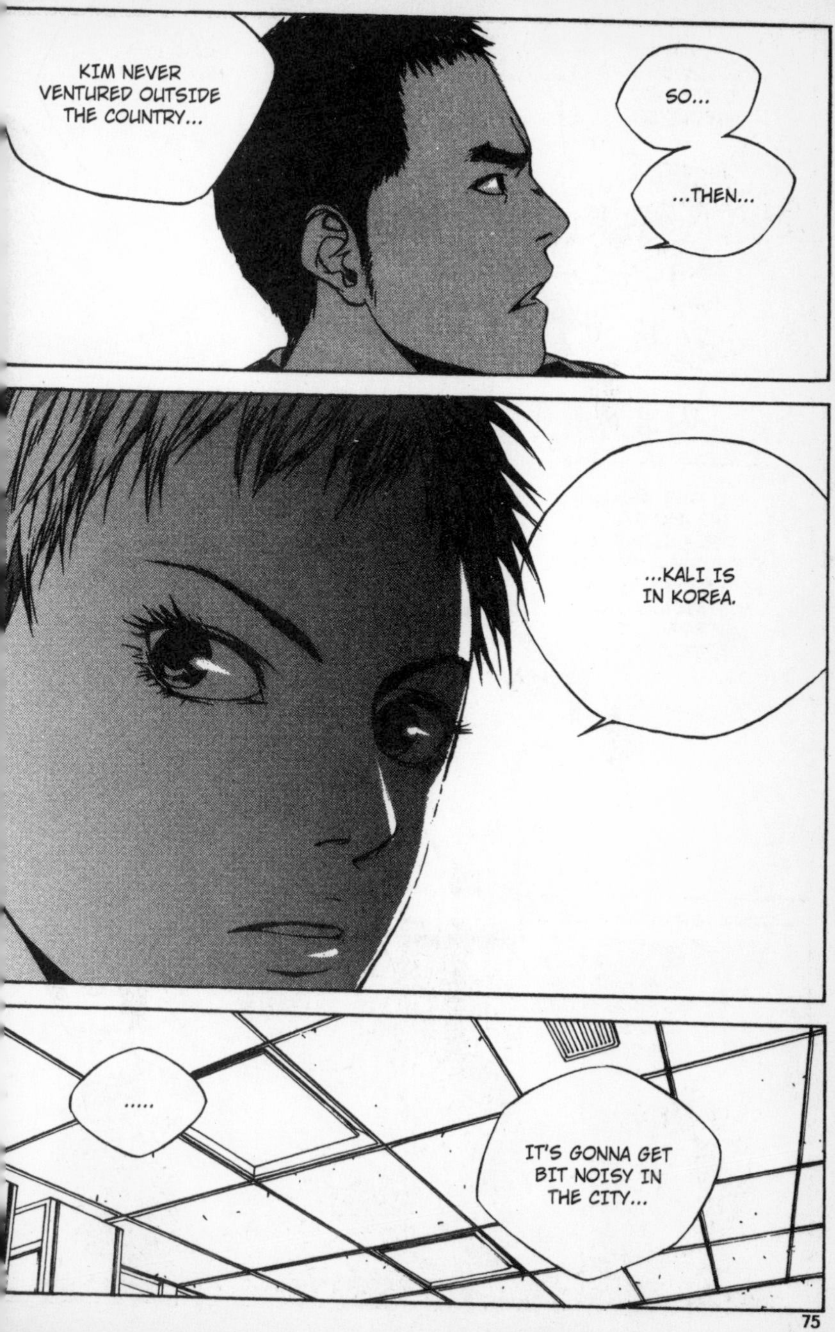
KIM NEVER VENTURED OUTSIDE THE COUNTRY...
SO...
...THEN...
...KALI IS IN KOREA.
.....
IT'S GONNA GET BIT NOISY IN THE CITY...

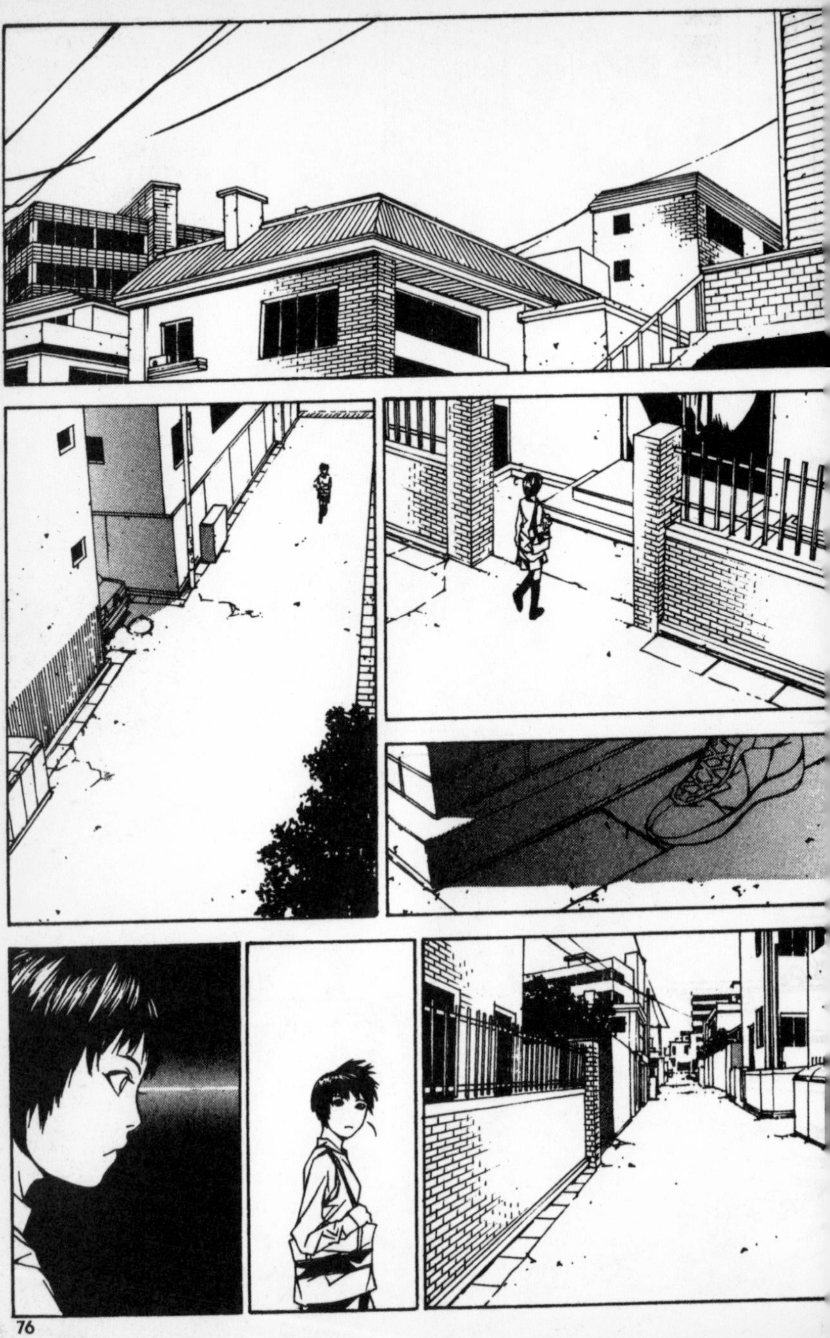

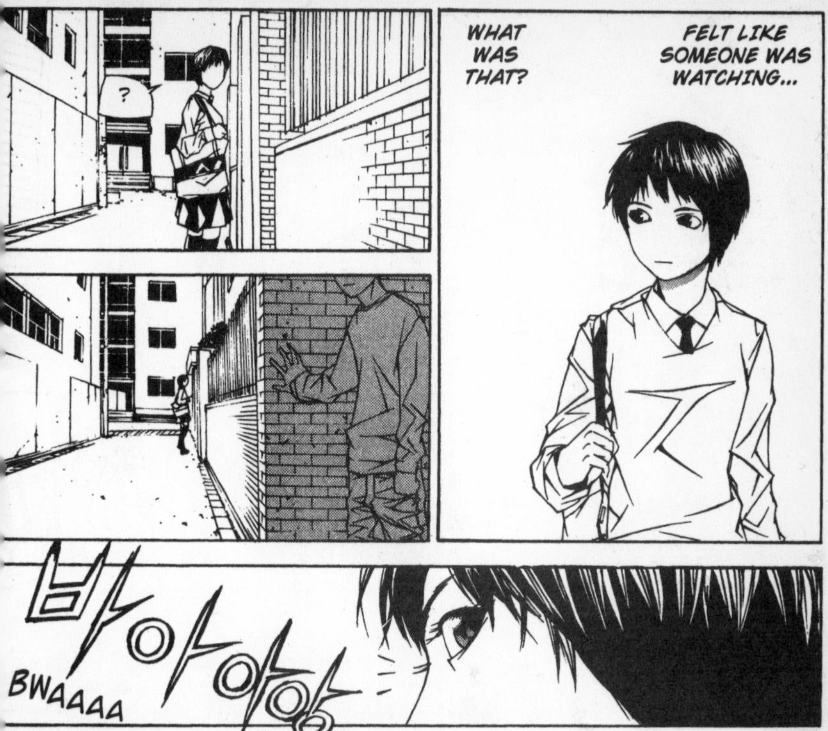
?
WHAT WAS THAT?
FELT LIKE SOMEONE WAS WATCHING...
바아아앙
BWAAAA

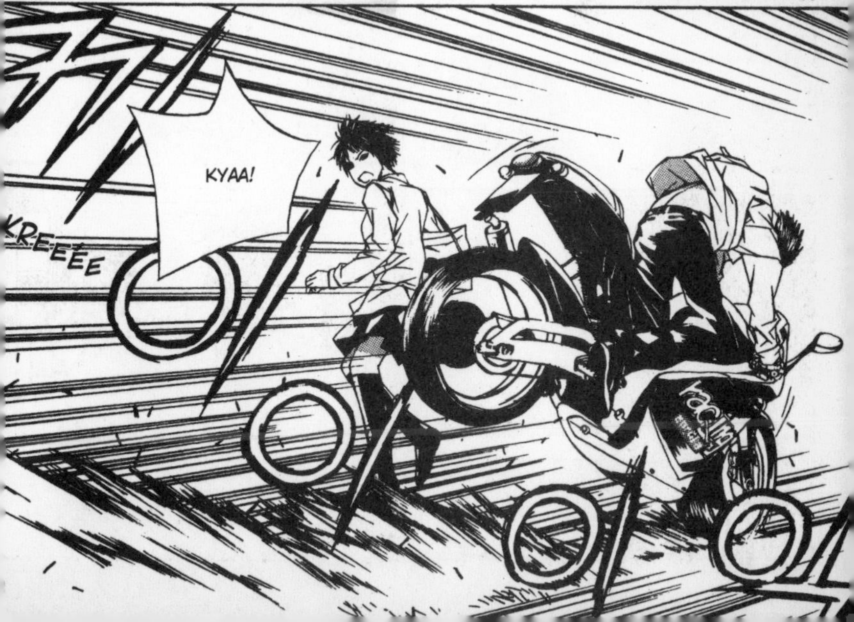
끼이이이
KREEEEE
KYAA!

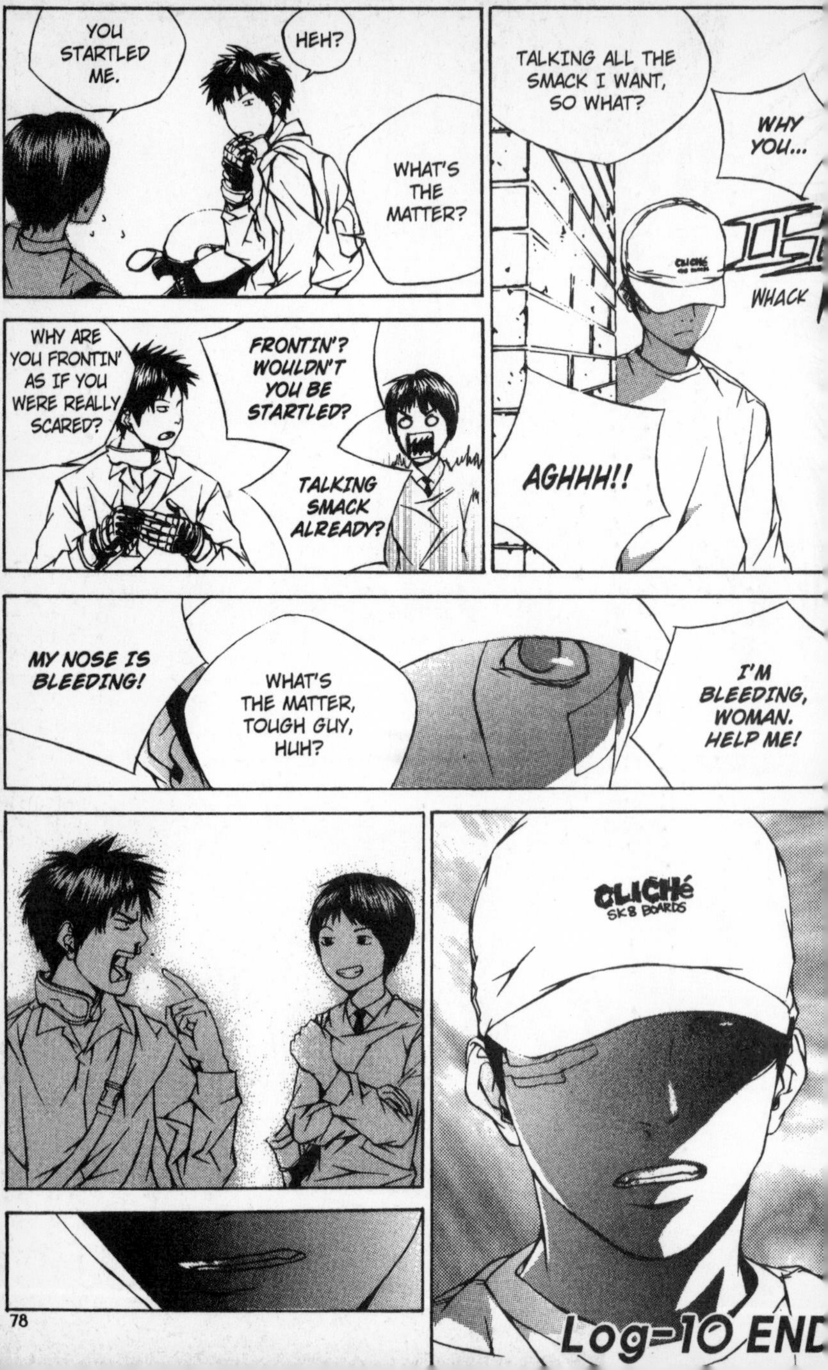
YOU STARTLED ME.
HEH?
WHAT'S THE MATTER?
WHY ARE YOU FRONTIN' AS IF YOU WERE REALLY SCARED?
FRONTIN'? WOULDN'T YOU BE STARTLED?
TALKING SMACK ALREADY?
TALKING ALL THE SMACK I WANT, SO WHAT?
WHY YOU...
WHACK
AGHHH!!
MY NOSE IS BLEEDING!
WHAT'S THE MATTER, TOUGH GUY, HUH?
I'M BLEEDING, WOMAN. HELP ME!
CLICHé SK8 BOARDS
Log-10 END

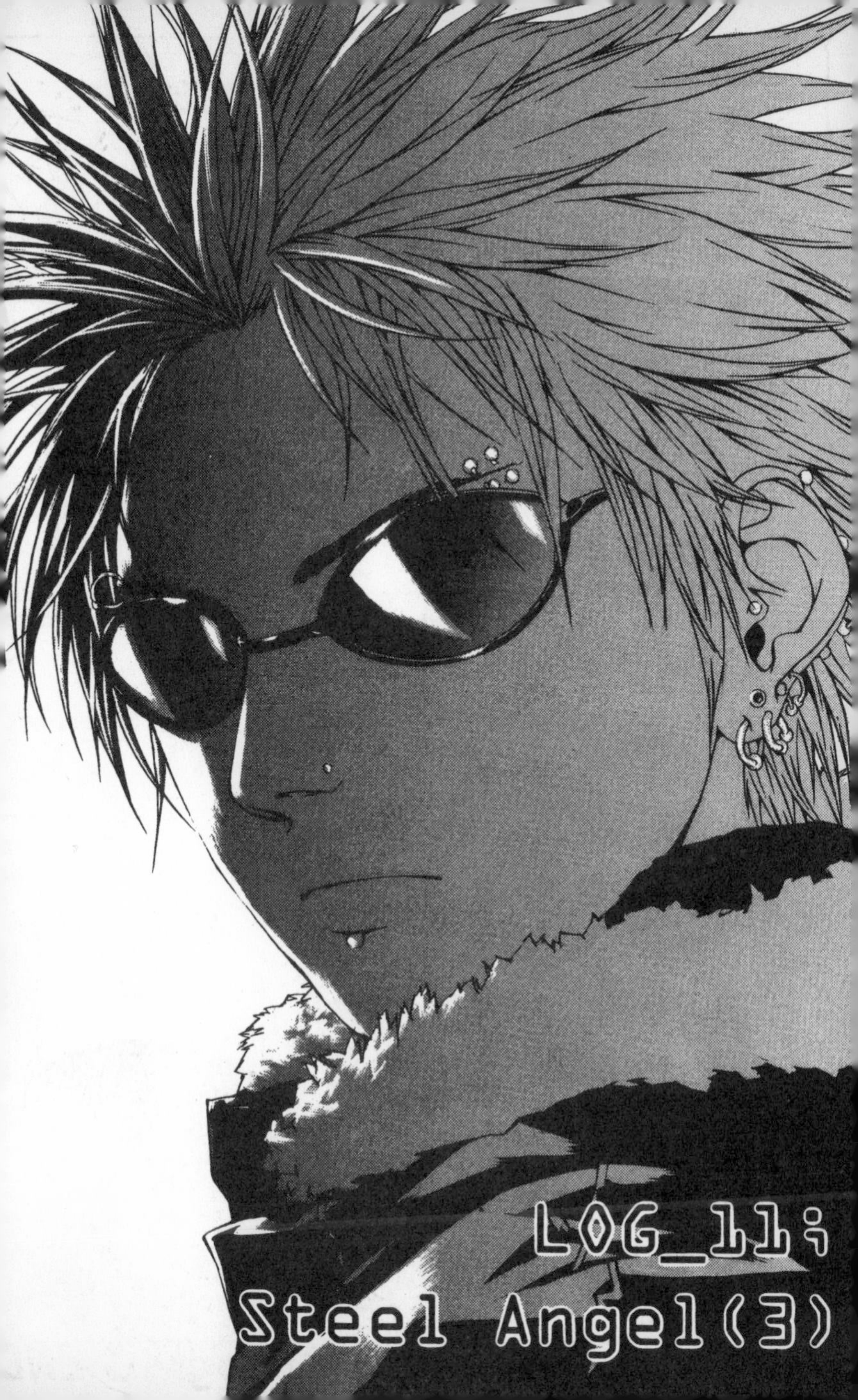

LOG_11: Steel Angel(3)

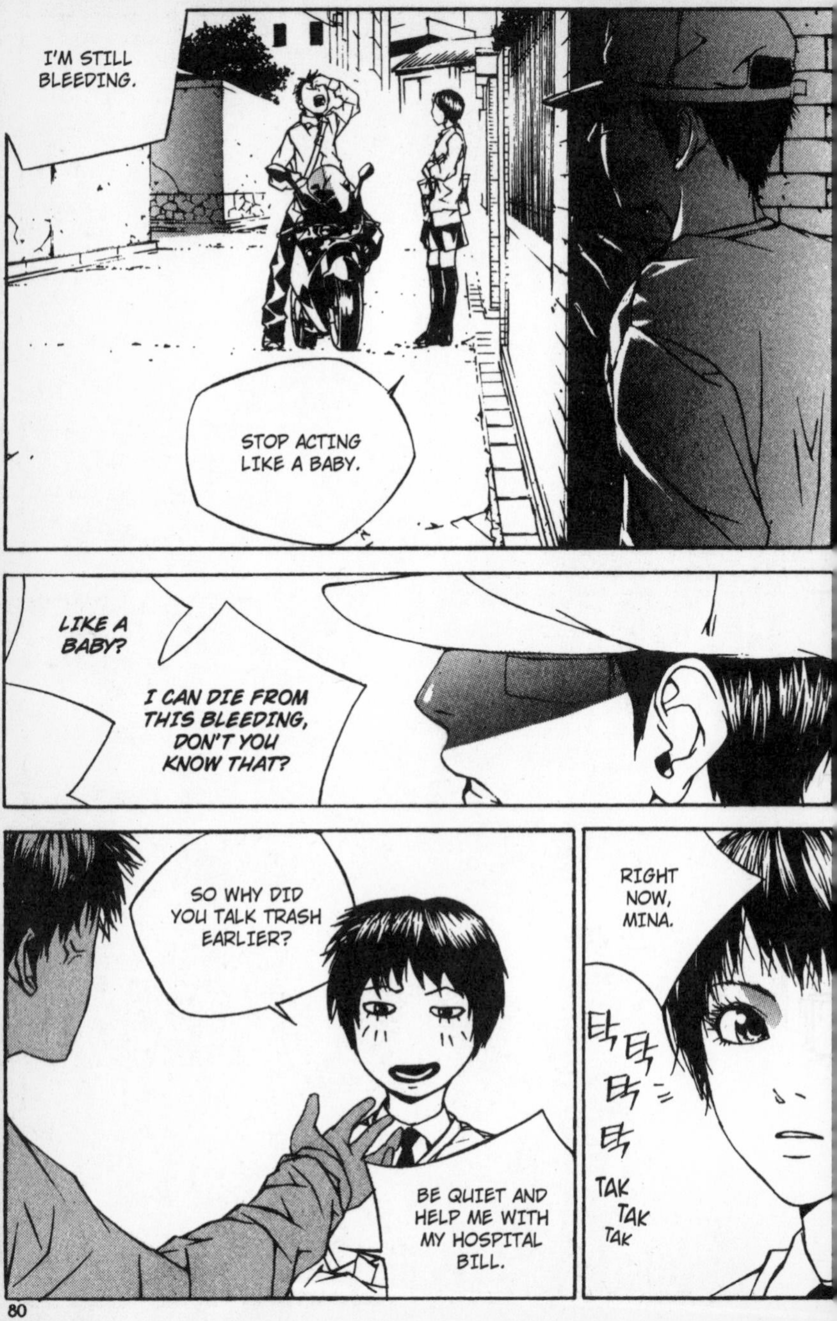
I'M STILL BLEEDING.
STOP ACTING LIKE A BABY.
LIKE A BABY?
I CAN DIE FROM THIS BLEEDING, DON'T YOU KNOW THAT?
SO WHY DID YOU TALK TRASH EARLIER?
BE QUIET AND HELP ME WITH MY HOSPITAL BILL.
RIGHT NOW, MINA.
탁
탁
탁
탁
TAK
TAK
TAK

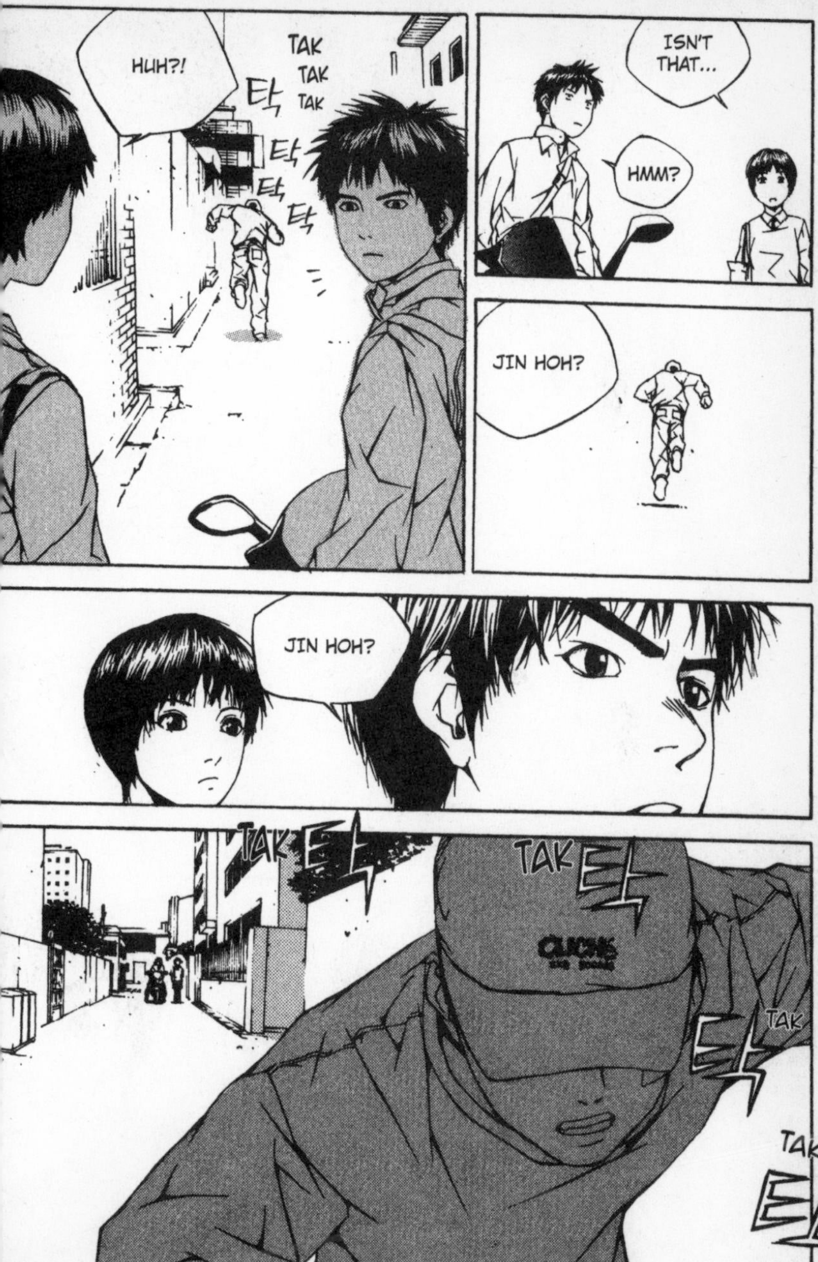
HUH?!
TAK
TAK
TAK
탁
탁
탁
탁
ISN'T THAT...
HMM?
JIN HOH?
JIN HOH?
TAK
TAK
TAK
TAK

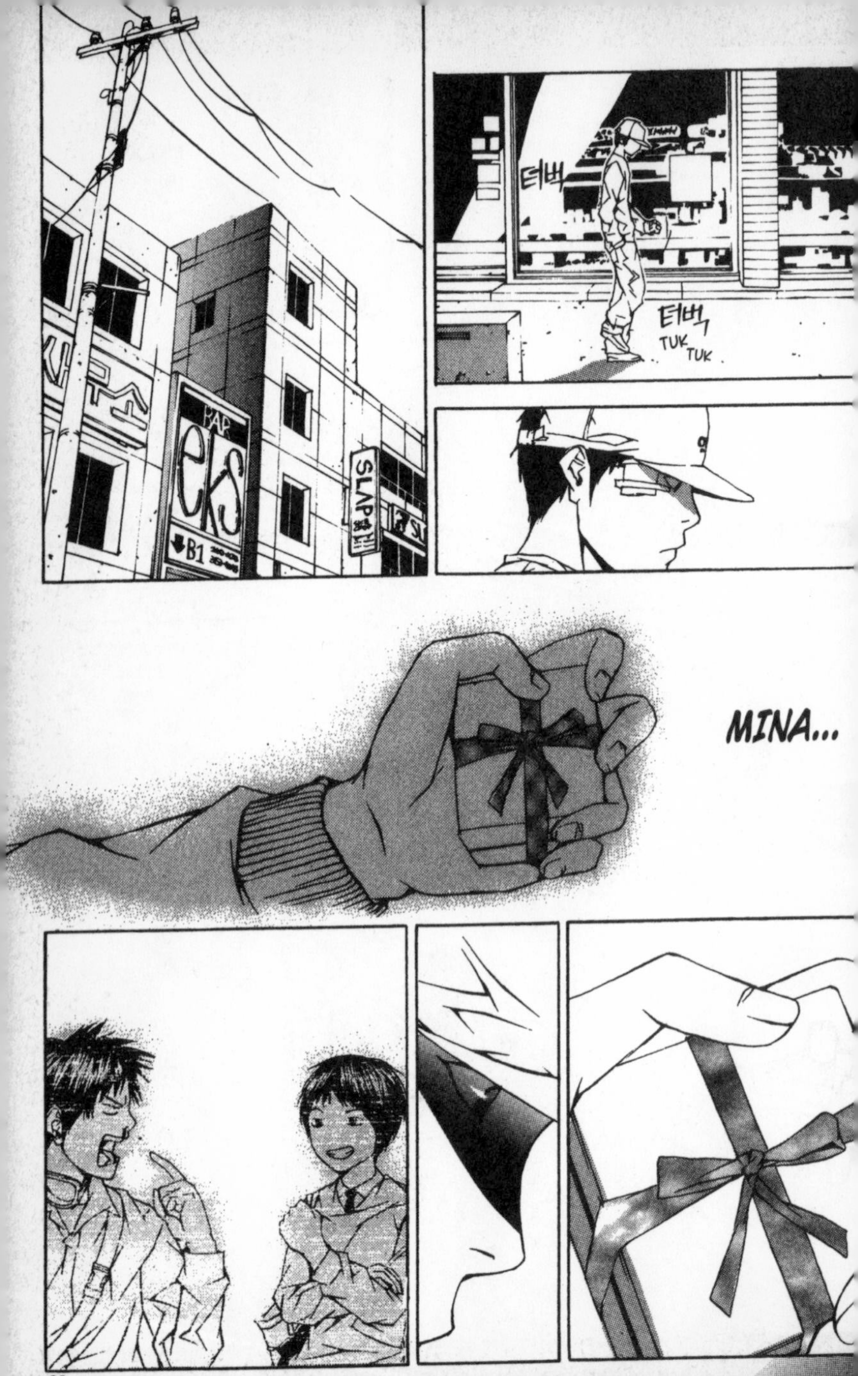
BAR
eks
B1
SLAP
터벅
터벅
TUK TUK
MINA...

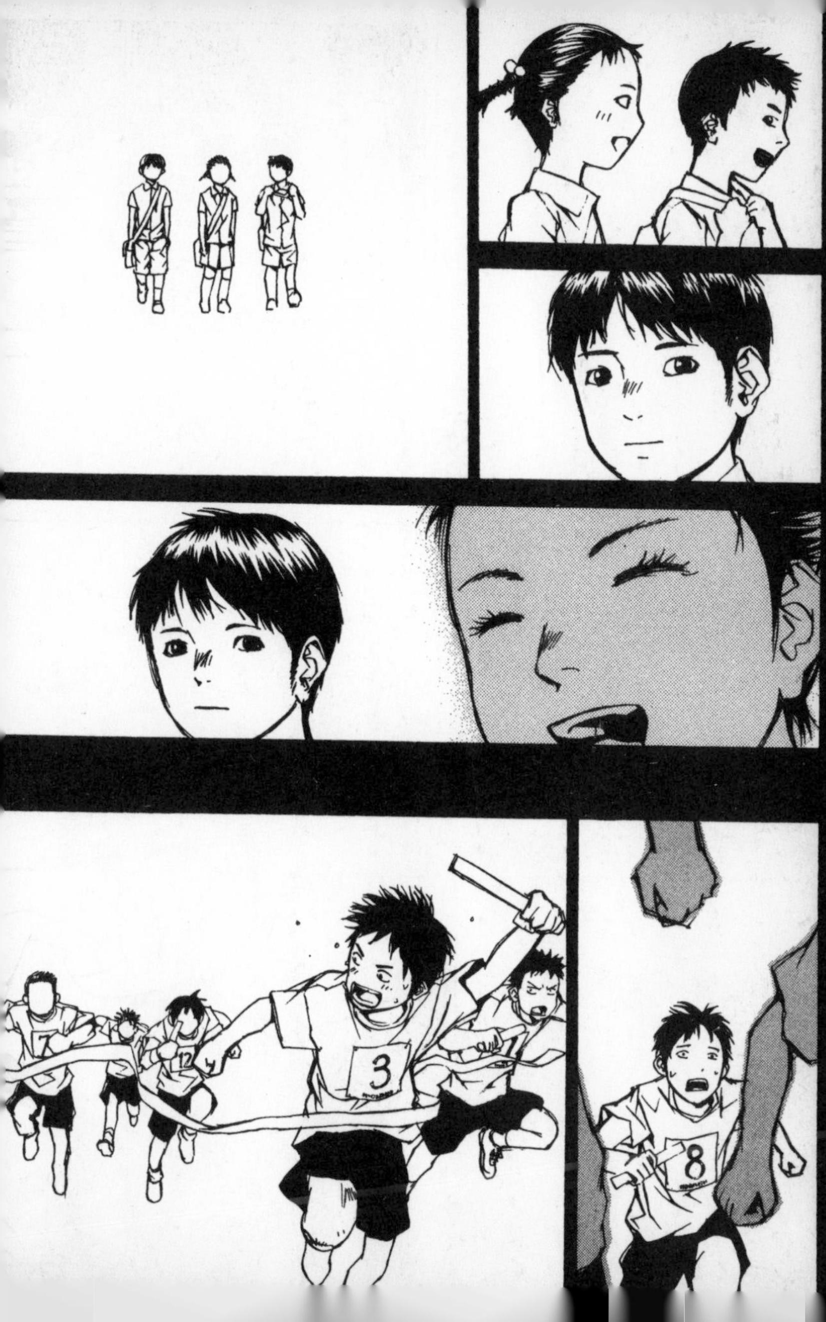
7
12
3
8

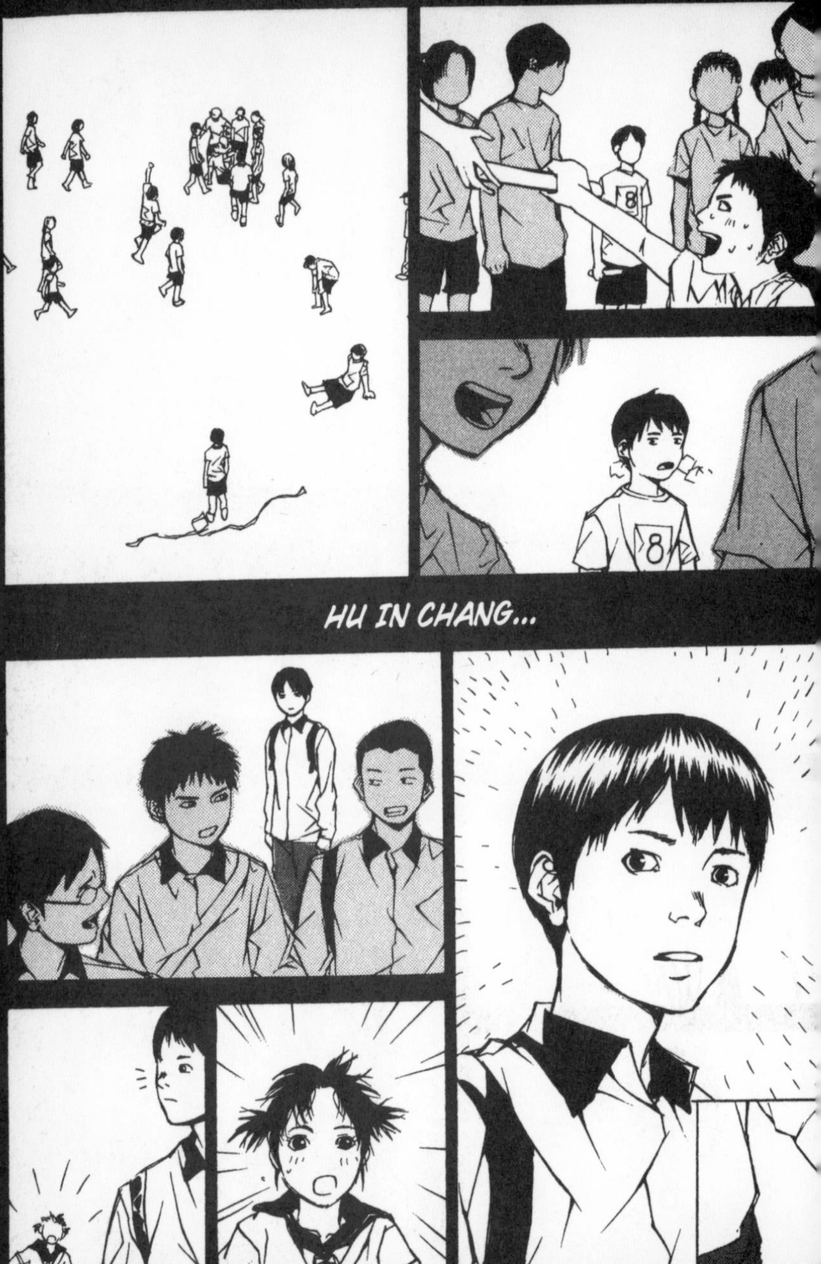
HU IN CHANG...

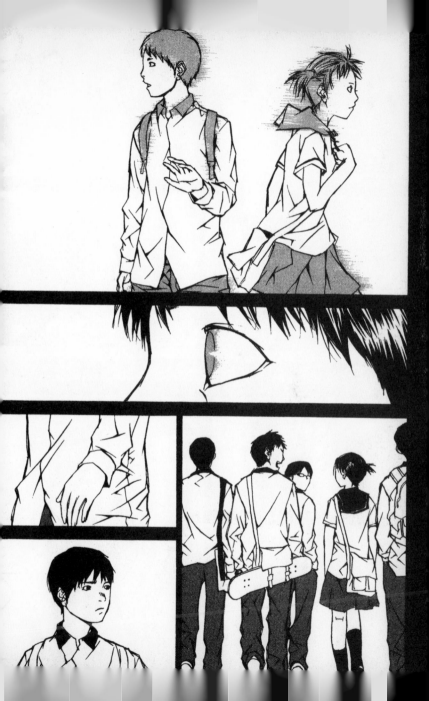

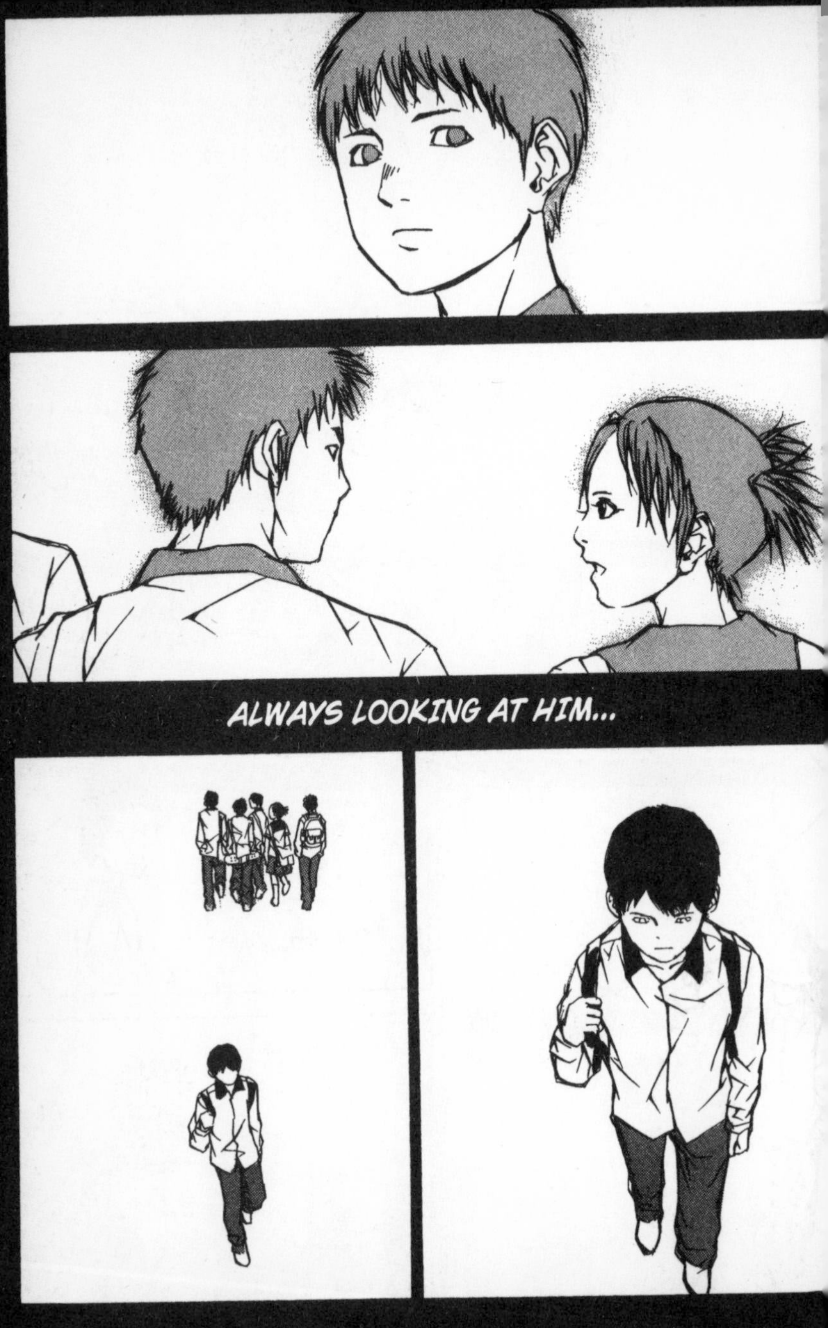
ALWAYS LOOKING AT HIM...

CLICHé
SK8 Boards

TUK

HEY!

.....

TUK

TUK

TUK

HUH?

HEY,
HEY!

WHAT'S
UP?

TUK

TUK

.....

LOOK
AT THIS
JACKASS.

VANS

?

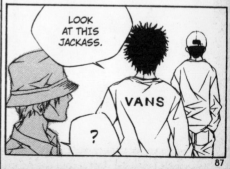

LISTEN, YOU DEAF, MUTE FUCK!

ARE YOU BLIND TOO?

PAK

YOU ALMOST DISLOCATED MY SHOULDER!

BBUNG

GRAB

YOU TESTING ME, BITCH?

STILL NO APOLOGIES?

C'MON, LET'S JUST GO.

I'M ALREADY PISSED OFF FROM THEM GIRLS REJECTING US. AND GUESS WHO'S GONNA PAY FOR IT.

I'M GONNA FUCK YOU UP.

LET'S GO!

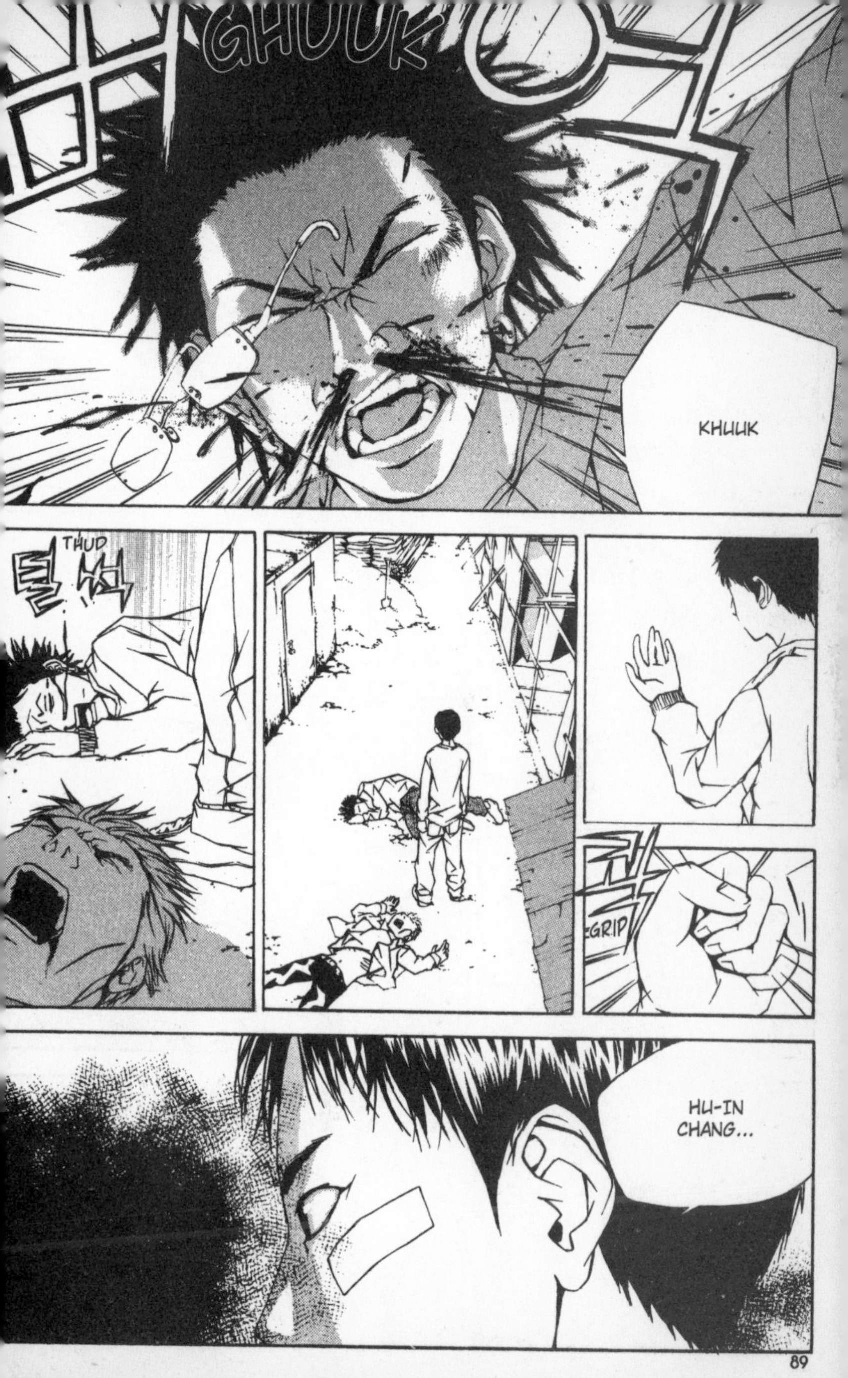
GHUUK
KHUUK
THUD
털썩
GRIP
HU-IN CHANG...

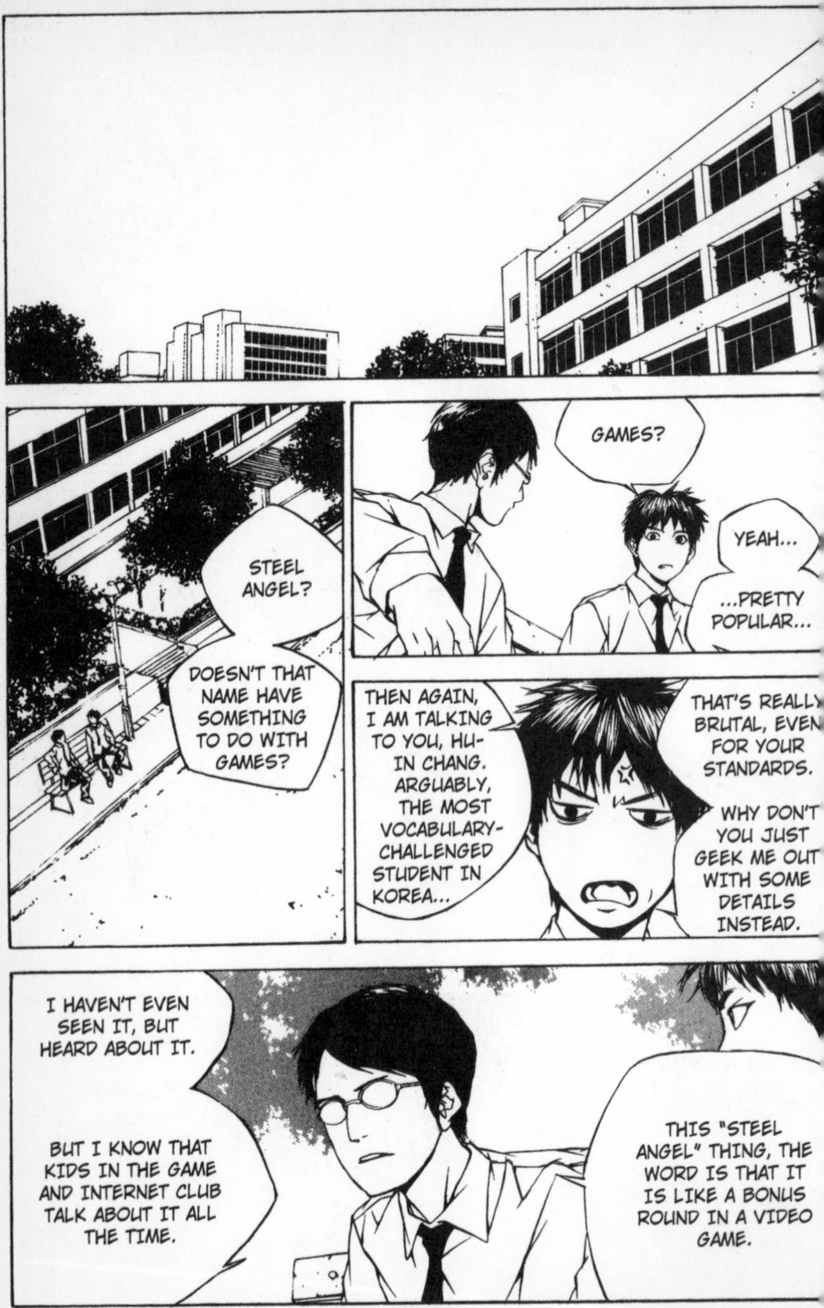
STEEL ANGEL?
DOESN'T THAT NAME HAVE SOMETHING TO DO WITH GAMES?
GAMES?
YEAH...
...PRETTY POPULAR...
THEN AGAIN, I AM TALKING TO YOU, HU-IN CHANG. ARGUABLY, THE MOST VOCABULARY-CHALLENGED STUDENT IN KOREA...
THAT'S REALLY BRUTAL, EVEN FOR YOUR STANDARDS.
WHY DON'T YOU JUST GEEK ME OUT WITH SOME DETAILS INSTEAD.
I HAVEN'T EVEN SEEN IT, BUT HEARD ABOUT IT.
BUT I KNOW THAT KIDS IN THE GAME AND INTERNET CLUB TALK ABOUT IT ALL THE TIME.
THIS "STEEL ANGEL" THING, THE WORD IS THAT IT IS LIKE A BONUS ROUND IN A VIDEO GAME.

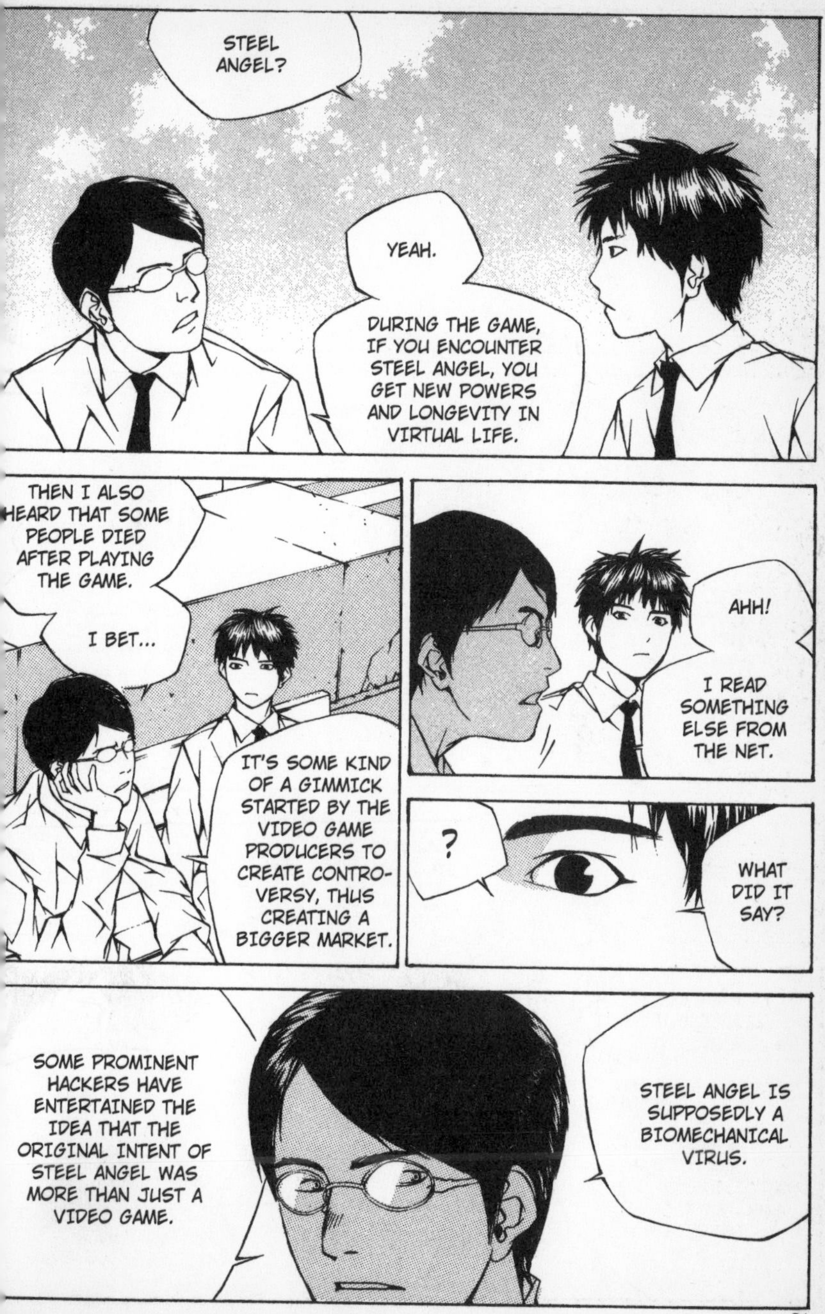
STEEL ANGEL?
YEAH.
DURING THE GAME, IF YOU ENCOUNTER STEEL ANGEL, YOU GET NEW POWERS AND LONGEVITY IN VIRTUAL LIFE.
THEN I ALSO HEARD THAT SOME PEOPLE DIED AFTER PLAYING THE GAME.
I BET...
IT'S SOME KIND OF A GIMMICK STARTED BY THE VIDEO GAME PRODUCERS TO CREATE CONTRO-VERSY, THUS CREATING A BIGGER MARKET.
AHH!
I READ SOMETHING ELSE FROM THE NET.
?
WHAT DID IT SAY?
SOME PROMINENT HACKERS HAVE ENTERTAINED THE IDEA THAT THE ORIGINAL INTENT OF STEEL ANGEL WAS MORE THAN JUST A VIDEO GAME.
STEEL ANGEL IS SUPPOSEDLY A BIOMECHANICAL VIRUS.

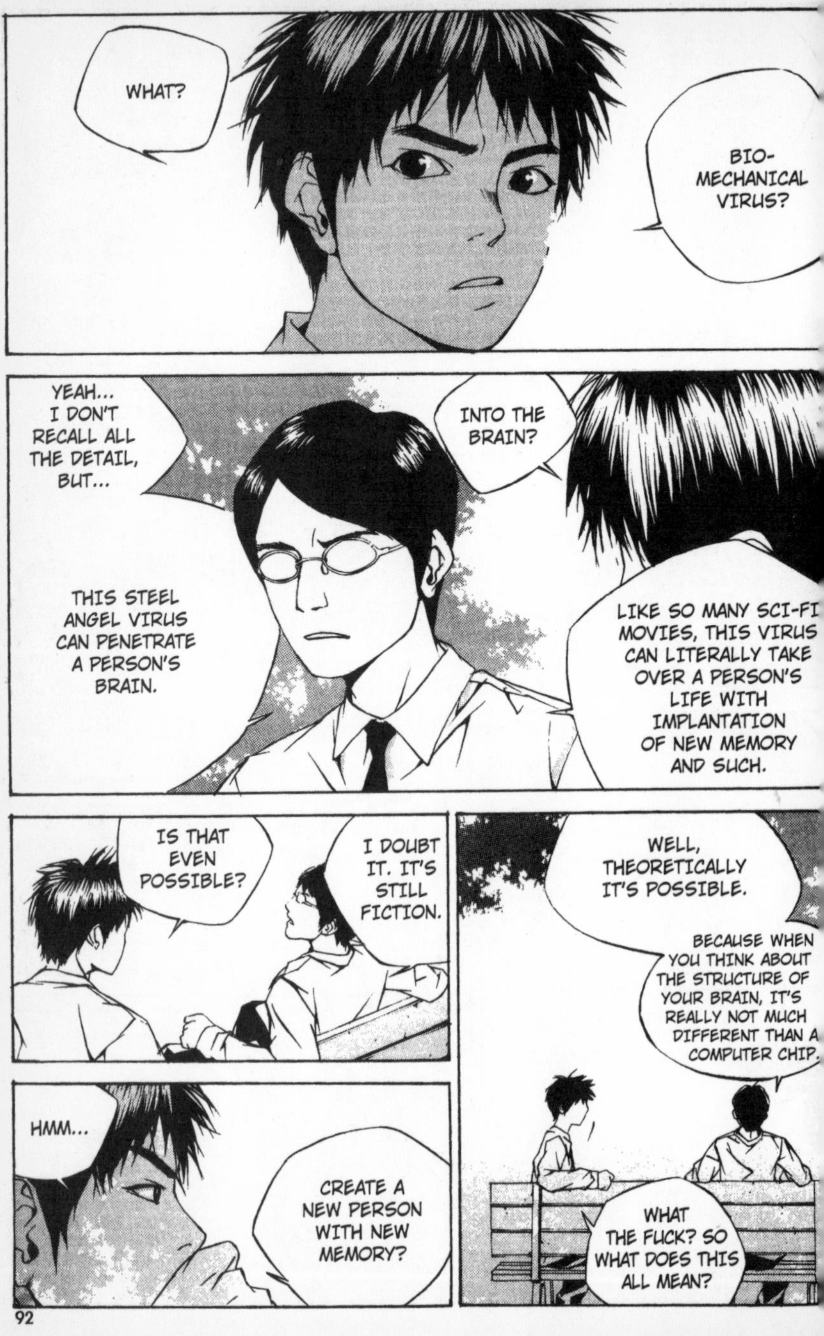
WHAT?
BIO-MECHANICAL VIRUS?
YEAH... I DON'T RECALL ALL THE DETAIL, BUT...
INTO THE BRAIN?
THIS STEEL ANGEL VIRUS CAN PENETRATE A PERSON'S BRAIN.
LIKE SO MANY SCI-FI MOVIES, THIS VIRUS CAN LITERALLY TAKE OVER A PERSON'S LIFE WITH IMPLANTATION OF NEW MEMORY AND SUCH.
IS THAT EVEN POSSIBLE?
I DOUBT IT. IT'S STILL FICTION.
HMM...
CREATE A NEW PERSON WITH NEW MEMORY?
WELL, THEORETICALLY IT'S POSSIBLE.
BECAUSE WHEN YOU THINK ABOUT THE STRUCTURE OF YOUR BRAIN, IT'S REALLY NOT MUCH DIFFERENT THAN A COMPUTER CHIP.
WHAT THE FUCK? SO WHAT DOES THIS ALL MEAN?

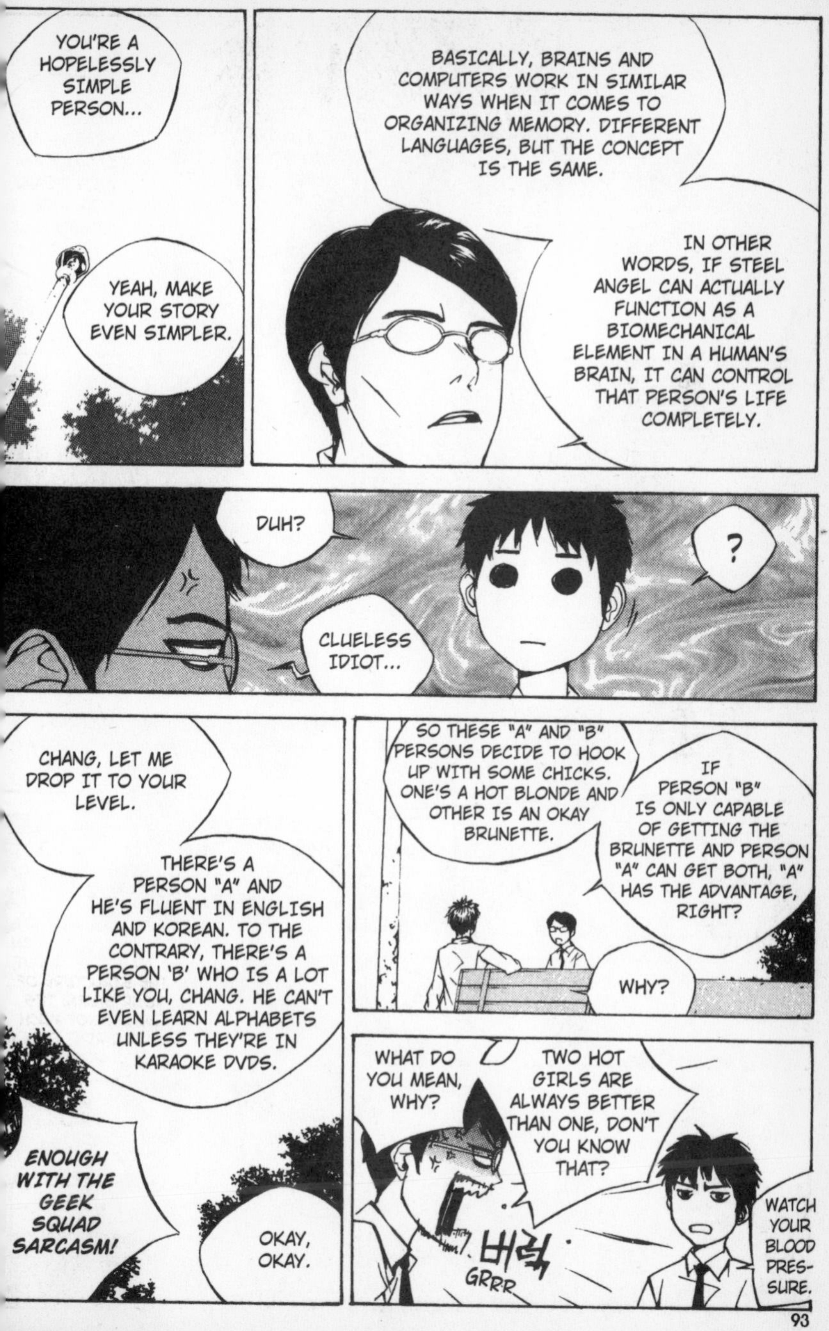
YOU'RE A HOPELESSLY SIMPLE PERSON...
YEAH, MAKE YOUR STORY EVEN SIMPLER.
BASICALLY, BRAINS AND COMPUTERS WORK IN SIMILAR WAYS WHEN IT COMES TO ORGANIZING MEMORY. DIFFERENT LANGUAGES, BUT THE CONCEPT IS THE SAME.
IN OTHER WORDS, IF STEEL ANGEL CAN ACTUALLY FUNCTION AS A BIOMECHANICAL ELEMENT IN A HUMAN'S BRAIN, IT CAN CONTROL THAT PERSON'S LIFE COMPLETELY.
DUH?
CLUELESS IDIOT...
?
CHANG, LET ME DROP IT TO YOUR LEVEL.
THERE'S A PERSON "A" AND HE'S FLUENT IN ENGLISH AND KOREAN. TO THE CONTRARY, THERE'S A PERSON 'B' WHO IS A LOT LIKE YOU, CHANG. HE CAN'T EVEN LEARN ALPHABETS UNLESS THEY'RE IN KARAOKE DVDS.
ENOUGH WITH THE GEEK SQUAD SARCASM!
OKAY, OKAY.
SO THESE "A" AND "B" PERSONS DECIDE TO HOOK UP WITH SOME CHICKS. ONE'S A HOT BLONDE AND OTHER IS AN OKAY BRUNETTE.
IF PERSON "B" IS ONLY CAPABLE OF GETTING THE BRUNETTE AND PERSON "A" CAN GET BOTH, "A" HAS THE ADVANTAGE, RIGHT?
WHY?
WHAT DO YOU MEAN, WHY?
TWO HOT GIRLS ARE ALWAYS BETTER THAN ONE, DON'T YOU KNOW THAT?
버럭
GRRR
WATCH YOUR BLOOD PRES-SURE.

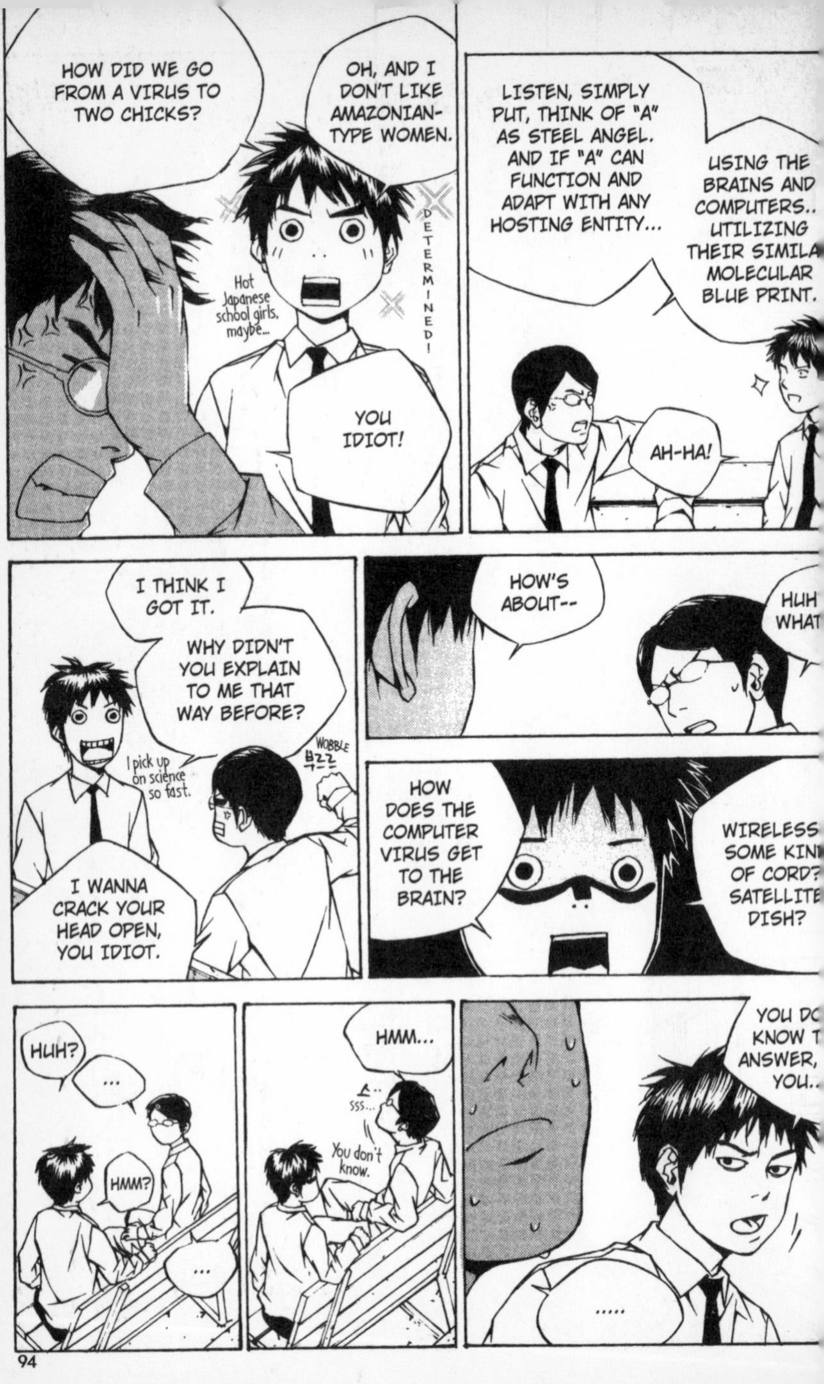
HOW DID WE GO FROM A VIRUS TO TWO CHICKS?
OH, AND I DON'T LIKE AMAZONIAN-TYPE WOMEN.
DETERMINED!
Hot Japanese school girls, maybe...
YOU IDIOT!
LISTEN, SIMPLY PUT, THINK OF "A" AS STEEL ANGEL. AND IF "A" CAN FUNCTION AND ADAPT WITH ANY HOSTING ENTITY...
USING THE BRAINS AND COMPUTERS... UTILIZING THEIR SIMILA MOLECULAR BLUE PRINT.
AH-HA!
I THINK I GOT IT.
WHY DIDN'T YOU EXPLAIN TO ME THAT WAY BEFORE?
I pick up on science so fast.
WOBBLE
I WANNA CRACK YOUR HEAD OPEN, YOU IDIOT.
HOW'S ABOUT--
HUH WHAT
HOW DOES THE COMPUTER VIRUS GET TO THE BRAIN?
WIRELESS SOME KIN OF CORD? SATELLITE DISH?
HUH?
...
HMM?
...
HMM...
sss...
You don't know.
YOU DO KNOW T ANSWER, YOU..
.....

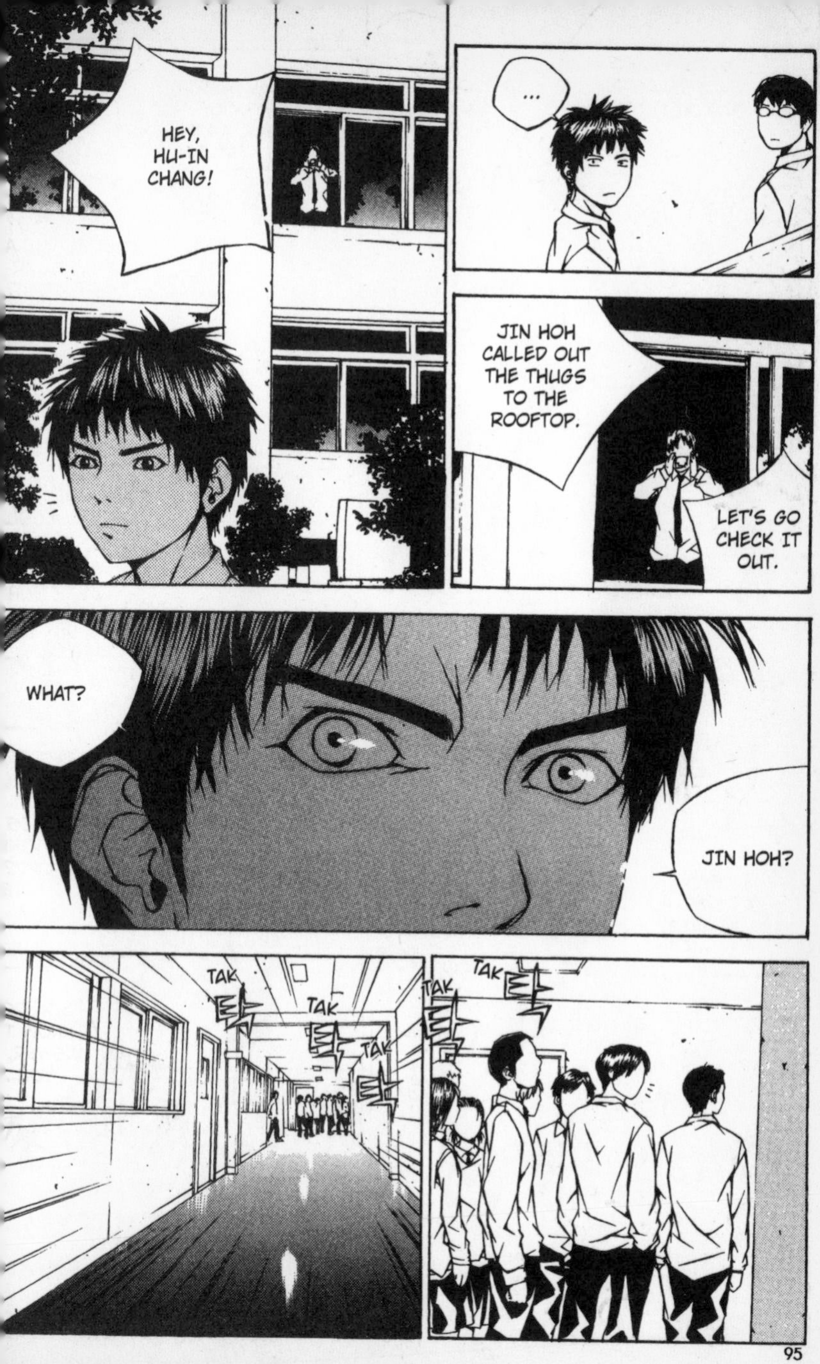
HEY, HU-IN CHANG!
...
JIN HOH CALLED OUT THE THUGS TO THE ROOFTOP.
LET'S GO CHECK IT OUT.
WHAT?
JIN HOH?
TAK
TAK
TAK
TAK
TAK

WHAT'S GOING ON?

HEY CHANG.

JIN HOH CAME INTO THE CLASSROOM AND JUST CALLED OUT THOSE THUGS.

THEY WENT UP A LITTLE WHILE AGO, BUT THE DOOR IS LOCKED UP THERE.

IT DON'T MAKE NO SENSE.

JIN HOH STARTING IT WITH THUGS?

TOLD YOU THE DOOR IS LOCKED.

KAANG

?

KAANG

KHAAK

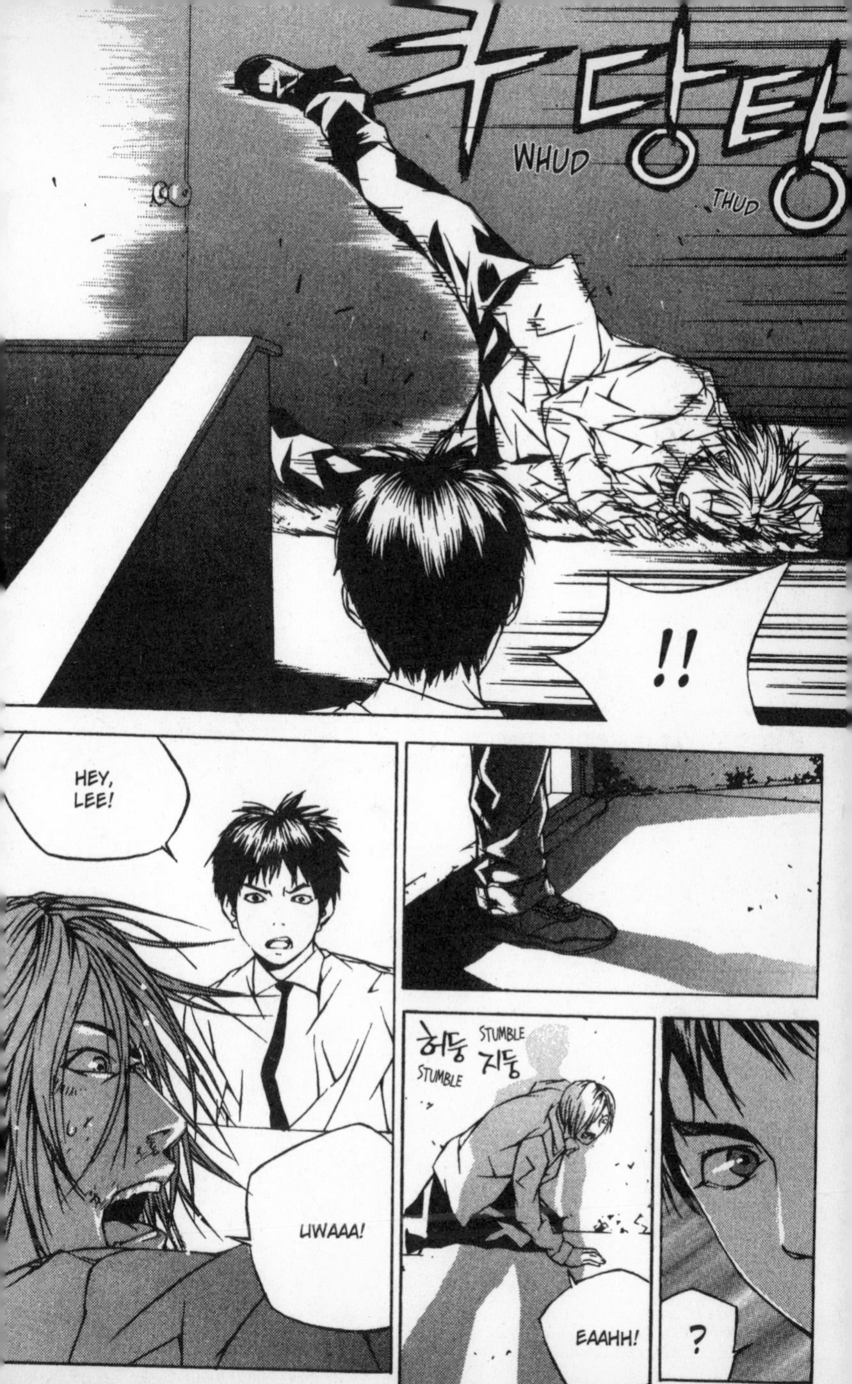
쿠당탕
WHUD
THUD
!!
HEY, LEE!
UWAAA!
허둥 지둥
STUMBLE
STUMBLE
EAAHH!
?

?!

JIN--HOH?

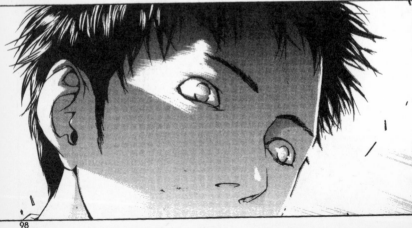

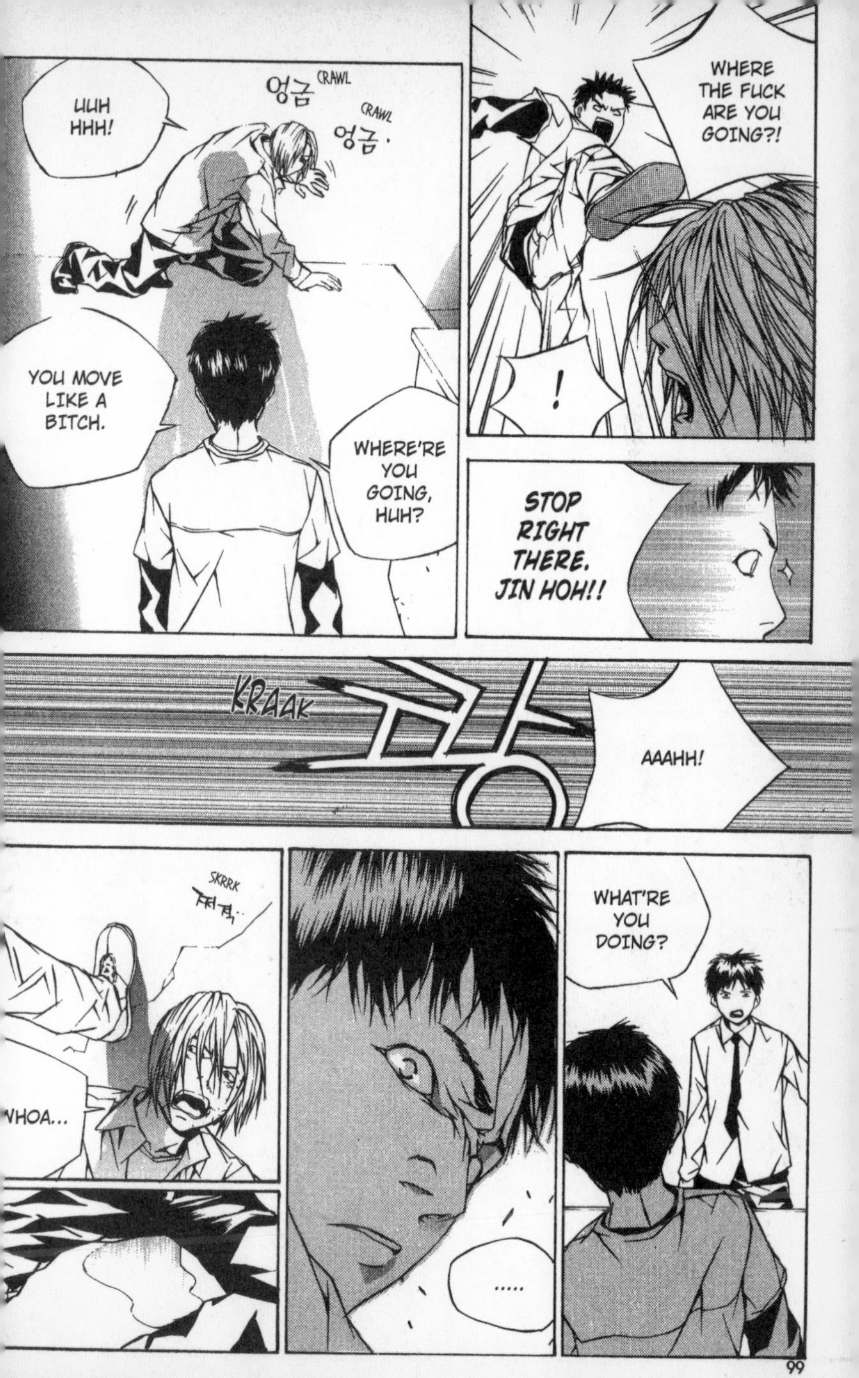
UUH HHH!
CRAWL
엉금
CRAWL
엉금.
YOU MOVE LIKE A BITCH.
WHERE'RE YOU GOING, HUH?
WHERE THE FUCK ARE YOU GOING?!
!
STOP RIGHT THERE. JIN HOH!!
KRAAK
AAAHH!
SKRRK
WHOA...
.....
WHAT'RE YOU DOING?

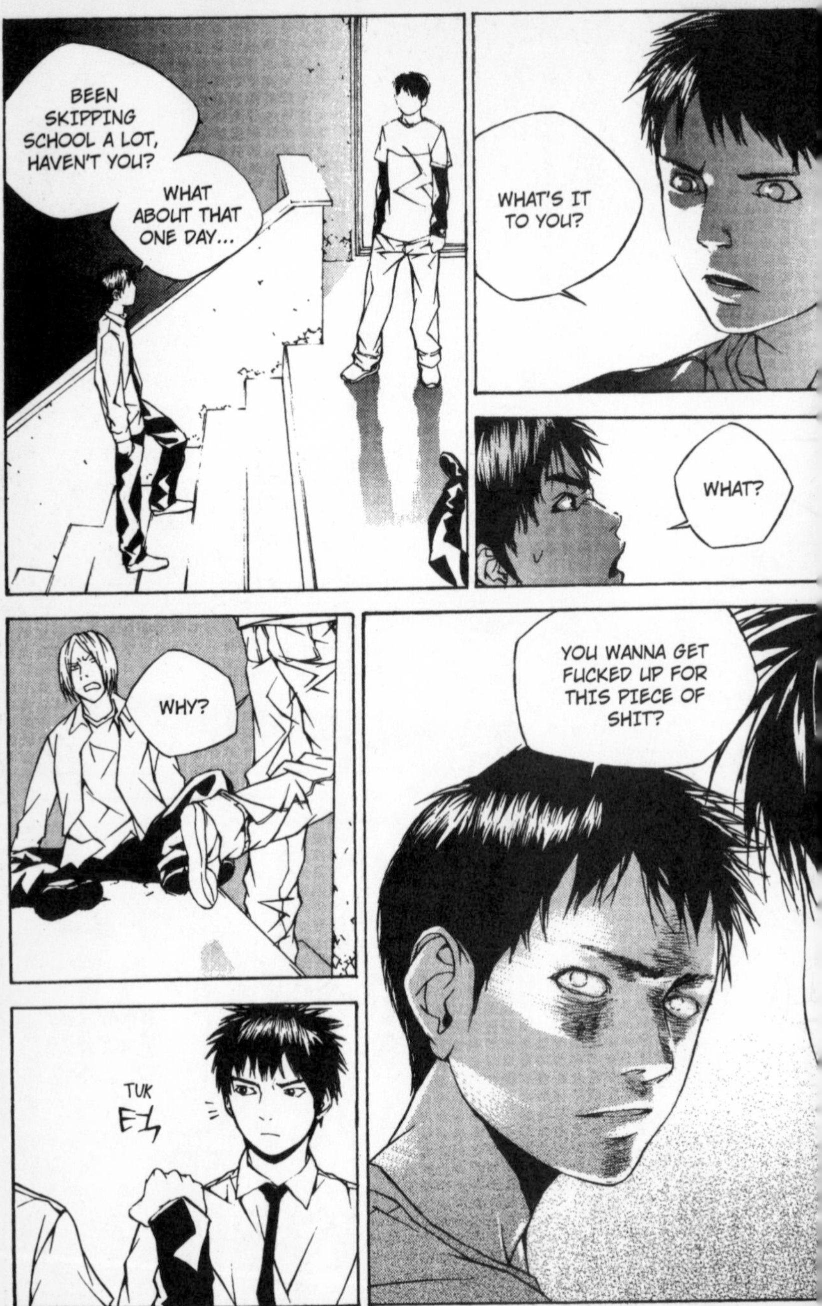
BEEN SKIPPING SCHOOL A LOT, HAVEN'T YOU?
WHAT ABOUT THAT ONE DAY...
WHAT'S IT TO YOU?
WHAT?
WHY?
YOU WANNA GET FUCKED UP FOR THIS PIECE OF SHIT?
TUK

HOW DO YOU MEAN...?

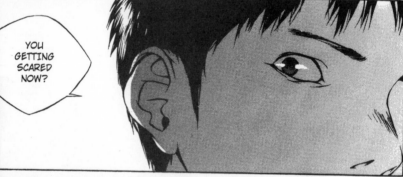

YOU GETTING SCARED NOW?

UP K!

PAK

YOU MUST BE HIGH!

TCH!

MUST BE HIGH...

YEAH, YOU STONED PUNK BITCH.

WHAT THE FUCK ARE YOU TWO DOING?

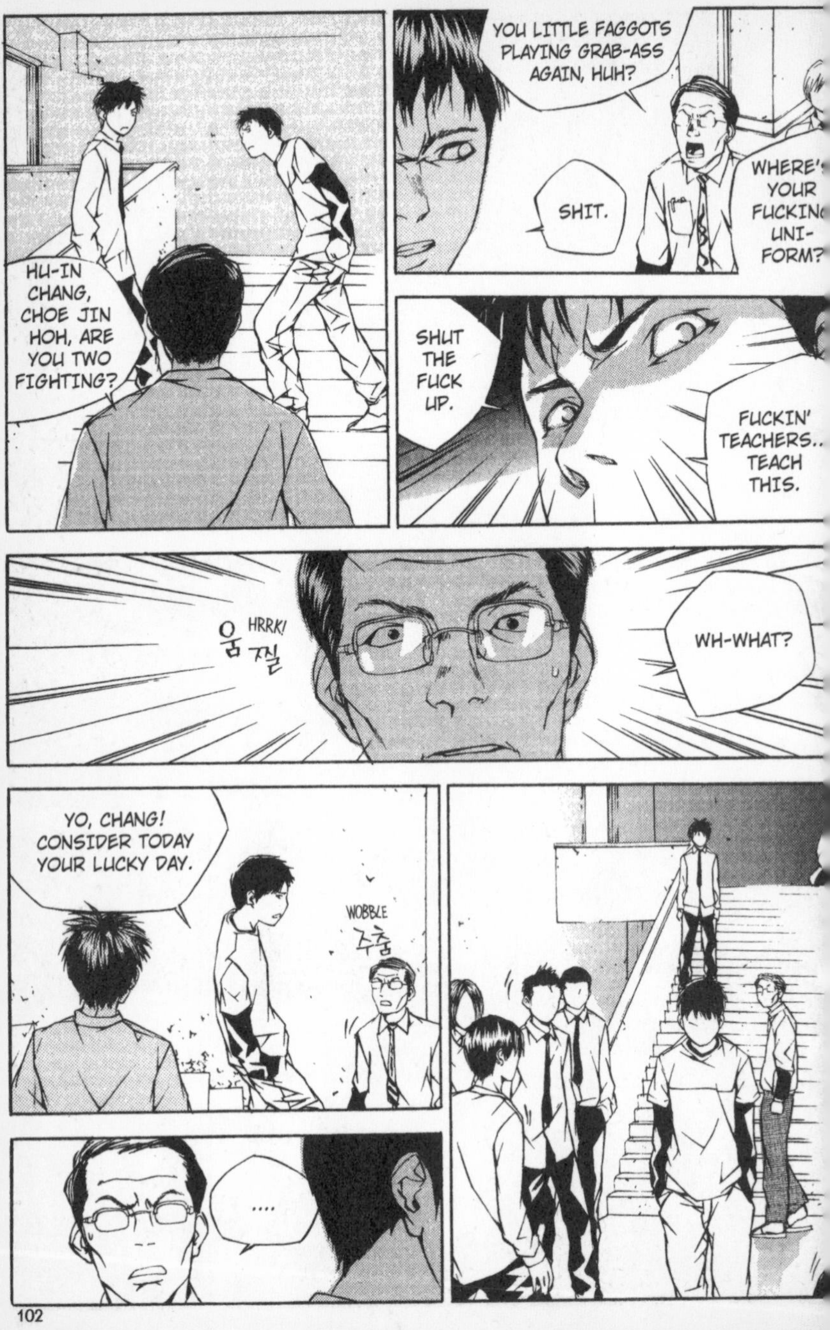
HU-IN CHANG, CHOE JIN HOH, ARE YOU TWO FIGHTING?
YOU LITTLE FAGGOTS PLAYING GRAB-ASS AGAIN, HUH?
WHERE'S YOUR FUCKING UNI-FORM?
SHIT.
SHUT THE FUCK UP.
FUCKIN' TEACHERS.. TEACH THIS.
움찔
HRRK!
WH-WHAT?
YO, CHANG! CONSIDER TODAY YOUR LUCKY DAY.
주춤
WOBBLE
....

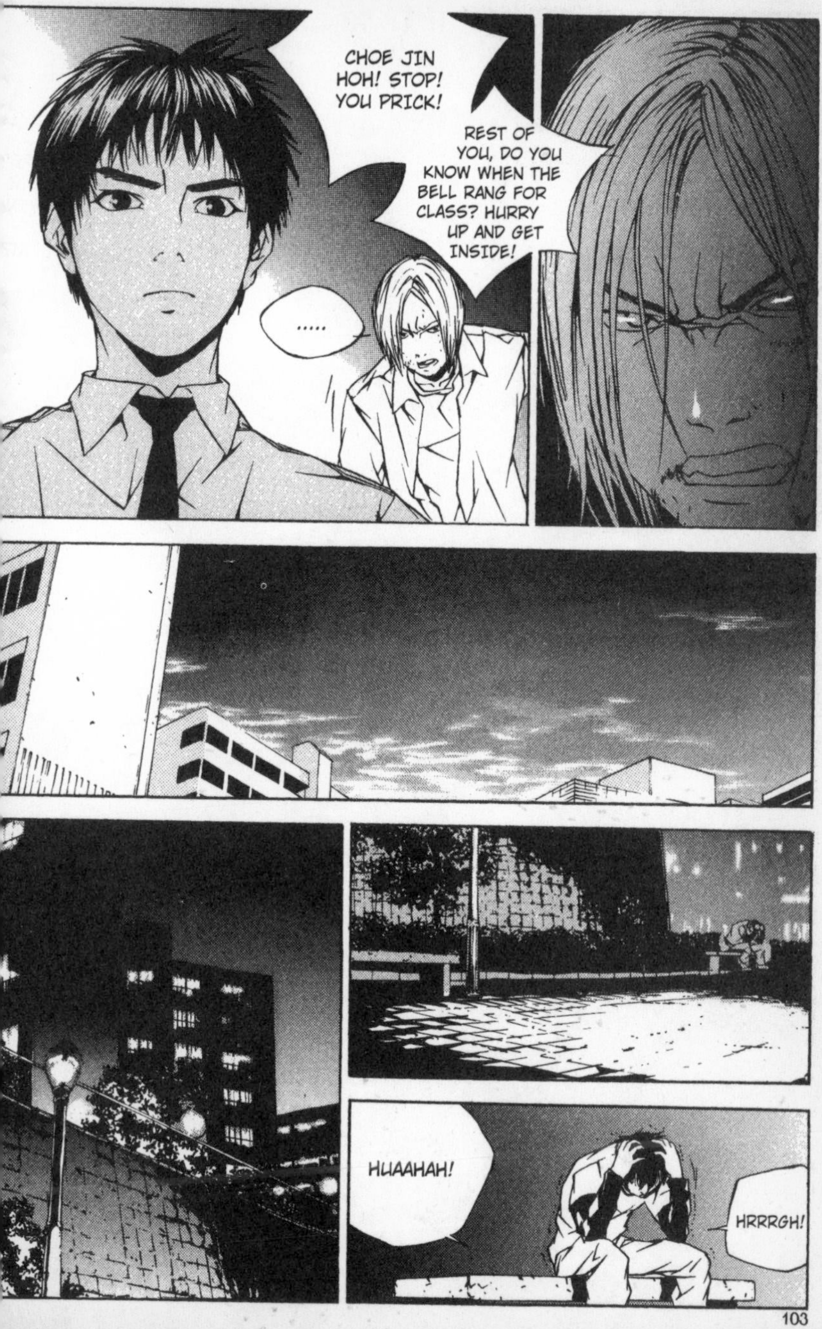
CHOE JIN HOH! STOP! YOU PRICK!
REST OF YOU, DO YOU KNOW WHEN THE BELL RANG FOR CLASS? HURRY UP AND GET INSIDE!
.....
HUAAHAH!
HRRRGH!

BWAAA 후아아아

HWAAAH!

BWAAA

KEEEEKK 끼이이

BREEE

BOOROONG 부릉

?

B

KEEEKK 끼익 BOOROONG 부릉부릉

KEEEKK 끼익

THOO THOO THOO 드드드

BOOA 부

THOO THOO THOO 드드드

BWOOOO 부으으

IS THAT THE MOTHER-FUCKER?

BOORROONG 부으으

.....

THAT'S HIM.

Log-11 END

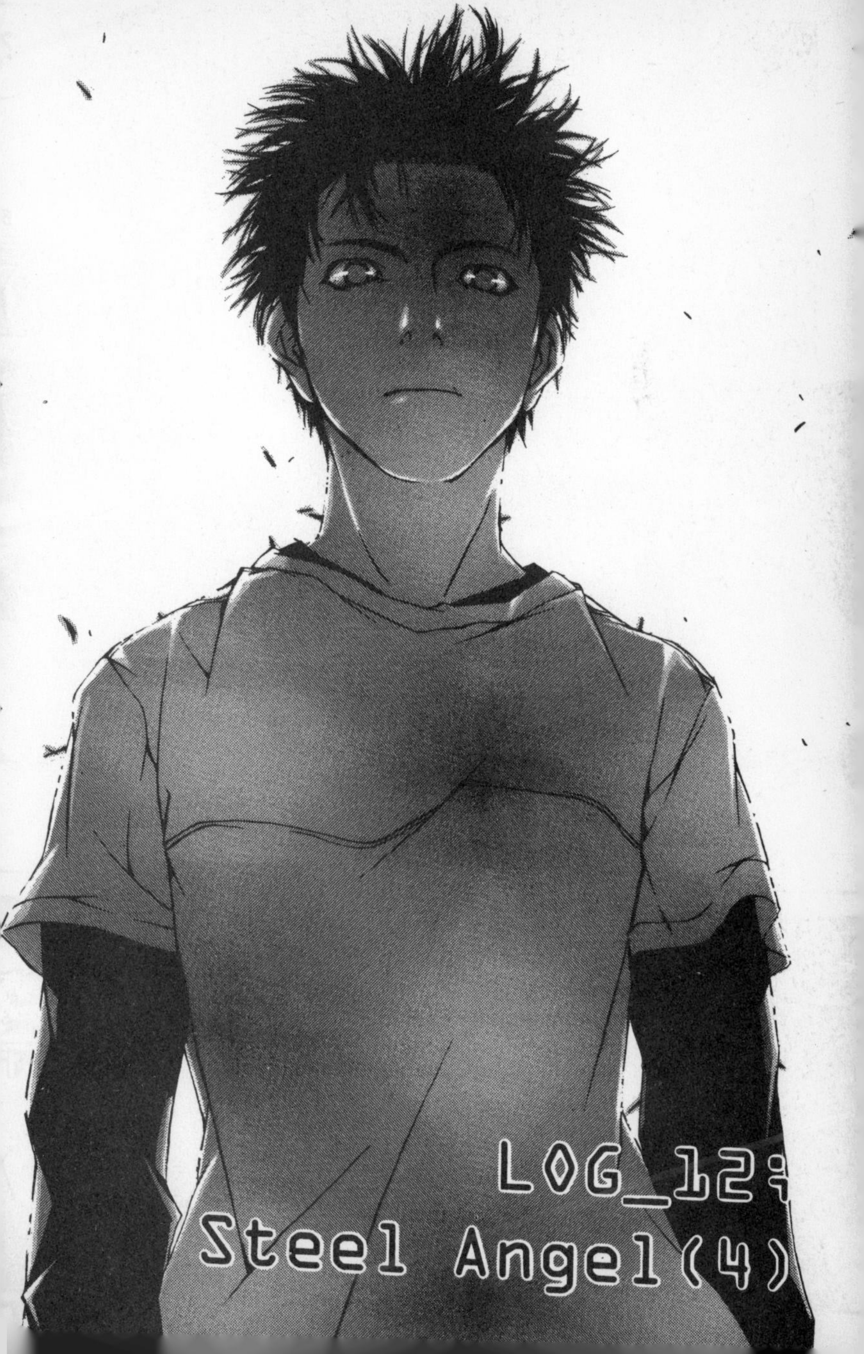
LOG_12:
Steel Angel(4)

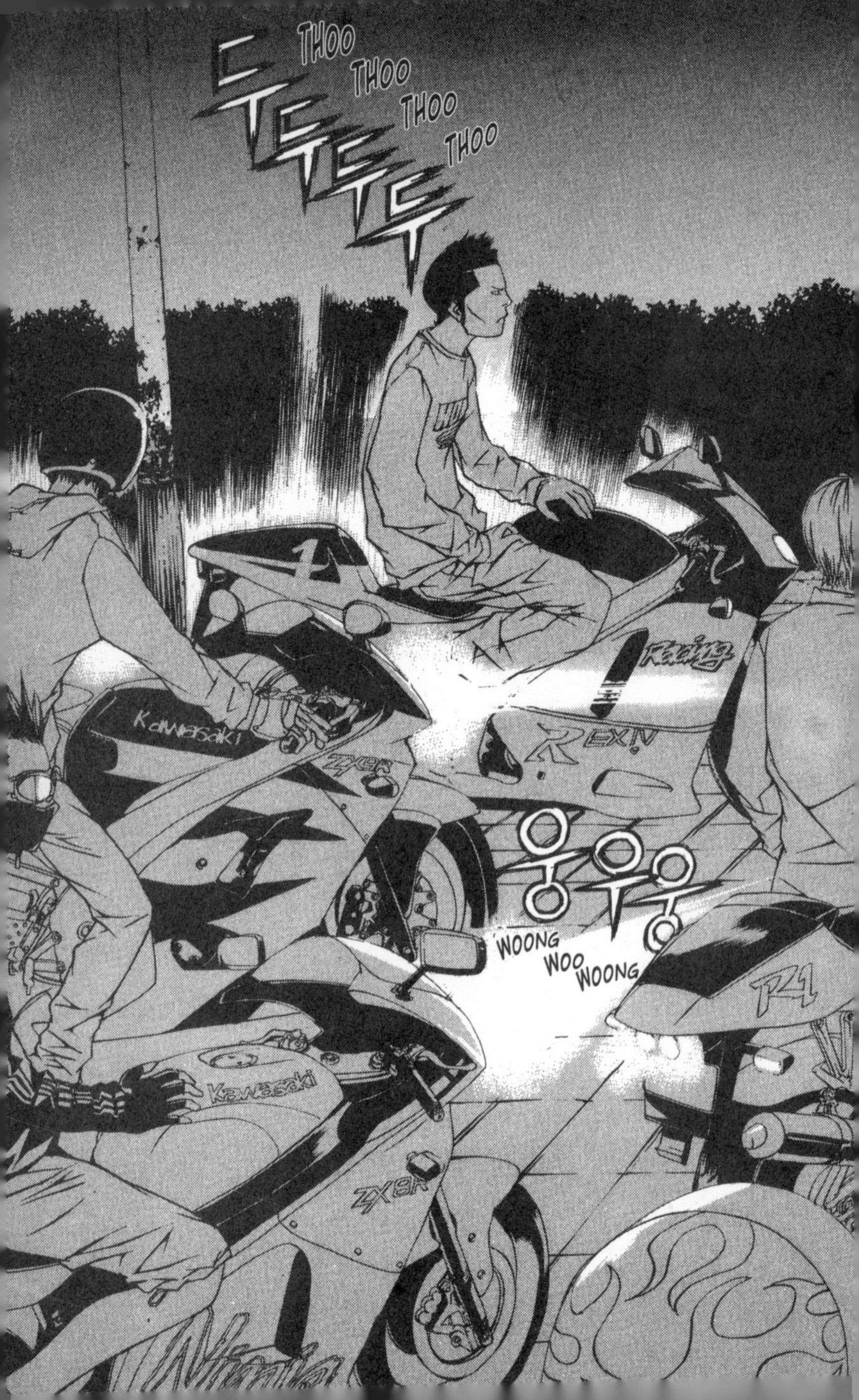
THOO
THOO
THOO
THOO
Kawasaki
Racing
WOONG
WOO
WOONG
Kawasaki

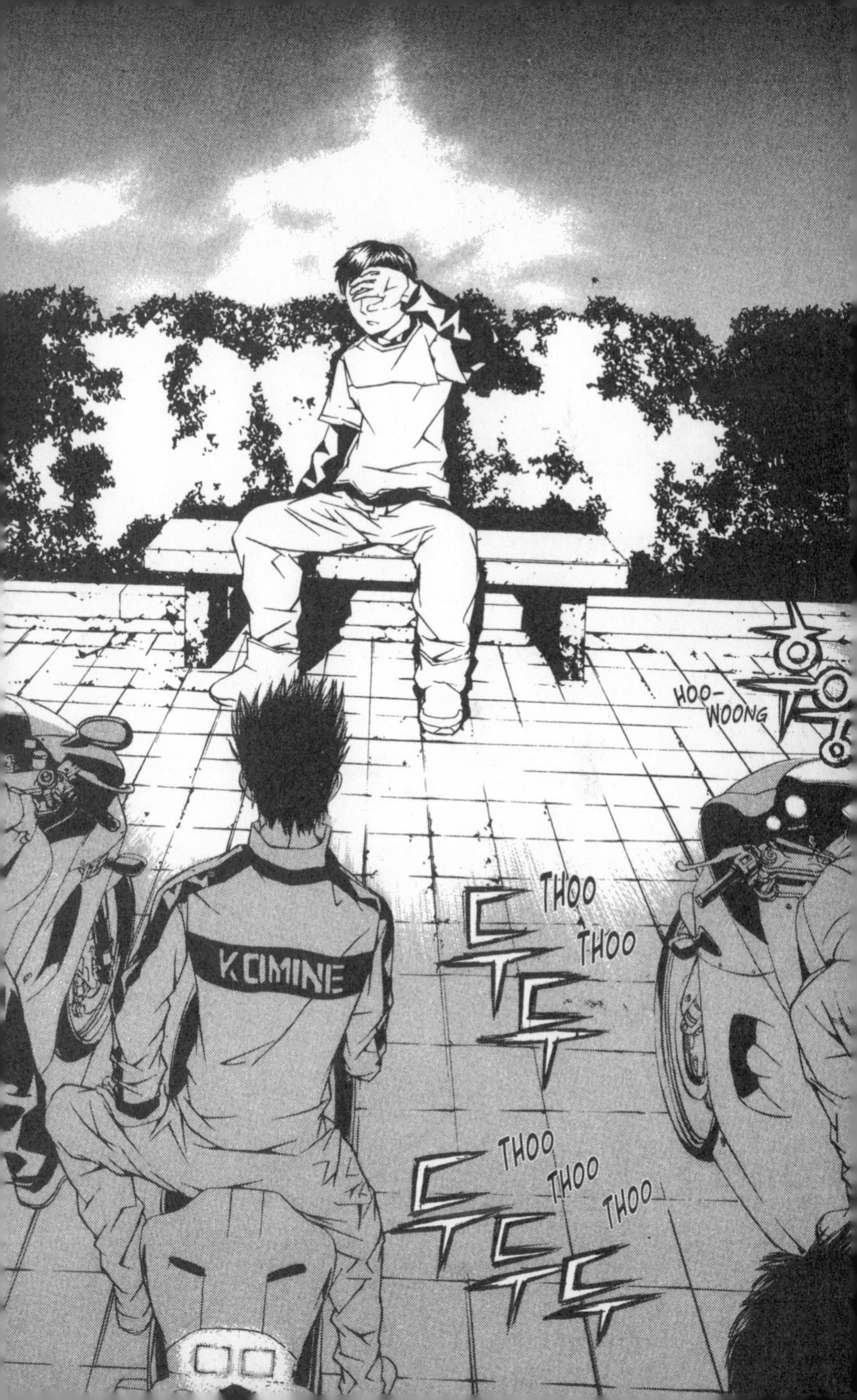
HOO-WOONG
KOMINE
THOO THOO
THOO THOO THOO

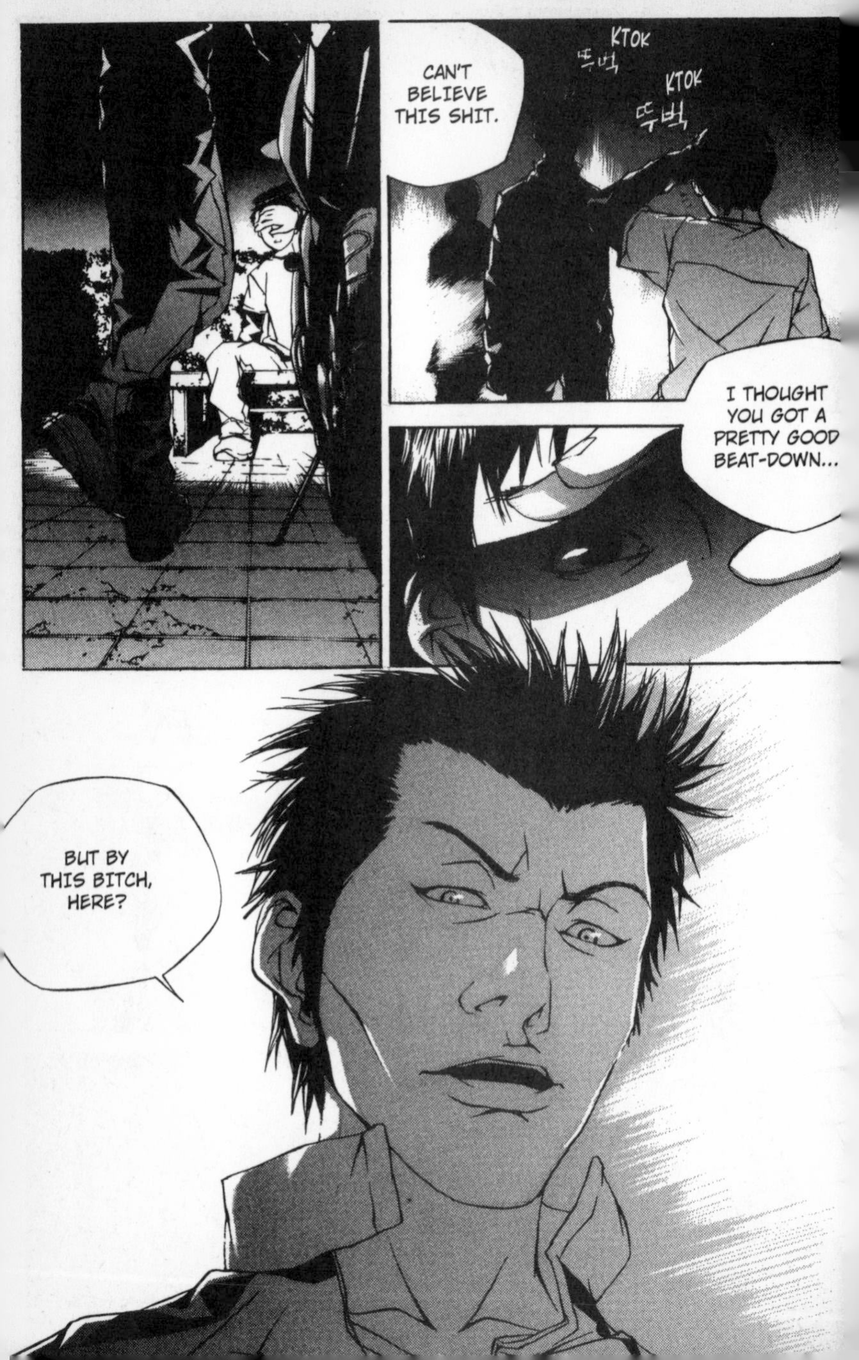
CAN'T BELIEVE THIS SHIT.
KTOK
뚜벅
KTOK
뚜벅
I THOUGHT YOU GOT A PRETTY GOOD BEAT-DOWN...
BUT BY THIS BITCH, HERE?

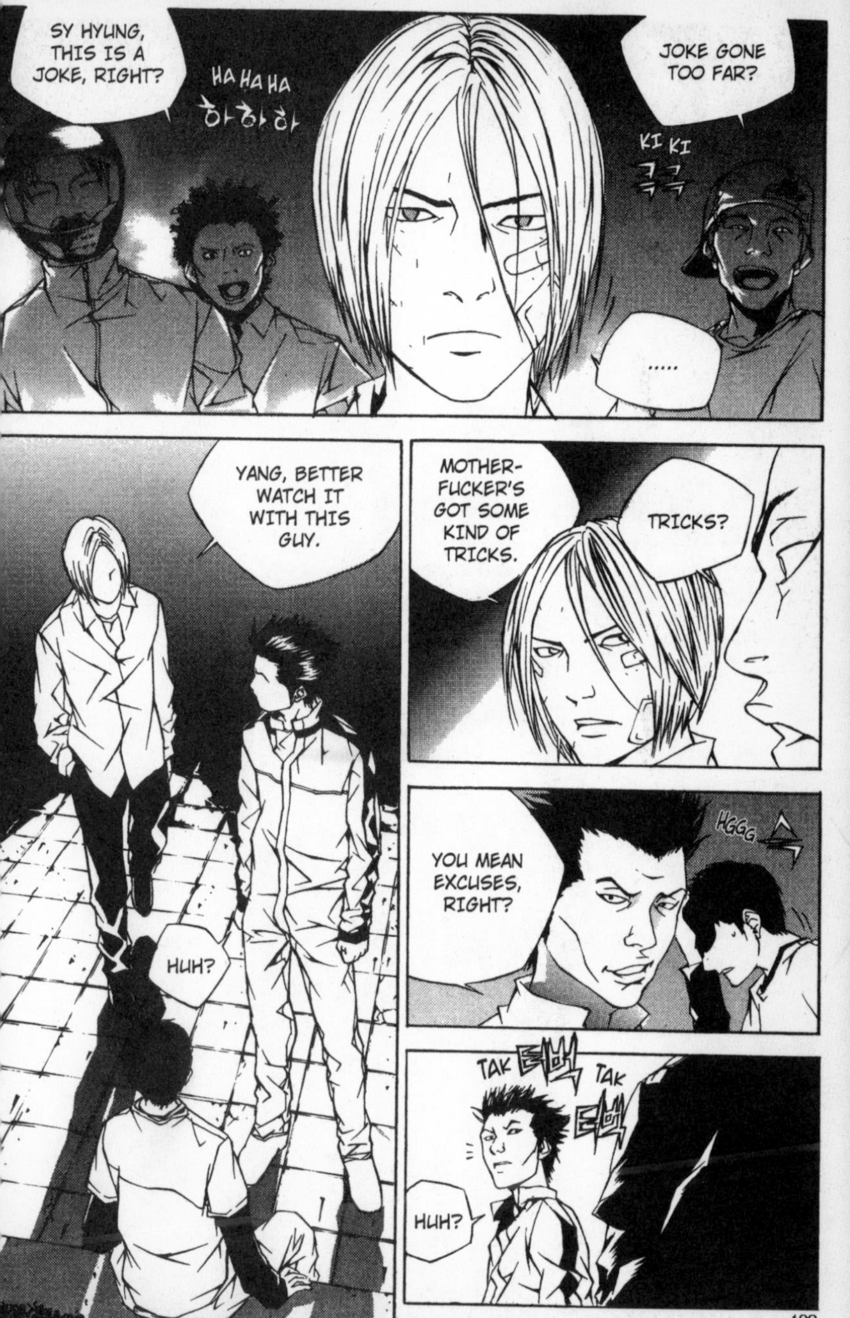
SY HYUNG, THIS IS A JOKE, RIGHT?
HA HA HA
하하하
JOKE GONE TOO FAR?
KI KI
큭큭
.....
YANG, BETTER WATCH IT WITH THIS GUY.
HUH?
MOTHER-FUCKER'S GOT SOME KIND OF TRICKS.
TRICKS?
YOU MEAN EXCUSES, RIGHT?
HGGG
TAK
탁
TAK
탁
HUH?

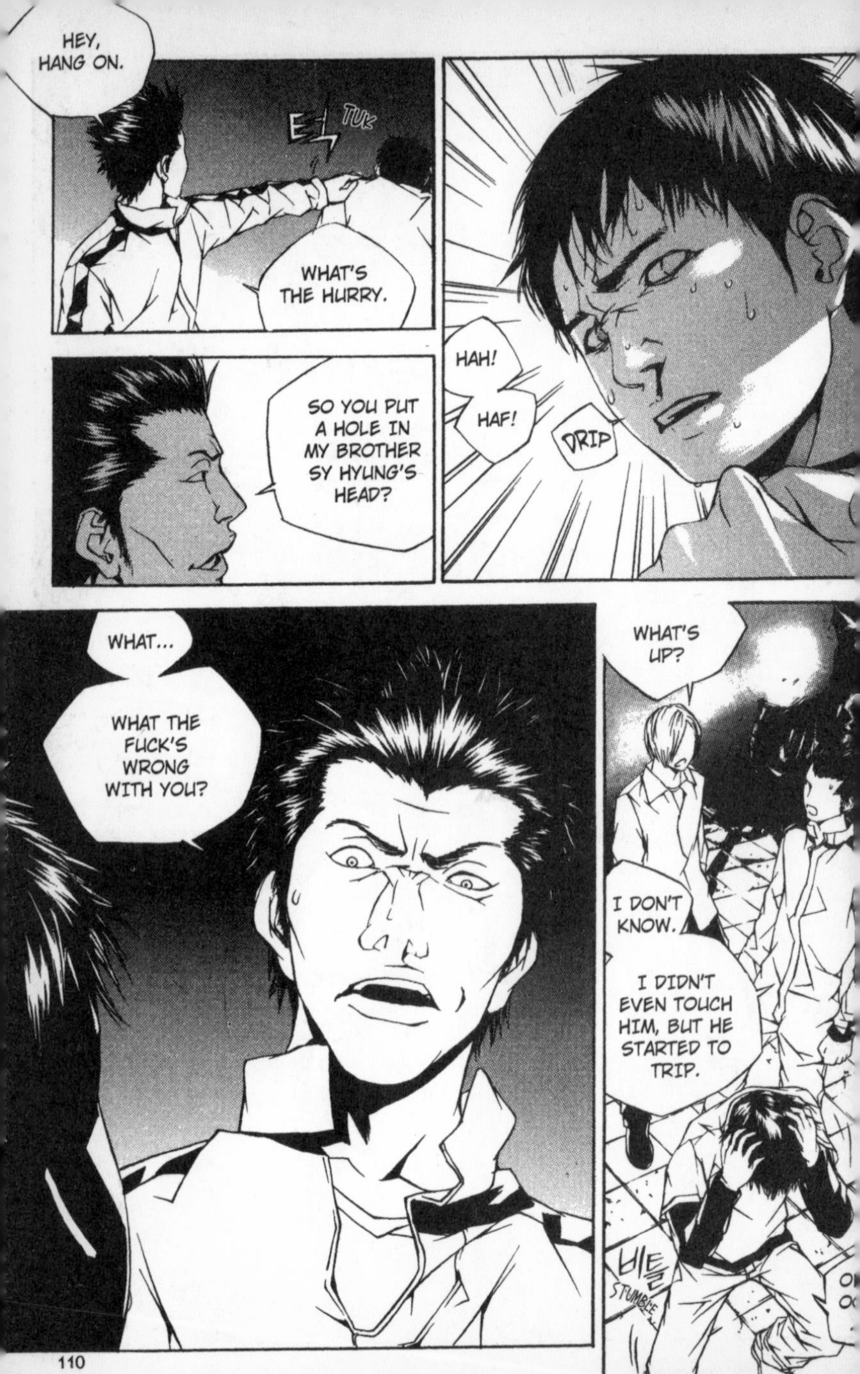
HEY, HANG ON.
TUK
WHAT'S THE HURRY.
SO YOU PUT A HOLE IN MY BROTHER SY HYUNG'S HEAD?
HAH!
HAF!
DRIP
WHAT...
WHAT THE FUCK'S WRONG WITH YOU?
WHAT'S UP?
I DON'T KNOW.
I DIDN'T EVEN TOUCH HIM, BUT HE STARTED TO TRIP.
비틀
STUMBLE

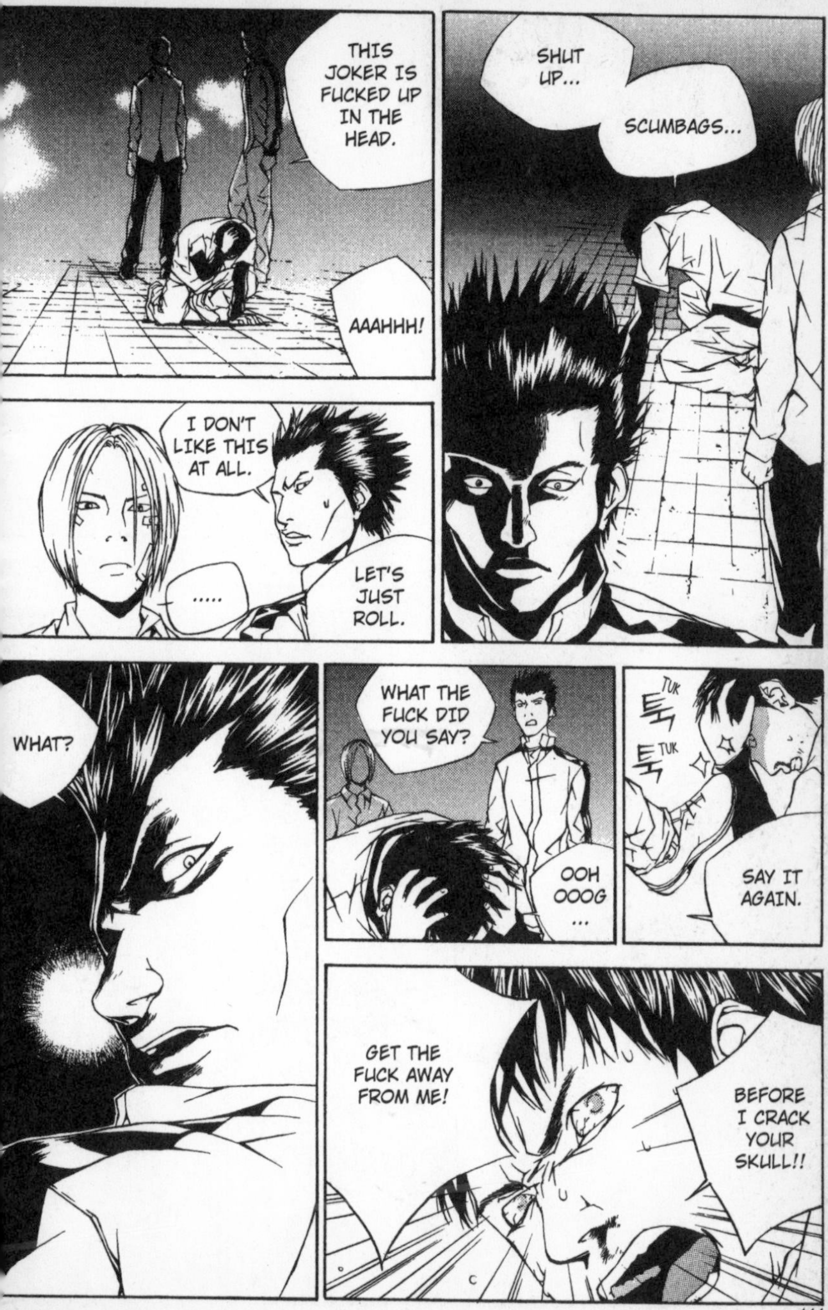
THIS JOKER IS FUCKED UP IN THE HEAD.
AAAHHH!
I DON'T LIKE THIS AT ALL.
.....
LET'S JUST ROLL.
SHUT UP...
SCUMBAGS...
WHAT?
WHAT THE FUCK DID YOU SAY?
OOH OOOG ...
TUK
TUK
SAY IT AGAIN.
GET THE FUCK AWAY FROM ME!
BEFORE I CRACK YOUR SKULL!!

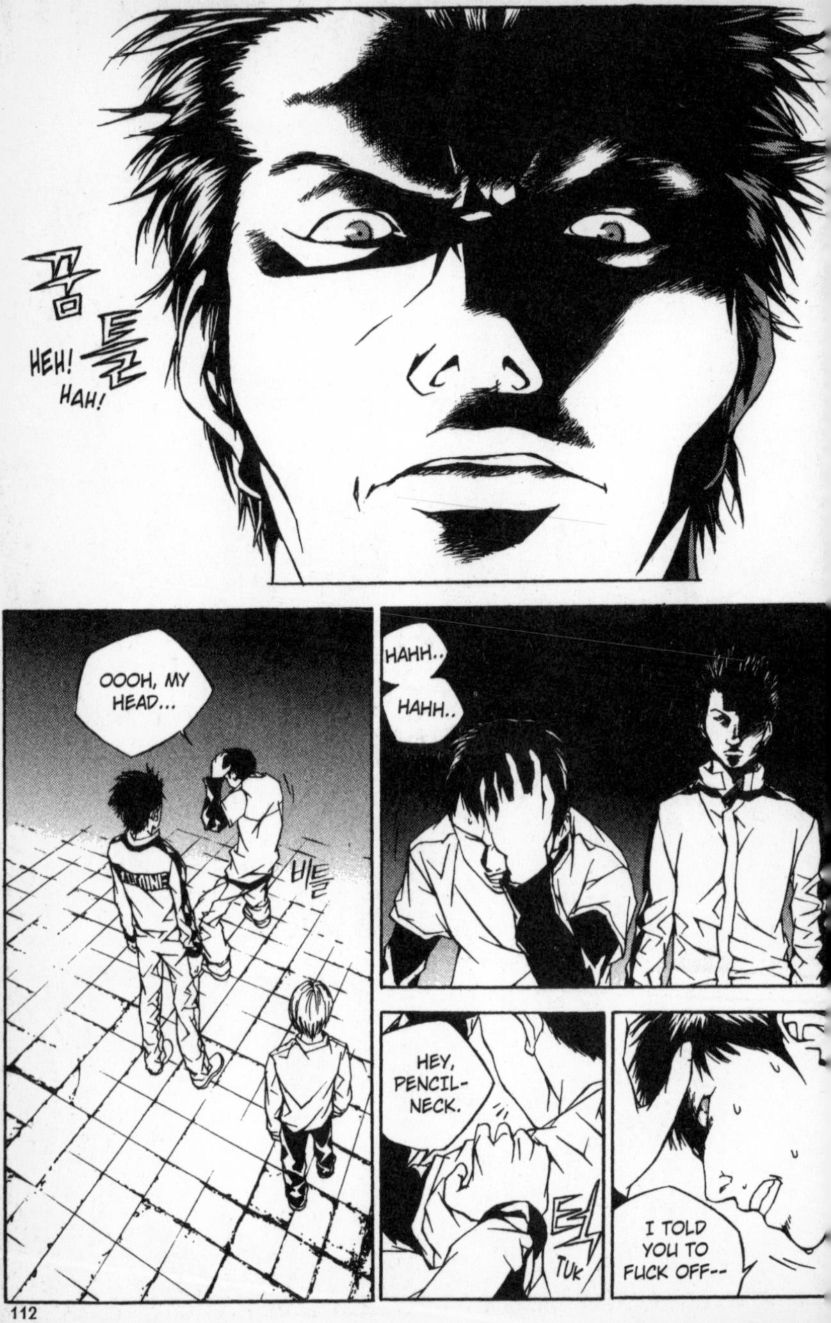
꿈틀
HEH!
HAH!
OOOH, MY HEAD...
비틀
HAHH..
HAHH..
HEY, PENCIL-NECK.
턱
TUK
I TOLD YOU TO FUCK OFF--

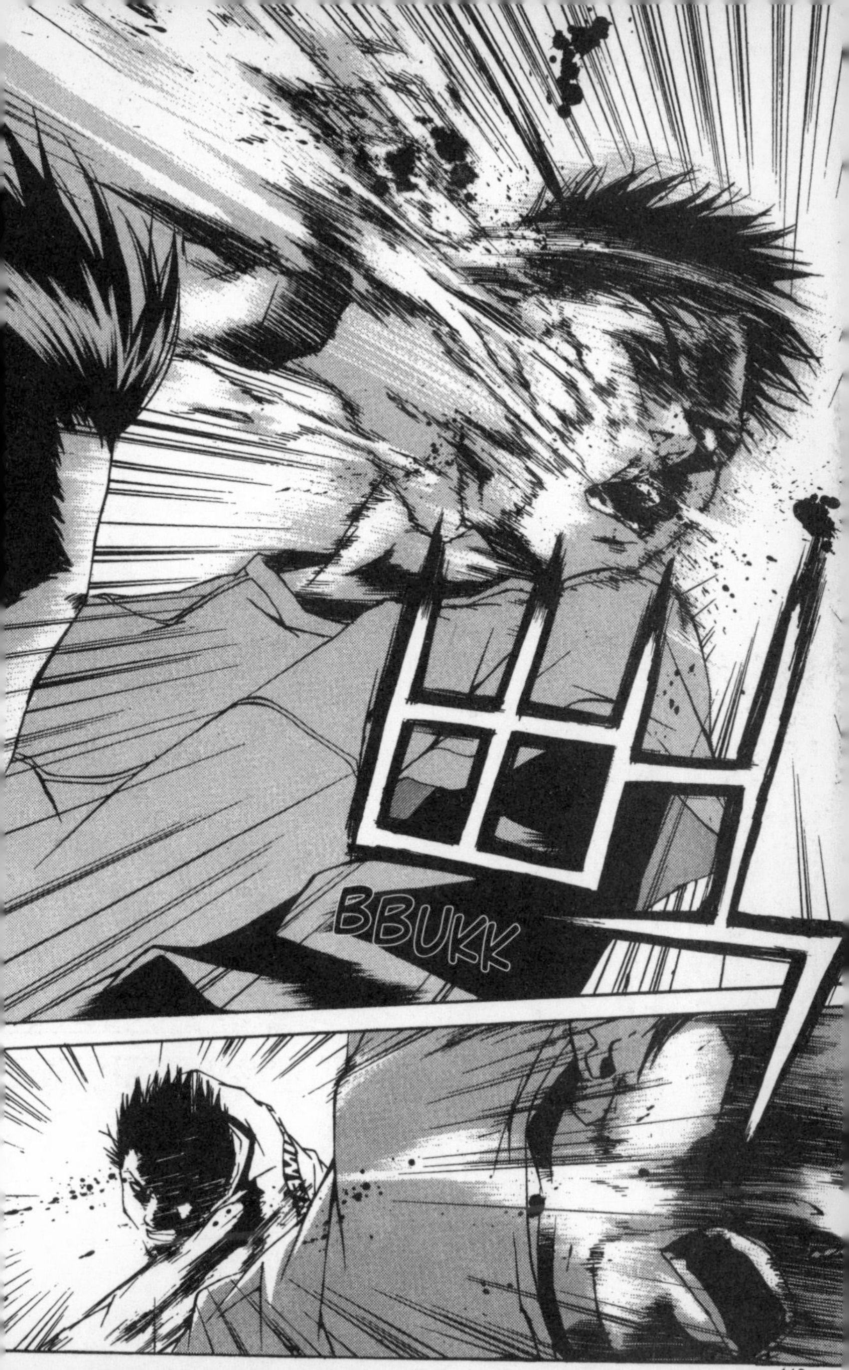
BBUKK

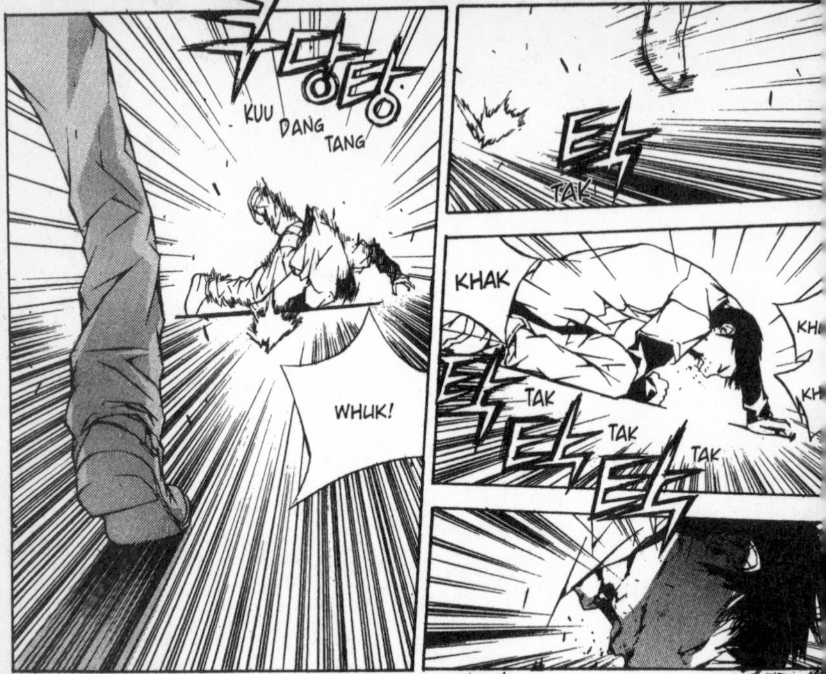
쿠당탕
KUU DANG TANG
WHUK!
탁
TAK
KHAK
탁
TAK
탁
TAK
탁
TAK

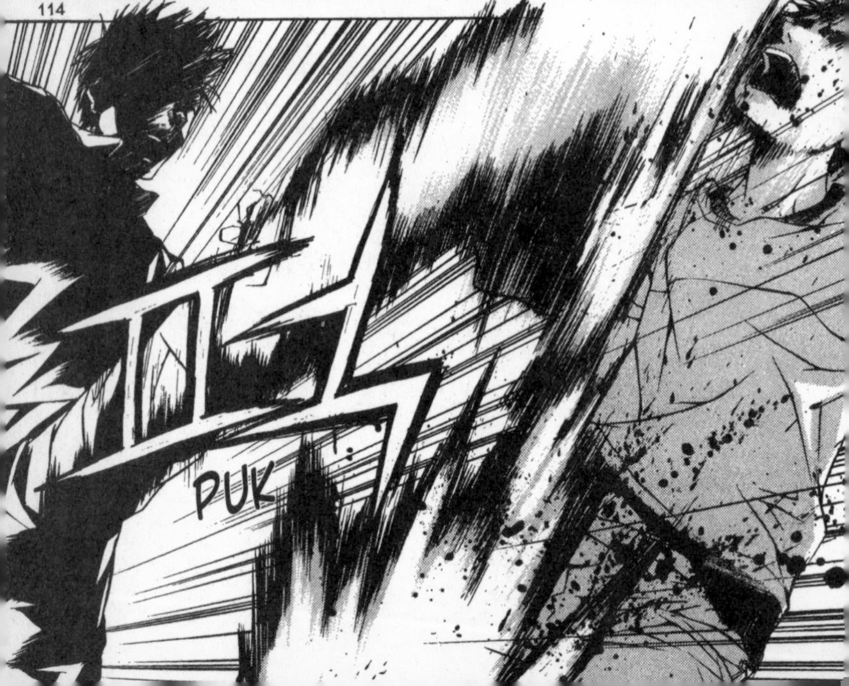
푹
PUK

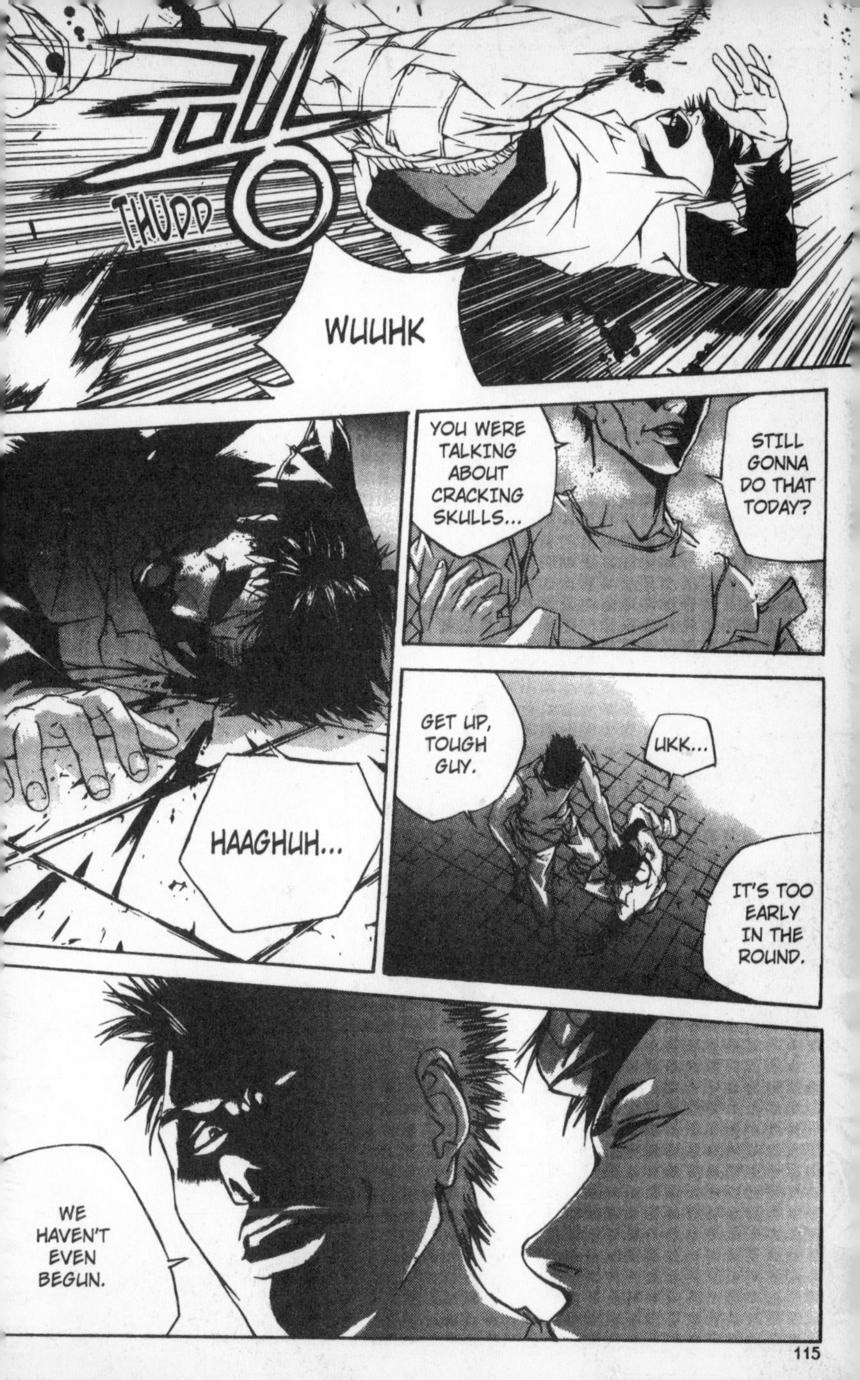
THUDD
WUUHK
HAAGHUH...
YOU WERE TALKING ABOUT CRACKING SKULLS...
STILL GONNA DO THAT TODAY?
GET UP, TOUGH GUY.
UKK...
IT'S TOO EARLY IN THE ROUND.
WE HAVEN'T EVEN BEGUN.

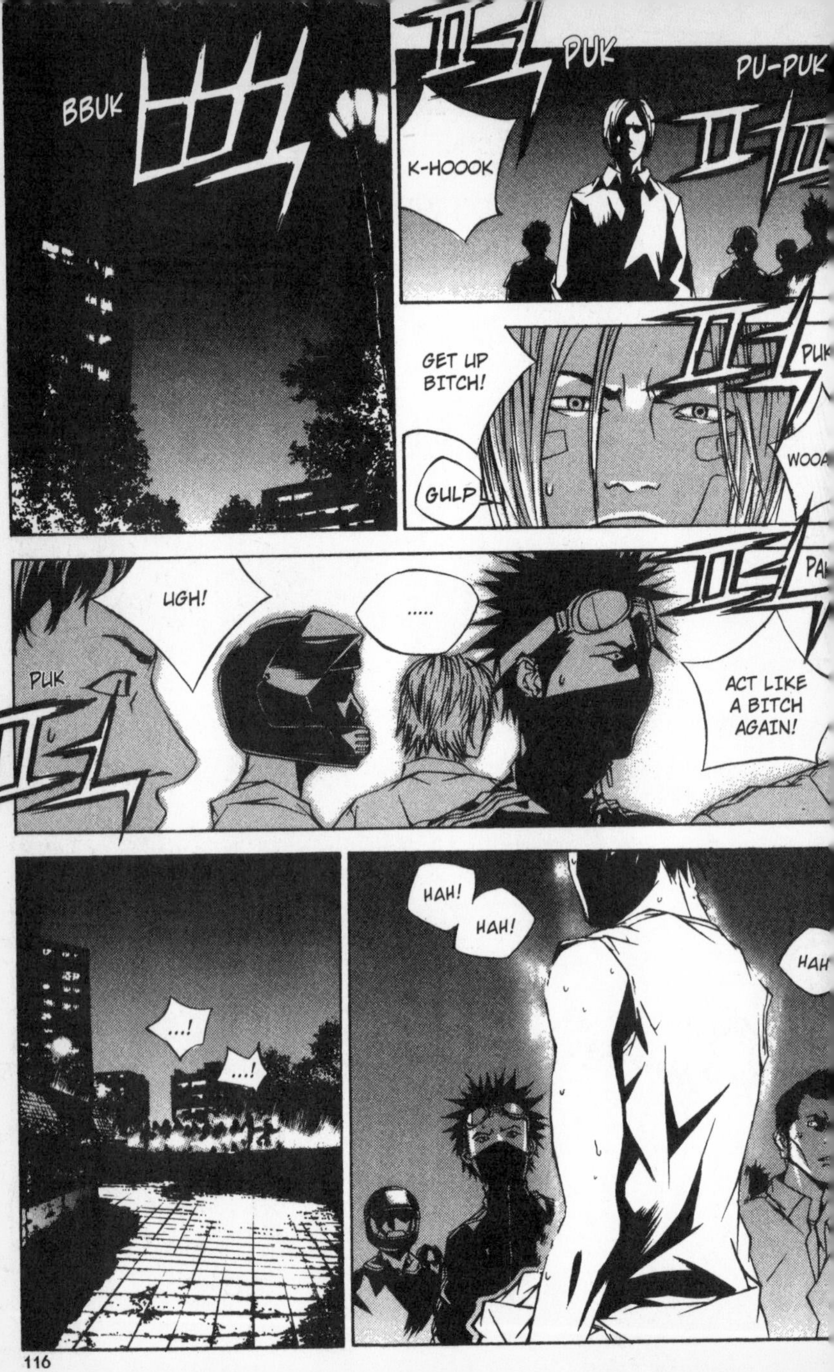

BBUK
PUK
PU-PUK
K-HOOOK
GET UP BITCH!
PUK
WOOA
GULP
UGH!
PUK
.....
PA
ACT LIKE A BITCH AGAIN!
...!
...!
HAH!
HAH!
HAH

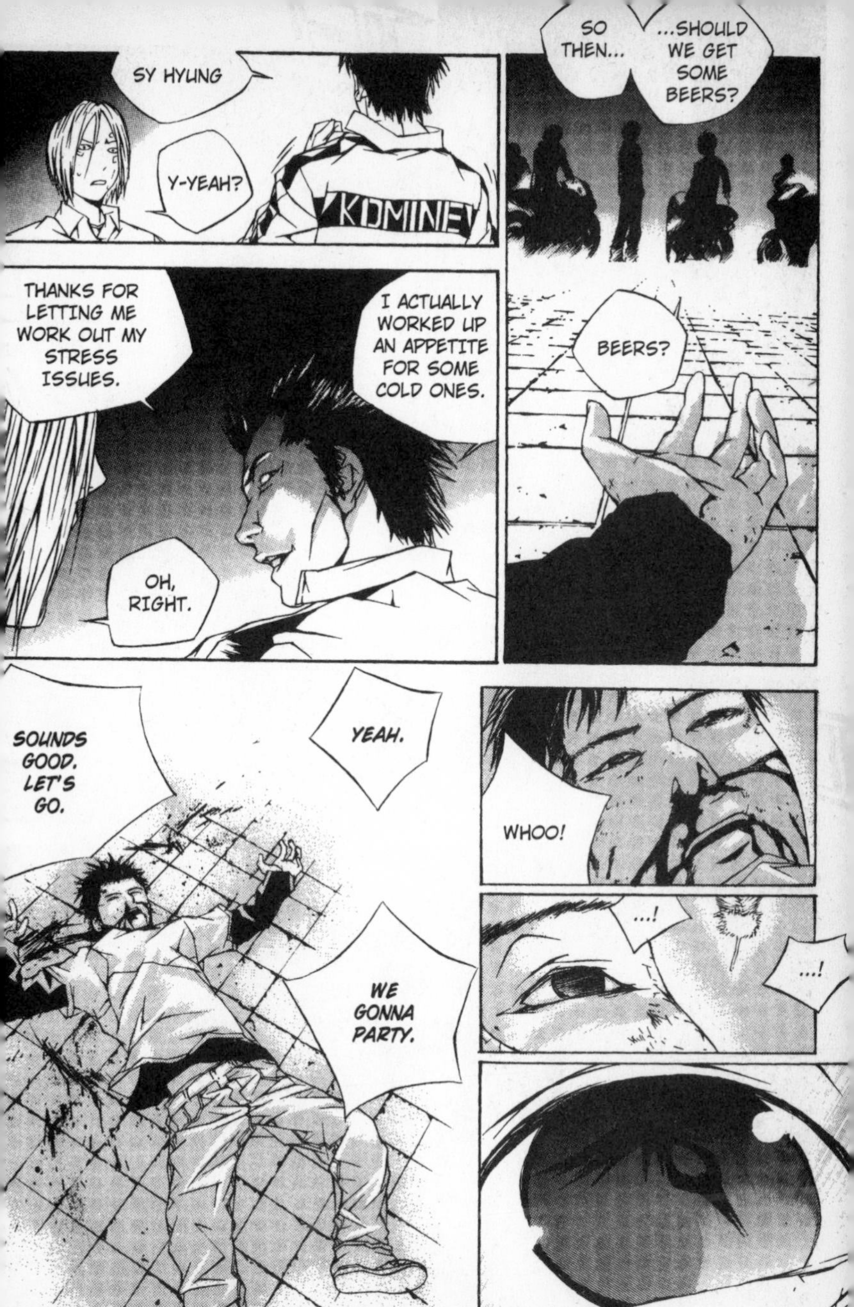
SY HYUNG
Y-YEAH?
SO THEN...
...SHOULD WE GET SOME BEERS?
THANKS FOR LETTING ME WORK OUT MY STRESS ISSUES.
I ACTUALLY WORKED UP AN APPETITE FOR SOME COLD ONES.
OH, RIGHT.
BEERS?
SOUNDS GOOD. LET'S GO.
YEAH.
WE GONNA PARTY.
WHOO!
...!
...!

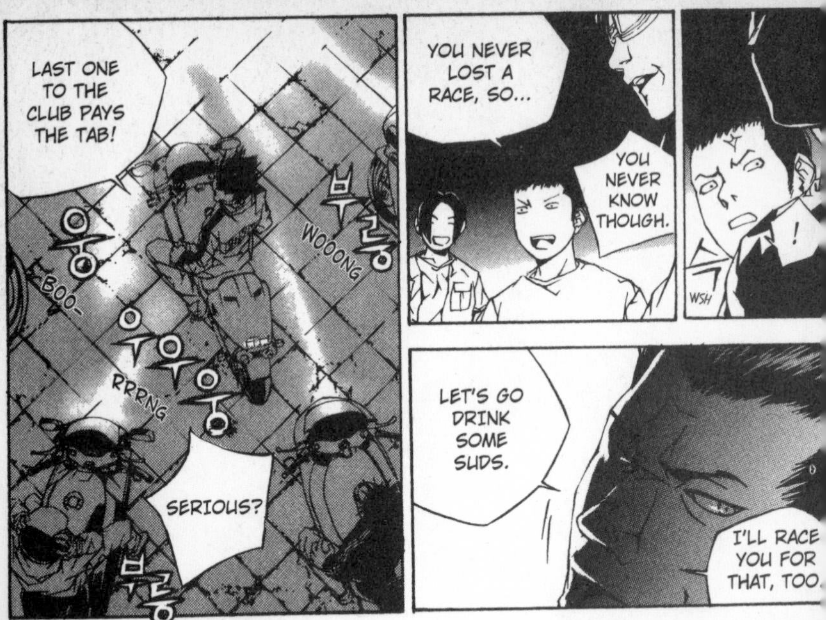
LAST ONE TO THE CLUB PAYS THE TAB!
WOOONG
BOO-
RRRNG
SERIOUS?
YOU NEVER LOST A RACE, SO...
YOU NEVER KNOW THOUGH.
WSH
LET'S GO DRINK SOME SUDS.
I'LL RACE YOU FOR THAT, TOO.

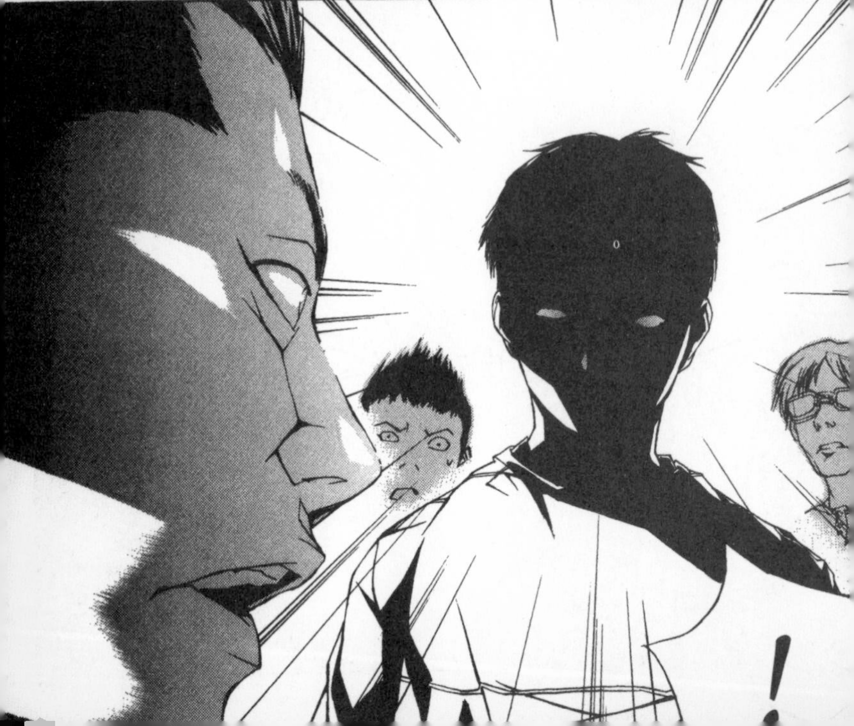

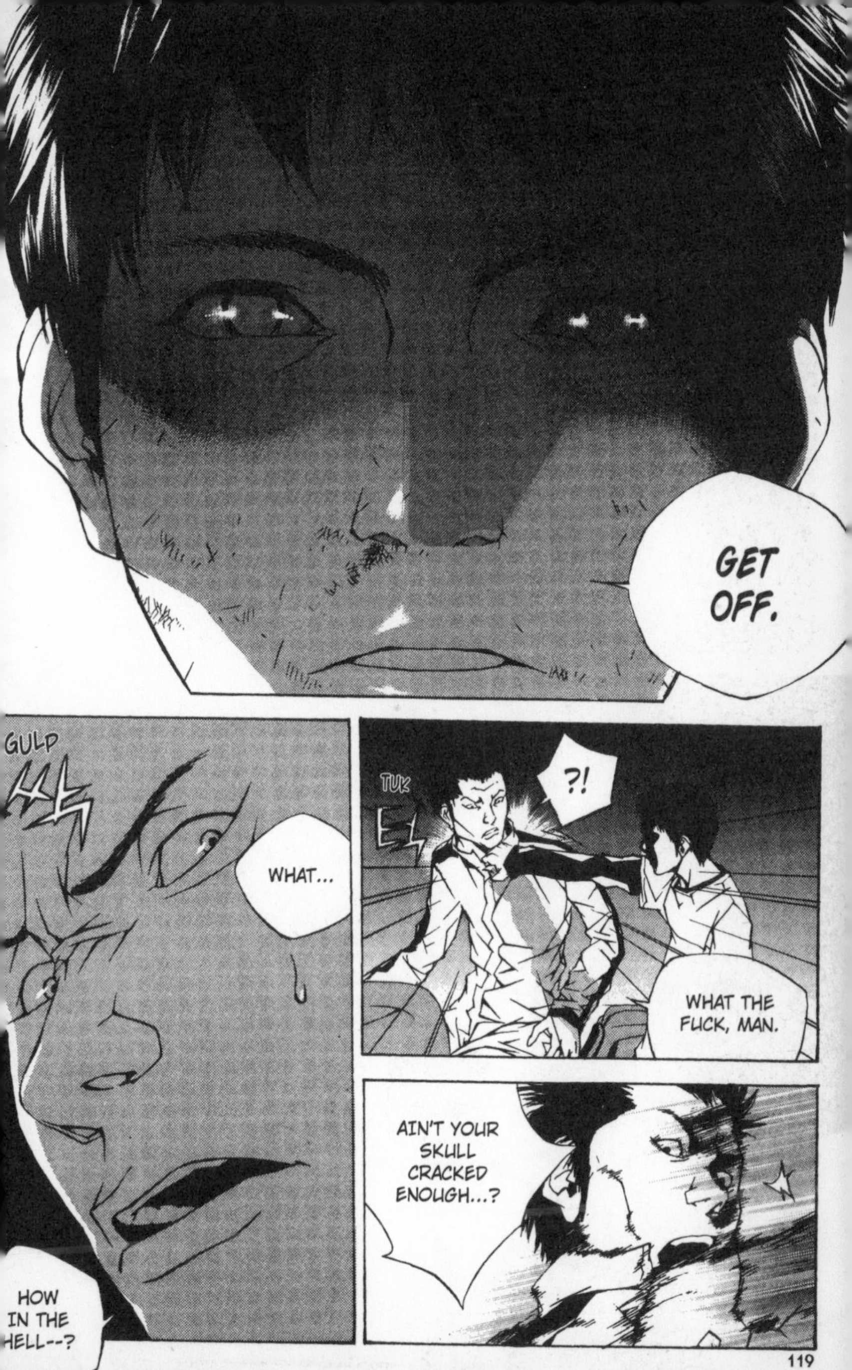
GET OFF.
GULP
WHAT...
HOW IN THE HELL--?
TUK
?!
WHAT THE FUCK, MAN.
AIN'T YOUR SKULL CRACKED ENOUGH...?

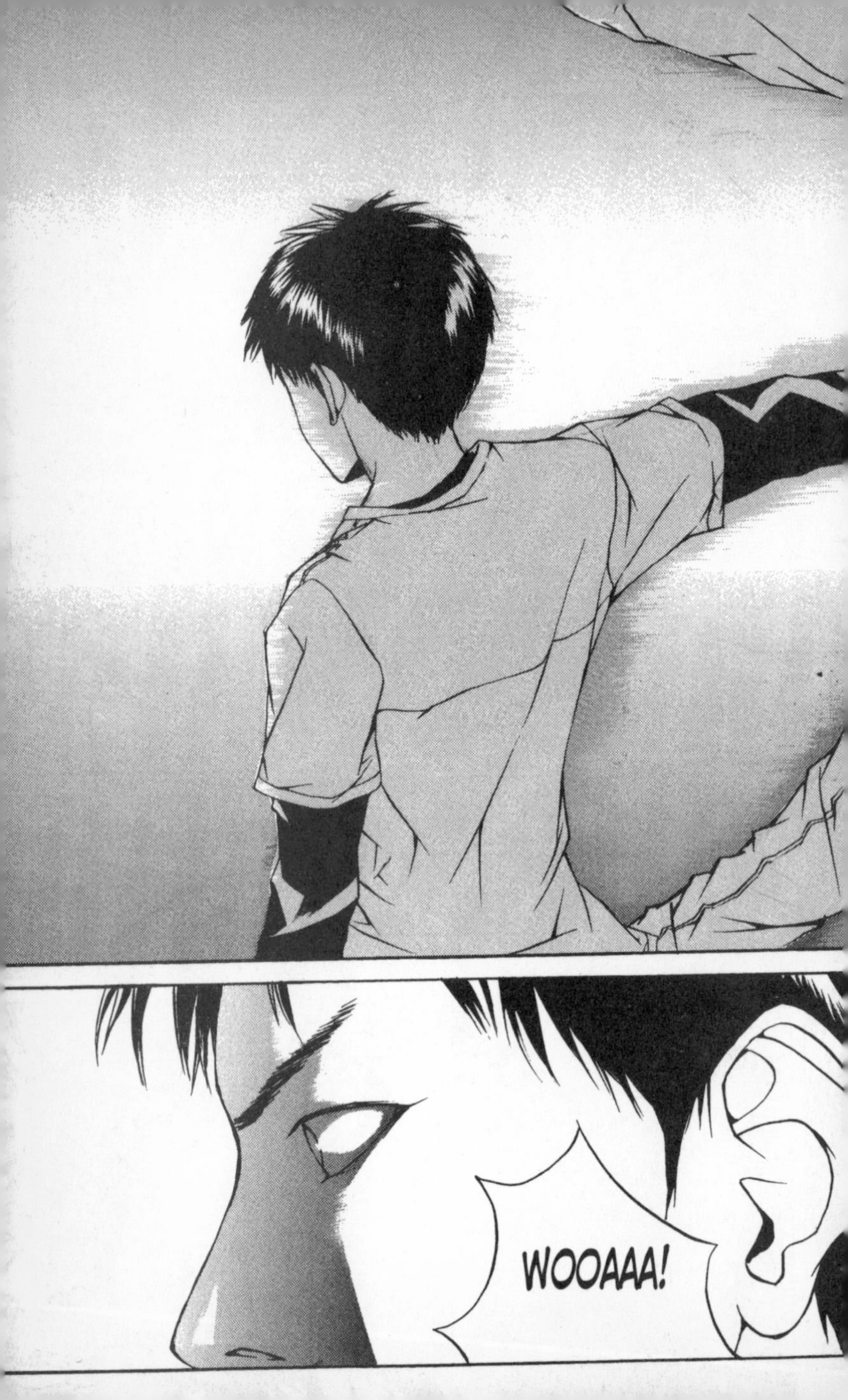
WOOAAA!

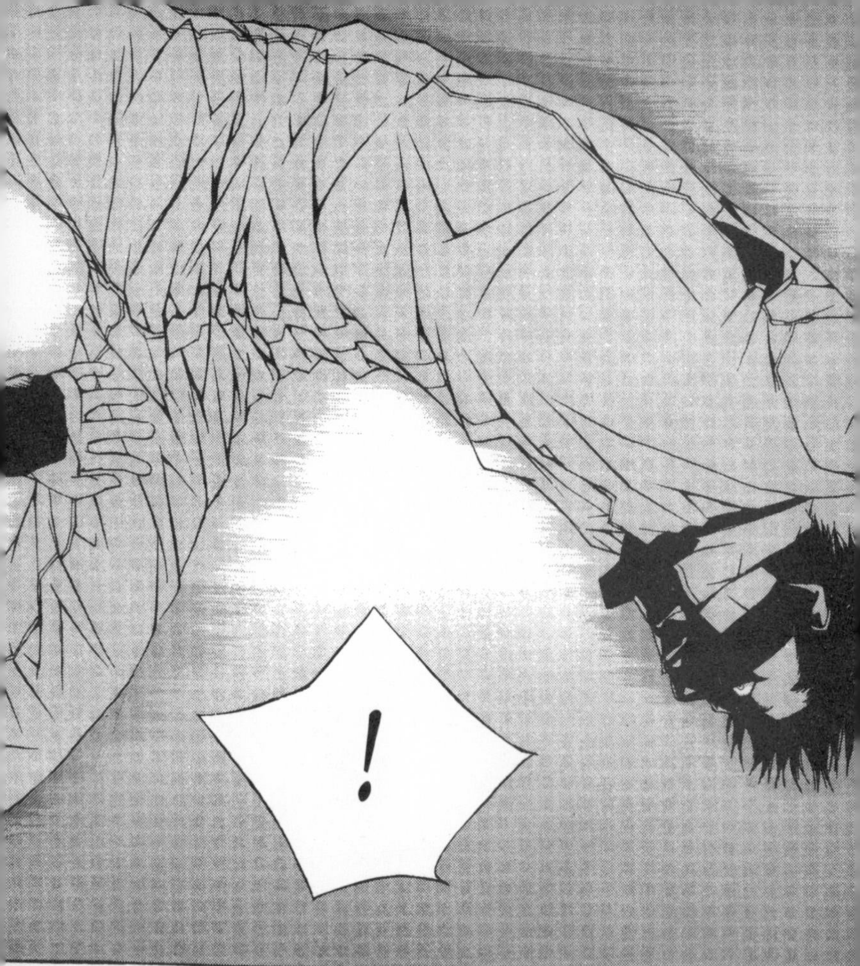
!

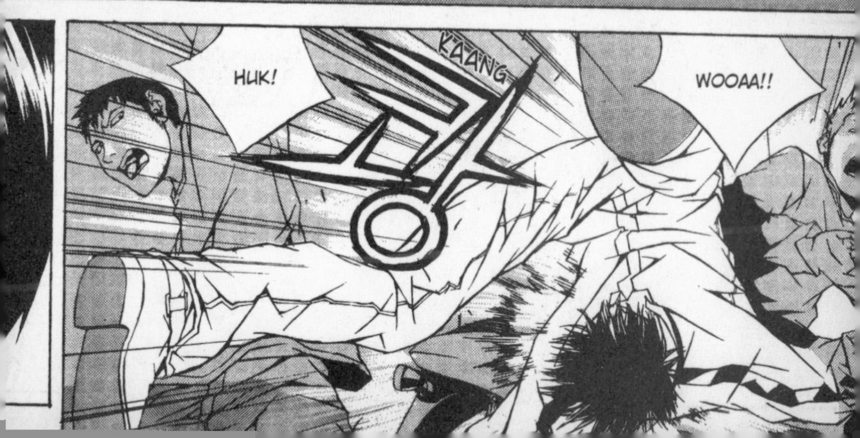
HUK!
KAANG
WOOAA!!

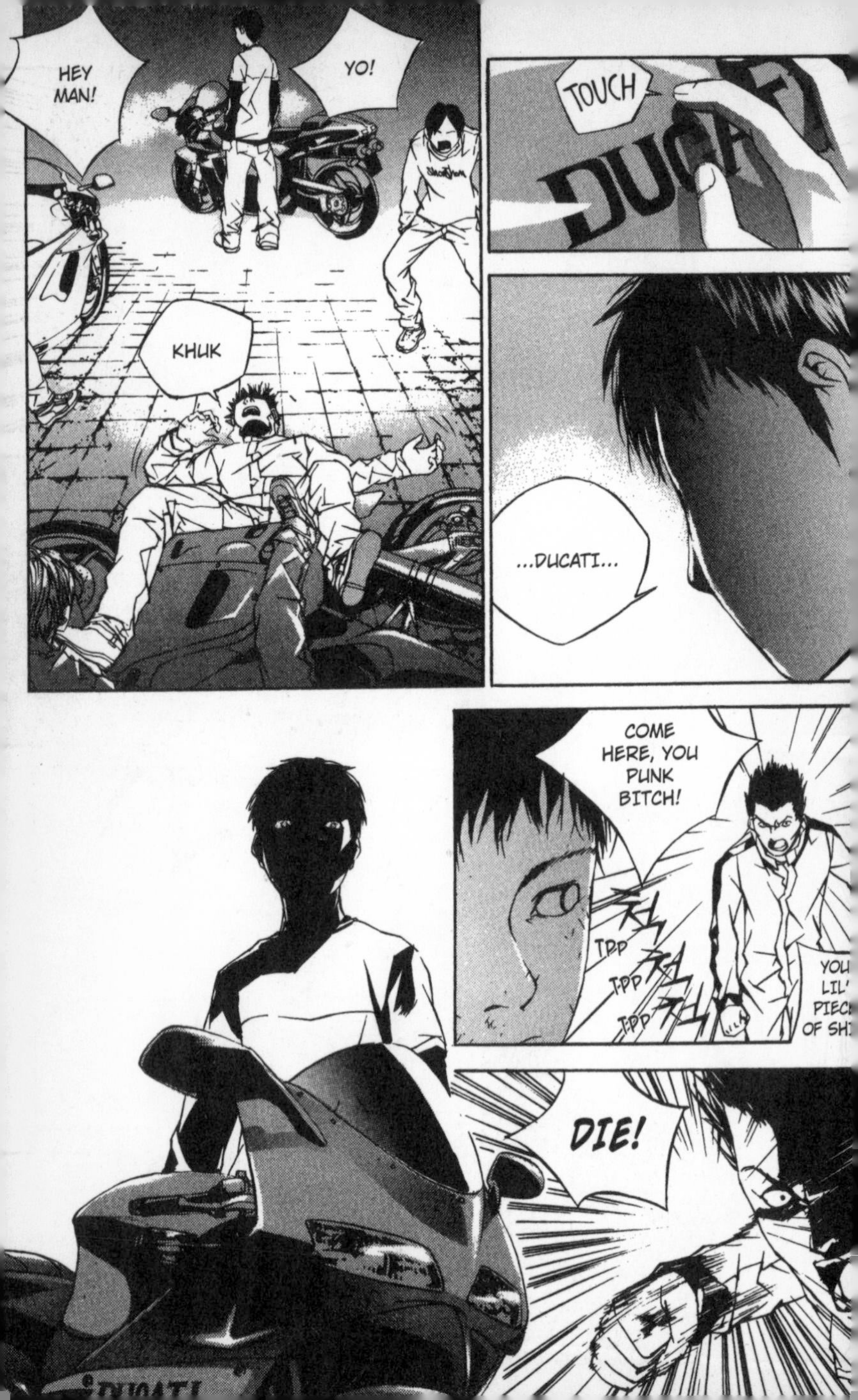
TOUCH
...DUCATI...
HEY MAN!
YO!
KHUK
COME HERE, YOU PUNK BITCH!
TPP
TPP
TPP
YOU LIL' PIEC OF SHI
DIE!

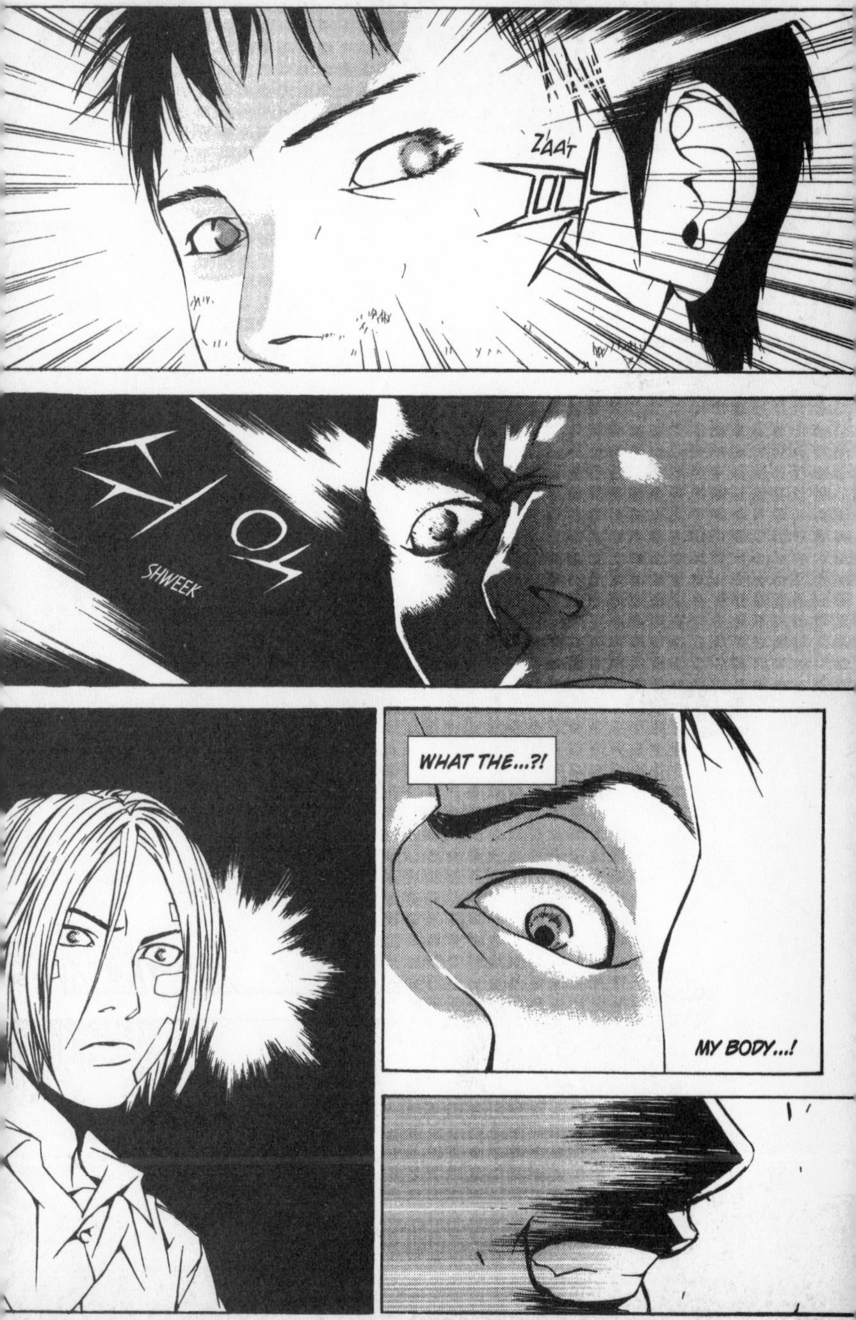
ZAAT
SHWEEK
WHAT THE...?!
MY BODY...!

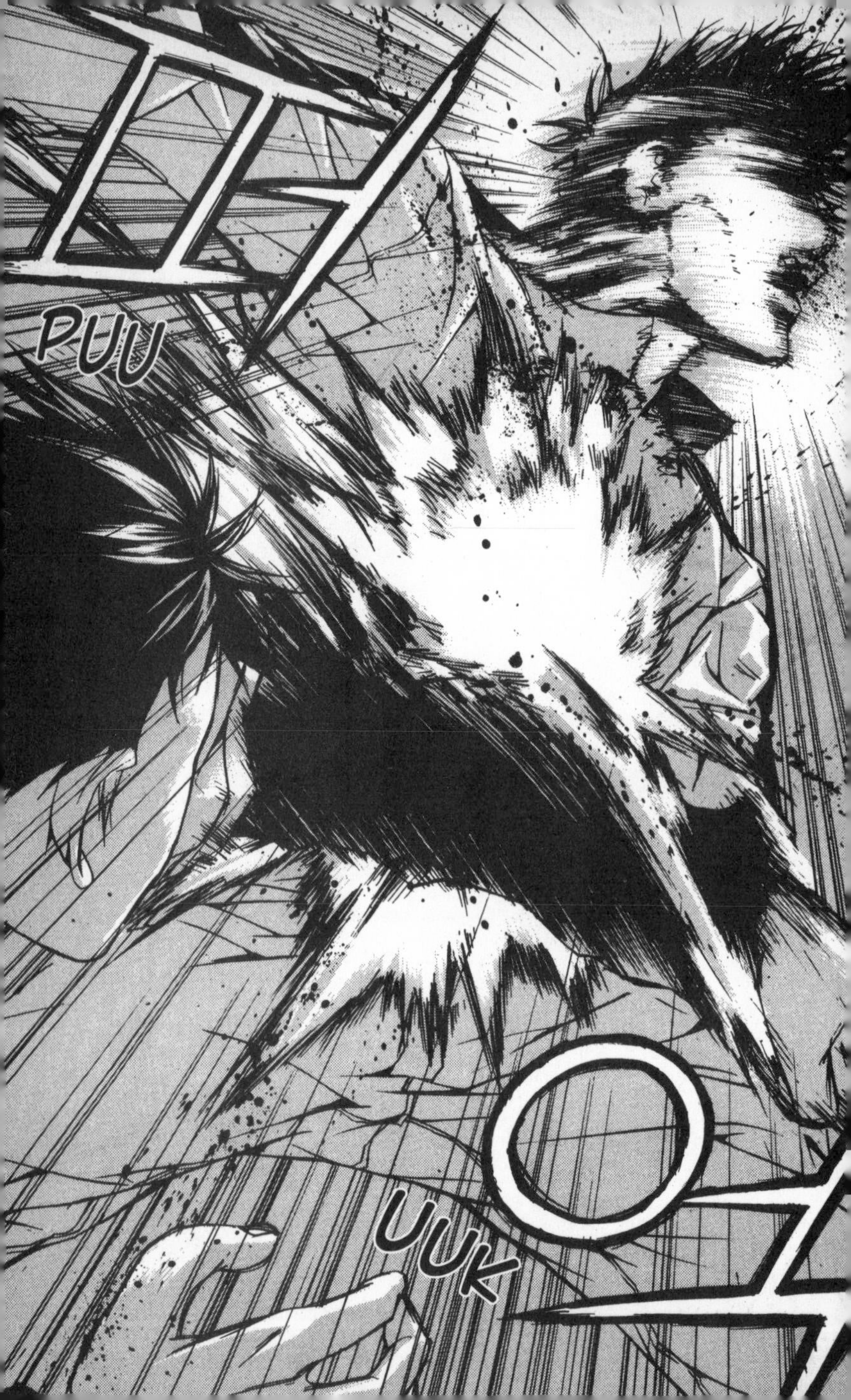
PUU
UUK

KAN

KAN

KHAKK!

KAN

OOMP

HEY, YOU OKAY?

OH, MAN. HE'S ALL FUCKED UP.

LOOK AT ALL THE BLOOD.

HEY!

SWGG

WAKE UP MAN!

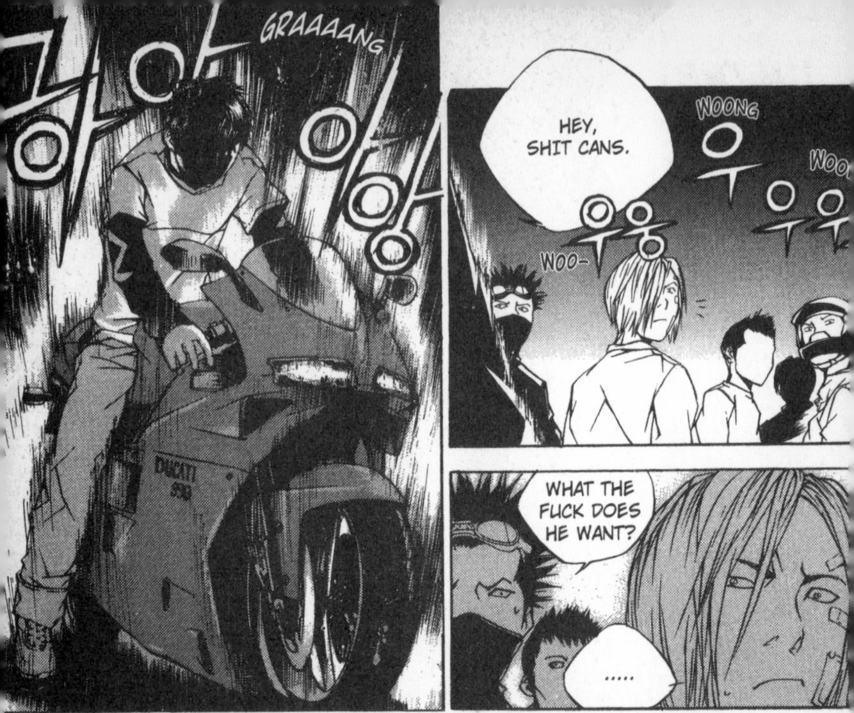
GRAAAANG
HEY, SHIT CANS.
WOONG
WOO-
WOO
WHAT THE FUCK DOES HE WANT?
.....

126

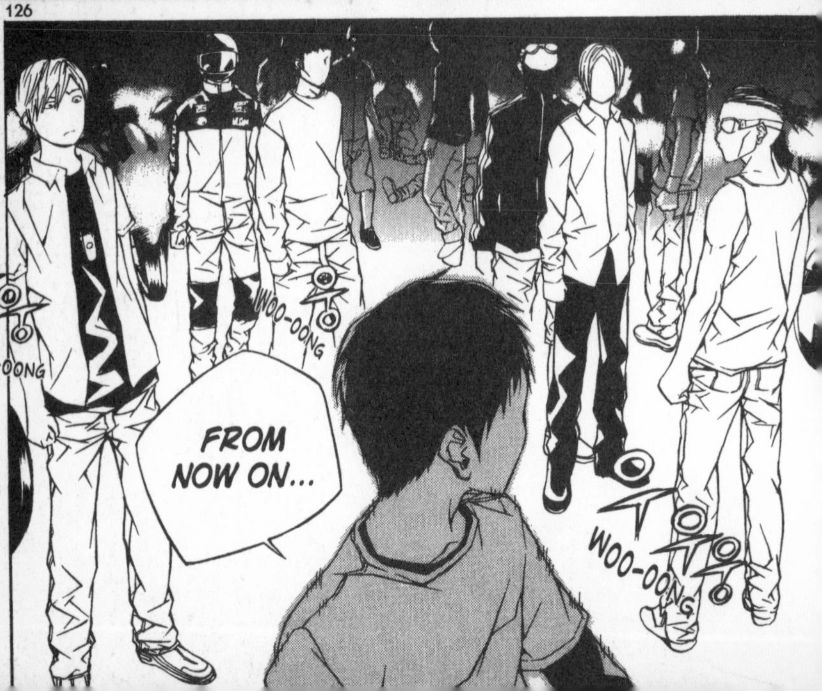
OO-OONG
WOO-OONG
FROM NOW ON...
WOO-OONG

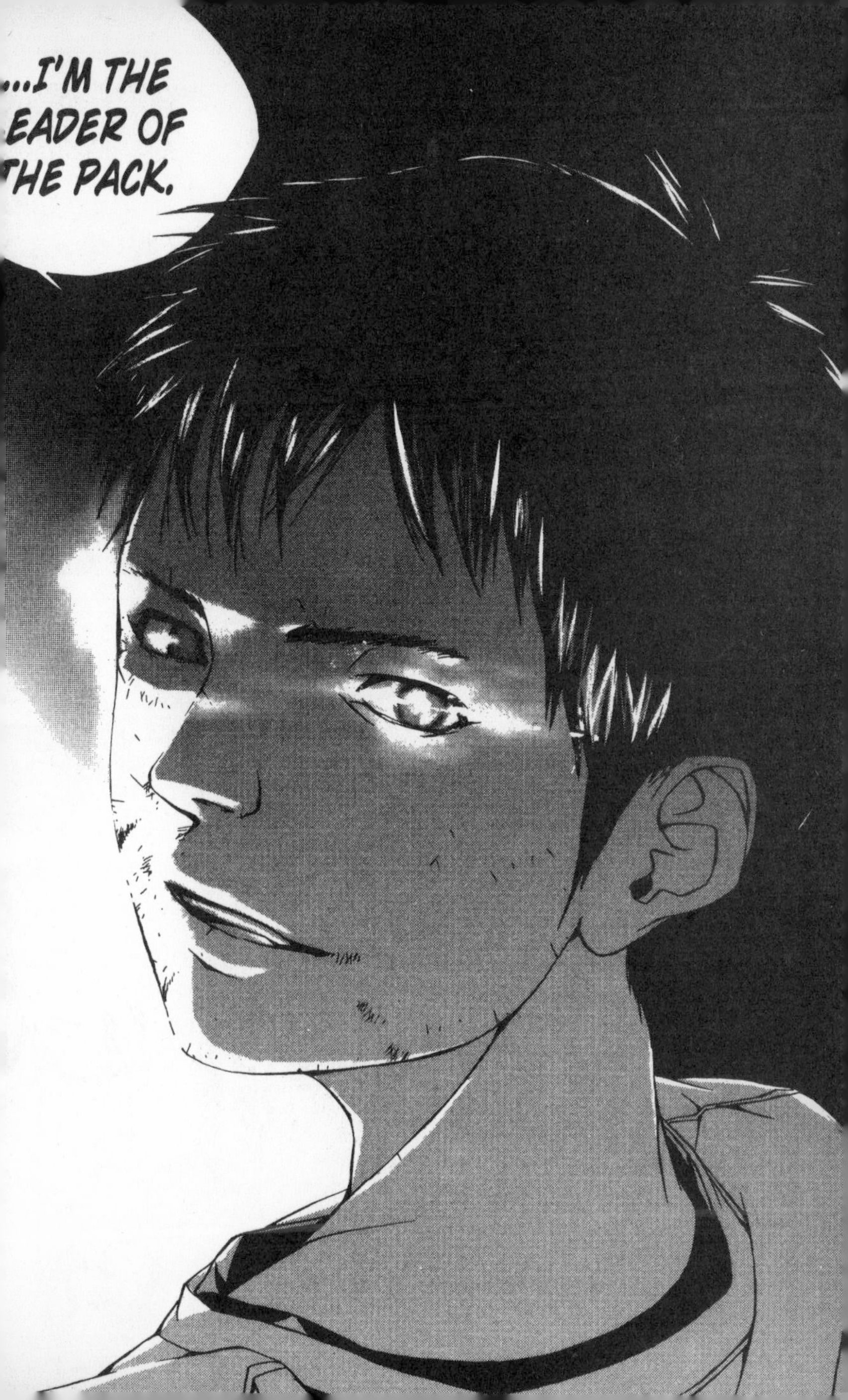
...I'M THE EADER OF THE PACK.

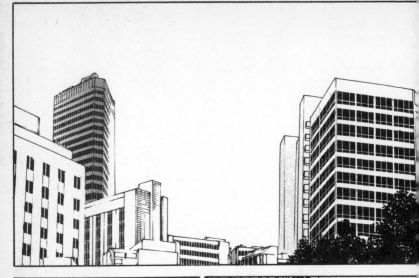

HAHA, REALLY? WAS HE FOR REAL?

I'M TELLING YOU. IT WAS EMBAR-RASSING.

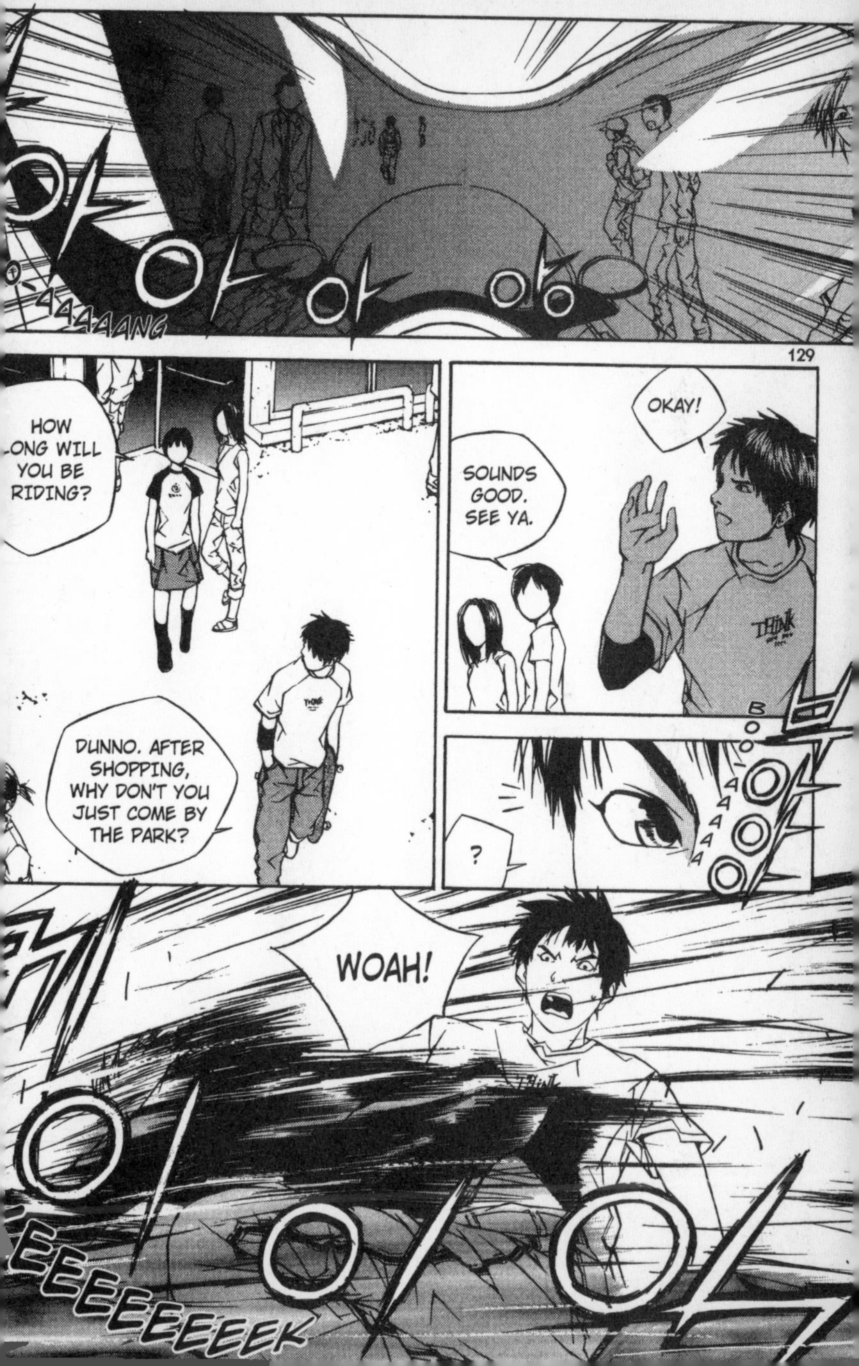
HOW LONG WILL YOU BE RIDING?
DUNNO. AFTER SHOPPING, WHY DON'T YOU JUST COME BY THE PARK?
SOUNDS GOOD. SEE YA.
OKAY!
?
WOAH!
EEEEEEEEEEK

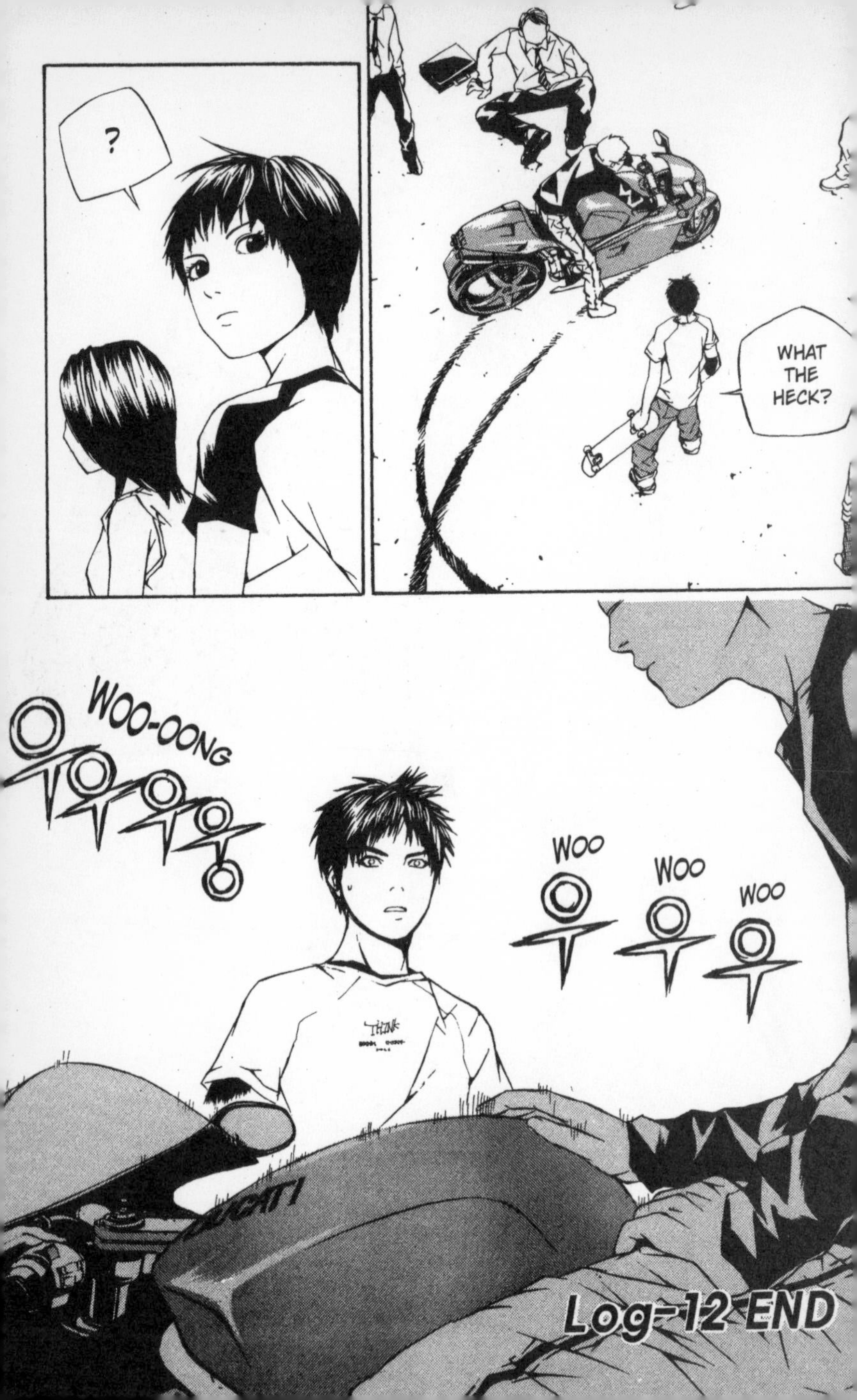
?
WHAT THE HECK?
WOO-OONG
WOO
WOO
WOO
Log-12 END

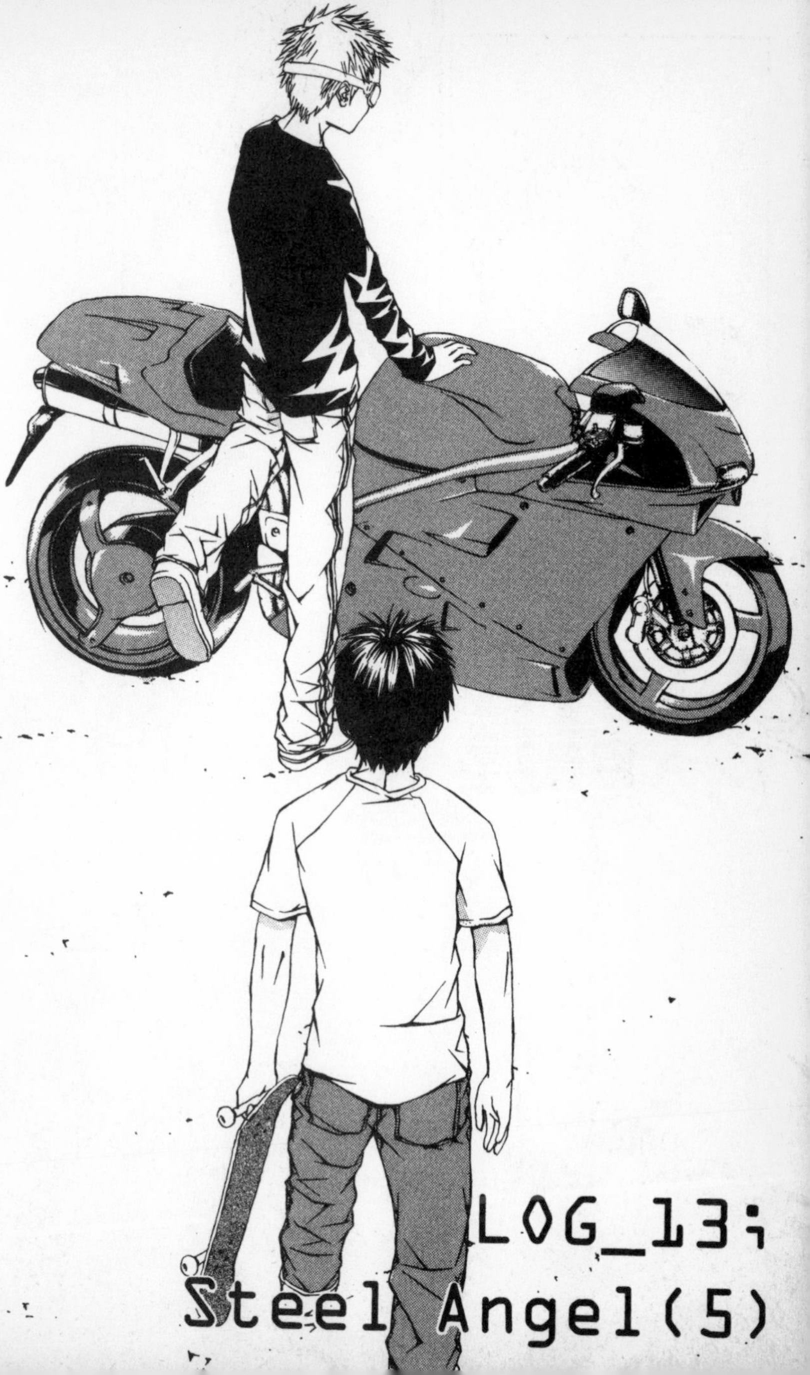
LOG_13;
Steel Angel(5)

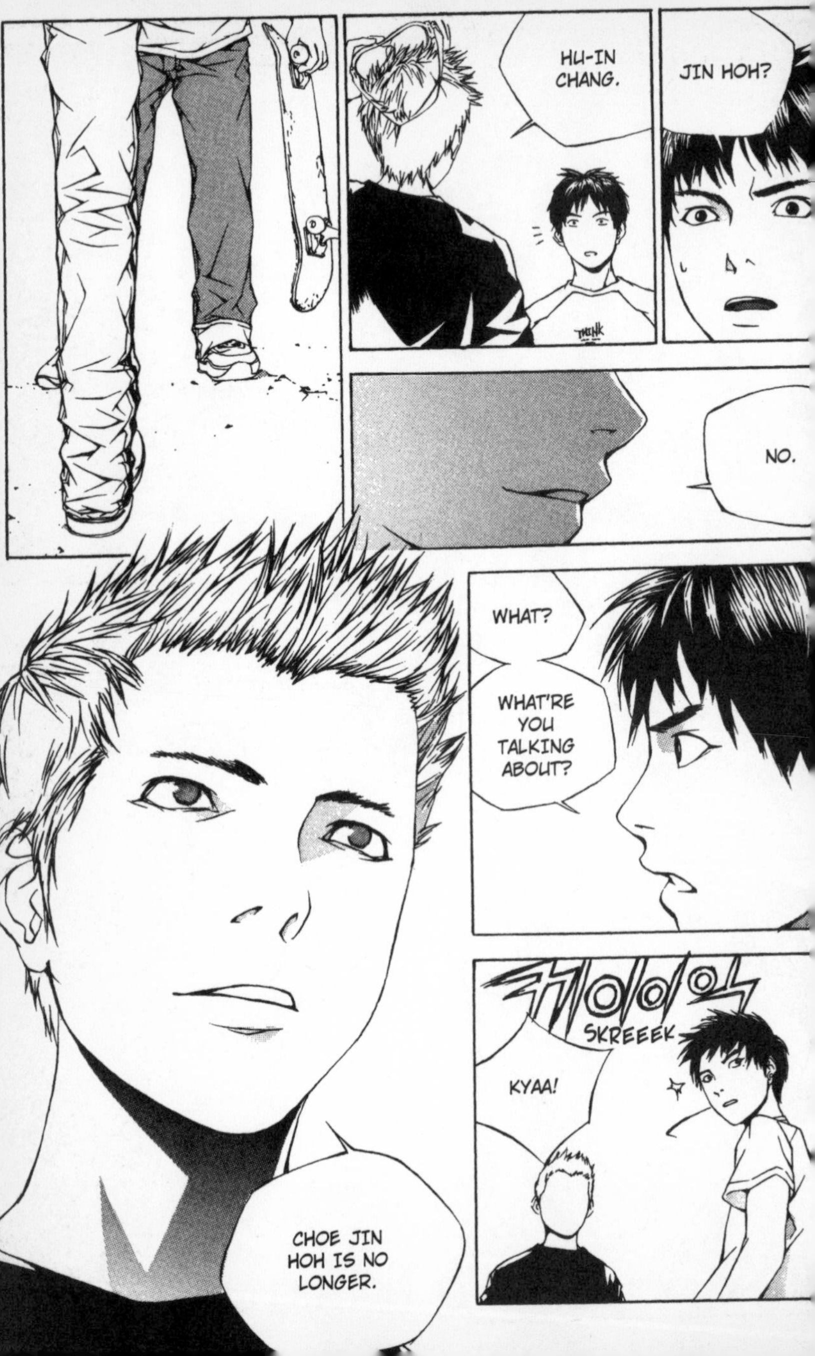
HU-IN CHANG.
JIN HOH?
NO.
CHOE JIN HOH IS NO LONGER.
WHAT?
WHAT'RE YOU TALKING ABOUT?
끼이이익
SKREEEK
KYAA!

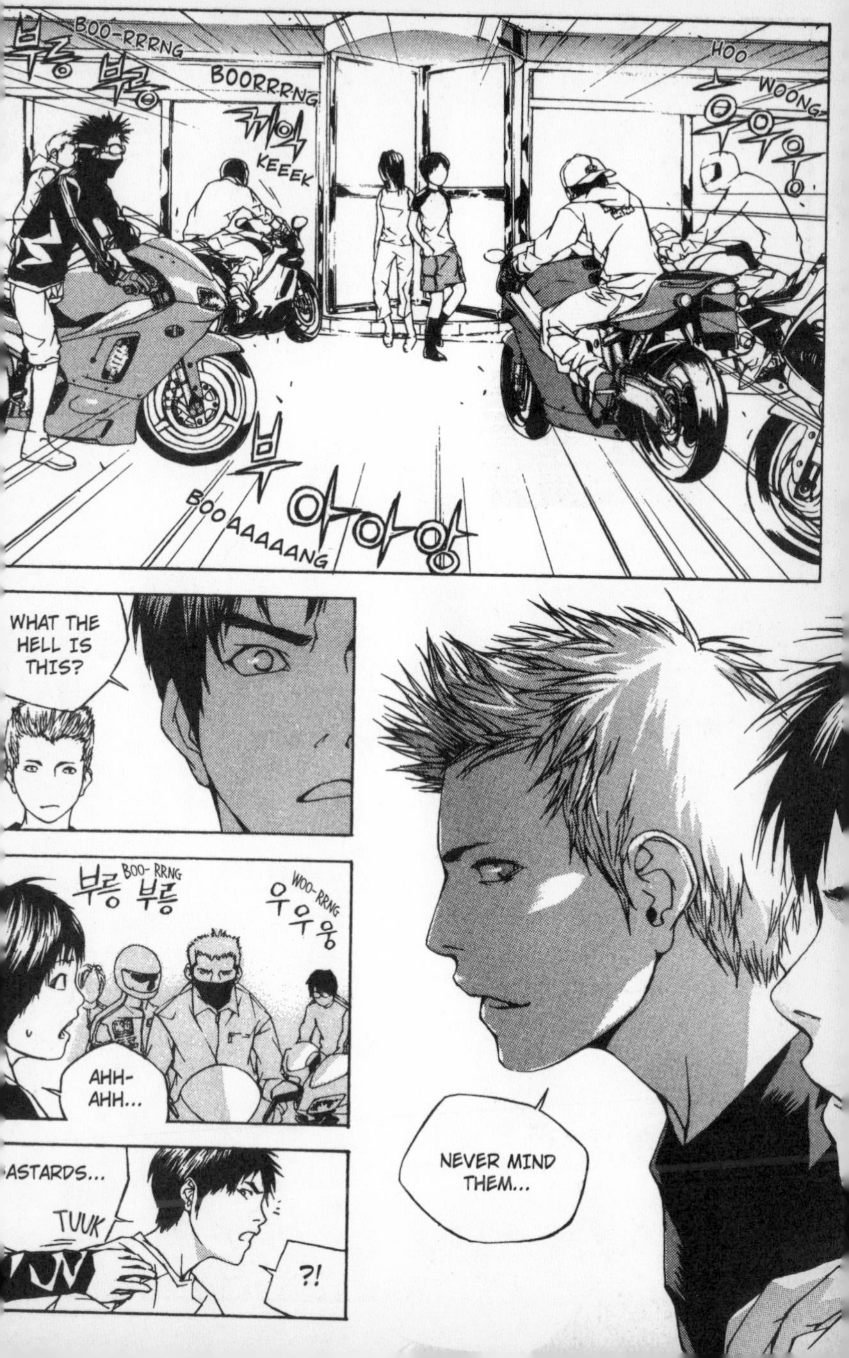
부릉 부릉
BOO-RRRNG
BOORRRRNG
KEEEK
HOO WOONG
BOOAAAAAANG
WHAT THE HELL IS THIS?
부릉 부릉
BOO-RRNG
우우웅
WOO-RRNG
AHH-AHH...
ASTARDS...
TUUK
?!
NEVER MIND THEM...

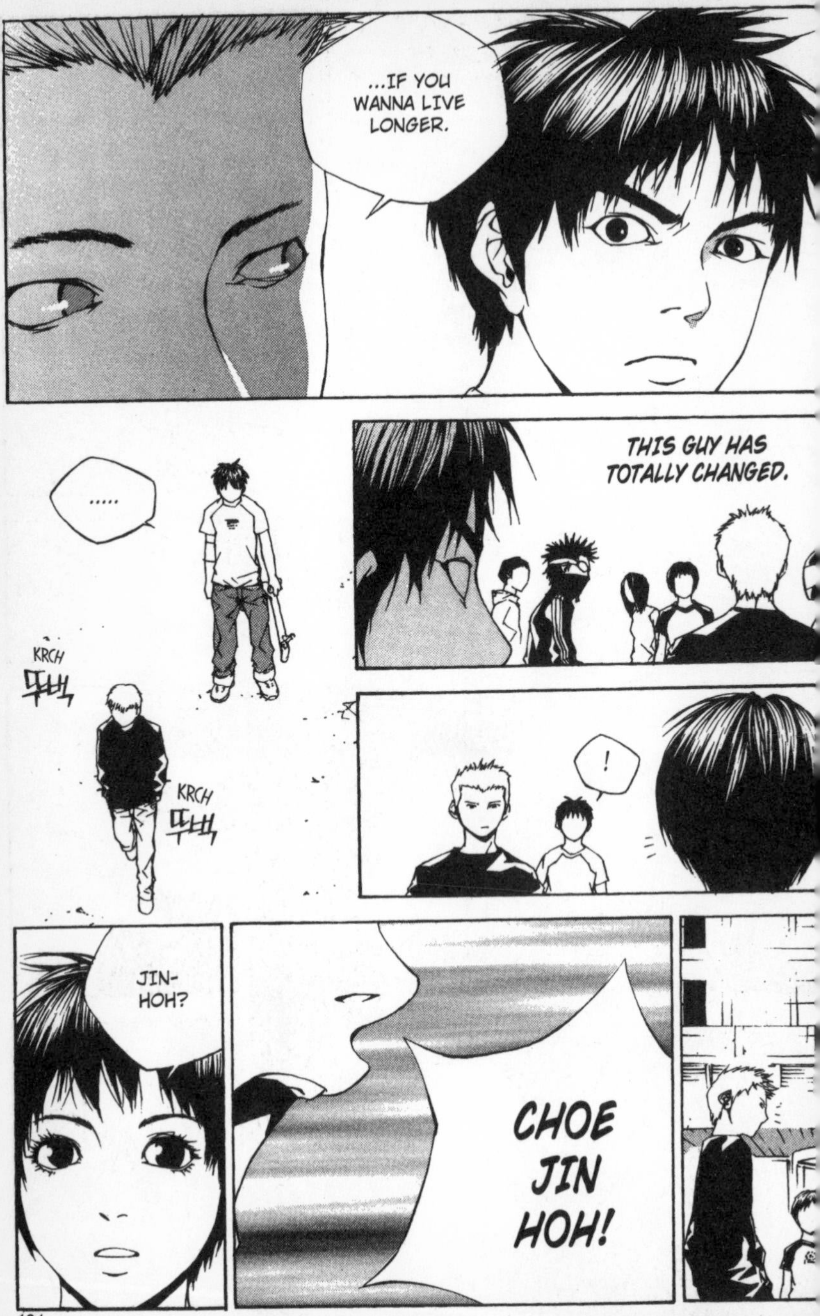
...IF YOU WANNA LIVE LONGER.
.....
KRCH
뚜벅
KRCH
뚜벅
THIS GUY HAS TOTALLY CHANGED.
!
JIN-HOH?
CHOE JIN HOH!

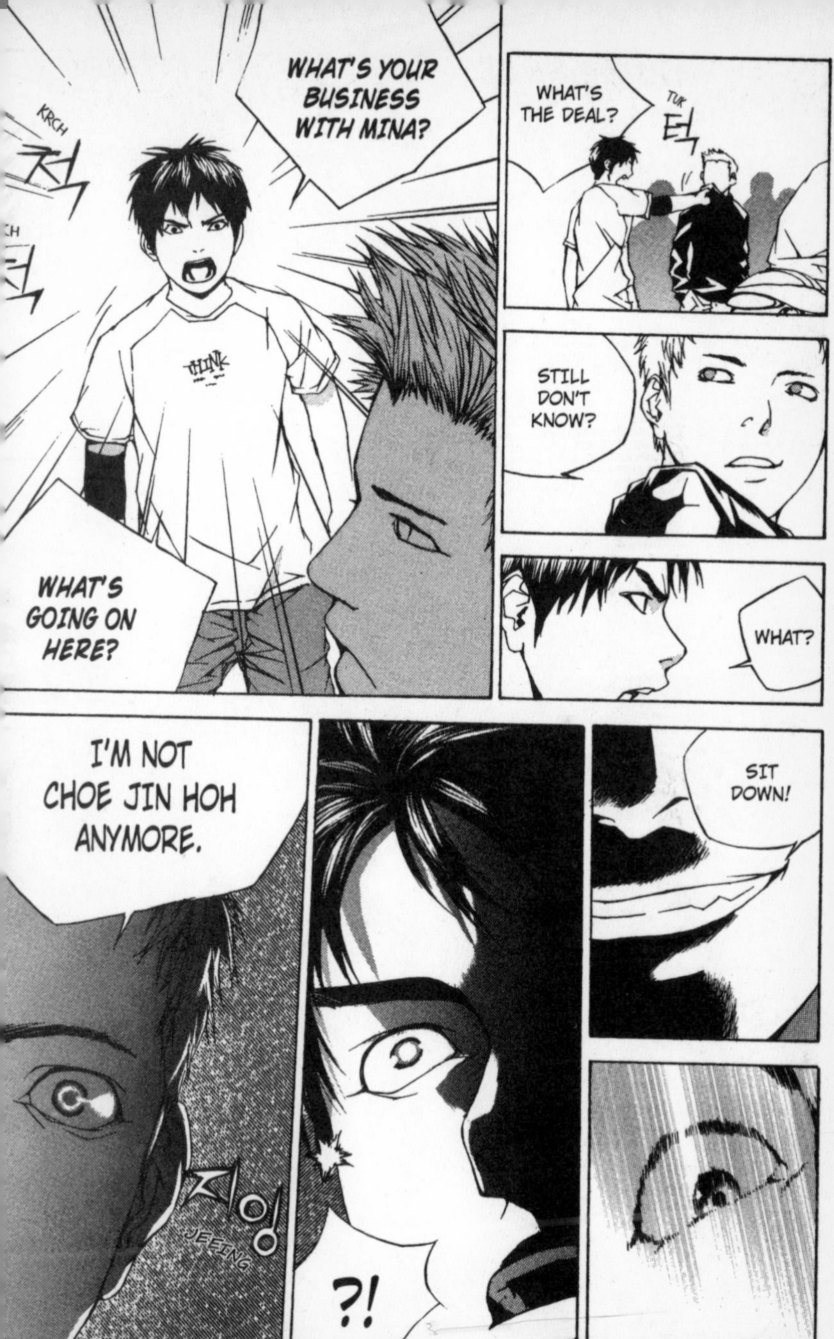
WHAT'S YOUR BUSINESS WITH MINA?
KRCH
WHAT'S GOING ON HERE?
WHAT'S THE DEAL?
TUK
STILL DON'T KNOW?
WHAT?
I'M NOT CHOE JIN HOH ANYMORE.
JEEING
?!
SIT DOWN!

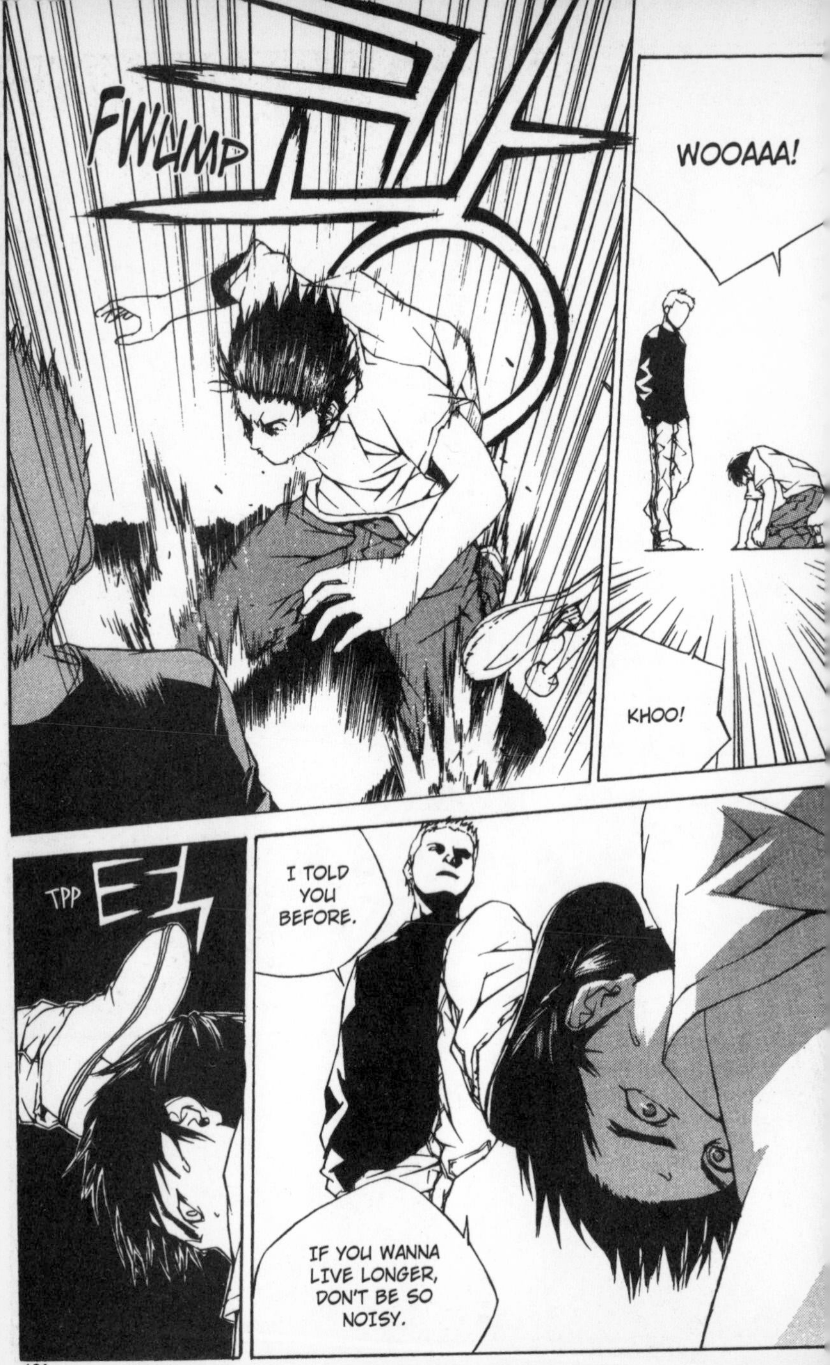
FWUMP
WOOAAA!
KHOO!
TPP
I TOLD YOU BEFORE.
IF YOU WANNA LIVE LONGER, DON'T BE SO NOISY.

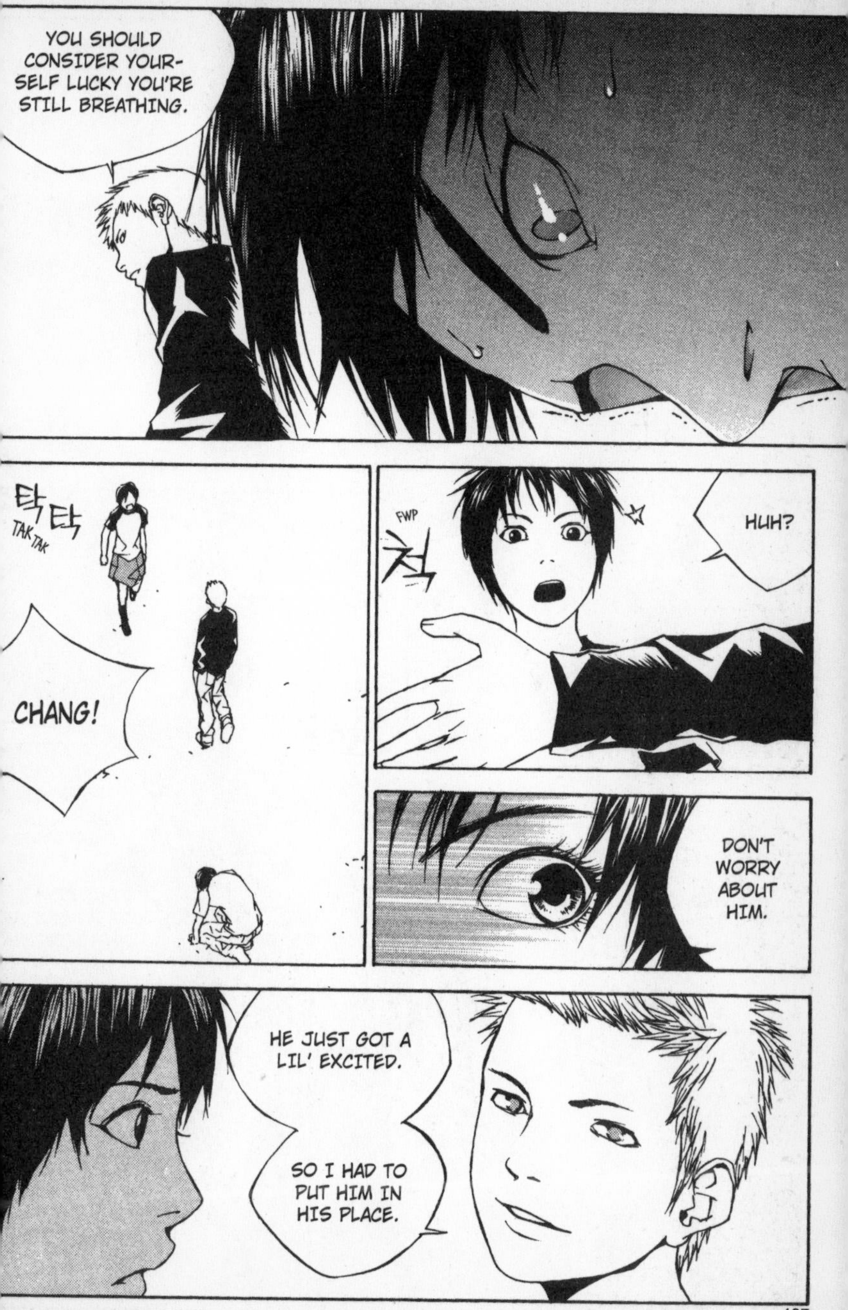

YOU SHOULD CONSIDER YOUR-SELF LUCKY YOU'RE STILL BREATHING.
탁 탁
TAK TAK
CHANG!
FWP
척
HUH?
DON'T WORRY ABOUT HIM.
HE JUST GOT A LIL' EXCITED.
SO I HAD TO PUT HIM IN HIS PLACE.

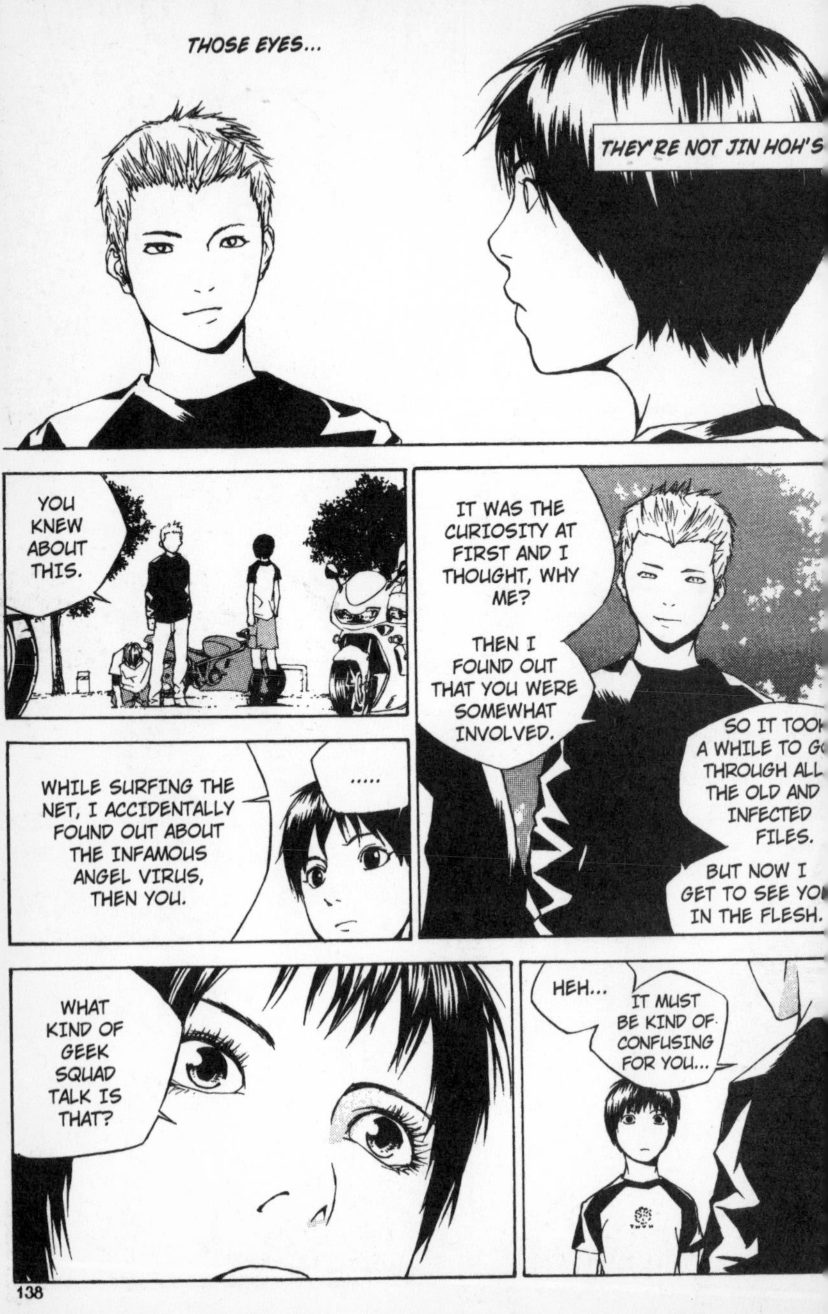
THOSE EYES...
THEY'RE NOT JIN HOH'S
YOU KNEW ABOUT THIS.
WHILE SURFING THE NET, I ACCIDENTALLY FOUND OUT ABOUT THE INFAMOUS ANGEL VIRUS, THEN YOU.
.....
IT WAS THE CURIOSITY AT FIRST AND I THOUGHT, WHY ME?
THEN I FOUND OUT THAT YOU WERE SOMEWHAT INVOLVED.
SO IT TOOK A WHILE TO GO THROUGH ALL THE OLD AND INFECTED FILES.
BUT NOW I GET TO SEE YOU IN THE FLESH.
WHAT KIND OF GEEK SQUAD TALK IS THAT?
HEH...
IT MUST BE KIND OF CONFUSING FOR YOU...

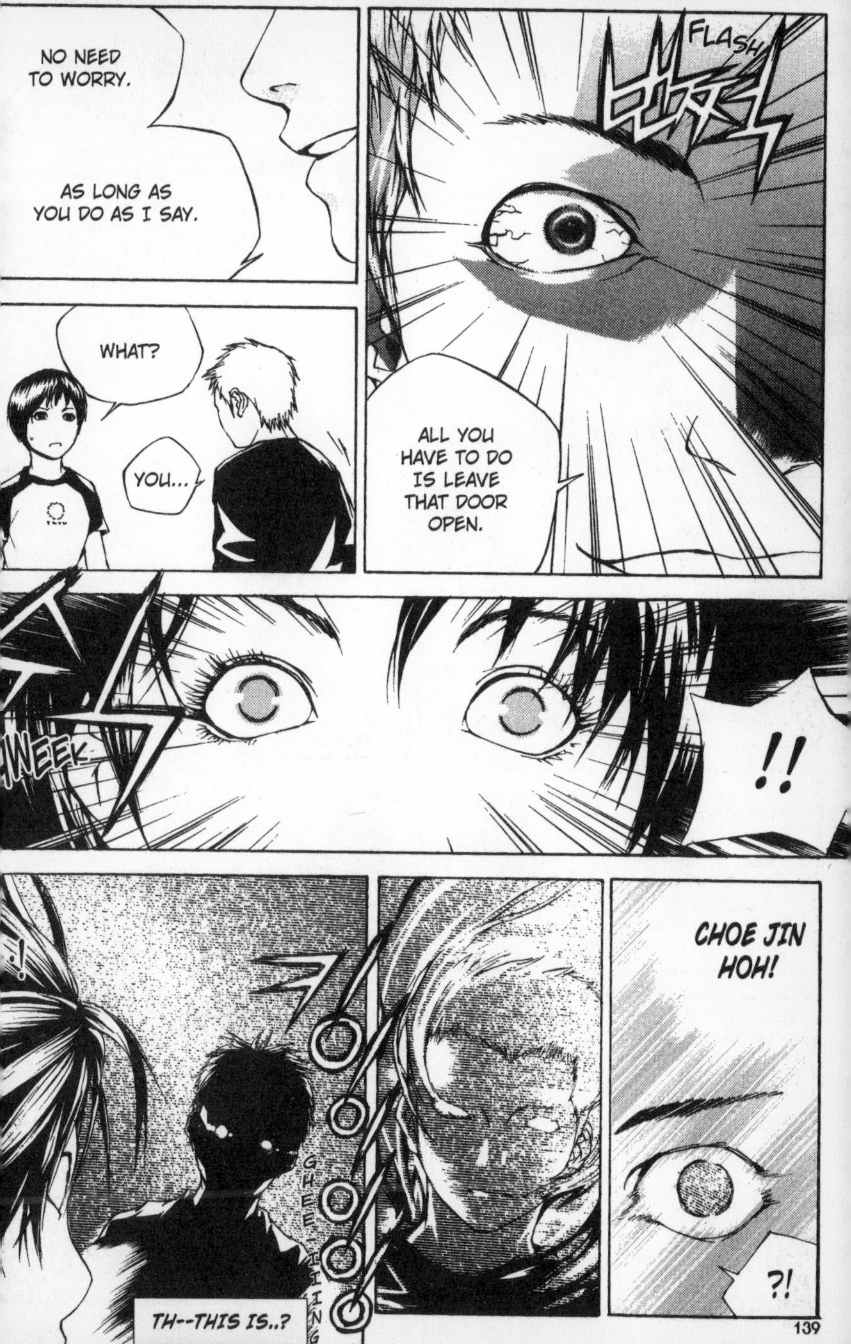
NO NEED TO WORRY.
AS LONG AS YOU DO AS I SAY.
WHAT?
YOU...
FLASH
ALL YOU HAVE TO DO IS LEAVE THAT DOOR OPEN.
!!
!
TH--THIS IS..?
GHEEIIING
CHOE JIN HOH!
?!

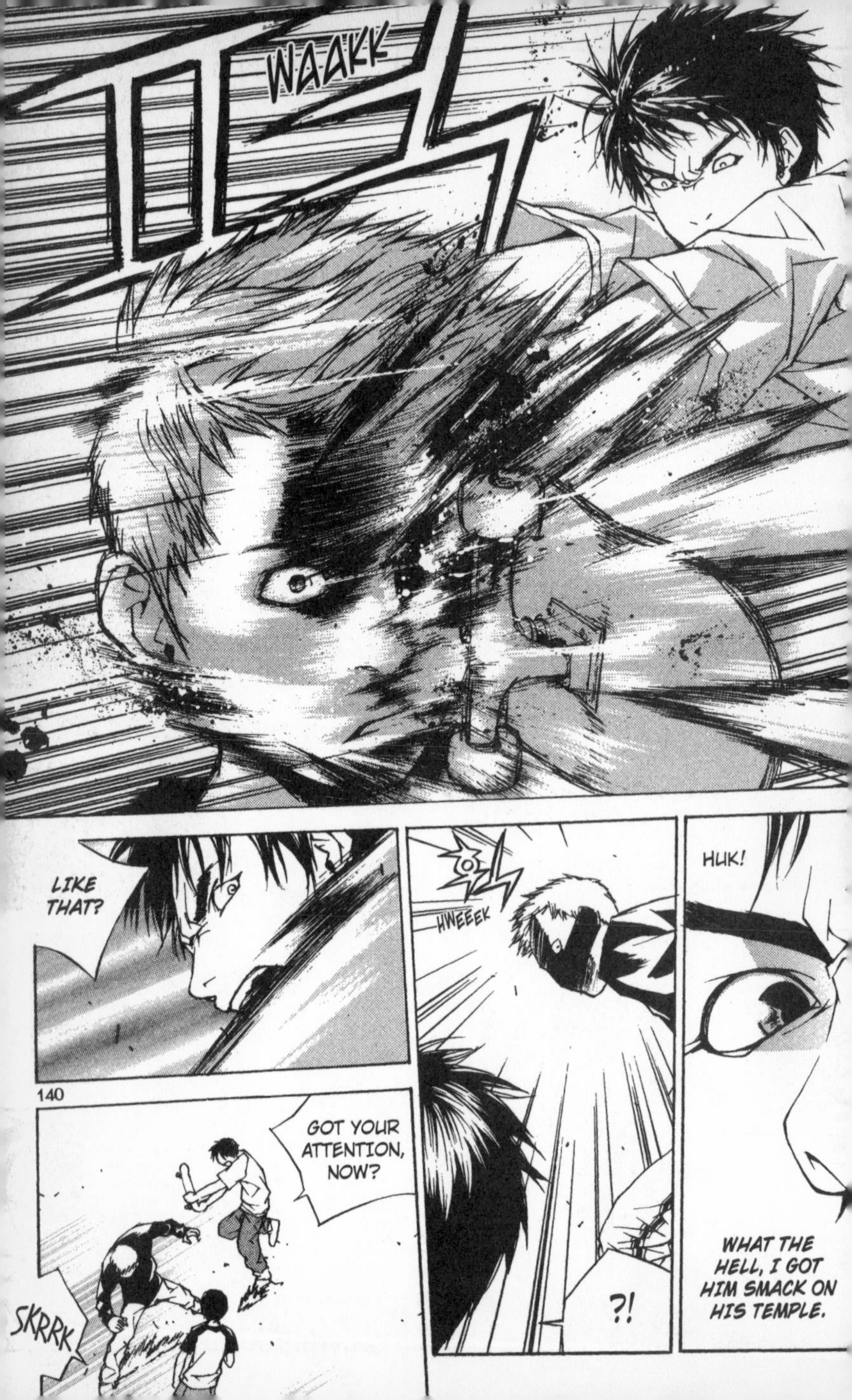
WAAKK
LIKE THAT?
GOT YOUR ATTENTION, NOW?
SKRRK
HWEEEK
?!
HUK!
WHAT THE HELL, I GOT HIM SMACK ON HIS TEMPLE.

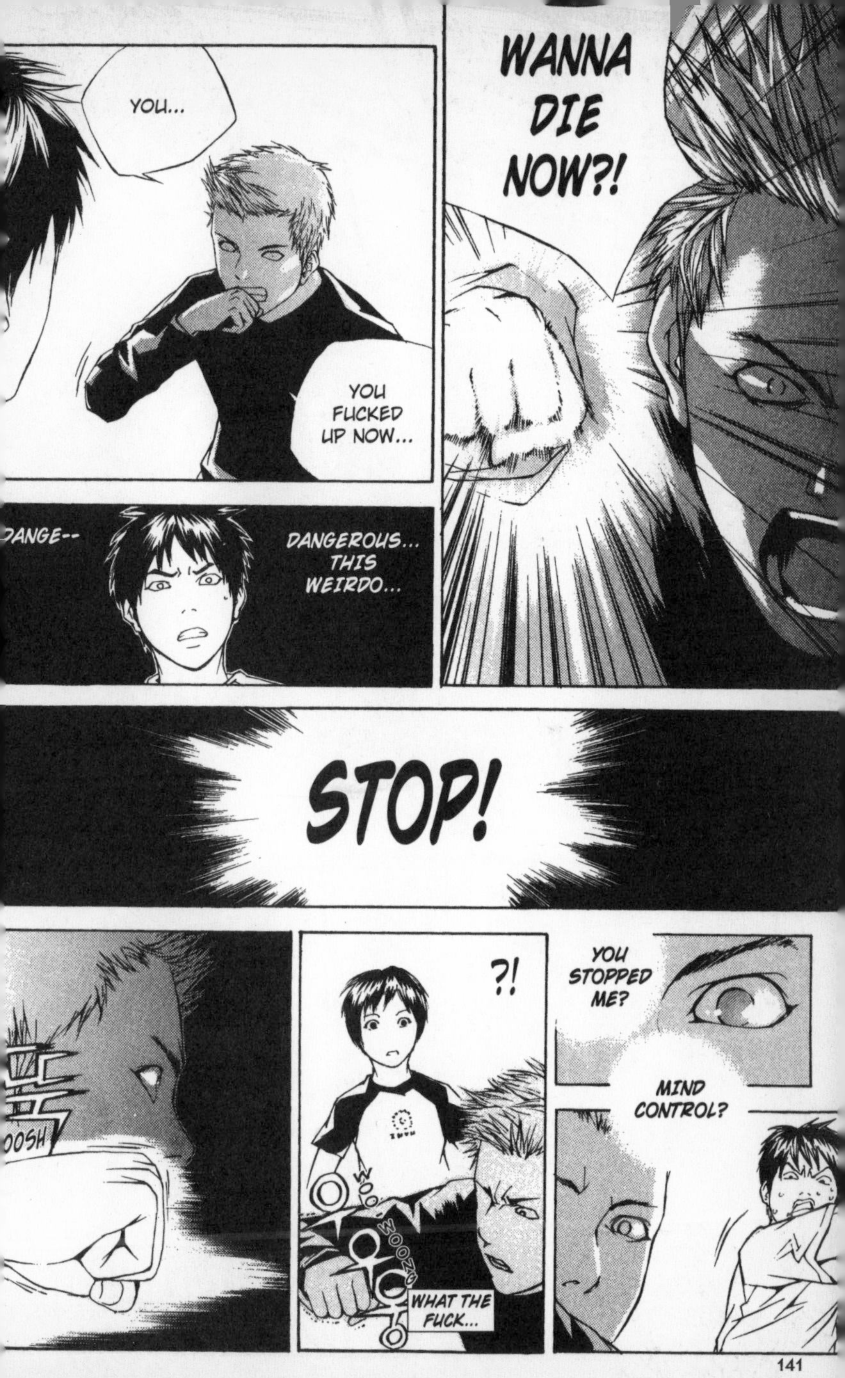
YOU...
YOU FUCKED UP NOW...
DANGE--
DANGEROUS... THIS WEIRDO...
WANNA DIE NOW?!
STOP!
OOSH
?!
WOO
WOONG
WHAT THE FUCK...
YOU STOPPED ME?
MIND CONTROL?

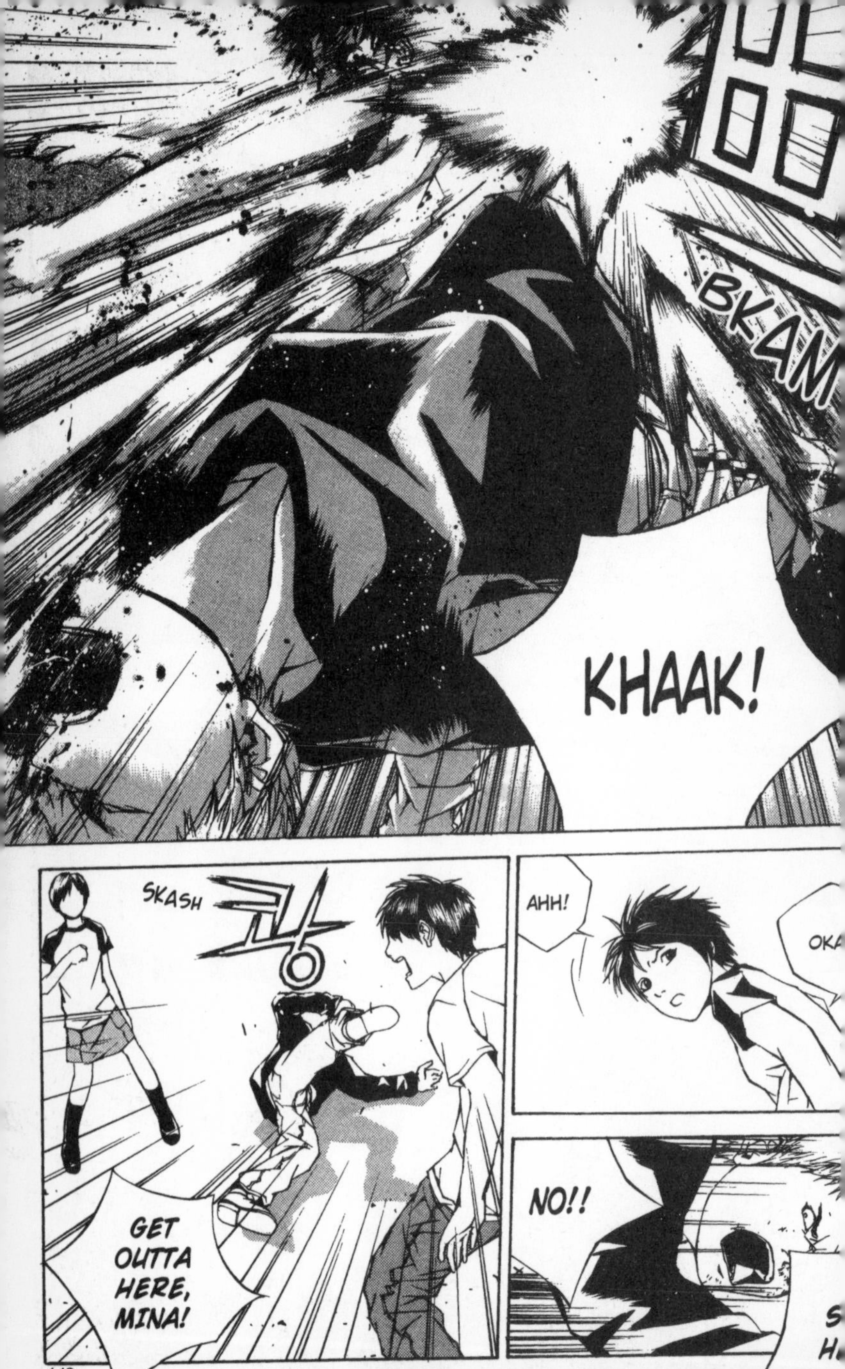
BKAM
KHAAK!
SKASH
GET OUTTA HERE, MINA!
AHH!
NO!!

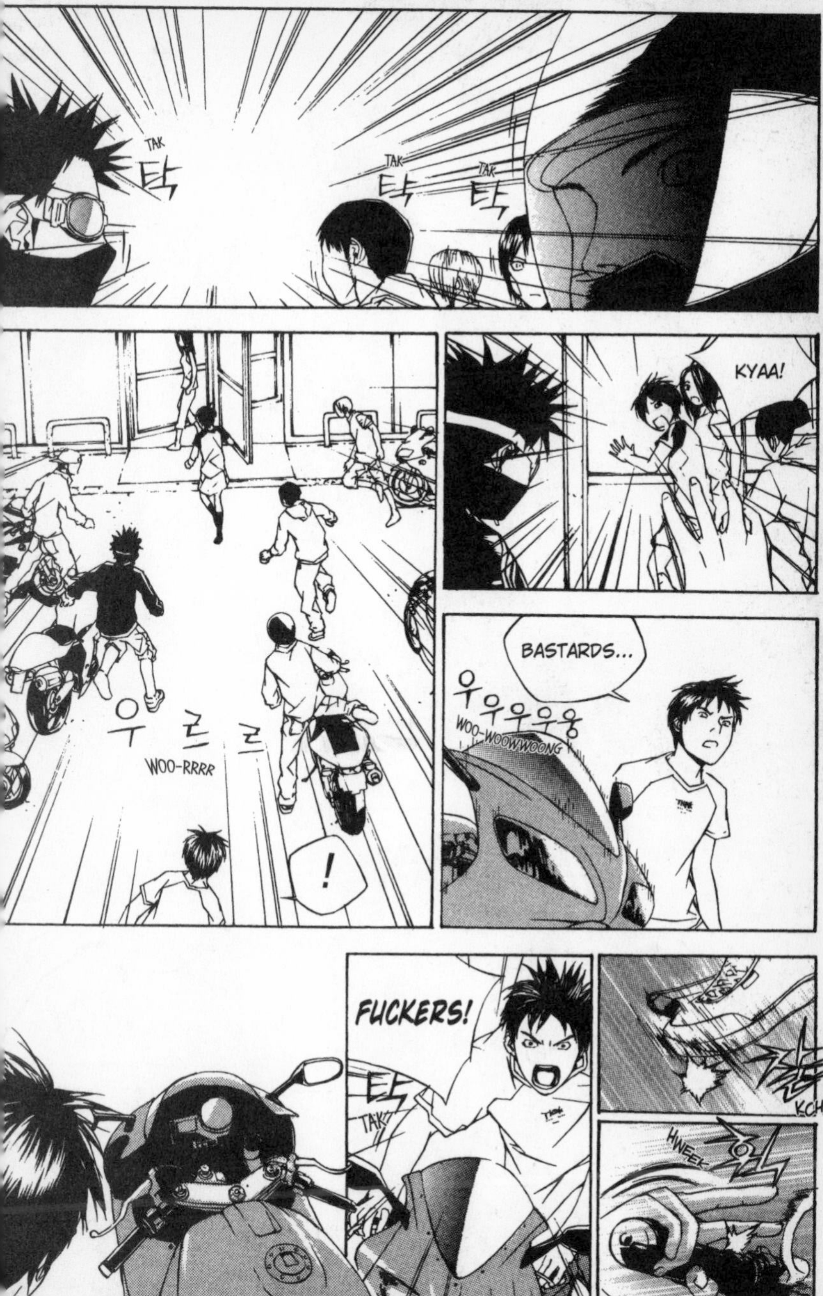
TAK
탁
TAK
탁
TAK
탁
우르르
WOO-RRRR
!
KYAA!
BASTARDS...
우우우우웅
WOO-WOOWWOONG
FUCKERS!
탁
TAK
KCHAK
HWEEK

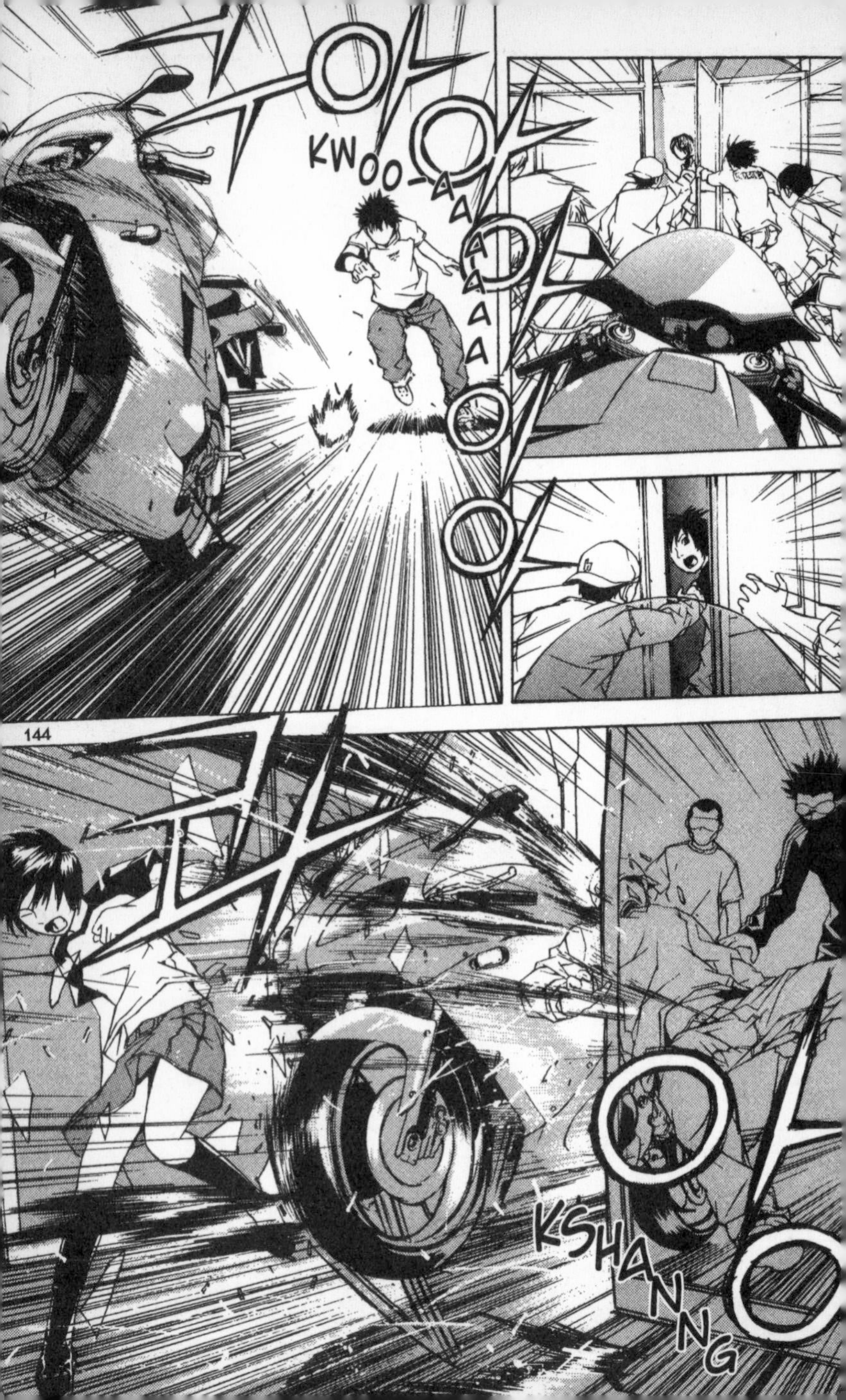
KWOO-AAAAAAAA
KSHANNG

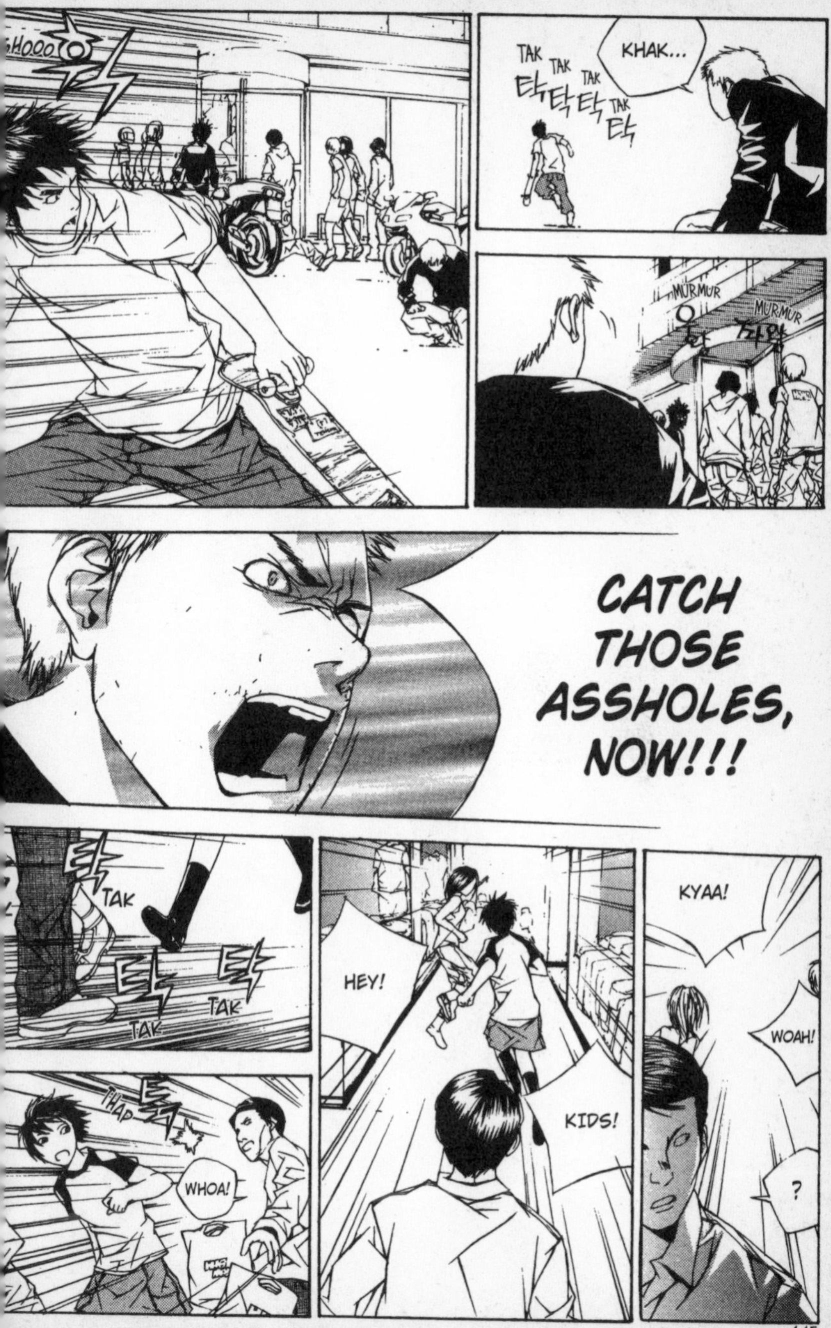
SHOOOO
TAK
TAK
TAK
TAK
KHAK...
MURMUR
MURMUR
CATCH THOSE ASSHOLES, NOW!!!
TAK
TAK
TAK
THAP
WHOA!
HEY!
KIDS!
KYAA!
WOAH!
?

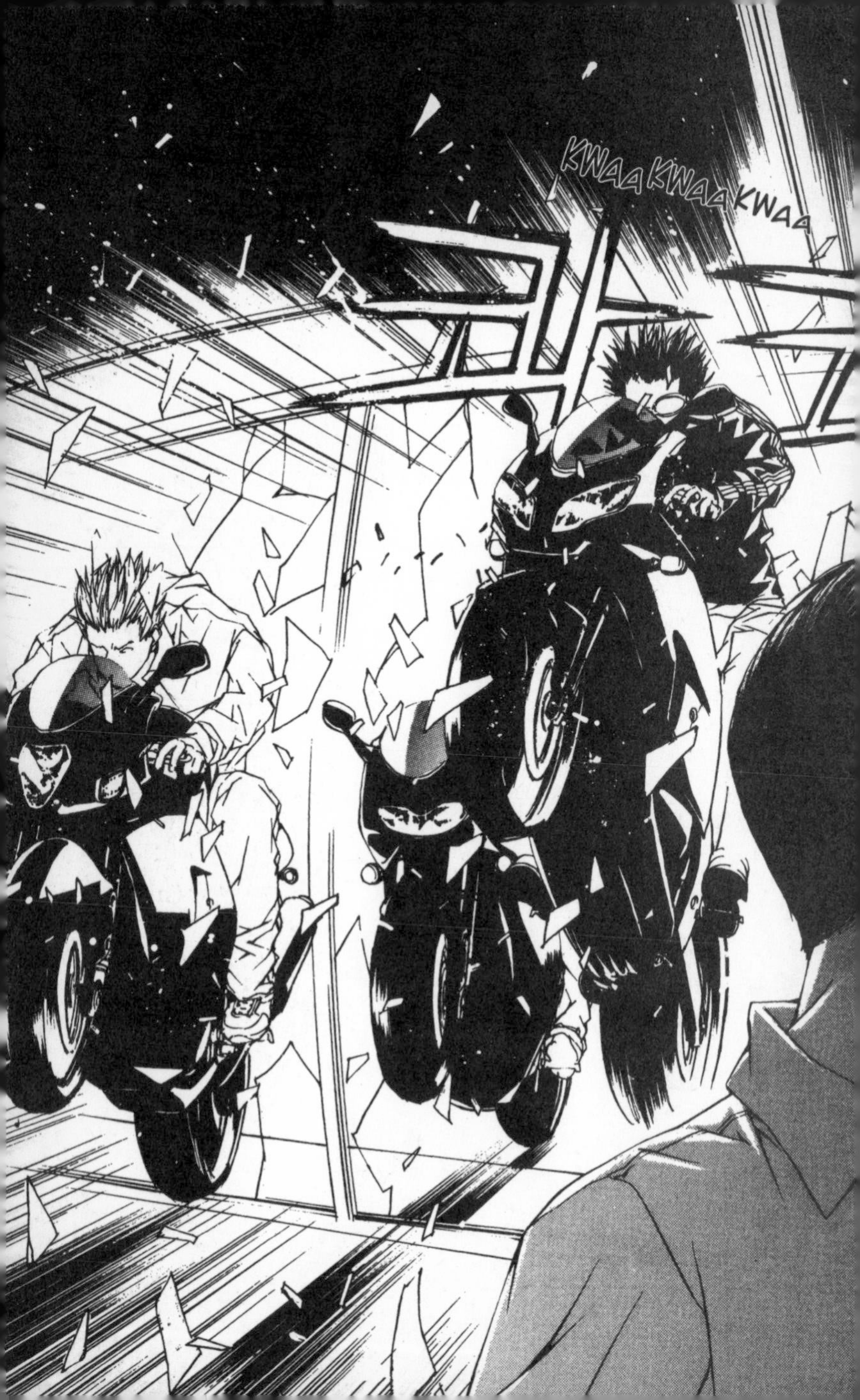
KWAA KWAA KWAA

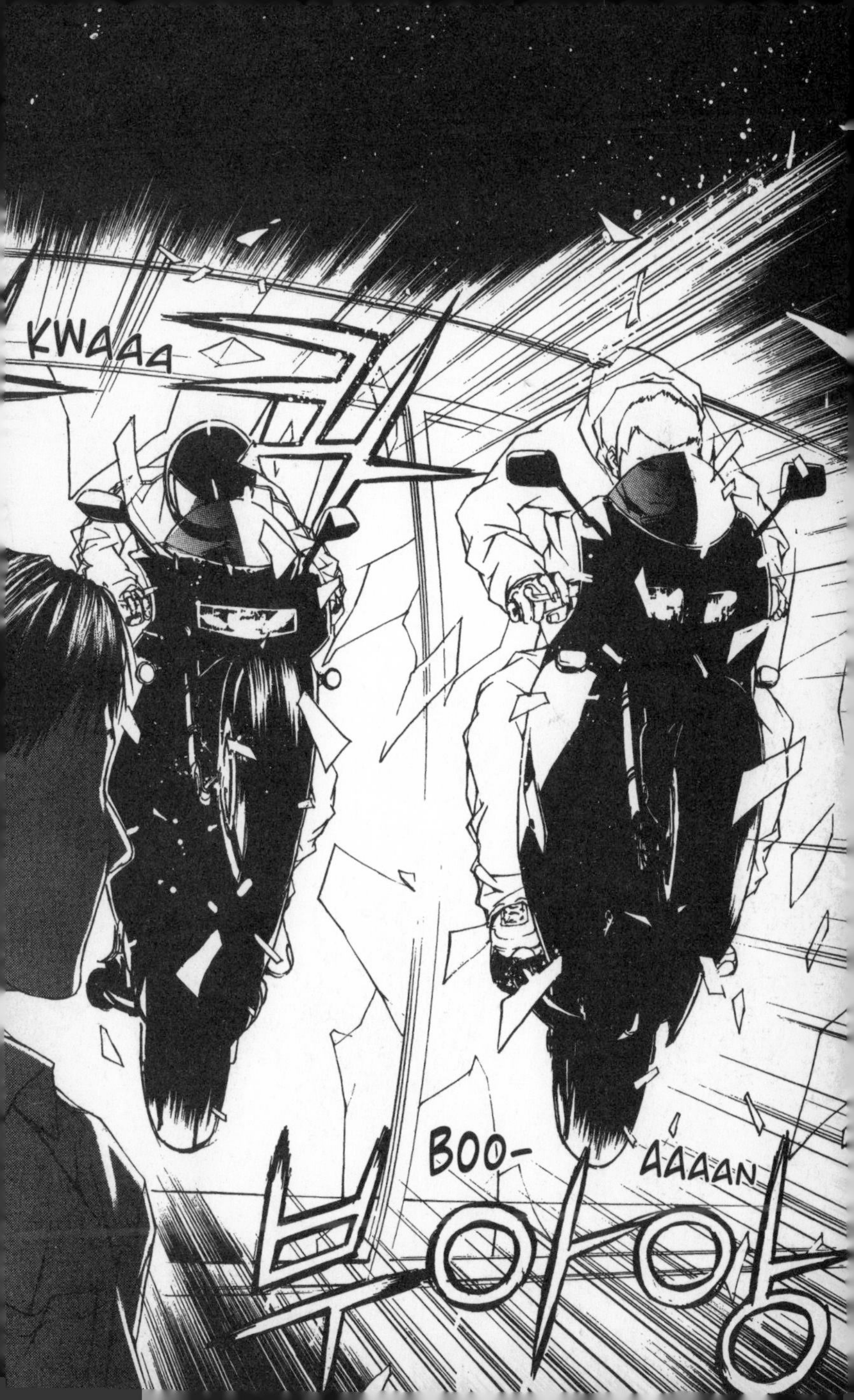
KWAAA
BOO-
AAAAN

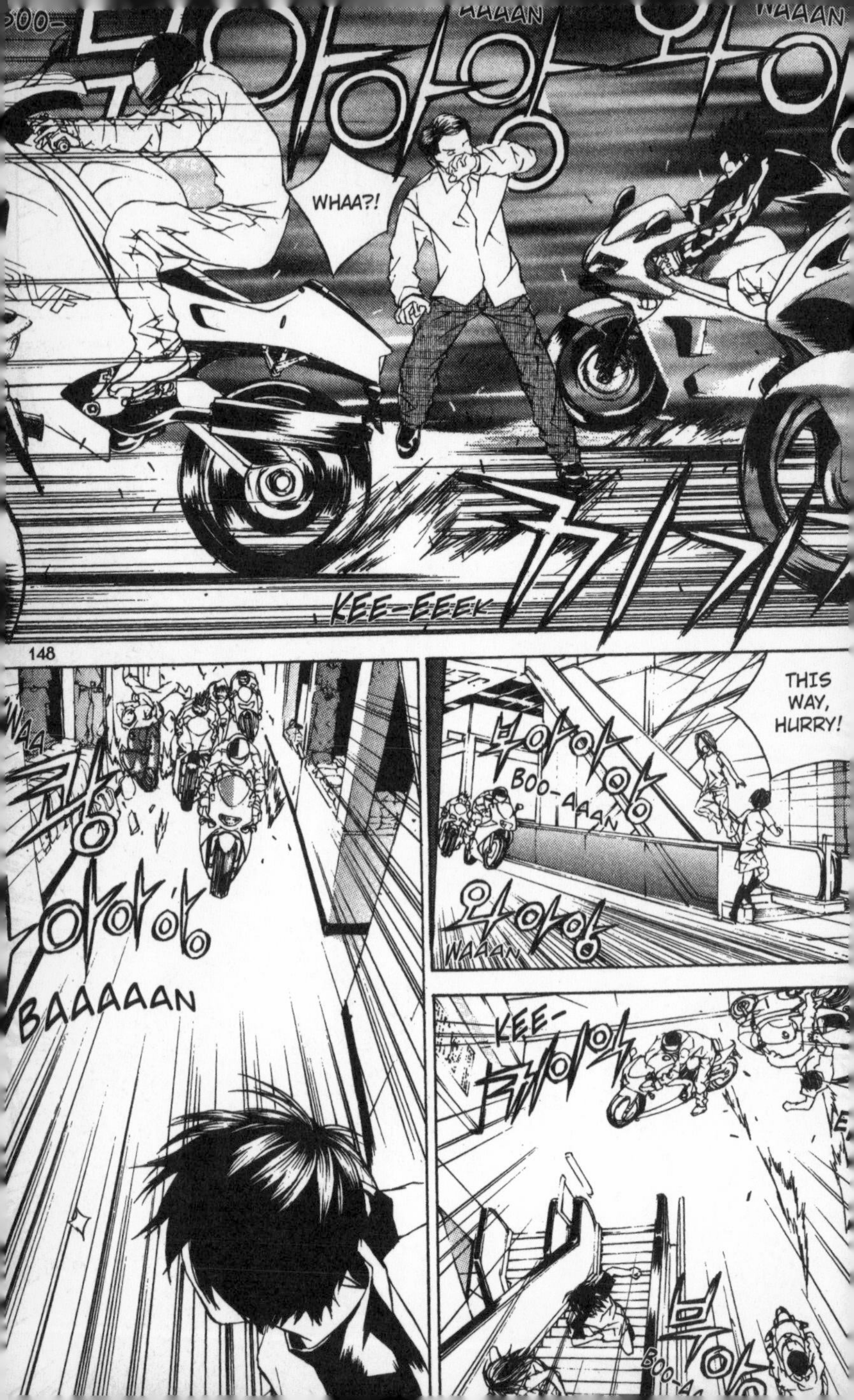
AAAAN
NAAAN
WHAA?!
KEE-EEEK
BAAAAAN
THIS WAY, HURRY!
BOO-AAAN
WAAAN
KEE-

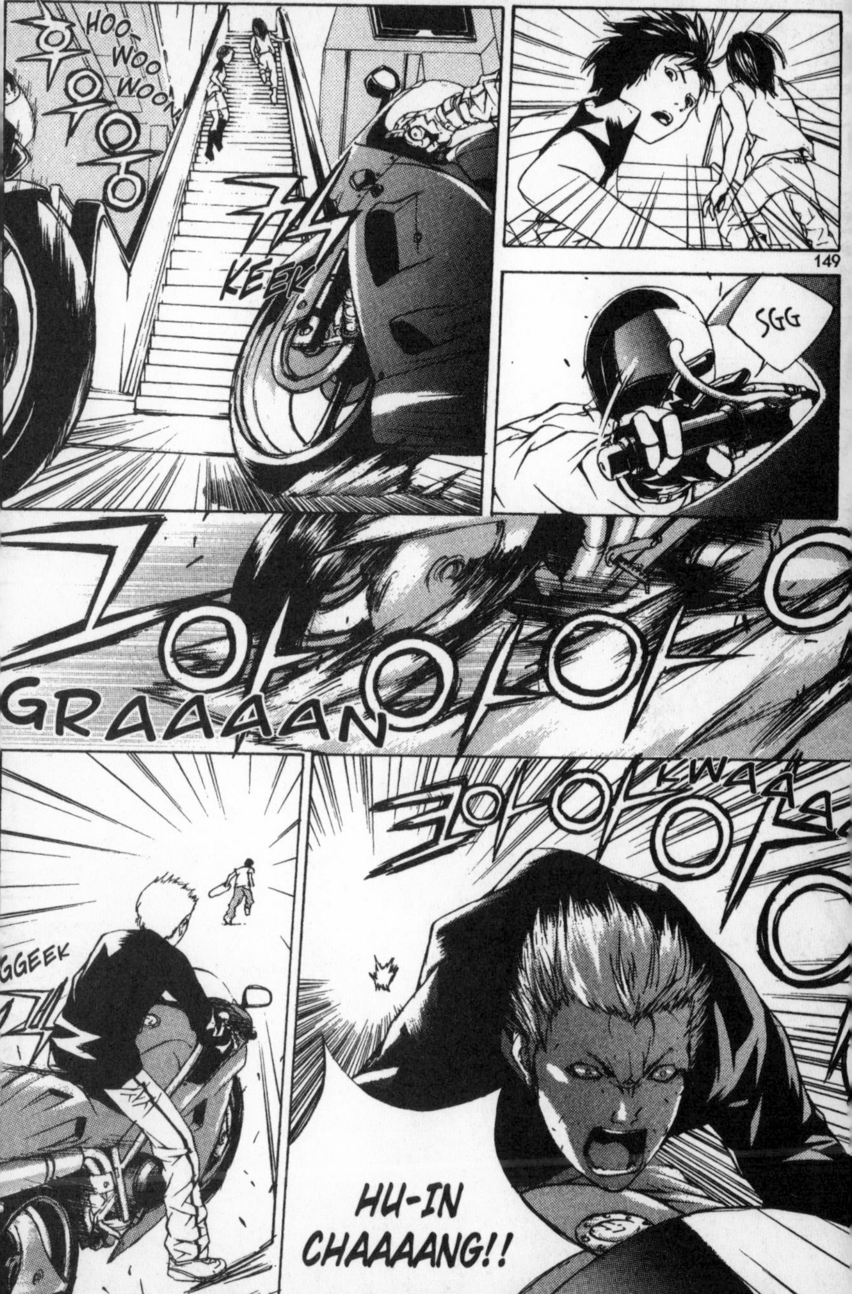
HOO-WOO-WOON
KEEK
SGG
GRAAAAAN
GGEEK
KWAAA...
HU-IN CHAAAANG!!

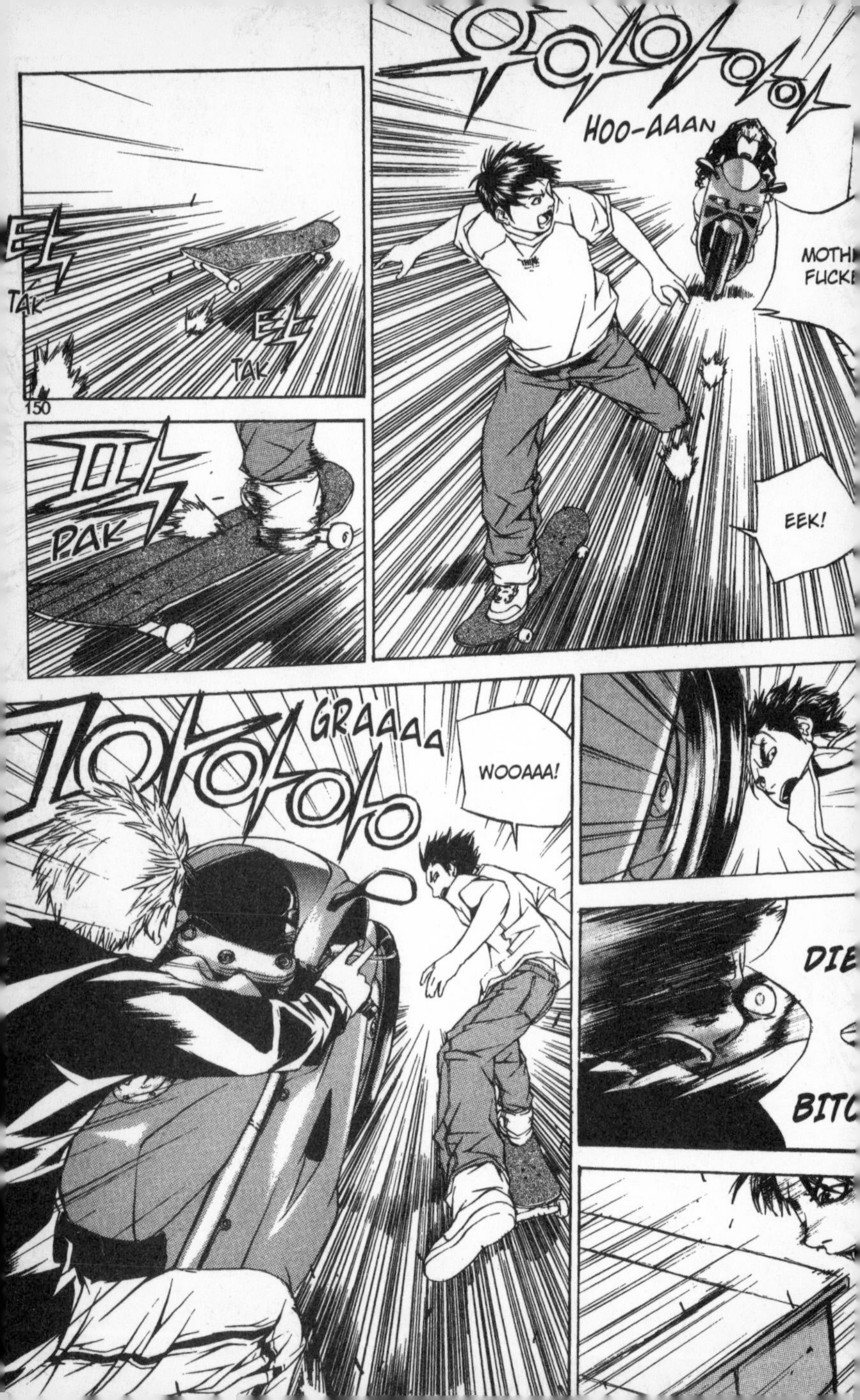

탁
TAK
탁
TAK
PAK
HOO-AAAN
MOTHI
FUCKI
EEK!
GRAAAAA
WOOAAA!
DIE
BITC

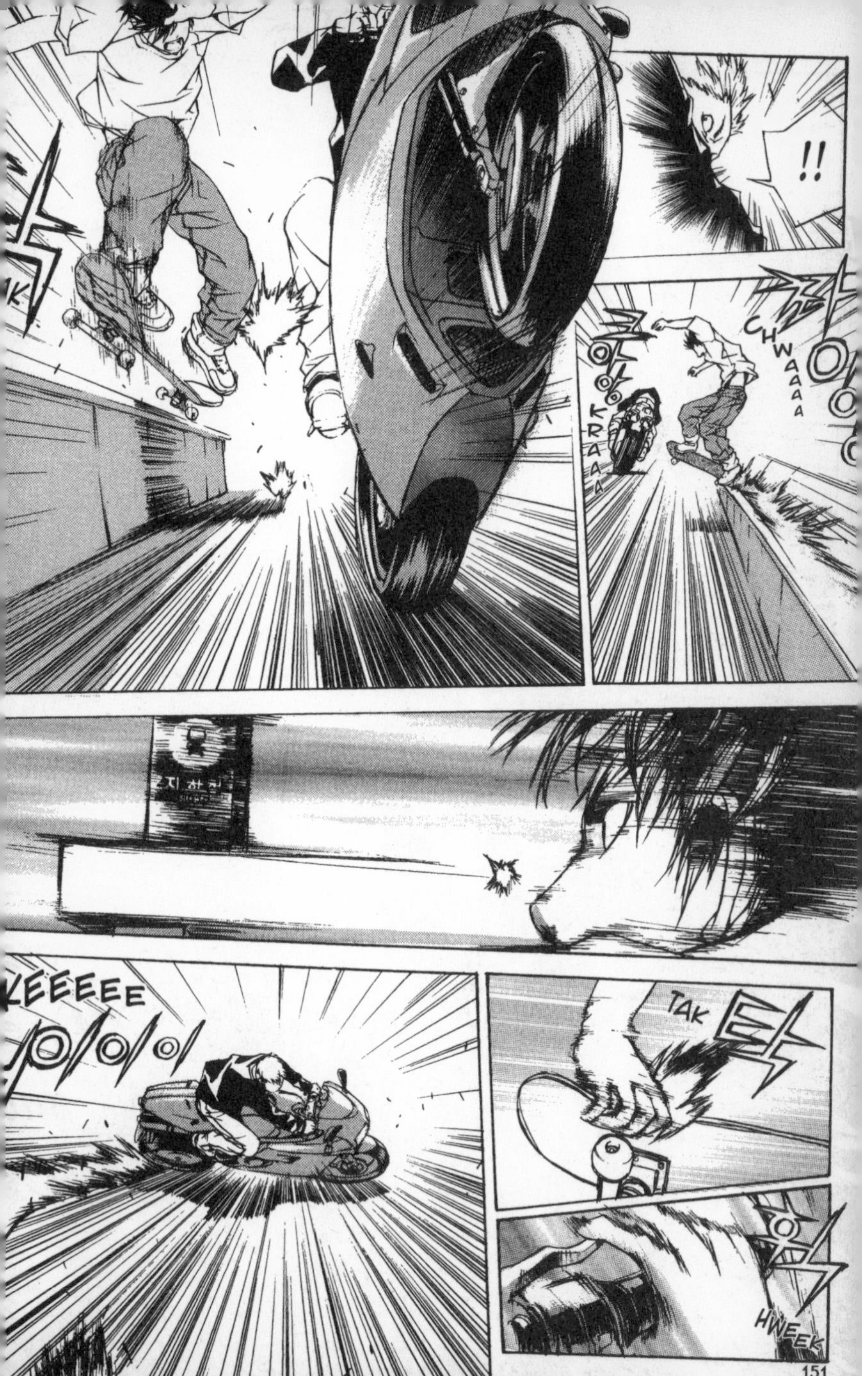
!!
CHWAAAA
KRAAAA
EEEEEE
TAK
HWEEK

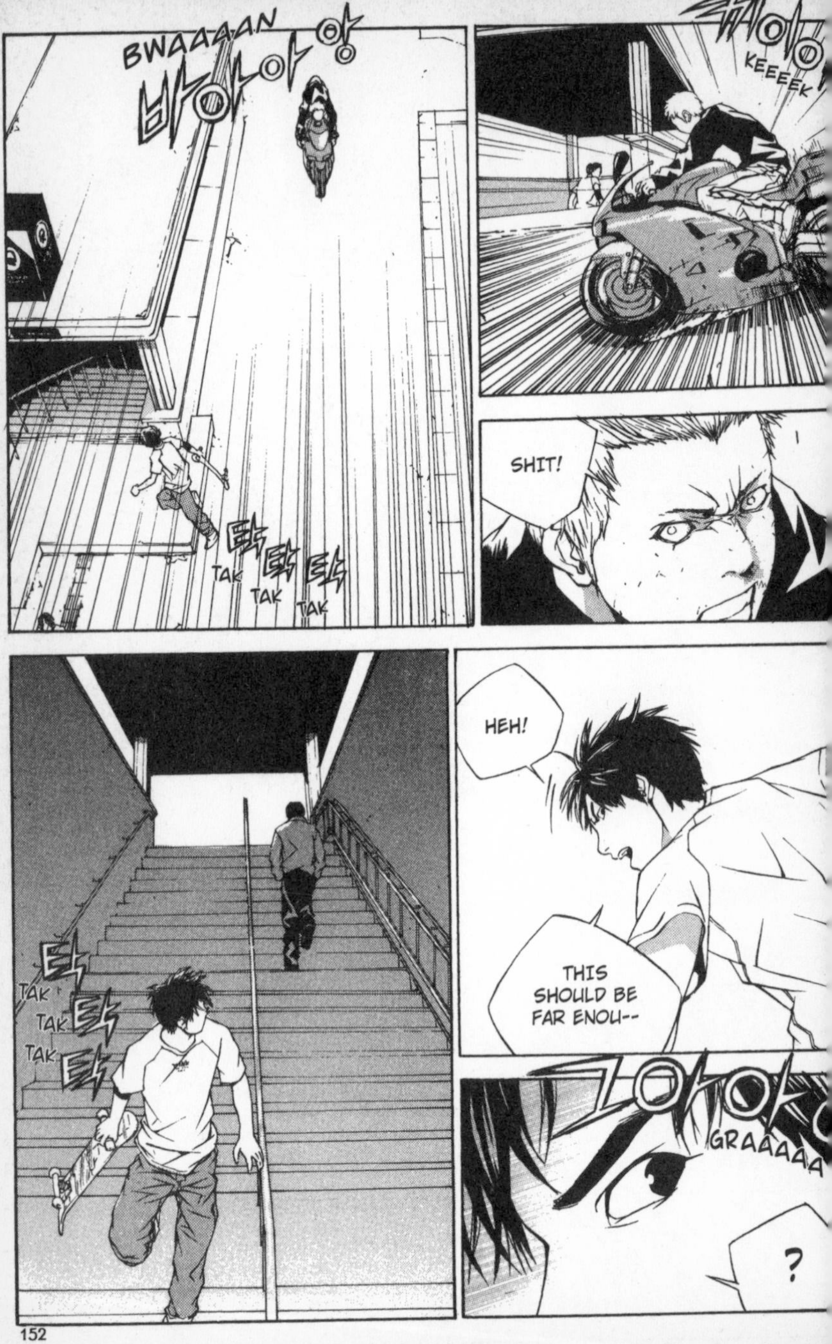
BWAAAAN
TAK
TAK
TAK
KEEEEEK
SHIT!
TAK
TAK
TAK
HEH!
THIS SHOULD BE FAR ENOU--
GRAAAAA
?

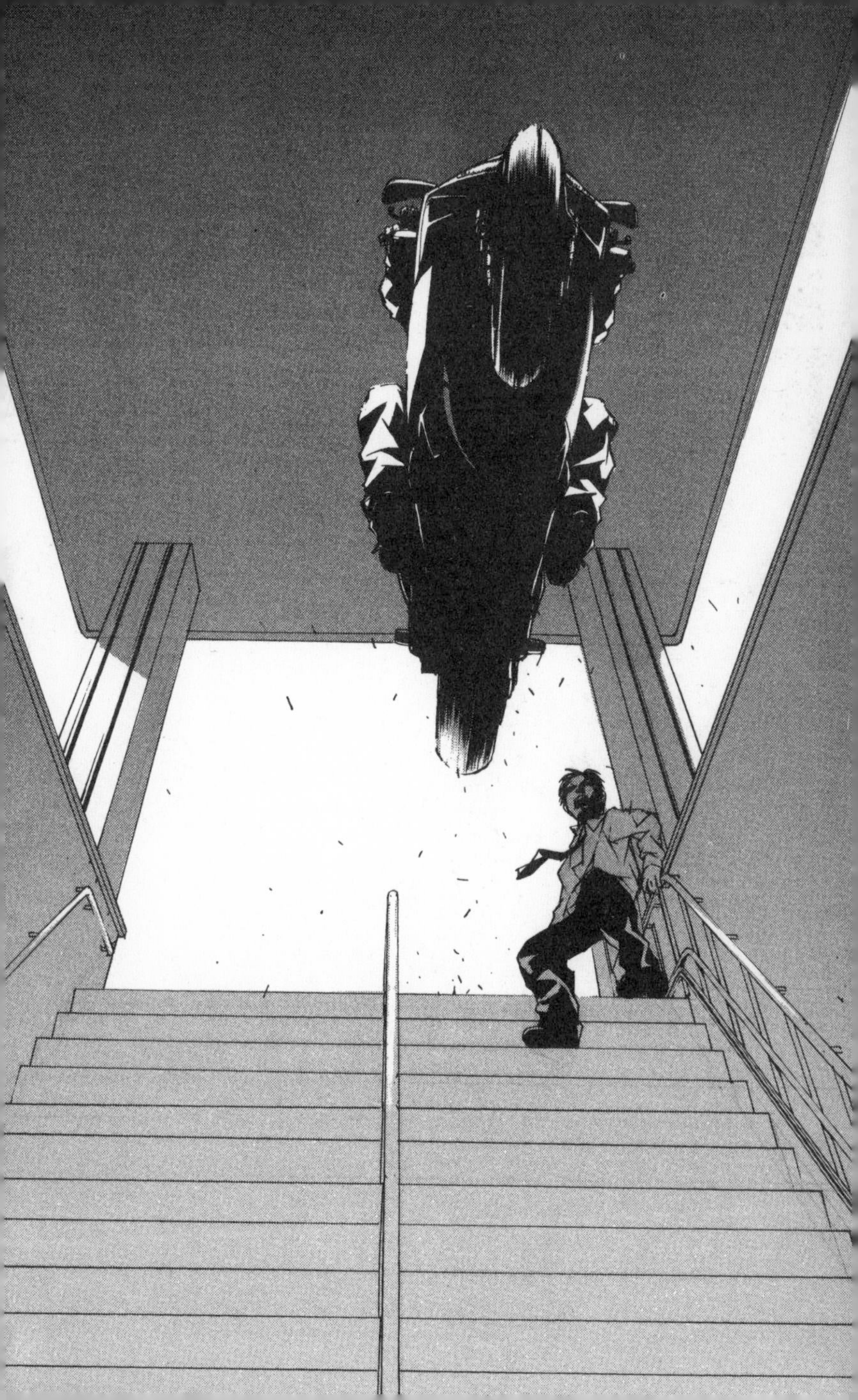

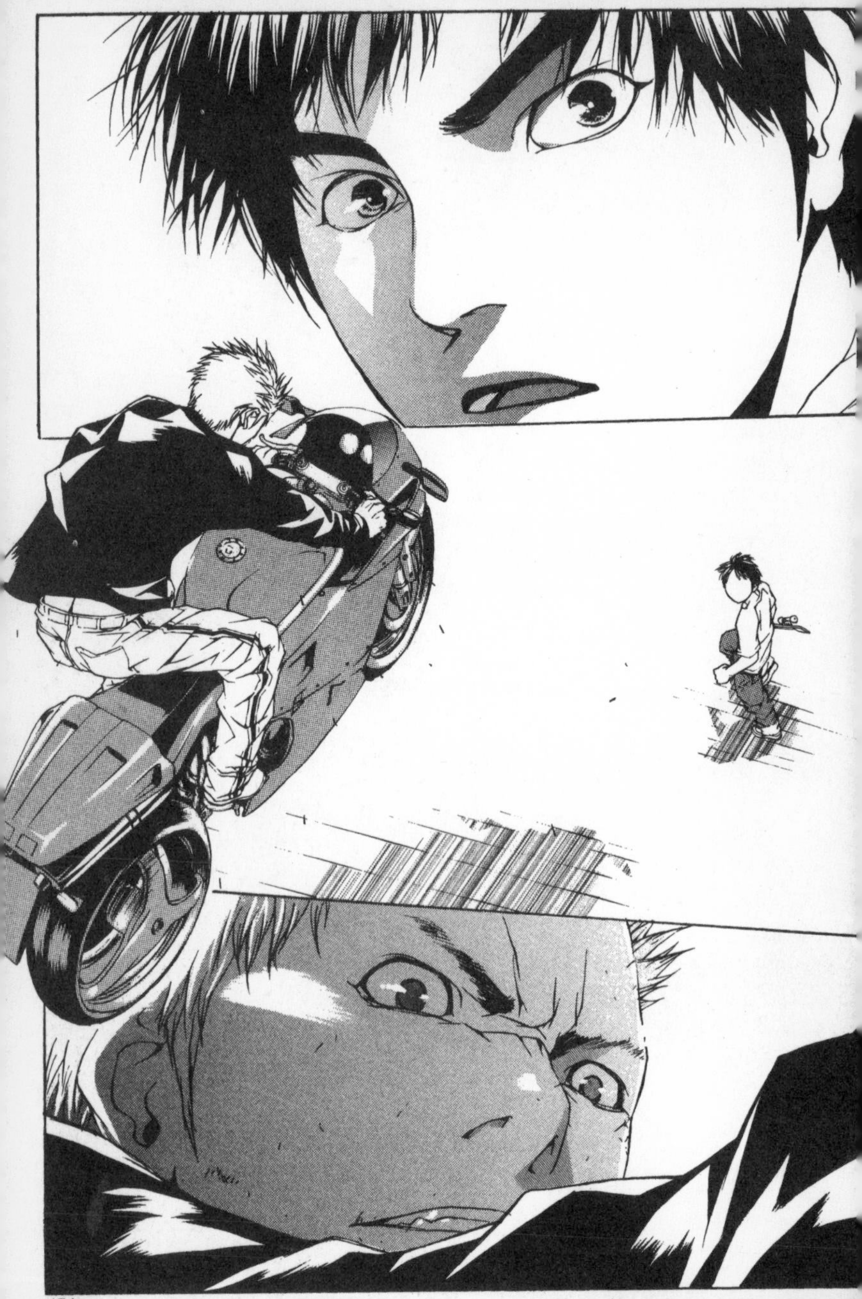

Log-13 END

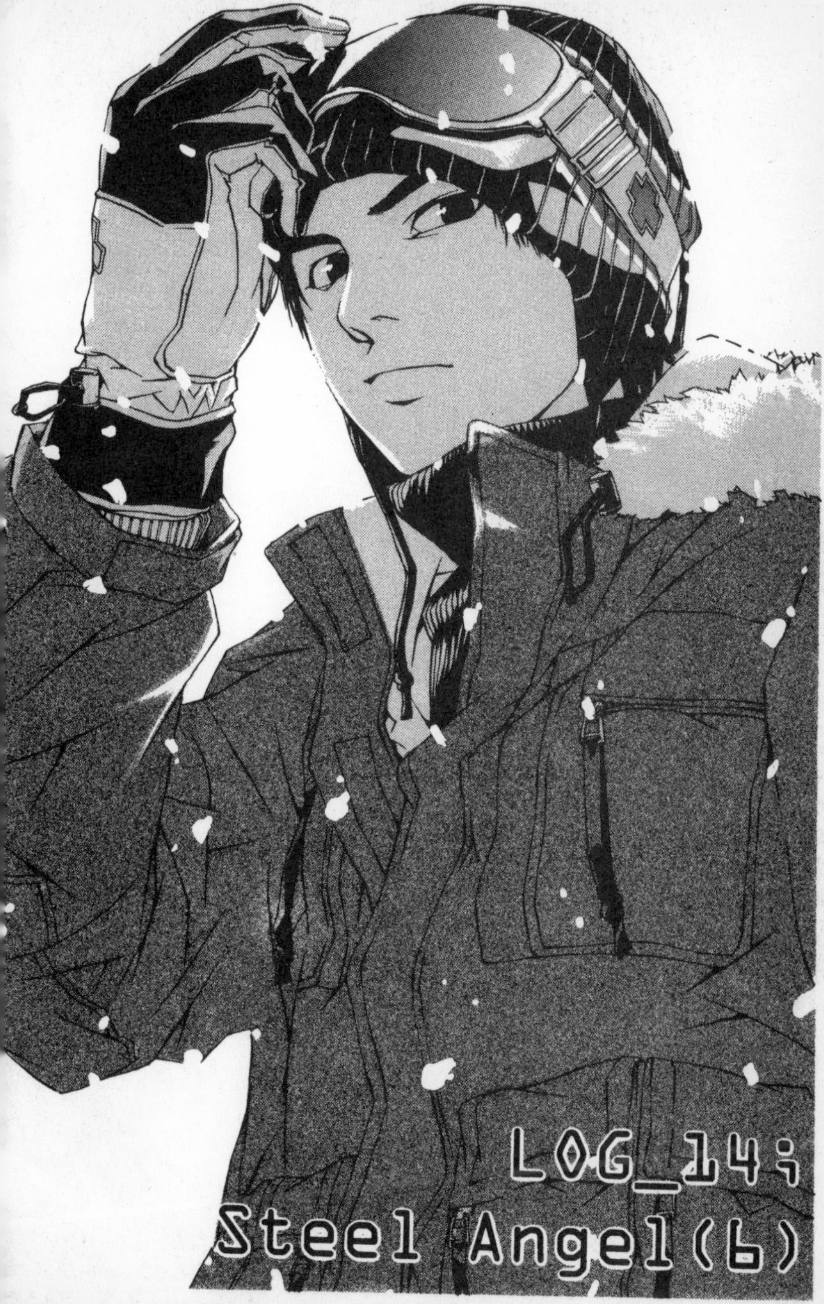
LOG_14;
Steel Angel(6)

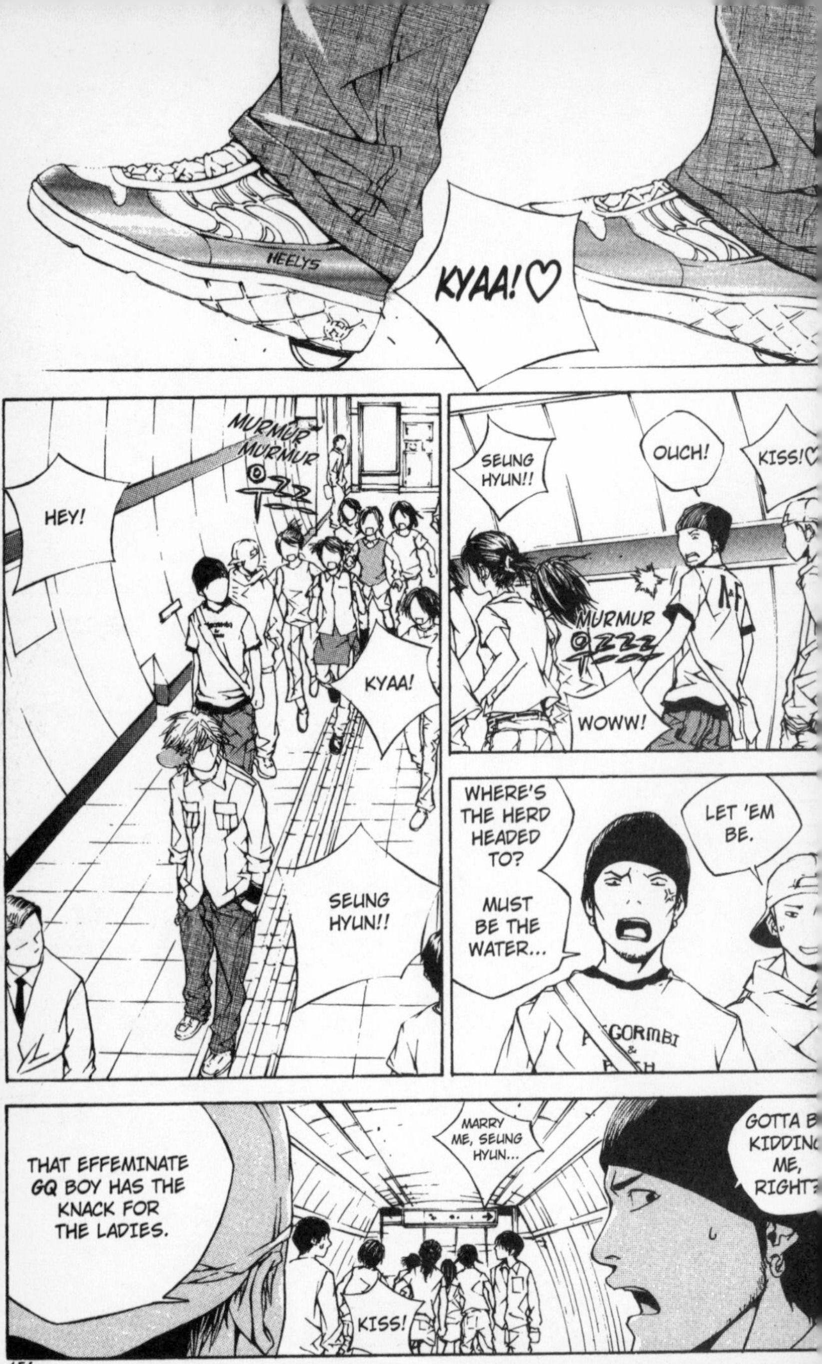
HEELYS
KYAA!♡
MURMUR MURMUR
HEY!
KYAA!
SEUNG HYUN!!
SEUNG HYUN!!
OUCH!
KISS!♡
MURMUR
WOWW!
WHERE'S THE HERD HEADED TO?
MUST BE THE WATER...
LET 'EM BE.
THAT EFFEMINATE GQ BOY HAS THE KNACK FOR THE LADIES.
MARRY ME, SEUNG HYUN...
KISS!
GOTTA B KIDDIN ME, RIGHT?

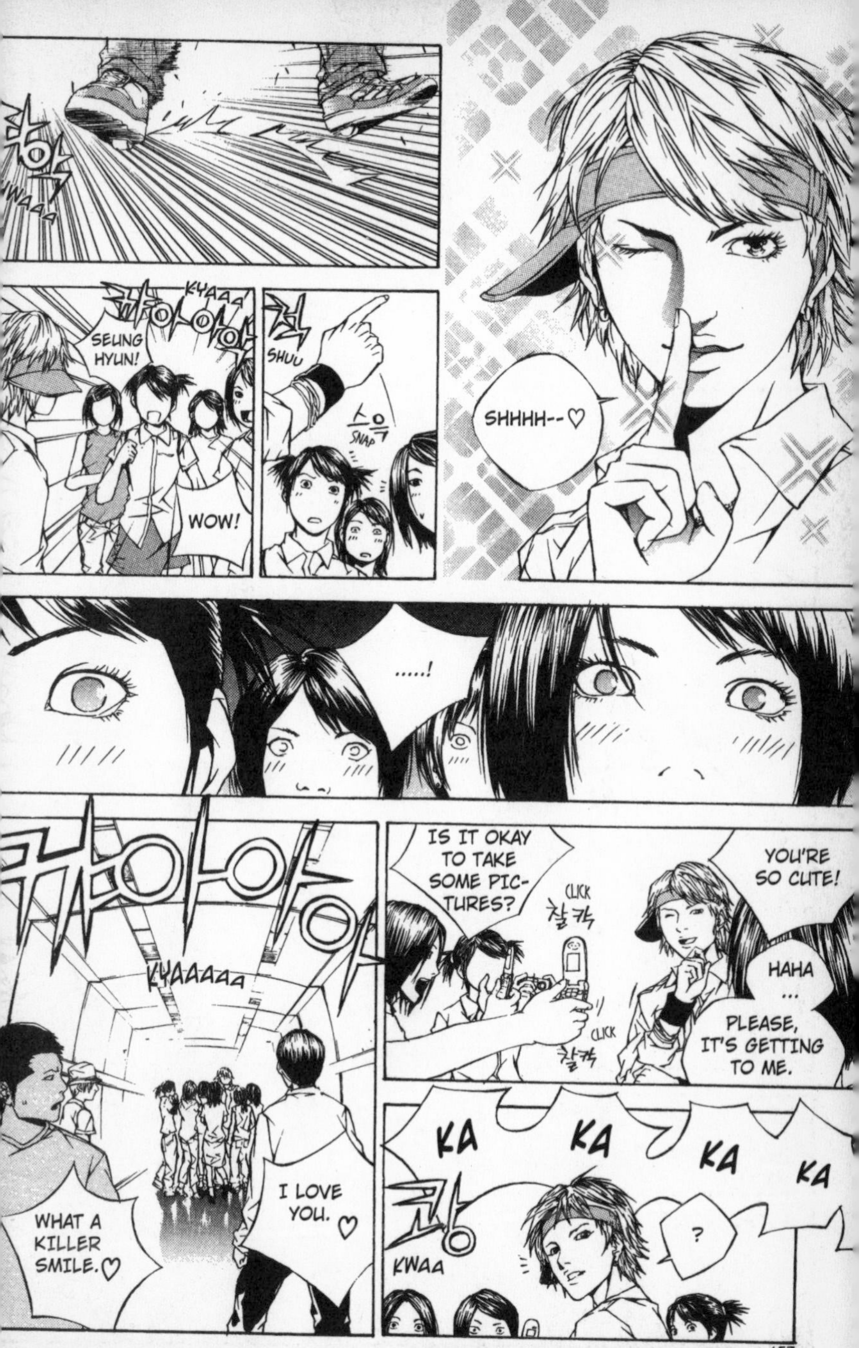

꺄아아아아악
KYAAAA
SEUNG HYUN!
WOW!
척
SHUU
스윽
SNAP
SHHHH--♡
.....!
꺄아아아아
KYAAAAA
WHAT A KILLER SMILE.♡
I LOVE YOU. ♡
IS IT OKAY TO TAKE SOME PIC-TURES?
CLICK
찰칵
CLICK
찰칵
YOU'RE SO CUTE!
HAHA ...
PLEASE, IT'S GETTING TO ME.
쾅
KWAA
KA KA KA KA
?

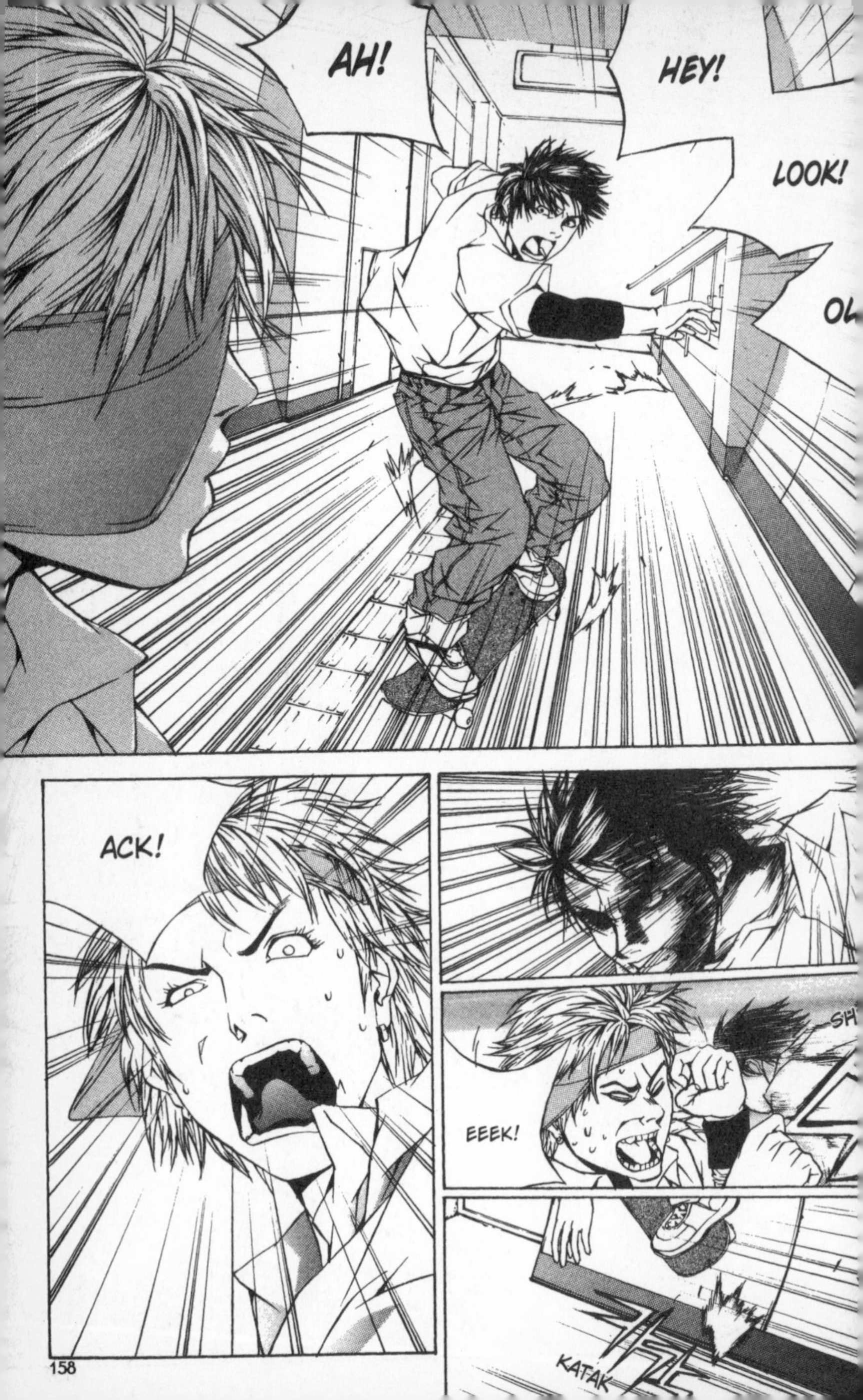
AH!
HEY!
LOOK!
ACK!
EEEK!
KATAK

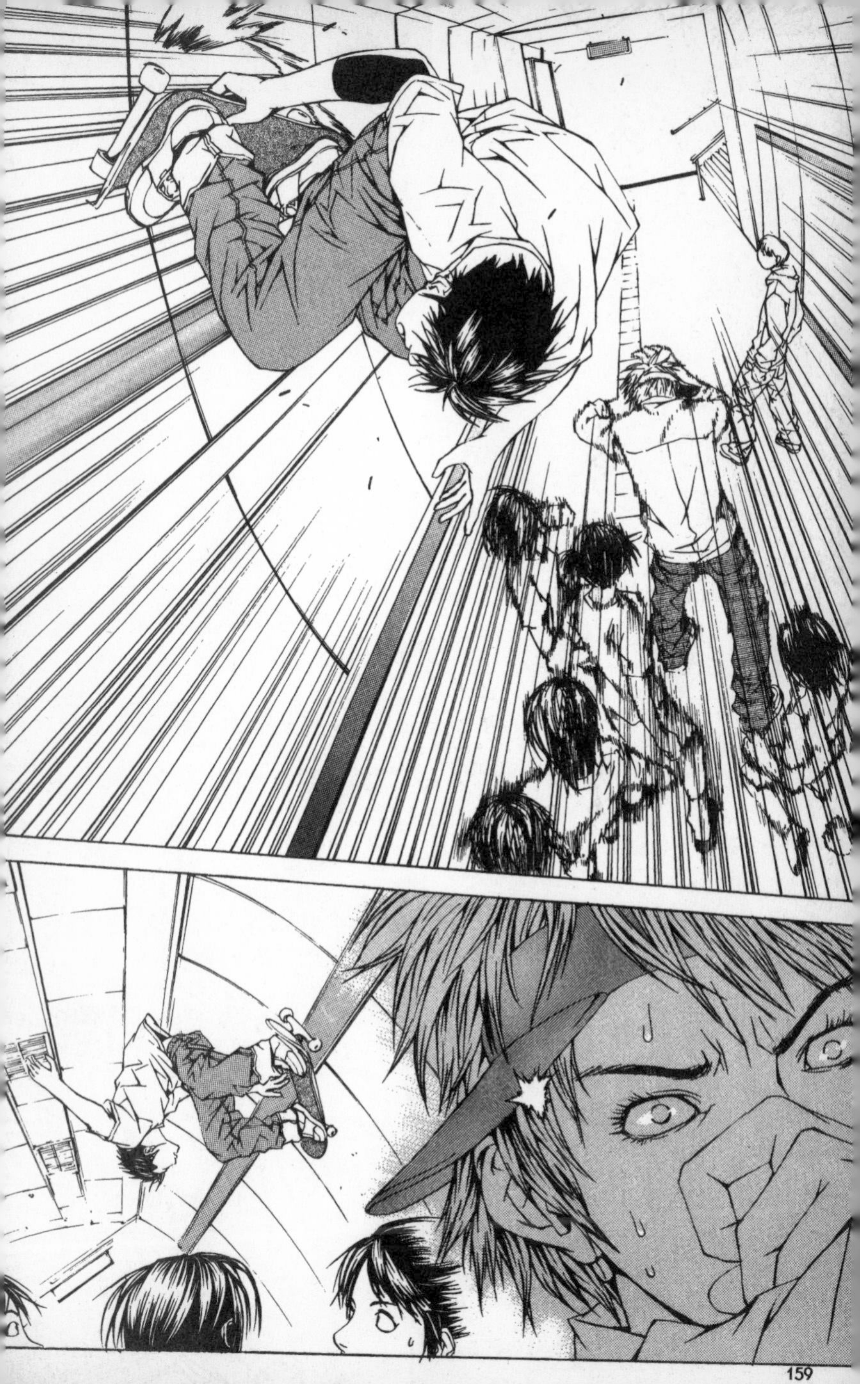

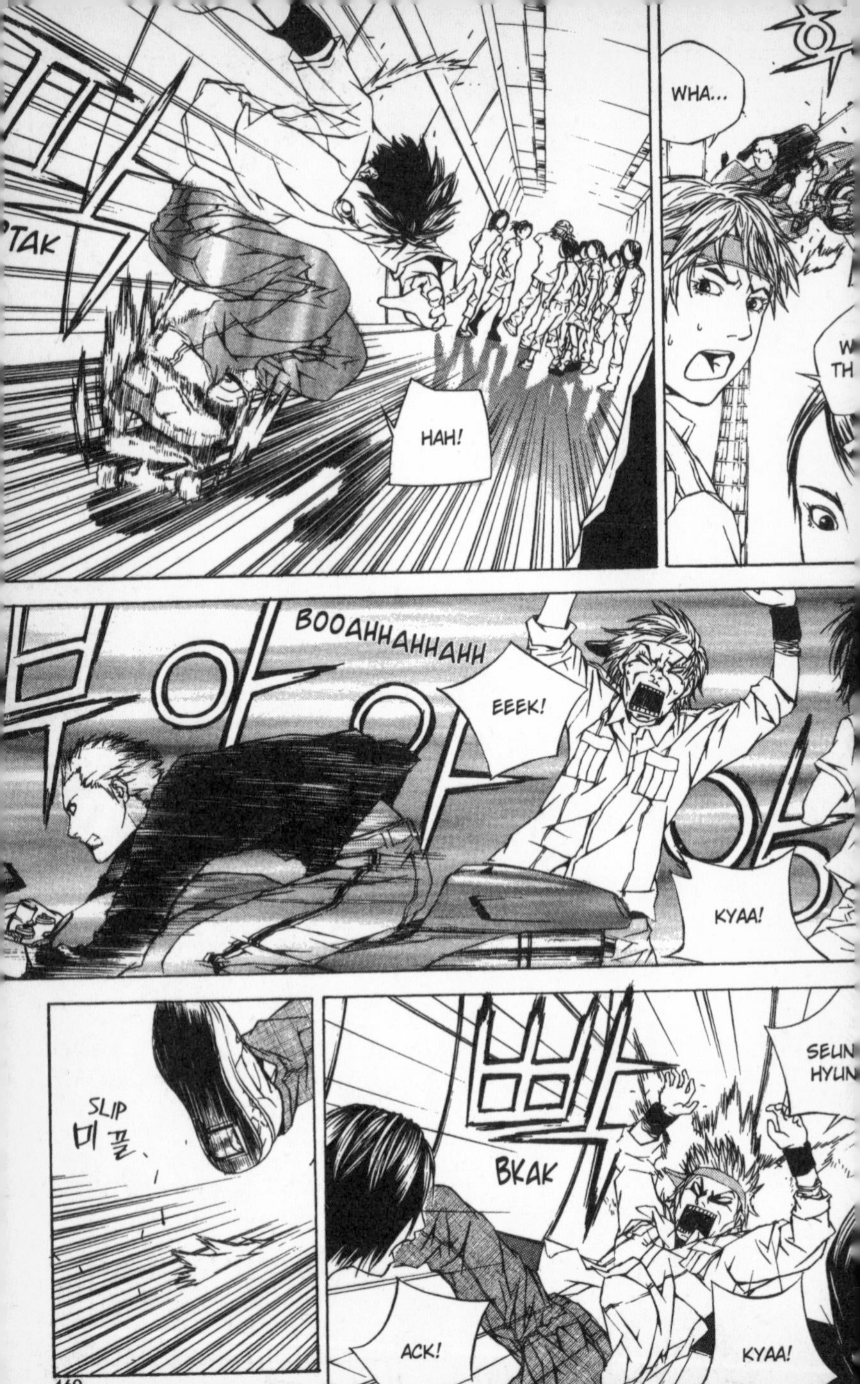
PTAK
HAH!
WHA...
BOOAHHAHHAHH
EEEK!
KYAA!
SLIP
미끌
BKAK
ACK!
KYAA!

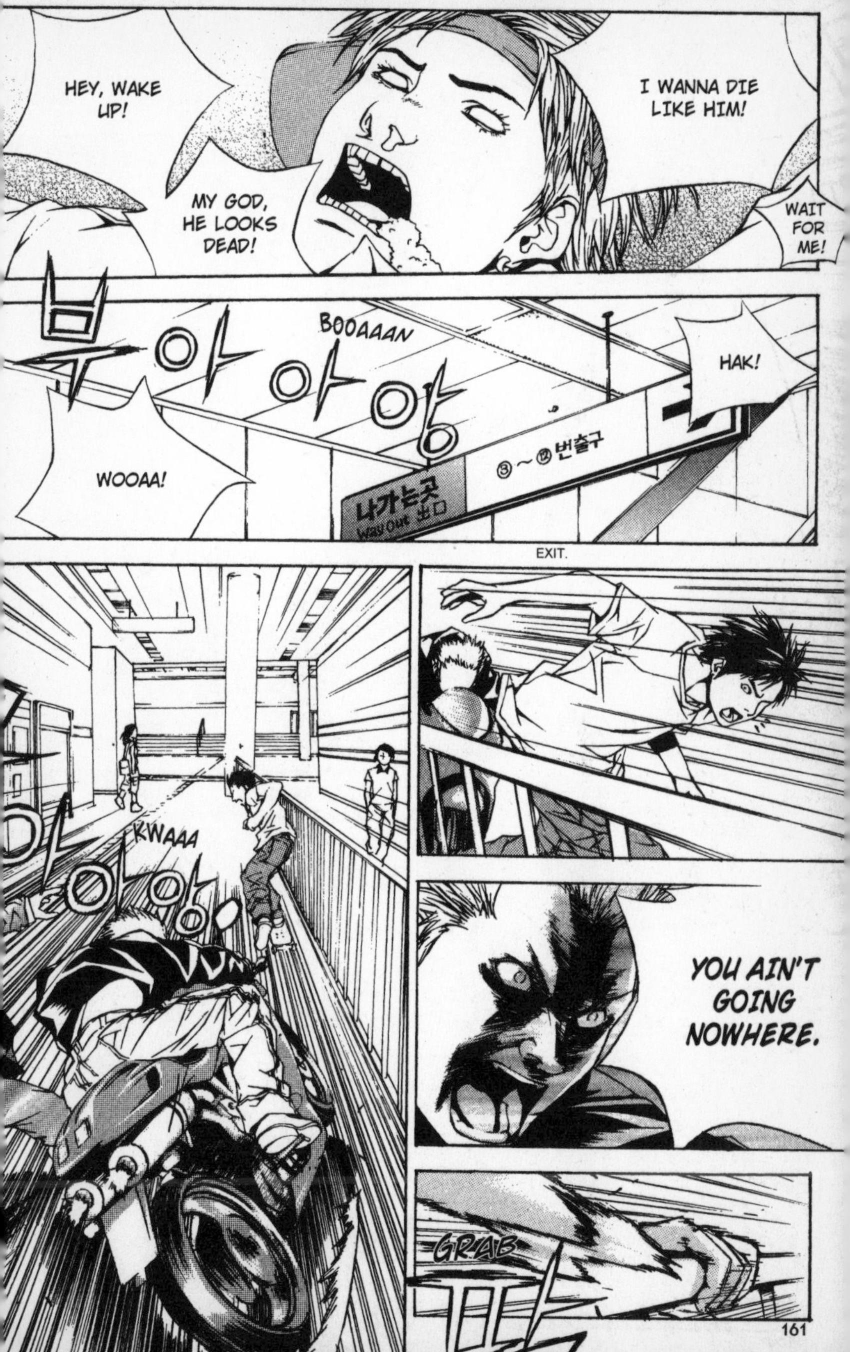
HEY, WAKE UP!
MY GOD, HE LOOKS DEAD!
I WANNA DIE LIKE HIM!
WAIT FOR ME!
부아아앙
BOOAAAN
WOOAA!
HAK!
나가는곳 出口 Way Out
③~⑫ 번출구
EXIT.
KWAAA
YOU AIN'T GOING NOWHERE.
GRAB

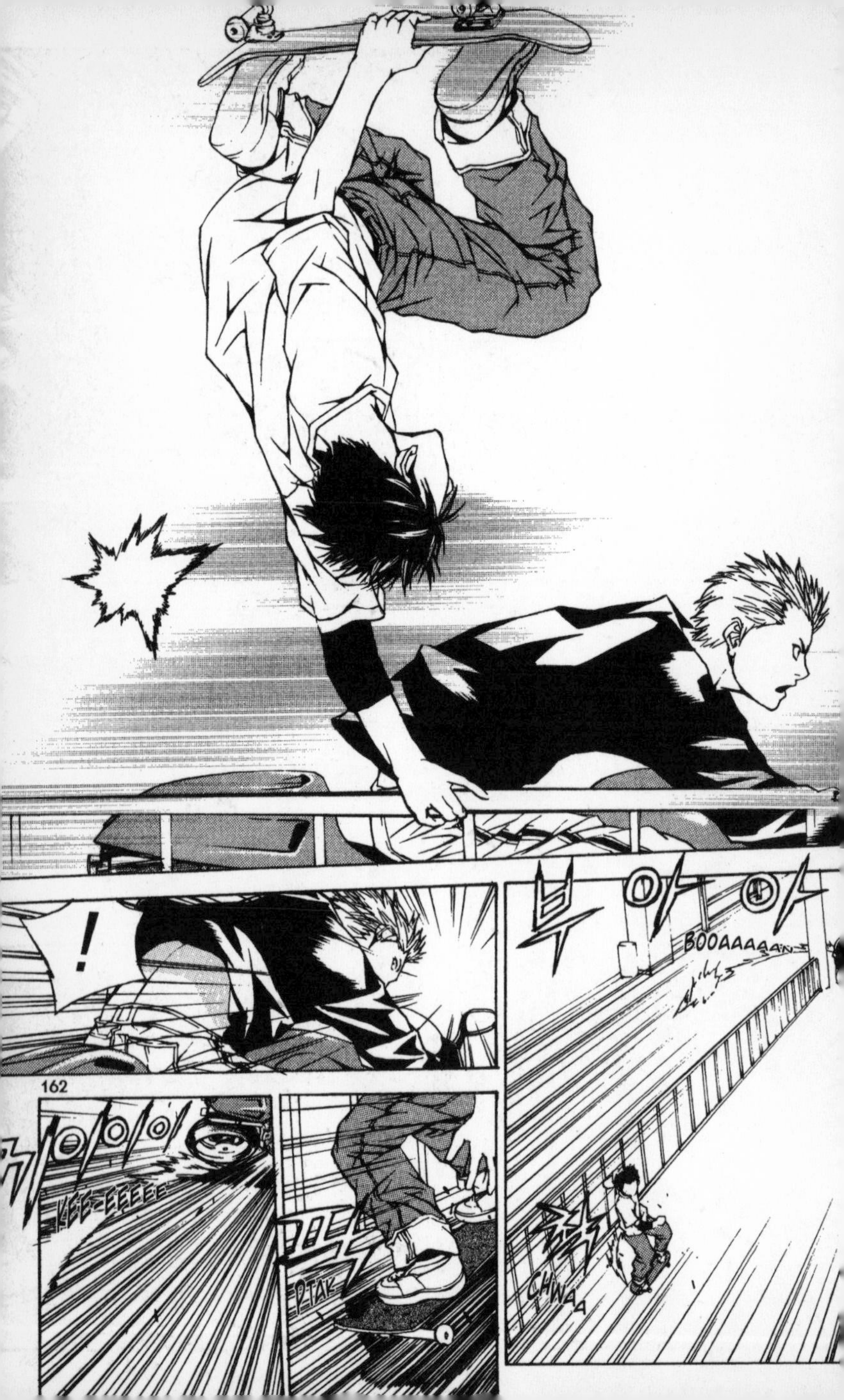
!
KEE-EEEEE
TAK
BOOAAAAAAN
CHWAA

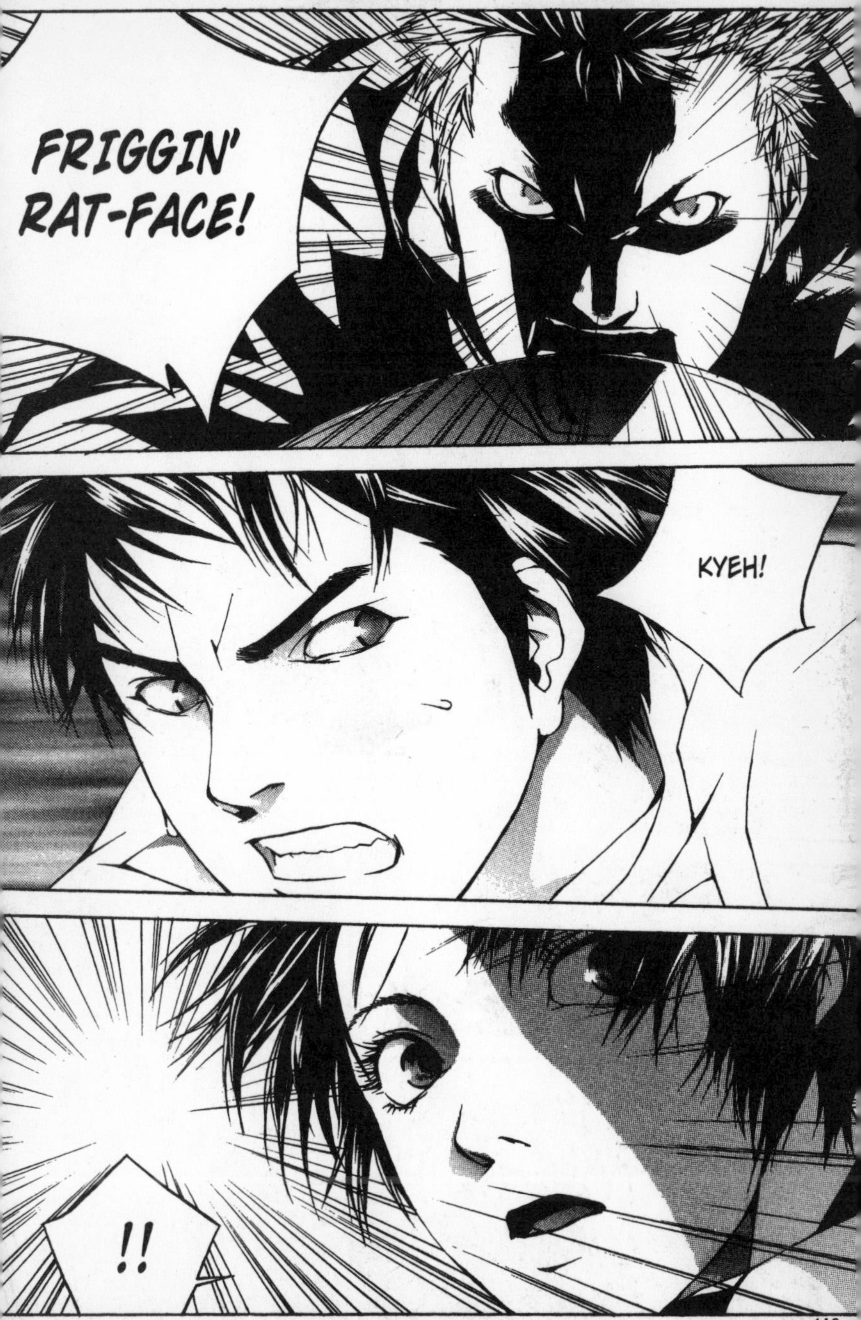
FRIGGIN' RAT-FACE!
KYEH!
!!

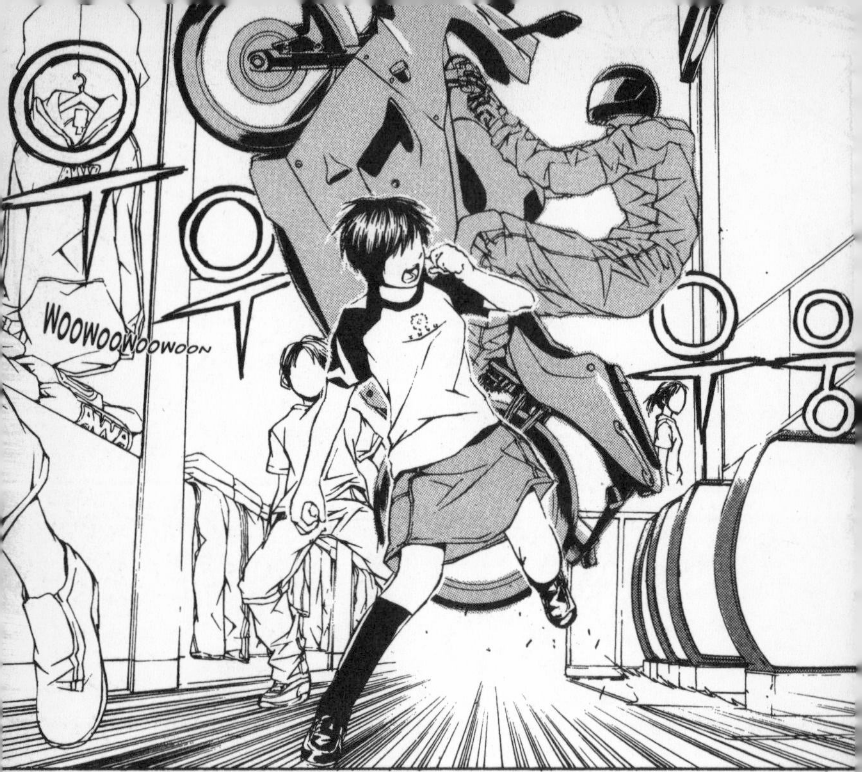
WOOWOOWOOWOON

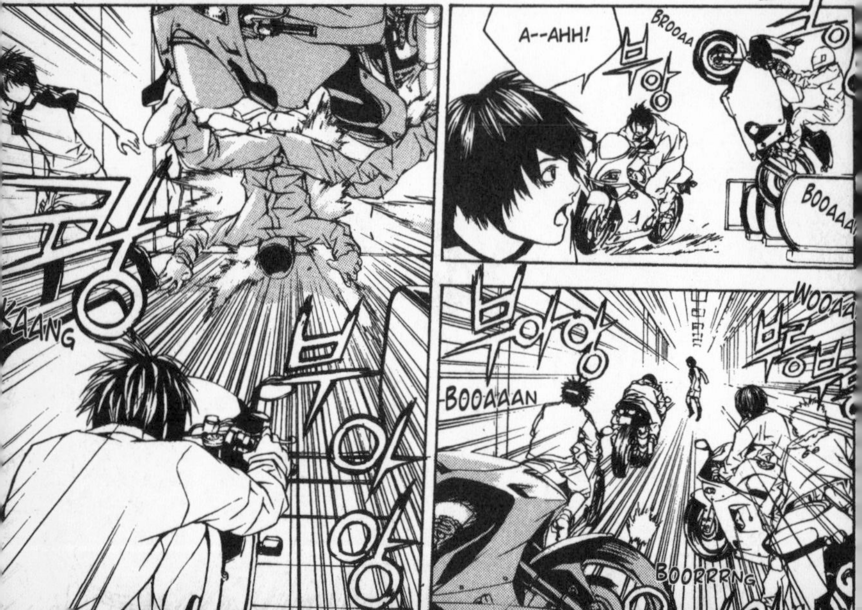
KAANG
A--AHH!
BROOAA
BOOAAA
WOOAA
BOOAAAN
BOORRRNG

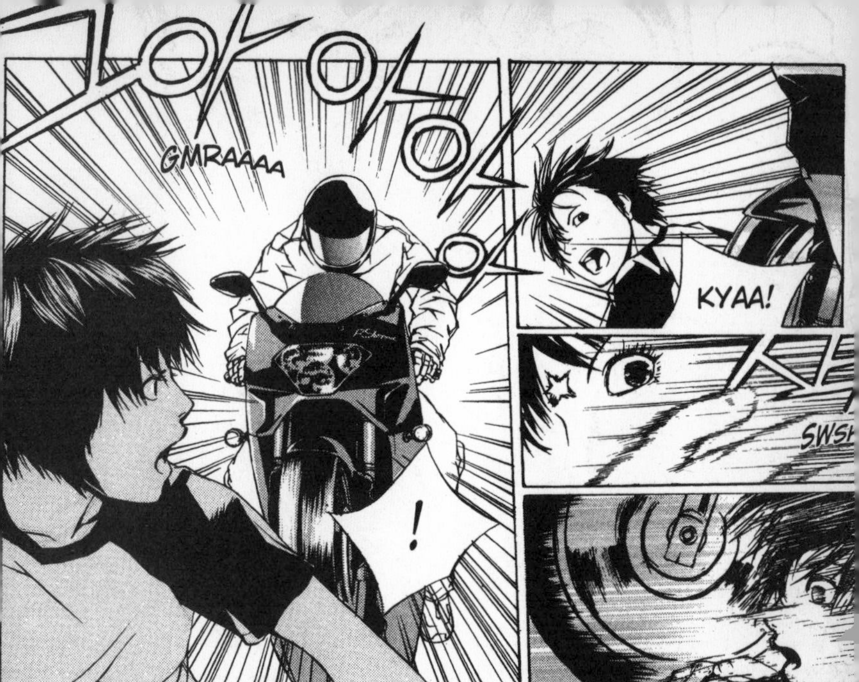
GMRAAAA
!
KYAA!
SWS

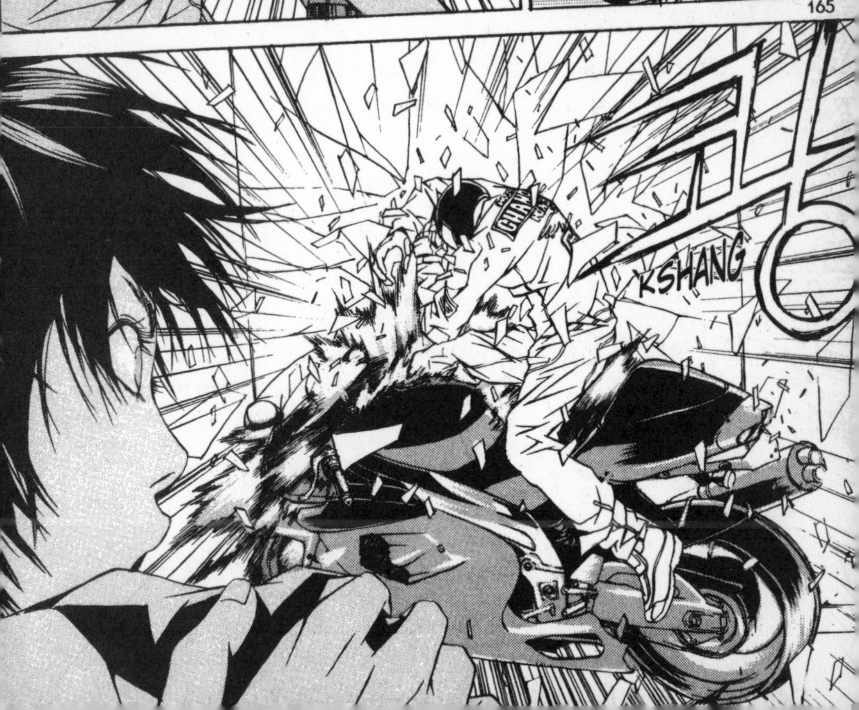
KSHANG

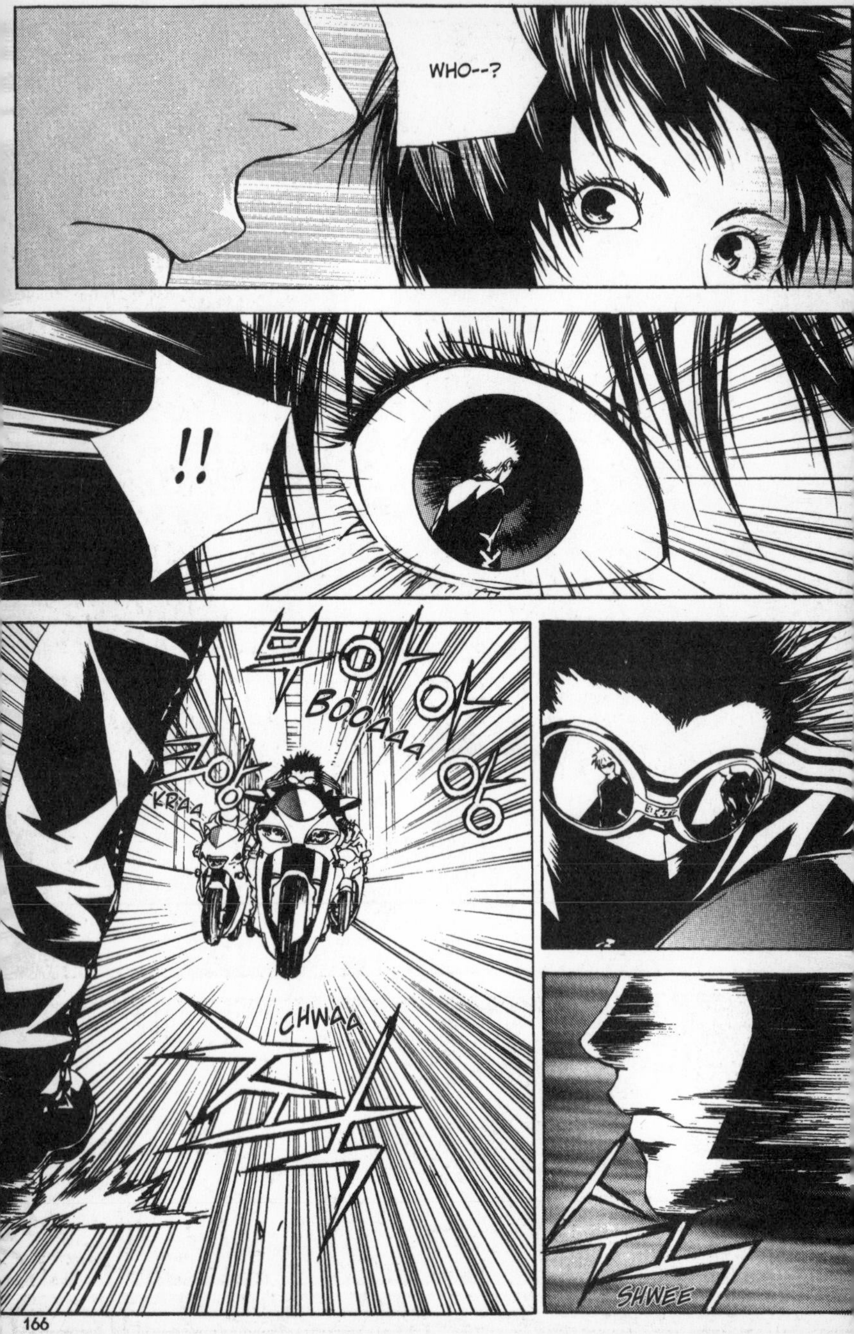
WHO--?
!!
BOOAAA
KRAA
CHWAA
SHWEE

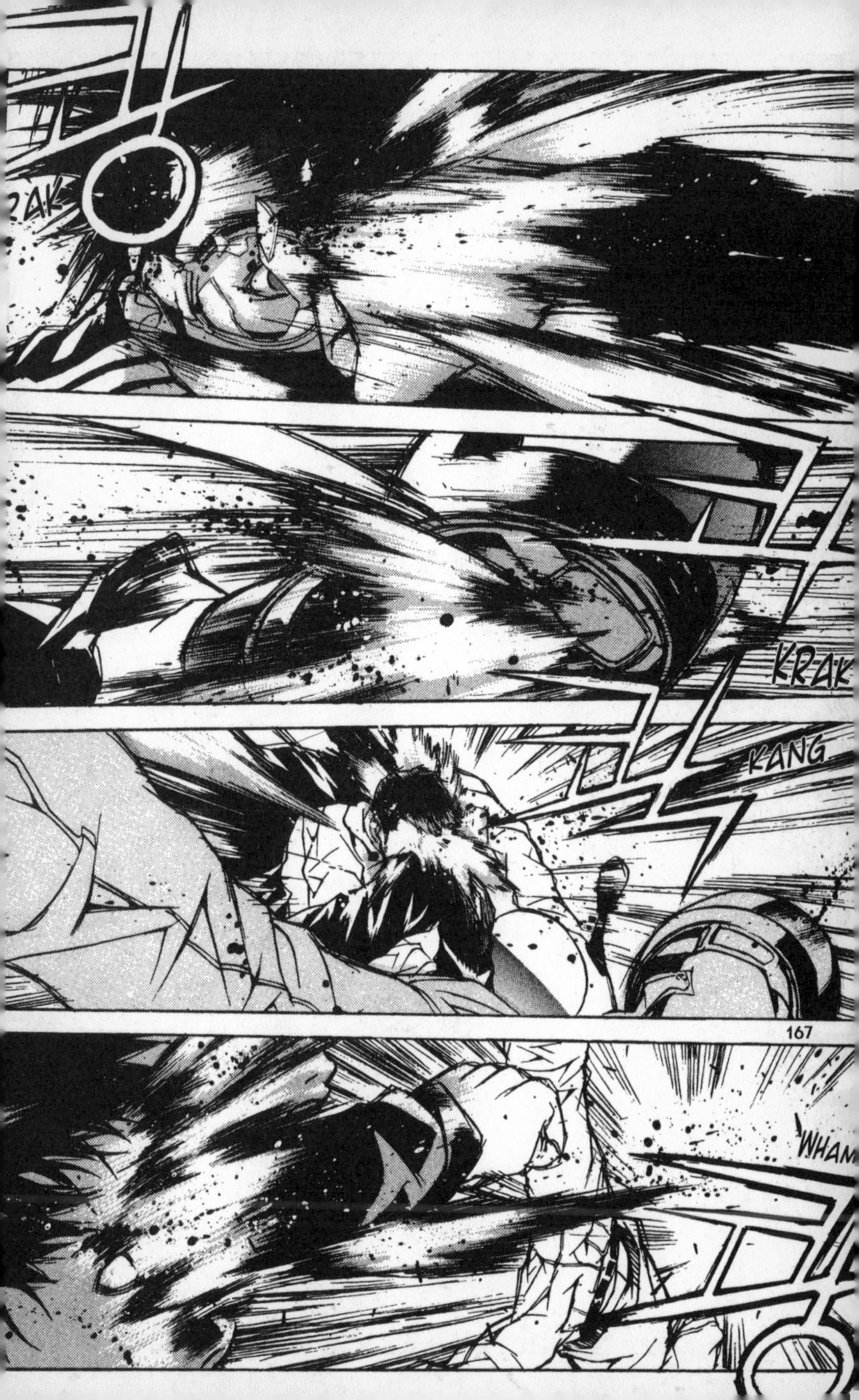
KRAK
KANG
WHAM

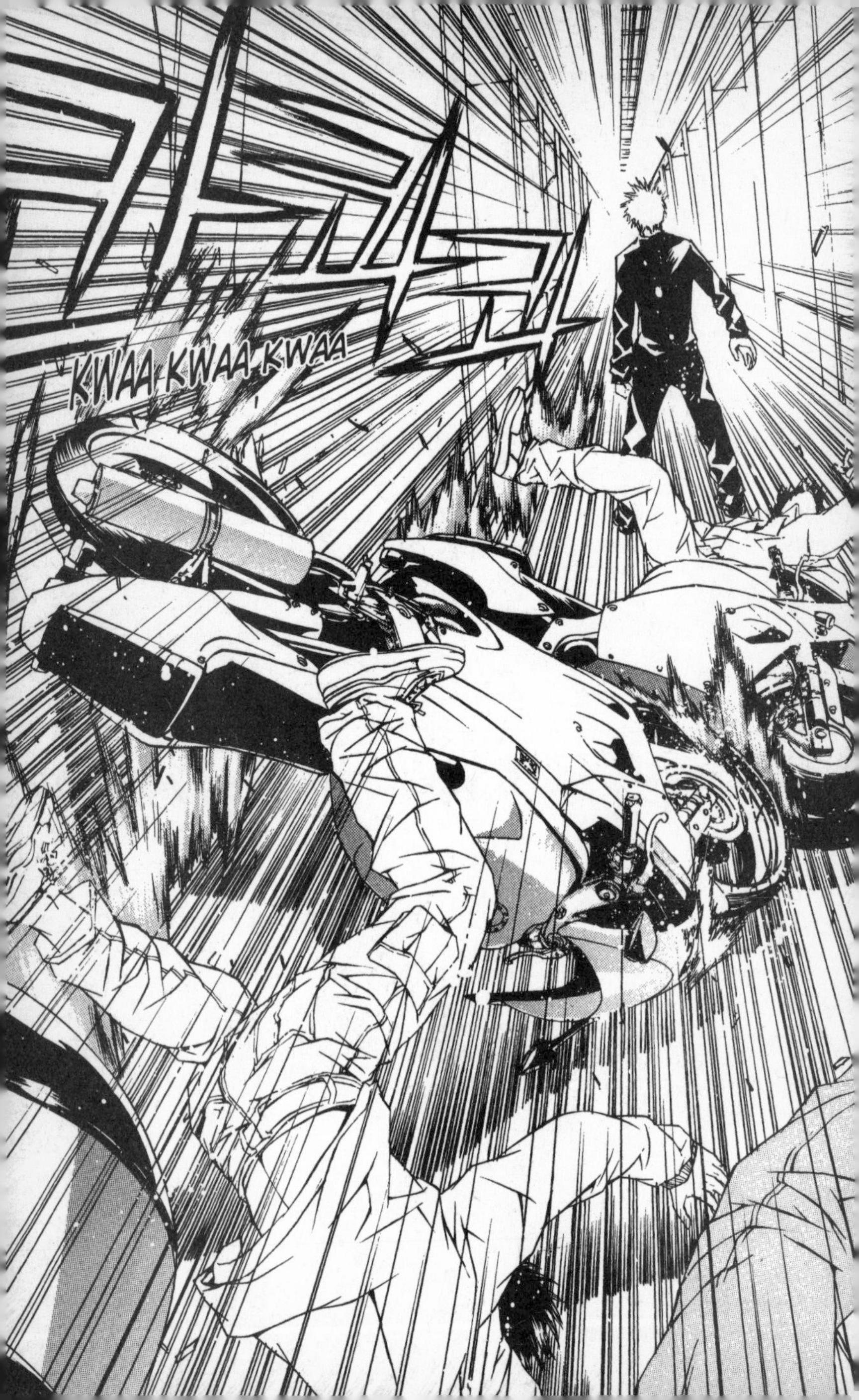
KWAA KWAA KWAA

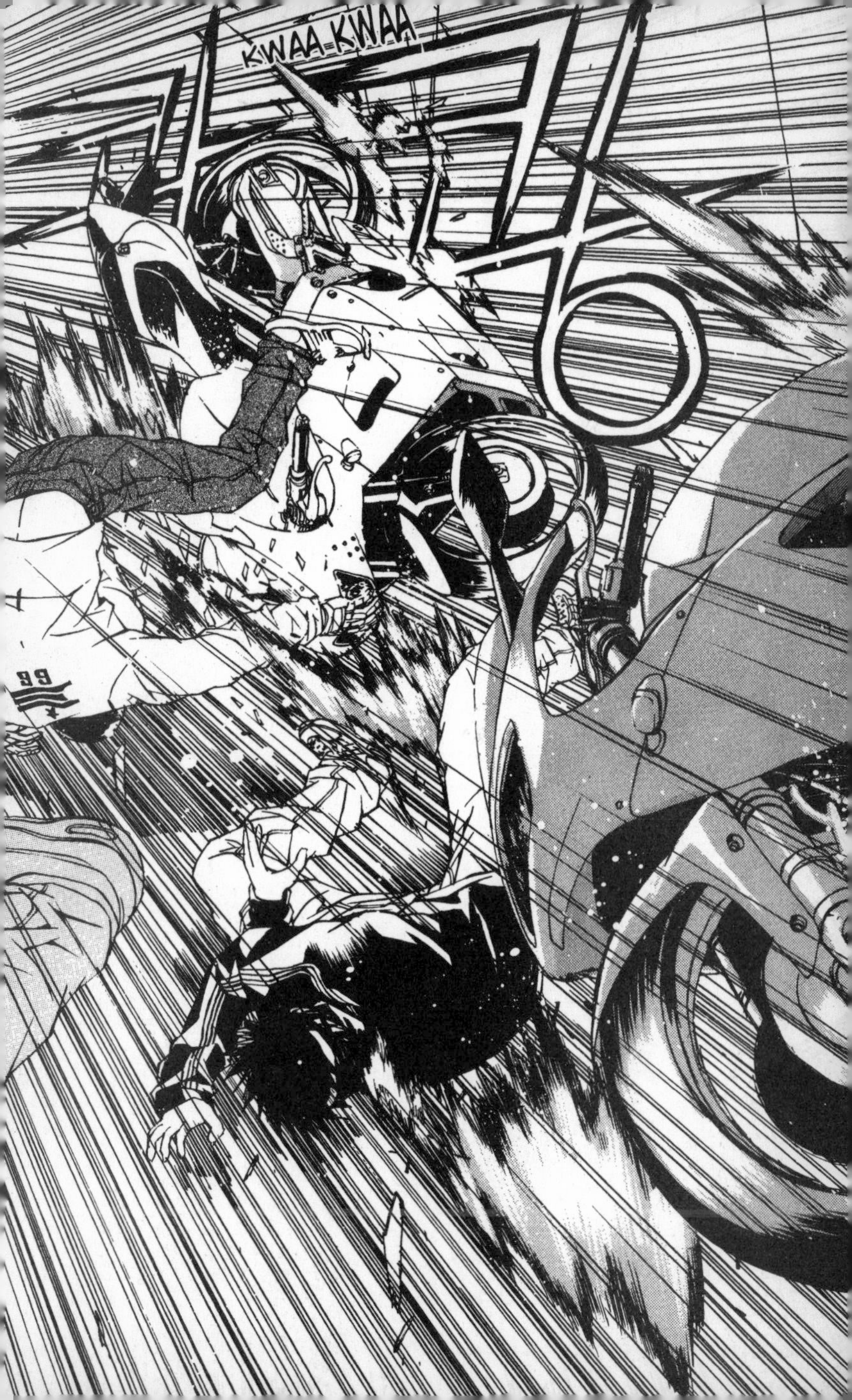
KWAA KWAA

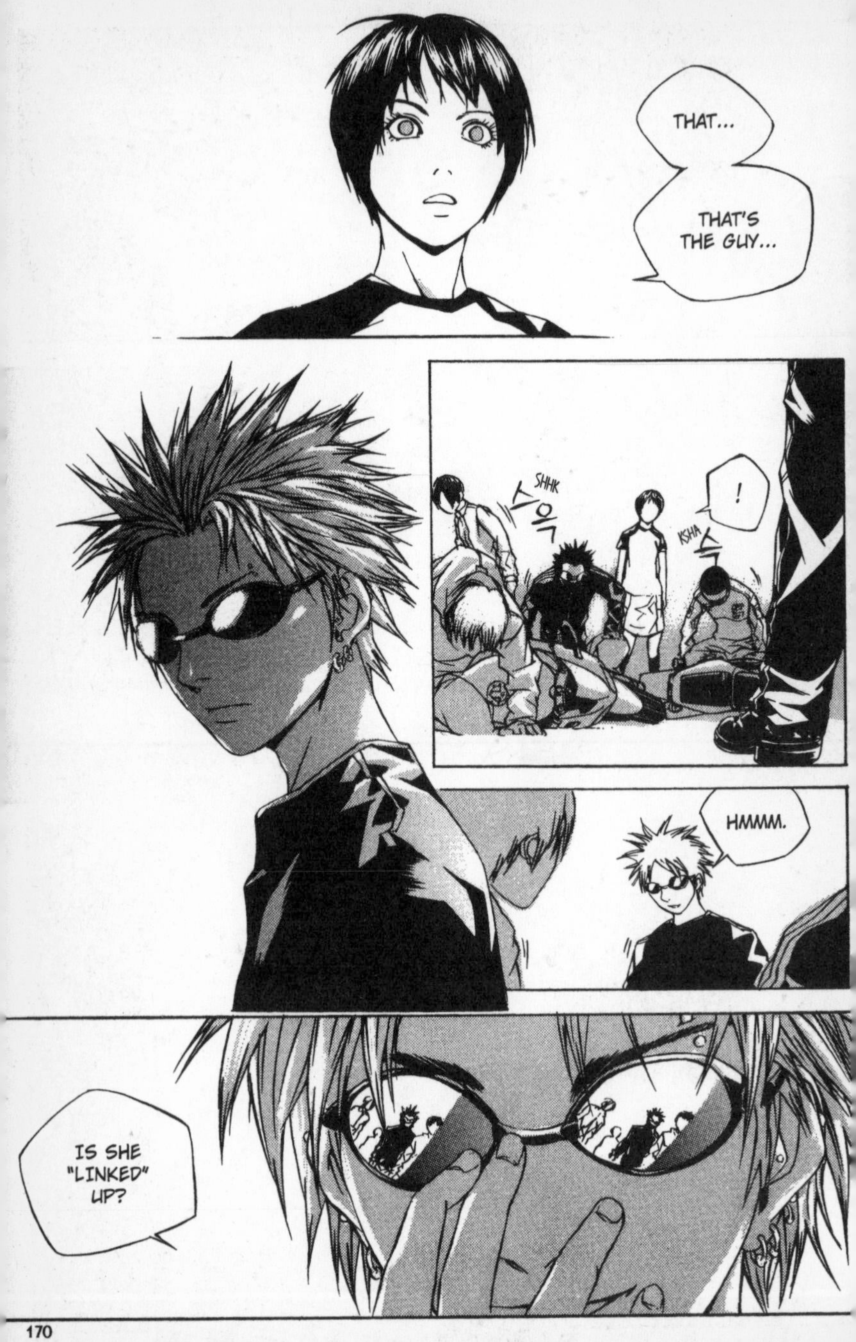
THAT...
THAT'S THE GUY...
SHHK
!
KSHA
HMMM.
IS SHE "LINKED" UP?

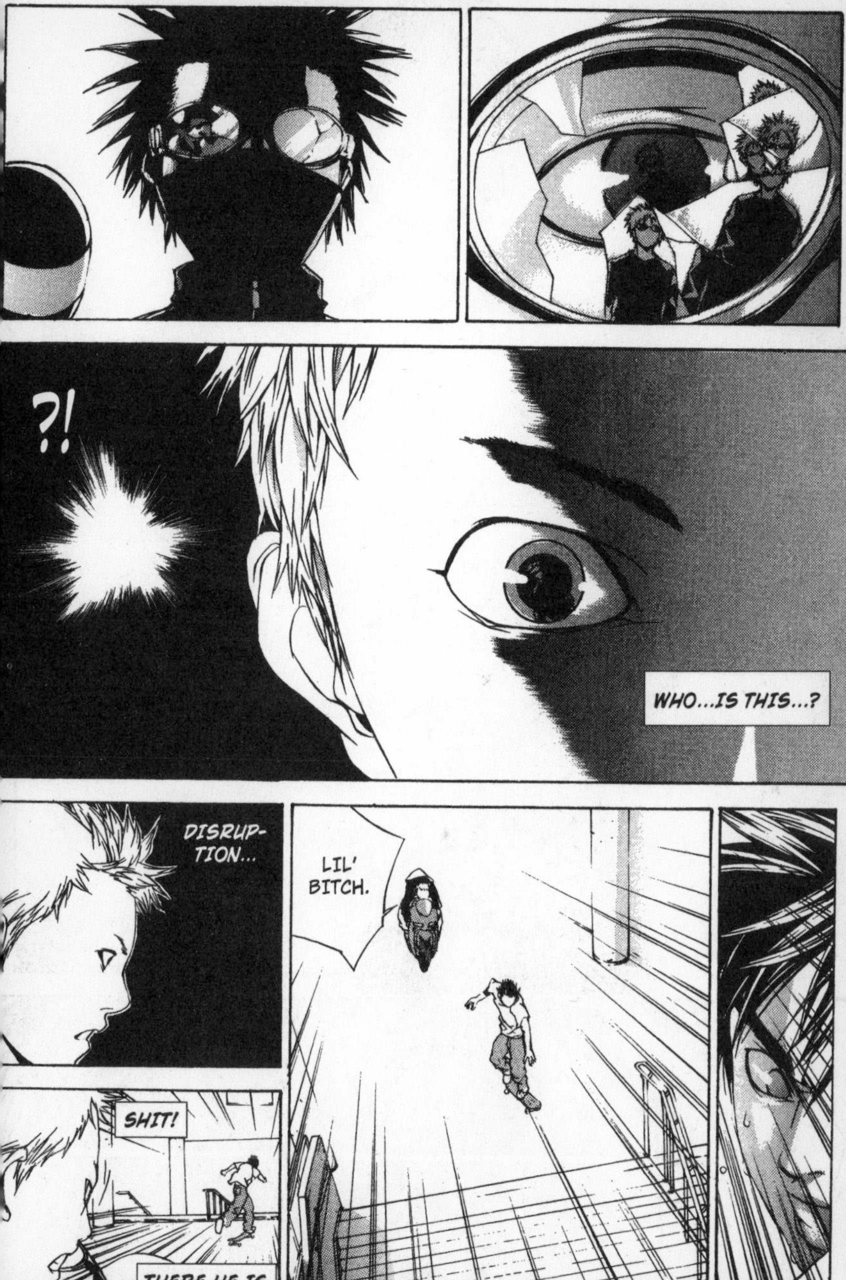
?!
WHO...IS THIS...?
DISRUP-TION...
SHIT!
THERE HE IS.
LIL' BITCH.

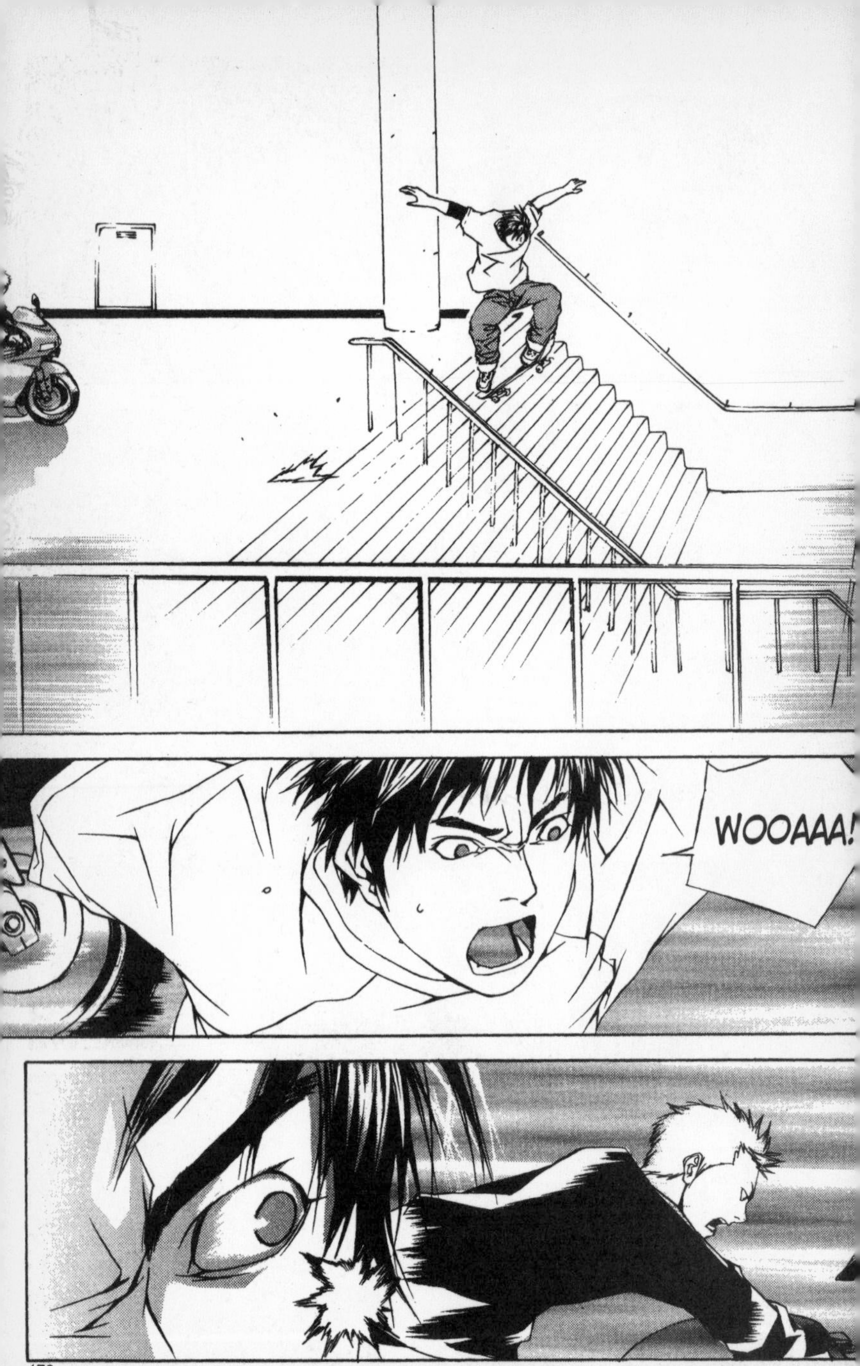
WOOAAA!

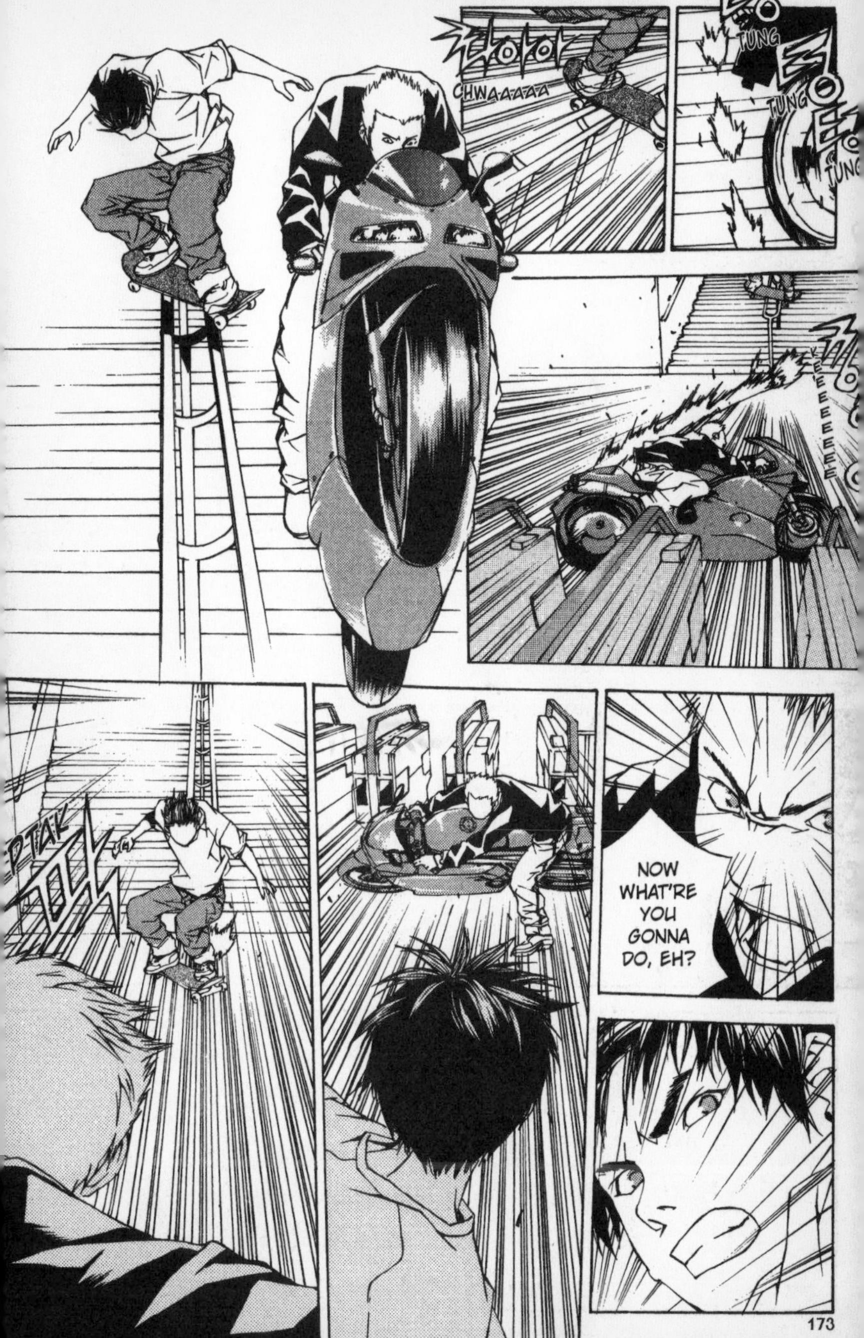
CHWAAAAAA
TUNG
TUNG
TUNG
KEEEEEEEEE
PTAK
NOW WHAT'RE YOU GONNA DO, EH?

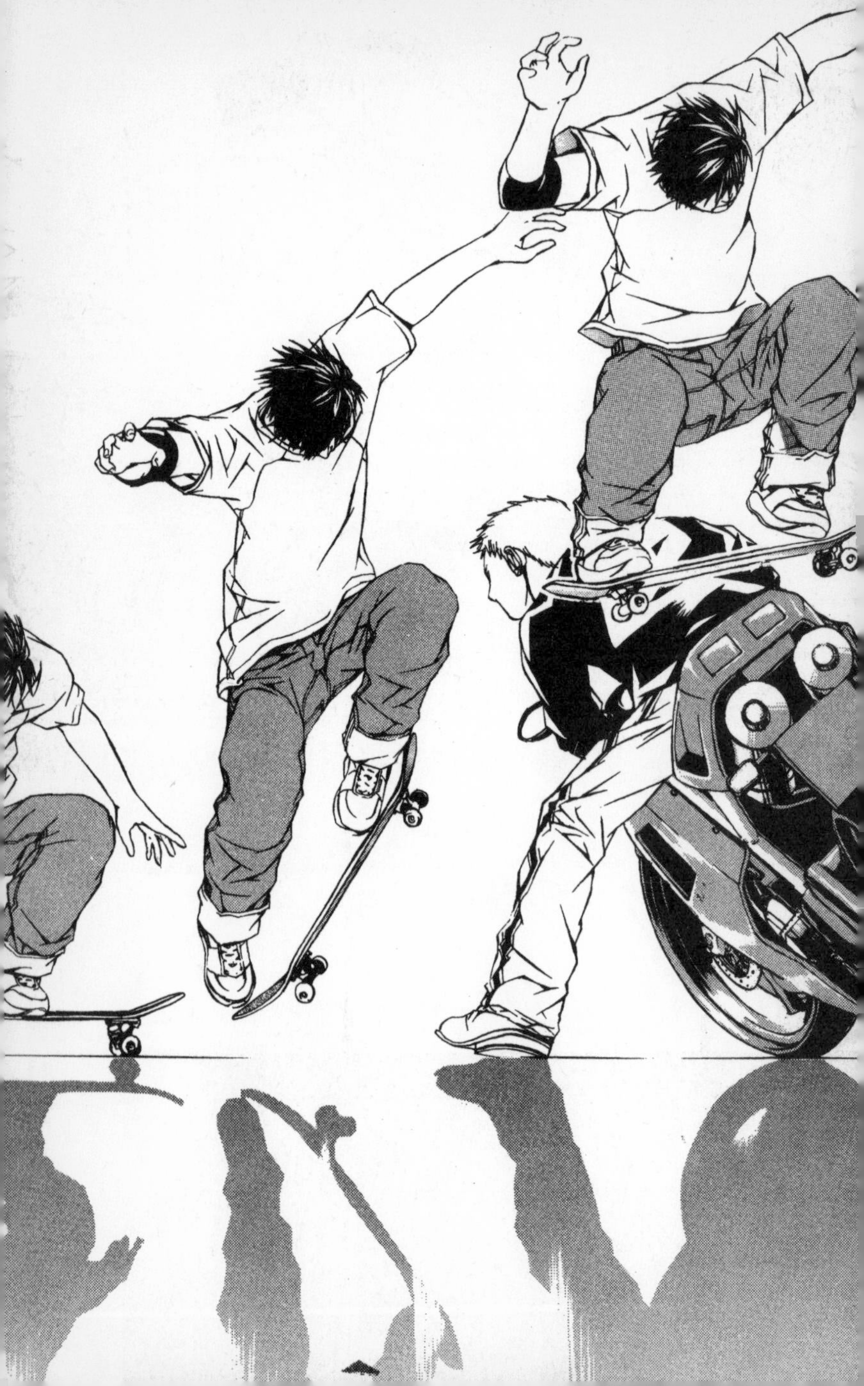

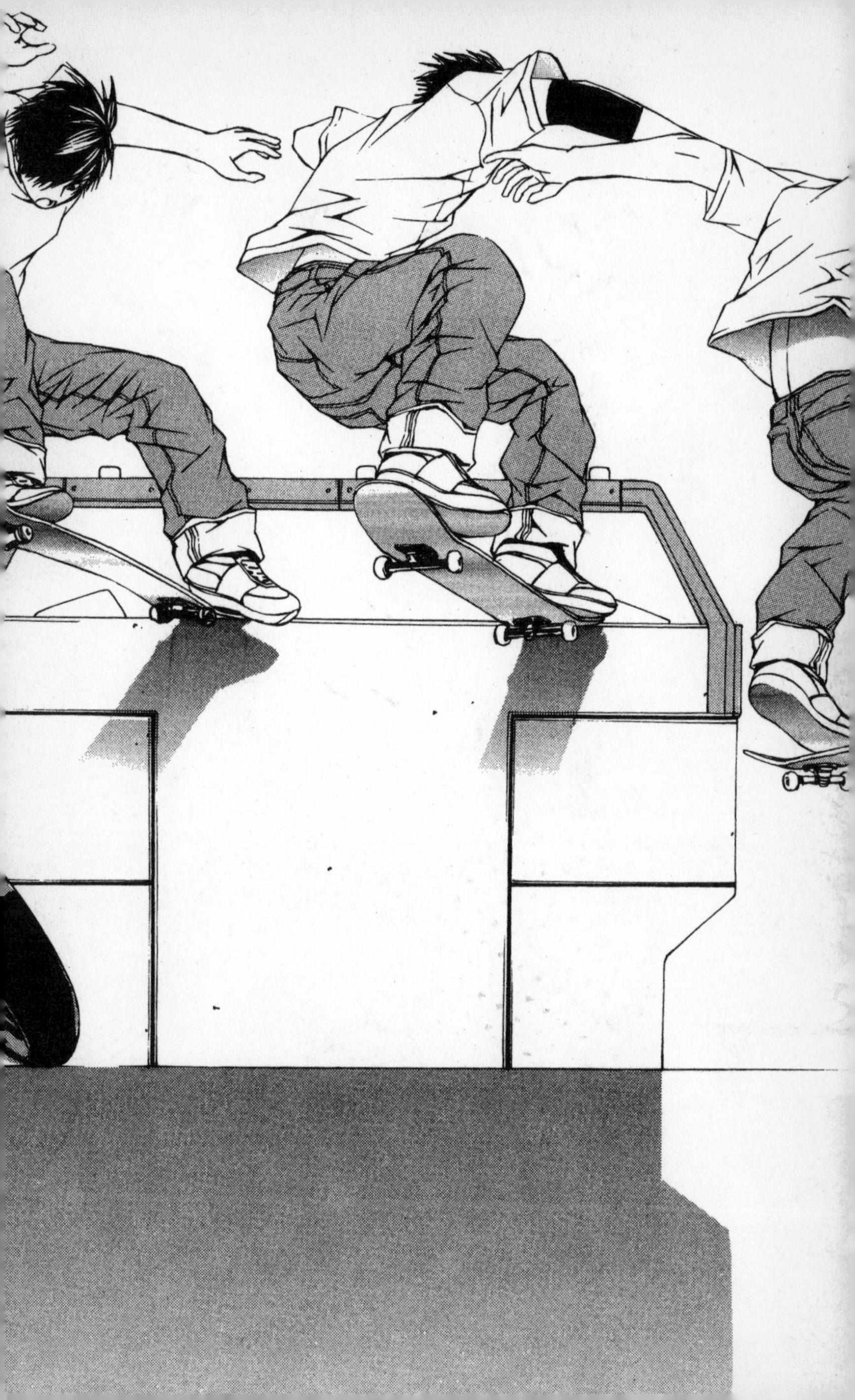

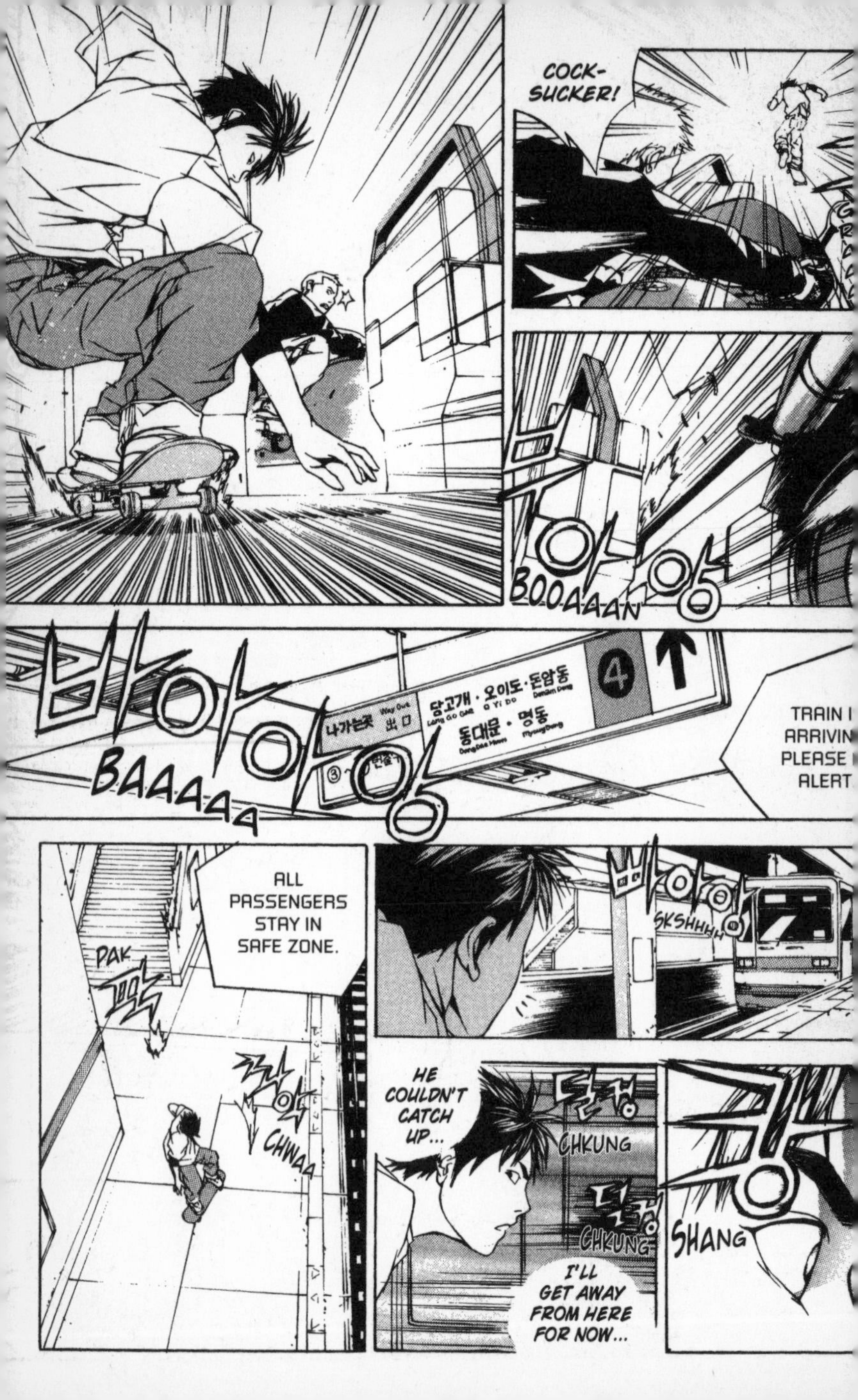
COCK-SUCKER!
BOOAAAAN
바아아앙
BAAAAAA
나가는곳 Way Out 出口
담고개 · 오이도 · 돈암동
동대문 · 명동
4
TRAIN I
ARRIVIN
PLEASE
ALERT
ALL PASSENGERS STAY IN SAFE ZONE.
PAK
CHWAA
SKSHHHH
HE COULDN'T CATCH UP...
CHKUNG
CHKUNG
I'LL GET AWAY FROM HERE FOR NOW...
SHANG

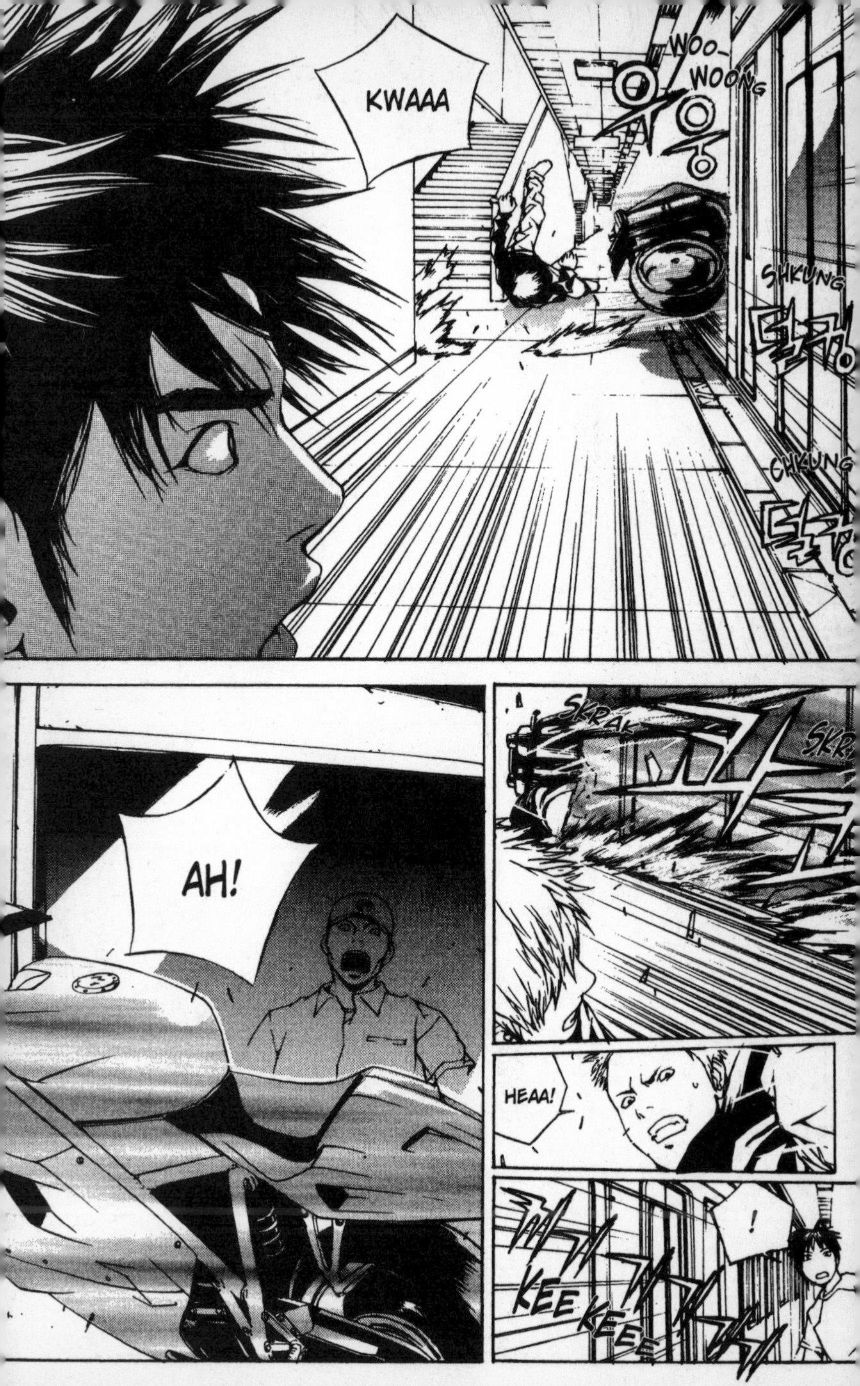

KWAAA
WOO-
WOONG
SHKUNG
CHKUNG
AH!
SKRAK
SKRA
HEAA!
!
KEE
KEEE

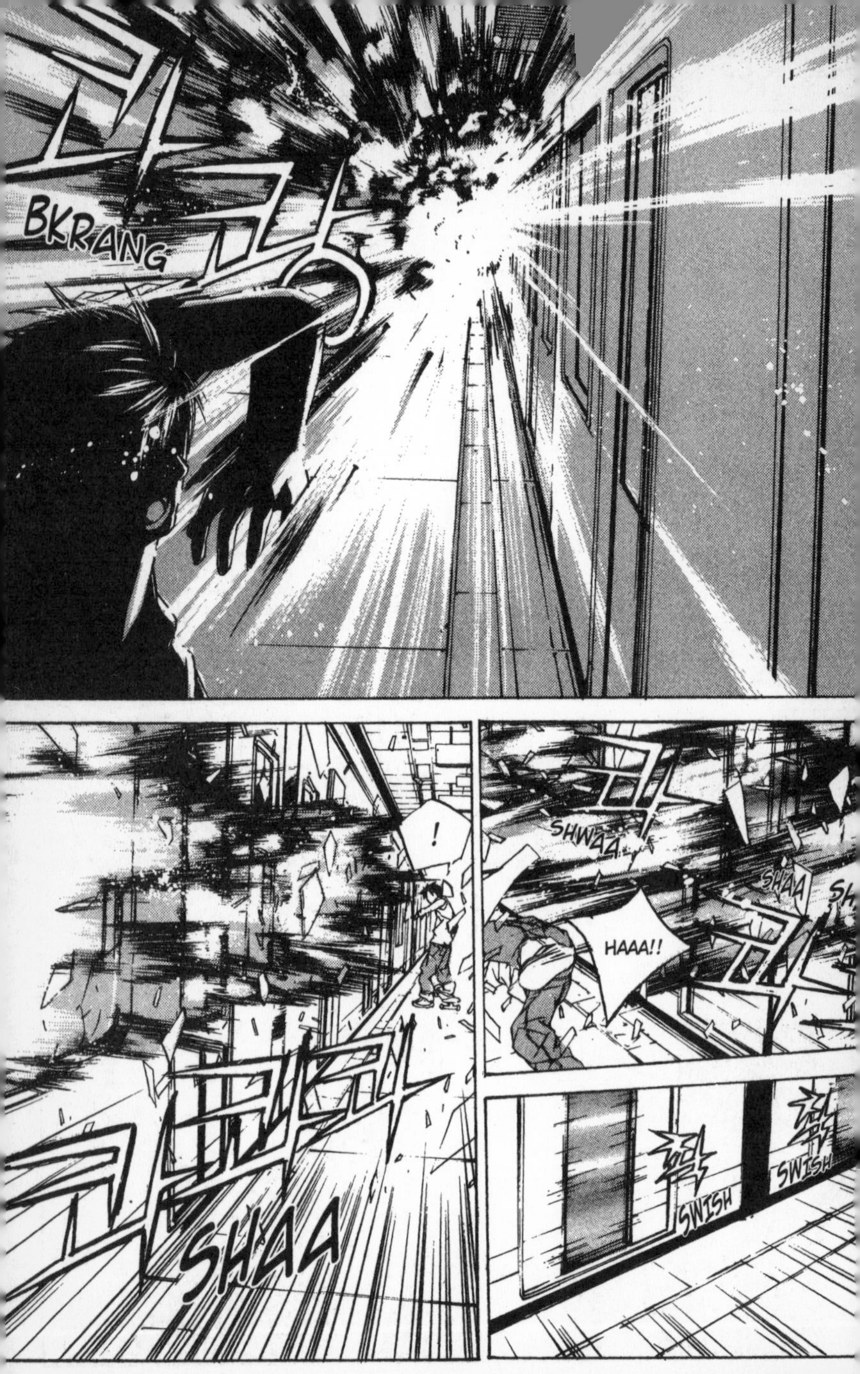
BKRANG
!
SHAA
SHWAA
SHAA
HAAA!!
SWISH
SWISH

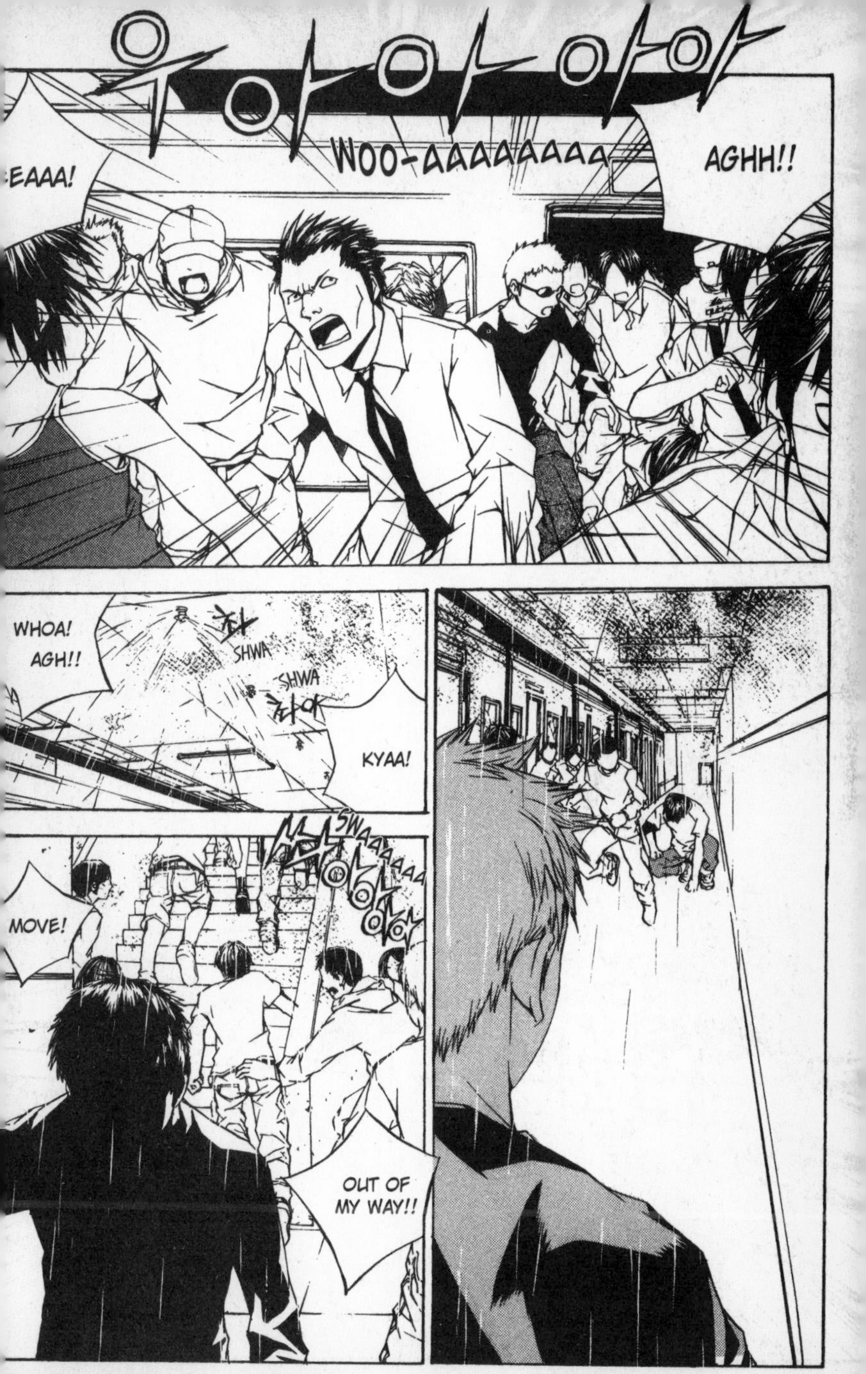
EAAA!
WOO-AAAAAAAA
AGHH!!
WHOA! AGH!!
SHWA
SHWA
KYAA!
MOVE!
SWAAAAAAA
OUT OF MY WAY!!

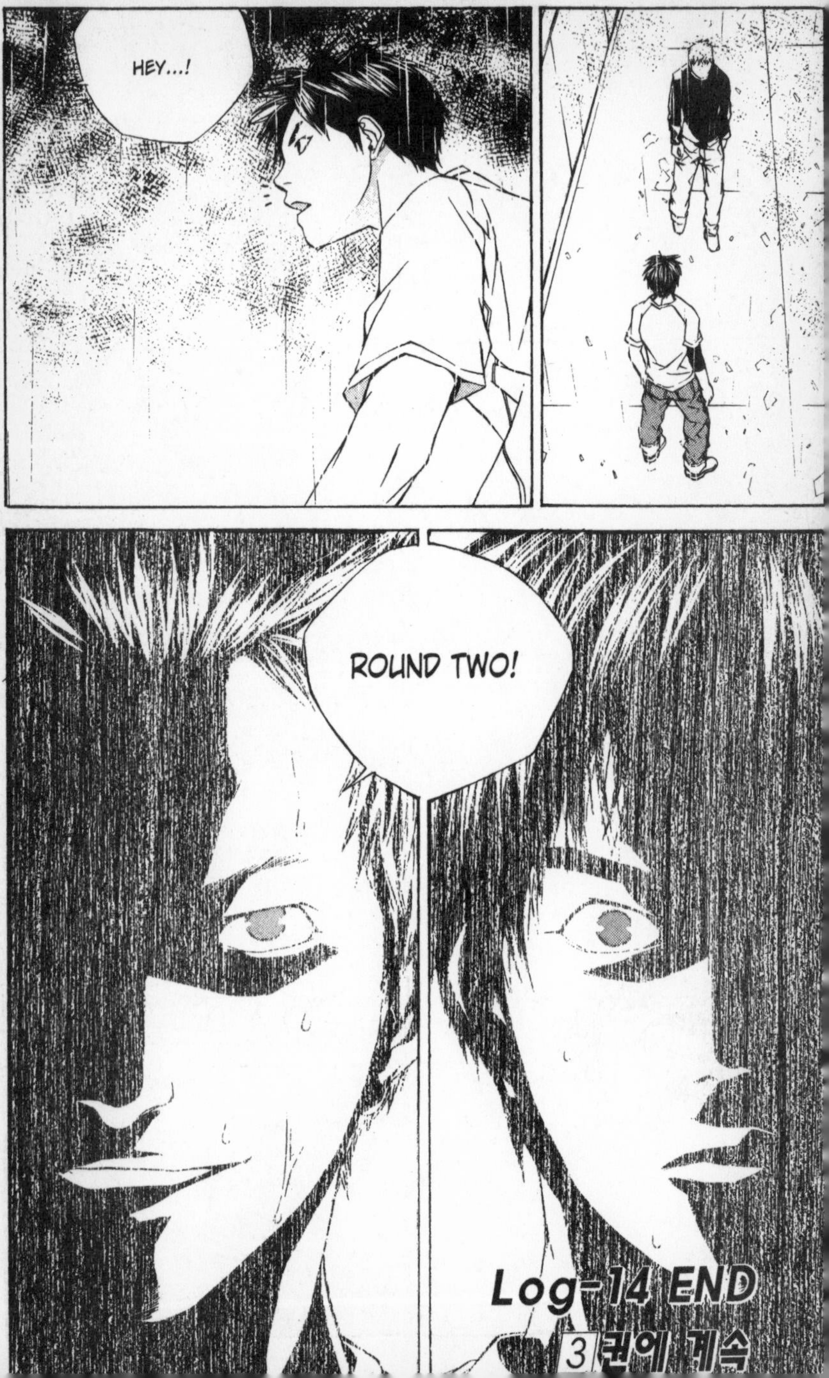
HEY...!
ROUND TWO!
Log-14 END
3권에 계속

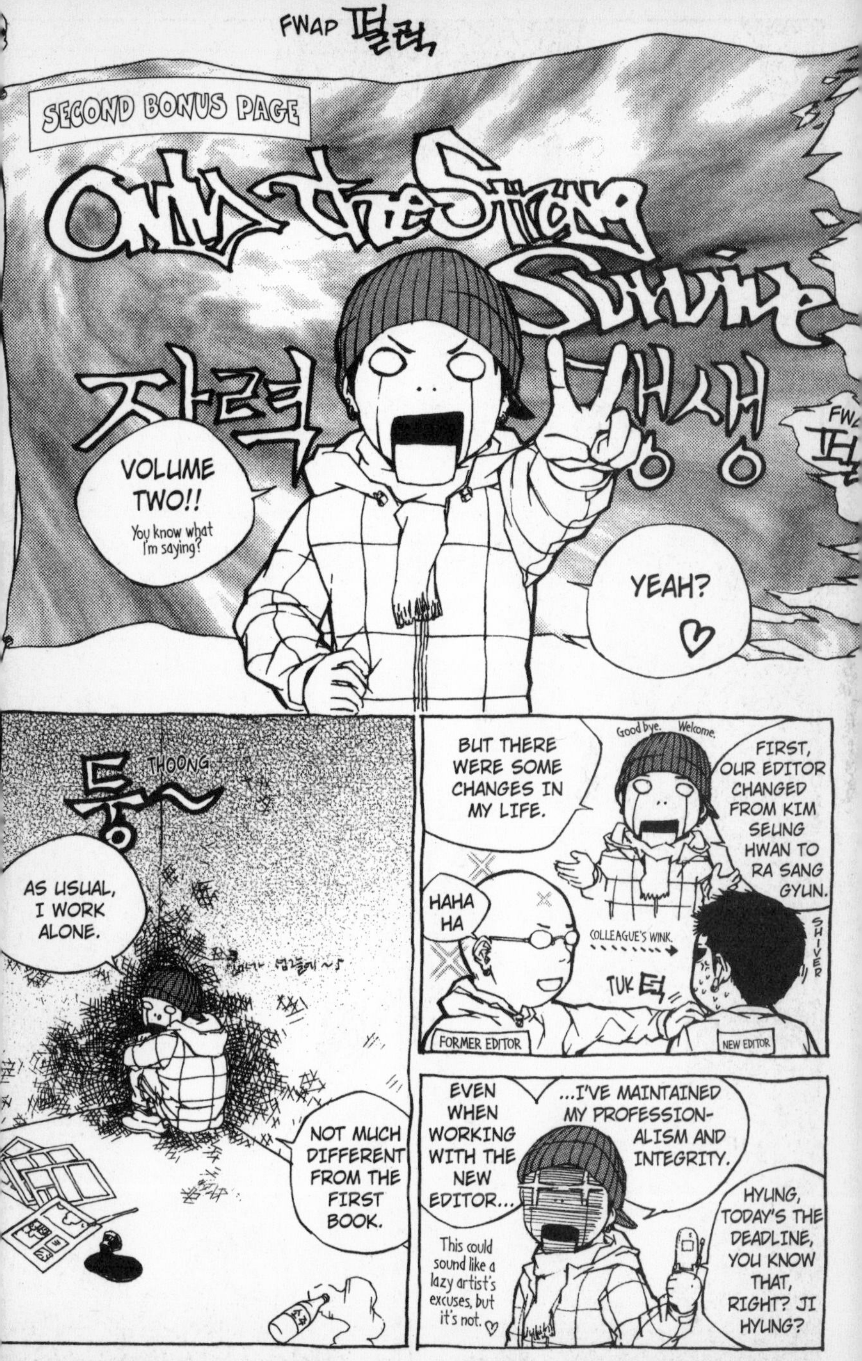
FWAP 펄럭
SECOND BONUS PAGE
ONLY the Strong Survive
자력갱생
VOLUME TWO!!
You know what I'm saying?
YEAH? ♥
THOONG 둥~
AS USUAL, I WORK ALONE.
NOT MUCH DIFFERENT FROM THE FIRST BOOK.
BUT THERE WERE SOME CHANGES IN MY LIFE.
Good bye.
Welcome.
FIRST, OUR EDITOR CHANGED FROM KIM SEUNG HWAN TO RA SANG GYUN.
HAHA HA
COLLEAGUE'S WINK.
TUK 툭
SHIVER
FORMER EDITOR
NEW EDITOR
EVEN WHEN WORKING WITH THE NEW EDITOR...
...I'VE MAINTAINED MY PROFESSION-ALISM AND INTEGRITY.
HYUNG, TODAY'S THE DEADLINE, YOU KNOW THAT, RIGHT? JI HYUNG?
This could sound like a lazy artist's excuses, but it's not. ♡

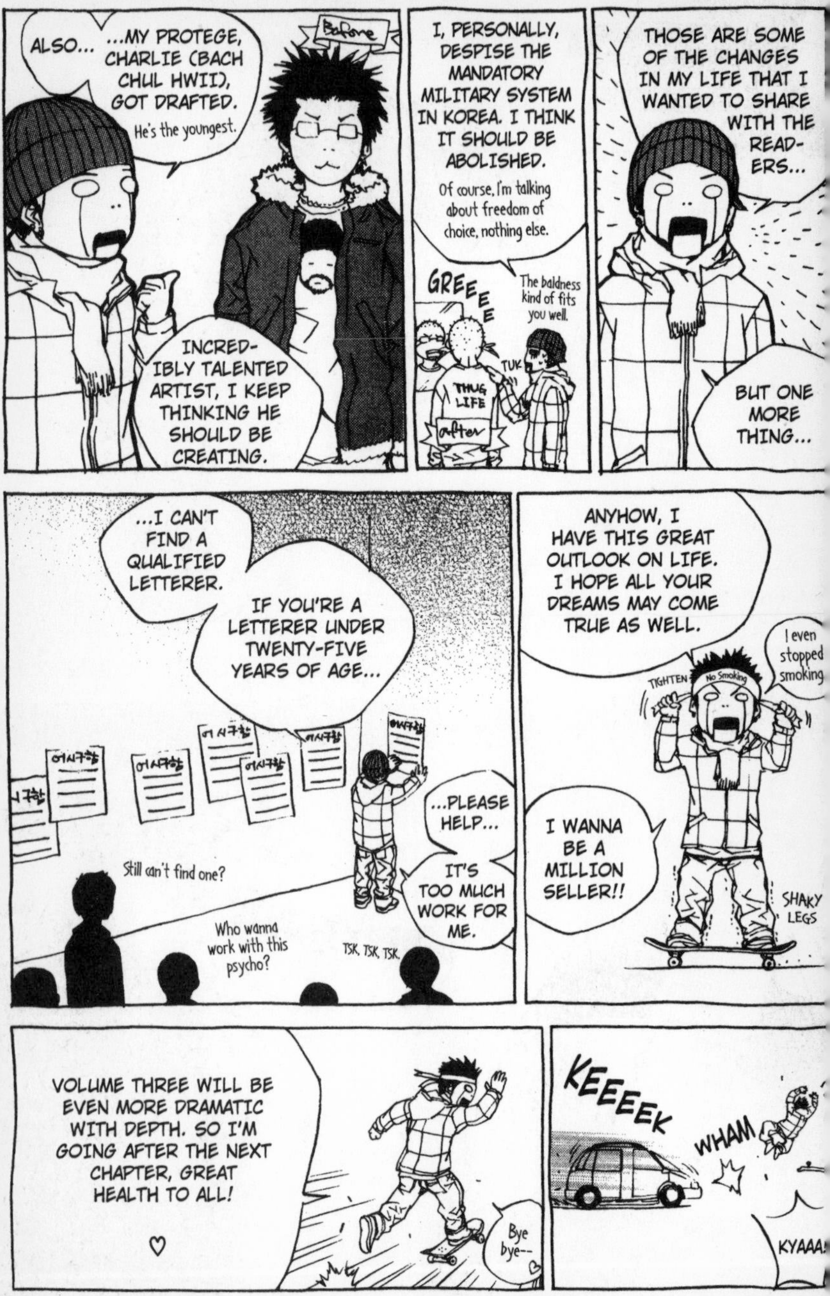
ALSO...
...MY PROTEGE, CHARLIE (BACH CHUL HWII), GOT DRAFTED.
He's the youngest.
Before
INCRED-IBLY TALENTED ARTIST, I KEEP THINKING HE SHOULD BE CREATING.
I, PERSONALLY, DESPISE THE MANDATORY MILITARY SYSTEM IN KOREA. I THINK IT SHOULD BE ABOLISHED.
Of course, I'm talking about freedom of choice, nothing else.
GREEEE
The baldness kind of fits you well.
TUK
THUG LIFE
after
THOSE ARE SOME OF THE CHANGES IN MY LIFE THAT I WANTED TO SHARE WITH THE READ-ERS...
BUT ONE MORE THING...
...I CAN'T FIND A QUALIFIED LETTERER.
IF YOU'RE A LETTERER UNDER TWENTY-FIVE YEARS OF AGE...
...PLEASE HELP...
IT'S TOO MUCH WORK FOR ME.
Still can't find one?
Who wanna work with this psycho?
TSK, TSK, TSK.
ANYHOW, I HAVE THIS GREAT OUTLOOK ON LIFE. I HOPE ALL YOUR DREAMS MAY COME TRUE AS WELL.
I even stopped smoking
TIGHTEN
No Smoking
I WANNA BE A MILLION SELLER!!
SHAKY LEGS
VOLUME THREE WILL BE EVEN MORE DRAMATIC WITH DEPTH. SO I'M GOING AFTER THE NEXT CHAPTER, GREAT HEALTH TO ALL!
♡
Bye bye--
KEEEEK
WHAM
KYAAA!

03.12

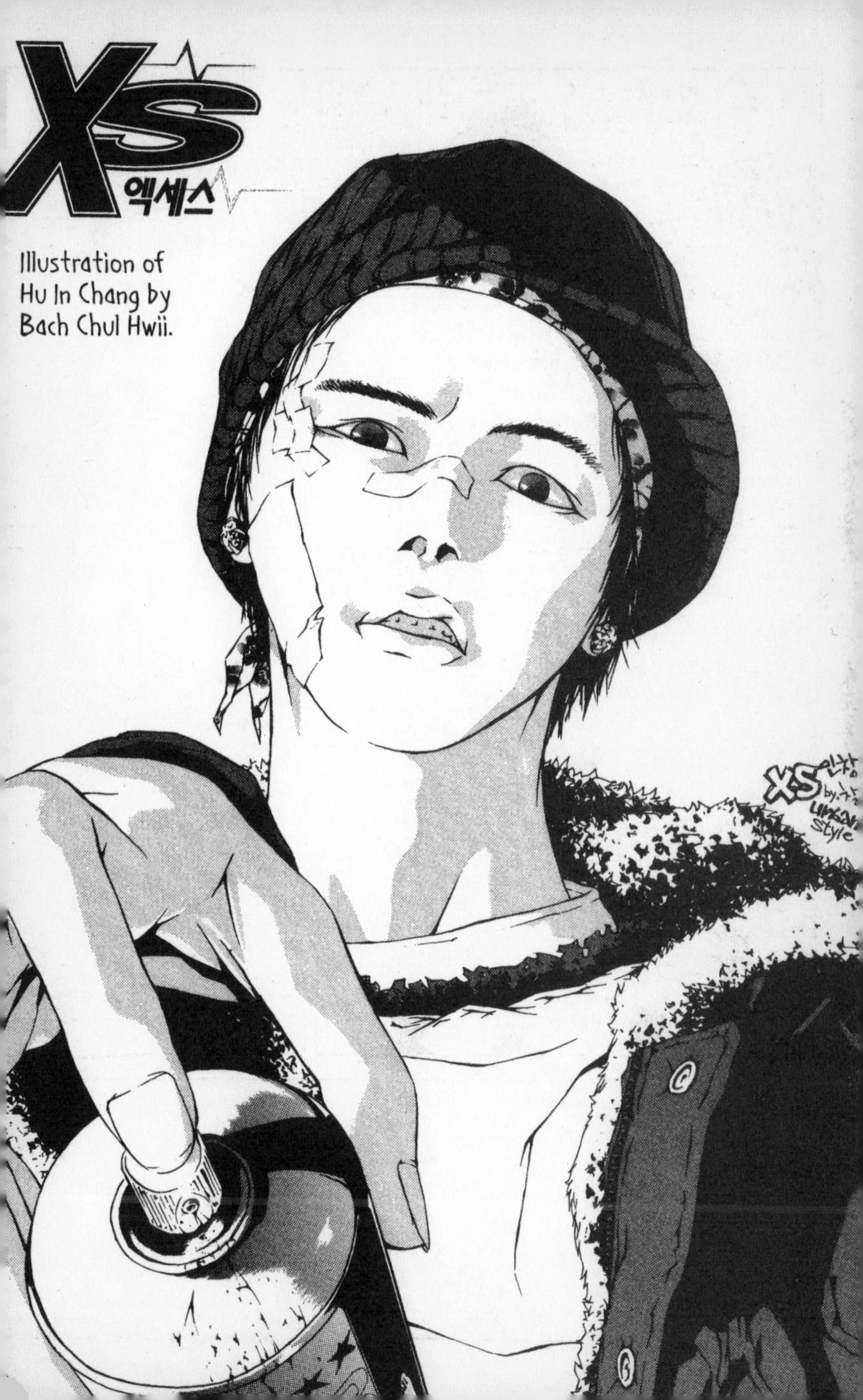
XS
엑세스

Illustration of Hu In Chang by Bach Chul Hwii.

Kim Young-Oh's

Banya
the explosive delivery man

With a worldwide war raging between humans and monsters, the young delivery men and women of the Gaya Desert Post Office do not pledge allegiance to any country or king. They are banded together by a pledge to *deliver* . . . "Fast. Precise. Secure." Banya, the craziest and craftiest of the bunch, will stop at nothing to get a job done. All five volumes are now available, so check out the complete series!

Volume 1
ISBN-10: 1-59307-614-2
ISBN-13: 978-1-59307-614-6

Volume 2
ISBN-10: 1-59307-688-6
ISBN-13: 978-1-59307-688-7

Volume 3
ISBN-10: 1-59307-705-X
ISBN-13: 978-1-59307-705-1

Volume 4
ISBN-10: 1-59307-774-2
ISBN-13: 978-1-59307-774-7

Volume 5
ISBN-10: 1-59307-841-2
ISBN-13: 978-1-59307-841-6

$12.95 EACH!

Previews for *BANYA: THE EXPLOSIVE DELIVERY MAN* and other DARK HORSE MANHWA titles can be found at darkhorse.com!

AVAILABLE AT YOUR LOCAL COMICS SHOP OR BOOKSTORE. To find a comics shop in your area, call 1-888-266-4226. For more information or to order direct: On the web: darkhorse.com. E-mail: mailorder@darkhorse.com. Phone: 1-800-862-0052 Mon.–Fri. 9 A.M. to 5 P.M. Pacific Time.

the KUROSAGI corpse delivery service

黒鷺死体宅配便

If you enjoyed this book, be sure to check out *The Kurosagi Corpse Delivery Service*, a new mature-readers manga series from the creator of *Mail*!

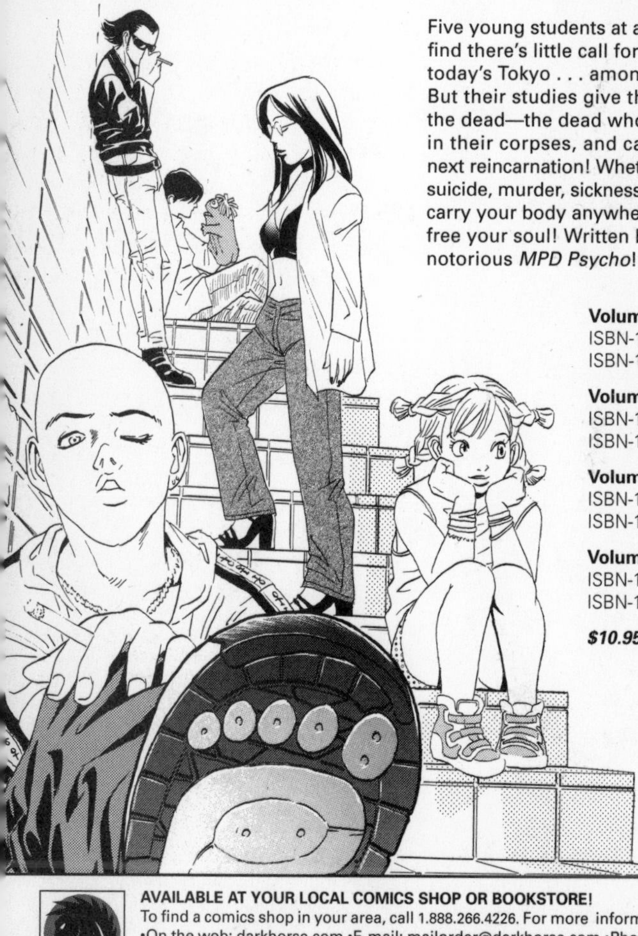

Five young students at a Buddhist university find there's little call for their job skills in today's Tokyo . . . among the *living*, that is! But their studies give them a direct line to the dead—the dead who are still trapped in their corpses, and can't move on to the next reincarnation! Whether you died from suicide, murder, sickness, or madness, they'll carry your body anywhere it needs to go to free your soul! Written by Eiji Otsuka of the notorious *MPD Psycho*!

Volume 1:
ISBN-10: 1-59307-555-3
ISBN-13: 978-1-59307-555-2

Volume 2:
ISBN-10: 1-59307-593-6
ISBN-13: 978-1-59307-593-4

Volume 3:
ISBN-10: 1-59307-594-4
ISBN-13: 978-1-59307-594-1

Volume 4:
ISBN-10: 1-59307-595-2
ISBN-13: 978-1-59307-595-8

$10.95 each!

DARK HORSE MANGA

AVAILABLE AT YOUR LOCAL COMICS SHOP OR BOOKSTORE!

To find a comics shop in your area, call 1.888.266.4226. For more information or to order direct: •On the web: darkhorse.com •E-mail: mailorder@darkhorse.com •Phone: 1.800.862.0052 Mon.-Fri. 9 A.M. to 5 P.M. Pacific Time. *Prices and availability subject to change without notice.

PARK JOONG-KI'S
S·H·A·M·A·N
WARRIOR

One of Korea's top five best-selling manhwa titles! From the desert wastelands emerge two mysterious warriors, master wizard Yarong and his faithful servant Batu. On a grave mission from their king, they have yet to realize the whirlwind of political movements and secret plots which will soon engulf them and change their lives forever. When Yarong is injured in battle, Batu must fulfill a secret promise to leave Yarong's side and protect his master's child. As Batu seeks to find and hide the infant, Yarong reveals another secret to those who have tracked him down to finish him off—the deadly, hidden power of a Shaman Warrior!

Volume 1
ISBN-10: 1-59307-638-X
ISBN-13: 978-1-59307-638-2

Volume 2
ISBN-10: 1-59307-749-1
ISBN-13: 978-1-59307-749-5

Volume 3
ISBN-10: 1-59307-769-6
ISBN-13: 978-1-59307-769-3

Volume 4
ISBN-10: 1-59307-819-6
ISBN-13: 978-1-59307-819-5

$12.95 EACH!

**Previews for *SHAMAN WARRIOR* and other
DARK HORSE MANHWA titles can be found at darkhorse.com!**

AVAILABLE AT YOUR LOCAL COMICS SHOP OR BOOKSTORE. To find a comics shop in your area, call 1-888-266-4226.
For more information or to order direct: On the web: darkhorse.com. E-mail: mailorder@darkhorse.com.
Phone: 1-800-862-0052 Mon.–Fri. 9 A.M. to 5 P.M. Pacific Time.

DARK HORSE MANHWA

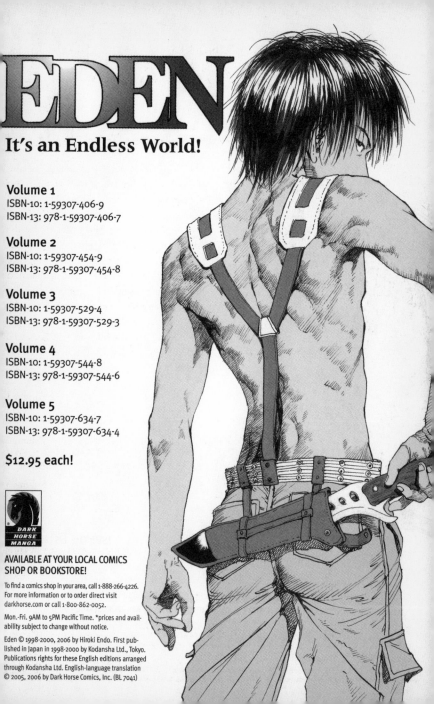

EDEN

It's an Endless World!

Volume 1
ISBN-10: 1-59307-406-9
ISBN-13: 978-1-59307-406-7

Volume 2
ISBN-10: 1-59307-454-9
ISBN-13: 978-1-59307-454-8

Volume 3
ISBN-10: 1-59307-529-4
ISBN-13: 978-1-59307-529-3

Volume 4
ISBN-10: 1-59307-544-8
ISBN-13: 978-1-59307-544-6

Volume 5
ISBN-10: 1-59307-634-7
ISBN-13: 978-1-59307-634-4

$12.95 each!

DARK HORSE MANGA

OLD BOY

Ten years ago, he was abducted and confined to a private prison. He was never told why he was there, or who put him there. Suddenly his incarceration has ended, again without explanation. He is sedated, stuffed inside a trunk, and dumped in a park. When he awakes, he is free to reclaim what's left of his life . . . and what's left is revenge.

This series is the inspiration of the *Oldboy* film directed by Chan-wook Park, which was awarded the Grand Jury prize at the 2004 Cannes Film Festival!

VOLUME 1:
ISBN-10: 1-59307-568-5
ISBN-13: 978-1-59307-568-2

VOLUME 2:
ISBN-10: 1-59307-569-3
ISBN-13: 978-1-59307-569-9

VOLUME 3:
ISBN-10: 1-59307-570-7
ISBN-13: 978-1-59307-570-5

VOLUME 4:
ISBN-10: 1-59307-703-3
ISBN-13: 978-1-59307-703-7

VOLUME 5:
ISBN-10: 1-59307-714-9
ISBN-13: 978-1-59307-714-3

VOLUME 6:
ISBN-10: 1-59307-720-3
ISBN-13: 978-1-59307-720-4

VOLUME 7:
ISBN-10: 1-59307-721-1
ISBN-13: 978-1-59307-721-1

VOLUME 8:
ISBN-10: 1-59307-722-X
ISBN-13: 978-1-59307-722-8

$12.95 EACH!

B U R S T

Don't miss the latest adventures of the most fun-loving, well-armed bounty hunters in Chicago! Rally Vincent and Minnie-May Hopkins return with Kenichi Sonoda's *Gunsmith Cats: Burst*, back in action and back in trouble!

Presented in the authentic right-to-left reading format, and packed full of bounty-hunting, gun-slinging, property-damaging action, *Gunsmith Cats: Burst* aims to please.

VOLUME 1
ISBN-10: 1-59307-750-5
ISBN-13: 978-59307-750-1

VOLUME 2
ISBN-10: 1-59307-767-X
ISBN-13: 978-1-59307-767-9

$10.95 EACH!

DARK HORSE MANGA

AVAILABLE AT YOUR LOCAL COMICS SHOP OR BOOKSTORE!

To find a comics shop in your area, call 1-888-266-4226. For more information or to order direct visit darkhorse.com or call 1-800-862-0052 Mon.-Fri. 9 A.M. to 5 P.M. Pacific Time. *Prices and availability subject to change without notice.

Gunsmith Cats Burst © Kenichi Sonoda 2005, 2007. First published in Japan in 2005 by Kodansha Ltd., Tokyo. Publication rights for English edition arranged through Kodansha Ltd. All rights reserved. (BL 7045)

GUNSMITH CATS

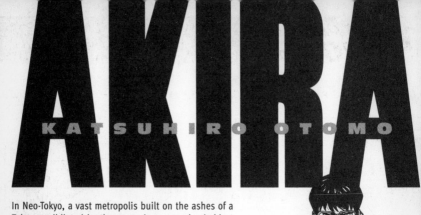

AKIRA

KATSUHIRO OTOMO

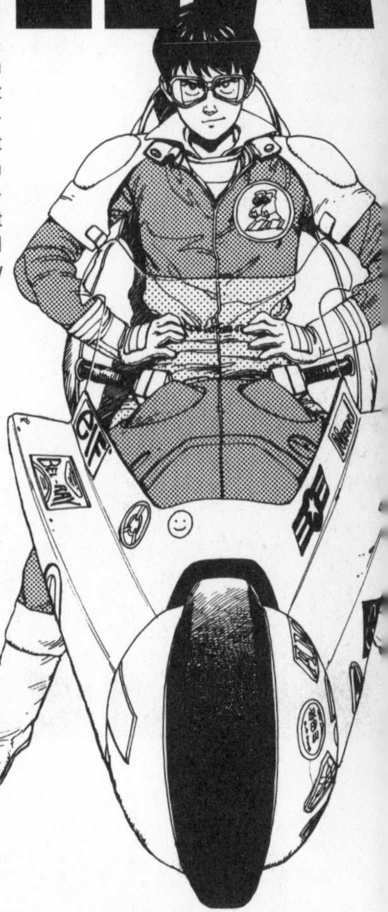

In Neo-Tokyo, a vast metropolis built on the ashes of a Tokyo annihilated by the mysterious apocalyptic blast that triggered World War III, the lives of two street-wise teenage friends, Tetsuo and Kaneda, are about to change forever. Paranormal abilities begin to waken in Tetsuo, and he becomes a target of a shadowy government operation that will stop at nothing to prevent another catastrophe like that which leveled Tokyo, and is terrified of someone—or something—of unthinkably monstrous power known only as . . . Akira.

VOLUME 1:
ISBN-10: 1-56971-498-3
ISBN-13: 978-1-56971-498-0
$24.95

VOLUME 2:
ISBN-10: 1-56971-499-1
ISBN-13: 978-1-56971-499-7
$24.95

VOLUME 3:
ISBN-10: 1-56971-525-4
ISBN-13: 978-1-56971-525-3
$24.95

VOLUME 4:
ISBN-10: 1-56971-526-2
ISBN-13: 978-1-56971-526-0
$27.95

VOLUME 5:
ISBN-10: 1-56971-527-0
ISBN-13: 978-1-56971-527-7
$27.95

VOLUME 6:
ISBN-10: 1-56971-528-9
ISBN-13: 978-1-56971-528-4
$29.95

KATSUHIRO OTOMO
AKIRA
CLUB

AND CHECK OUT THE STUNNING NEW ART BOOK, *AKIRA CLUB*
ISBN-10: 1-59307-741-6
ISBN-13: 978-1-59307-741-9
$29.95

DARK HORSE MANGA

AVAILABLE AT YOUR LOCAL COMICS SHOP OR BOOKSTORE!
To find a comics shop in your area, call 1-888-266-4226. For more information or to order direct visit darkhorse.com or call 1-800-862-00
Mon.–Fri. 9 A.M. to 5 P.M. Pacific Time. *Prices and availability subject to change without notice.

darkhorse.com | DARK HORSE TWENTY YEARS

COMICS | BOOKS | PRODUCTS | REVIEWS | ZONES | NEWS | HELP | COMPANY | RESOURCES

VISIT THE MANGA ZONE ON
DARKHORSE.COM
TO EXPLORE GREAT FEATURES LIKE:

- Exclusive content from editors on upcoming projects!
- Download exclusive desktops!
- Online previews and animations!
- Message Boards!
- Up-to-date information on the latest releases!
- Links to other cool manga sites.

Visit DARKHORSE.COM/MANGA for more details!

publisher
MIKE RICHARDSON

editor
TIM ERVIN

book design
TONY ONG

art director
LIA RIBACCHI

English-language version produced by DARK HORSE COMICS.

XS Hybrid vol. 2

Dark Horse Manhwa
A division of Dark Horse Comics, Inc.
10956 SE Main Street
Milwaukie, OR 97222

darkhorse.com

First edition: September 2007
ISBN-10: 1-59307-757-2
ISBN-13: 978-1-59307-757-0

10 9 8 7 6 5 4 3 2 1
Printed in Canada

To find a comics shop in your area, call the Comic Shop Locator Service
toll-free at 1-888-266-4226.